Self-Efficacy Beliefs of Adolescents

a volume in
Adolescence and Education

Series Editors:
Tim Urdan, *Santa Clara University*
Frank Pajares, *Emory University*

Adolescence and Education

Tim Urdan and Frank Pajares, Series Editors

Self-Efficacy Beliefs of Adolescents

edited by

Frank Pajares
Emory University

and

Tim Urdan
Santa Clara University

INFORMATION AGE
PUBLISHING

Greenwich, Connecticut • www.infoagepub.com

Library of Congress Cataloging-in-Publication Data

Self-efficacy and adolescents / edited by Frank Pajares and Tim Urdan.
    p. cm.
 Includes bibliographical references.
 ISBN 1-59311-366-8 (pbk.) — ISBN 1-59311-367-6 (hardcover)
 1. Self-efficacy. 2. Adolescent psychology. I. Pajares, Frank. II.
Urdan, Timothy C.
 BF637.S38S44 2005
 155.5'1825—dc22

                        2005026421

Printed in the United States of America

For Albert Bandura, who charts the waters we navigate.
With appreciation, affection, and respect.
Frank Pajares and Tim Urdan

For Pat Ashton, John Bengston, Barry Guinagh,
David Miller, and Rod Webb, who gently guided my early efforts
and inspired my love for the work.
Frank Pajares

For Nancy, who does not read my work but is still proud of it.
Tim Urdan

LIST OF CONTRIBUTORS

Albert Bandura — Stanford University

Nancy E. Betz — The Ohio State University

Mimi Bong — Ehwa Womans University, South Korea

Steven D. Brown — Loyola University Chicago

Gian Vittorio Caprara — Università di Roma "La Sapienza" Italy

Timothy J. Cleary — University of Wisconsin Milwaukee

Heather A. Davis — The Ohio State University

Deborah L. Feltz — Michigan State University

Uichol Kim — Chung-Ang University South Korea

Robert M. Klassen — University of Alberta Canada

Robert W. Lent — University of Maryland

Aleksandra Luszczynska — University of Sussex, United Kingdom

T. Michelle Magyar — University of California at Los Angeles

Judith L. Meece — University of North Carolina at Chapel Hill

Gabriele Oettingen — New York University; University of Hamburg, Germany

Frank Pajares — Emory University

Young-Shin Park — Inha University South Korea

Camillo Regalia — Università Cattolica Milano Italy

Eugenia Scabini — Università Cattolica Milano Italy

Dale H. Schunk — University of North Carolina Greensboro

Ralf Schwarzer — Freie Universität Berlin Germany

Anita Woolfolk Hoy — The Ohio State University

Barry J. Zimmerman — City University of New York

Kristina M. Zosuls — New York University

CONTENTS

FOREWORD

The introduction of the psychological construct of self-efficacy is widely acknowledged as one of the most important developments in the history of psychology. Today, it is simply not possible to explain phenomena such as human motivation, learning, self-regulation, and accomplishment without discussing the role played by self-efficacy beliefs. In this, the fifth volume of our series on adolescence and education, we focus on the self-efficacy beliefs of adolescents. We are proud and fortunate to be able to bring together the most prominent voices in the study of self-efficacy, including that of the Father of Social Cognitive Theory and of self-efficacy, Professor Albert Bandura. It is our hope, and our expectation, that this volume will become required reading for all students and scholars in the areas of adolescence and of motivation and, of course, for all who play a pivotal role in the education and care of youth.

In an opening chapter certain to make a seminal contribution to theory and research on the social cognitive development of adolescents, Professor Bandura writes expansively on how the self-efficacy beliefs of adolescents profoundly influence their lives and aspirations, and he addresses adolescent development from an agentic perspective in which people are viewed as self-organizing, proactive, self-regulating, and self-reflecting. Professor Bandura traces the role of self-efficacy beliefs in family functioning, educational development, career aspirations and trajectories, health promotion, affect regulation, management of sexuality, management of high-risk activities, and political participation and social commitment. Finally, he places social cognitive theory in a cultural context.

Adolescence is a pivotal developmental period in which youth begin to form an enduring sense of personal identity and agency about themselves. In the second chapter of the volume, Barry Zimmerman and Timothy Cleary trace the role of self-efficacy beliefs and self-regulatory skills in the development of adolescents' personal agency. They discuss the historic origins of self-efficacy beliefs, clarify their nature, and sift out their distinctive features. Dale Schunk and Judith Meece then explore the development of self-efficacy beliefs during adolescence, discussing the major influences on children's self-efficacy beliefs. They provide an overview of research on self-efficacy during adolescence and discuss the critical roles played by parents, peers, and school influences, summarizing developmental and educational research that addresses each of the influences.

The next two chapters examine how the self-efficacy beliefs of parents and teachers influence adolescents. Drawing on findings from their own longitudinal project and numerous previous studies, Gian Vittorio Caprara, Eugenia Scabini, and Camillo Regalia explain how the filial efficacy, parental self-efficacy, and collective efficacy of families influence adolescents' well-being and adjustment. Anita Woolfolk Hoy and Heather Davis explore established, likely, and possible connections between teachers' efficacy judgments and adolescents' learning and development. They also examine emergent research on teachers' sense of efficacy for establishing and maintaining positive relationships with adolescents.

We then turn our attention to areas vital to adolescents that have received much attention from self-efficacy researchers—health and risk-taking, sport and physical activity, and special education. Adolescent health-related risk behaviors include smoking, alcohol consumption, poor diet, unsafe sex, reckless or drunk driving, and violence. Ralf Schwarzer and Aleksandra Luszczynska discuss risk prevention and risk behavior change from a developmental perspective and point to the influential role that self-efficacy beliefs and self-regulatory strategies play in translating desired goals into action. Deborah Feltz and Michelle Magyar examine the potential influence of self-efficacy on performance in sport and physical activity, considering the integration of self-efficacy and other achievement related theories, longitudinal changes in self-efficacy over time, and performance enhancement interventions that have resulting changes in efficacy beliefs. Robert Klassen reviews the literature on the self-efficacy beliefs of adolescents with learning disabilities, discusses the motivational and metacognitive difficulties of these students, and provides results of a multi-method study investigating the academic self-efficacy and motivational beliefs of adolescents with and without learning disabilities.

Self-efficacy is an important variable in career counseling, and two chapters address this area so critical to adolescent development. Nancy Betz describes how self-efficacy assessments can be used with parallel measures of vocational interests in basic domains of vocational activity, and she explains how career counseling interventions can increase the range of career options considered by adolescents. In the following chapter, Steven Brown and Bob Lent provide an overview of those parts of social cognitive career theory that have the most relevance for adolescents' career decision-making and transitions from school to college or work. They build on research findings and on their own work to suggest practical ways in which parents, teachers, and counselors can help to promote adolescents' career options.

In the next two chapters, noted scholars place self-efficacy in a cultural and international context. Gabriele Oettingen and Kristina Zosuls ask to what extent origins and consequences of self-efficacy beliefs in adolescence vary within cultural contexts. They consider the role that cultural factors play as both potential sources of self-efficacy appraisal and potential consequences of self-efficacy beliefs. They also discuss the variables that may moderate the influence of culture on adolescents' self-efficacy beliefs, and vice-versa. International studies of academic achievement place East Asian students at the top of mathematics and science achievement and near the top in reading literacy. However, some 80 years ago, Asians were considered "genetically inferior," and they were barred from immigrating to the United States until 1965. Uichol Kim and Young-Shin Park trace the success of East Asian students to traditional Confucian and family values and to a view of education as the basis for national development. They contend also that self-efficacy, relational efficacy, and social self-efficacy have direct and mediating influences on the educational achievement of Asian students.

The next two chapters focus on the assessment of self-efficacy beliefs. First, Mimi Bong discusses the errors sometimes made when assessing self-efficacy and the likely impact less-than-optimal procedures can have on results. Following the advice of Bandura and of other prominent researchers, she provides guidelines on how best to operationalize self-efficacy in research studies. In his never-before published *Guide for Creating Self-Efficacy Scales*, Professor Bandura provides theoretical guidelines, insights, and examples to help researchers and practitioners create self-efficacy scales in various domains. In this guide, he deals with issues of domain specification, gradations of change, content relevance, phrasing of items, response scale, item analysis, minimizing biases in responding, assessing collective efficacy, and validation. The appendix includes illustrative self-efficacy scales focusing on regulating exercise, regulating eating habits, pain management, driving, problem-solving, parenting, and teaching, as well as scales assessing collective efficacy for reading and for mathematics, and perceived collective family efficacy. The often-used Children's Self-Efficacy Scale is also included.

In our coda to the volume, Frank Pajares identifies some of the implications that emanate from research findings on the self-efficacy beliefs of adolescents, and he offers teachers and parents some ways to safeguard and, when appropriate, maximize the self-efficacy beliefs of the young people in their care. In doing so, he clarifies the defining characteristics of this important self-belief and briefly synthesizes the major findings on the relation between the adolescents' self-efficacy, motivation, and accomplishment.

We thank the scholars who contributed their insights to this endeavor, most especially Professor Bandura, without whose guidance, clarity of vision, and profound scholarship our own thoughts and efforts would find themselves without a roof. We also heartily thank our doctoral students, Ellen Usher and John Barich without whose extraordinary efforts our volume would still be in the draft stage. And we are especially grateful to Benjamin Gonzalez, whose expert and patient assistance throughout the publication process was invaluable to us.

Frank Pajares and Tim Urdan

CHAPTER 1

ADOLESCENT DEVELOPMENT FROM AN AGENTIC PERSPECTIVE

Albert Bandura

Different periods of life present certain prototypic challenges and competency demands for successful functioning. Changing aspirations, time perspectives, and societal systems over the course of the life span alter how people structure, regulate, and evaluate their lives. Psychosocial changes with age do not represent lock-step stages through which everyone must inevitably pass as part of a preordained developmental sequence. There are many pathways through life and, at any given period, people vary substantially in how successfully they manage their lives in the milieus in which they are immersed. The beliefs they hold about their capabilities to produce results by their actions are an influential personal resource in negotiating their lives through the life cycle.

Social cognitive theory analyzes developmental changes across the life span in terms of evolvement and exercise of human agency. When viewed from this perspective, the paths that lives take are shaped by the reciprocal interplay between personal factors and diverse influences in ever-changing societies. The environment in which people live their lives is not a situational entity that ordains their life course. Rather, it is a varied suc-

Self-Efficacy Beliefs of Adolescents, 1–43
Copyright © 2006 by Information Age Publishing
All rights of reproduction in any form reserved.

cession of transactional life events in which individuals play a role in shaping the course of their personal development (Baltes, 1983; Bandura, 1997; Hultsch & Plemons, 1979). Some of the influential events involve biological changes. Others are normative social events linked to people's age, status, and their roles in educational, familial, occupational, and other institutional systems. Virtually everyone engages in these latter activities at certain phases in their development. Other life events involve unpredictable occurrences in the physical environment or irregular life events such as career changes, divorce, migration, accidents, and illnesses

There is much that people do designedly to exercise some control over their self-development and life circumstances. But there is a lot of fortuity in the courses lives take (Bandura, 1982, 1998). People are often inaugurated into new life trajectories through fortuitous circumstances. Fortuity does not mean uncontrollability of its effects. There are ways that people capitalize on the fortuitous character of life. They make chance happen by pursuing an active life that increases the fortuitous encounters they will experience. People also make chance work for them by cultivating their interests, enabling beliefs, and competencies. These personal resources enable them to make the most of opportunities that arise unexpectedly.

Lives are historically placed and socially developed in milieus that present unique opportunities, constraints, and challenges. Elder (1994) has argued eloquently for the analysis of people's lives over time as they are shaped by the distinctive life experiences provided by the eras in which they live. For example, the adolescents of yesteryear grew up in an environment quite different from that of the youth of today. They are players in an electronic era of rapid social and technological change that is transforming how people communicate, educate, work, relate to each other, and conduct their business and daily affairs.

The youth culture in this multimedia electronic generation is immersed in new forms of social interactions (Oksman & Turtiainen, 2004). Contemporary teenagers are filling empty periods of their everyday lives using mobile communication, text messaging, and chat sites in expanded personal and virtual networks. In these disembodied communications, the participants can control their self-presentation and shape their personal identities. These private forms of communication permit independence from parental supervision of the virtual world of teenagers. Parents, in turn, favor these mobile devices for security reassurance, to monitor their children's whereabouts, and to try to influence them in extra-familial contexts. Some teenagers complain about the parental intrusion ("My mom's been texting me a lot").

Major sociocultural changes that make life markedly different—such as technological innovations, economic depressions, military conflicts, cultural upheavals, and political changes—modify the character of the society in ways that have strong impact on life courses. Life trajectories differ depending on where people are in their lives at the time of such changes (Elder, 1981). Whatever the social conditions might be, personal lives take varied directions at any given time and place. It is the way in which people take advantage of opportunity structures and manage constraints under the prevailing sociocultural conditions that make the difference.

The present chapter addresses adolescent development and self-renewal from an agentic perspective (Bandura, 1986, 2001). In this conception, people are self-organizing, proactive, self-regulating, and self-reflecting. They are contributors to their life circumstances not just products of them. To be an agent is to influence intentionally one's functioning and life circumstances. There are four core features of human agency. One such feature is intentionality. People form intentions that include action plans and strategies for realizing them. The second feature involves the temporal extension of agency through forethought. This includes more than future-directed plans. People set themselves goals and anticipate likely outcomes of prospective actions to guide and motivate their efforts anticipatorily. A future cannot be a cause of current behavior because it has no material existence. But by being represented cognitively in the present, visualized futures serve as current guides and motivators of behavior.

Agents are not only planners and forethinkers. They are also self-regulators. They adopt personal standards and monitor and regulate their actions by self-reactive influence. They do things that give them satisfaction and a sense of self-worth, and refrain from actions that bring self-censure. People are not only agents of action. They are self-examiners of their own functioning. Through functional self-awareness they reflect on their personal efficacy, the soundness of their thoughts and actions, and the meaning of their pursuits, and they make corrective adjustments if necessary. Forethought and self-influence are important parts of a causal structure.

FOUNDATION OF HUMAN AGENCY

Among the mechanisms of human agency, none is more central or pervasive than beliefs of personal efficacy. This core belief is the foundation of human motivation, well-being, and accomplishments. Unless people believe they can produce desired effects by their actions, they have little incentive to act or to persevere in the face of difficulties. Whatever other factors serve as guides and motivators, they are rooted in the core belief that one has the power to effect changes by one's actions.

Belief in one's efficacy is a key personal resource in self-development, successful adaptation, and change. It operates through its impact on cognitive, motivational, affective, and decisional processes. Efficacy beliefs affect whether individuals think optimistically or pessimistically, in self-enhancing or self-debilitating ways. Such beliefs affect people's goals and aspirations, how well they motivate themselves, and their perseverance in the face of difficulties and adversity. Efficacy beliefs also shape people's outcome expectations—whether they expect their efforts to produce favorable outcomes or adverse ones. In addition, efficacy beliefs determine how environmental opportunities and impediments are viewed. People of low efficacy are easily convinced of the futility of effort in the face of difficulties. They quickly give up trying. Those of high efficacy view impediments as surmountable by self-development and perseverant effort. They stay the course in the face of difficulties and remain resilient to adversity.

Efficacy beliefs also affect the quality of emotional life and vulnerability to stress and depression. And last, but not least, efficacy beliefs determine the choices people make at important decisional points. A factor that influences choice behavior can profoundly affect the courses lives take. This is because the social influences operating in the selected environments continue to promote certain competencies, values, and lifestyles.

Many meta-analyses have been conducted across diverse spheres of functioning in both laboratory and field studies, with diverse populations of varying ages and sociodemographic characteristics, in different cultural milieus, and for both individual and collective efficacy (Bandura, 2002). The evidence from these meta-analyses shows that efficacy beliefs contribute significantly to level of motivation, socio-cognitive functioning, emotional well-being, and performance accomplishments.

MODES OF AGENCY

Social cognitive theory distinguishes among three modes of agency, each of which is founded in people's beliefs that they can influence the course of events by their actions. These include *individual*, *proxy*, and *collective* agency. In personal agency exercised individually, people bring their influence to bear on their own functioning and on environmental events.

In many spheres of functioning, people do not have direct control over the social conditions and institutional practices that affect their everyday lives. Under these circumstances, they seek their well-being, security, and valued outcomes through the exercise of proxy agency. In this socially-mediated mode of agency, people try by one means or another to get those who have access to resources or expertise or who wield influence to act at their behest to secure the outcomes they desire (Baltes, 1996; Brandstädter, 1992). For example, children turn to parents, and marital partners to spouses to act for them. Proxy agency relies heavily on perceived social efficacy to enlist the mediative efforts of others.

People do not live their lives in isolation. Many of the things they seek are achievable only through socially interdependent effort. Social cognitive theory extends the conception of human agency to collective agency (Bandura, 2000, 2001). In the exercise of collective agency, people pool their knowledge, skills, and resources, provide mutual support, form alliances, and work together to secure what they cannot accomplish on their own. People's shared beliefs in their joint capabilities to bring about desired changes in their lives are the foundation of collective agency. Perceived collective efficacy raises people's vision of what they wish to achieve, enhances motivational commitment to their endeavors, strengthens resilience to adversity, and enhances group accomplishments.

INTERDEPENDENCE OF HUMAN AGENCY AND SOCIAL STRUCTURE

Human functioning is rooted in social systems. Therefore, human agency operates within a broad network of socio-structural influences. These social systems are not the workings of impersonal forces disembodied from the activities of individuals. Social structures are created by human activity to organize, guide, and regulate human affairs in given domains by authorized rules and sanctions (Giddens, 1984). Social systems necessarily operate through the activities of individuals who preside over them. The socio-structural practices, in turn, impose constraints and provide resources and opportunity structures for personal development and functioning. Given this dynamic bi-directionality of influence, social cognitive theory rejects a dualism between human agency and a disembodied social structure.

Socio-structural theories and psychological theories are often regarded as rival conceptions of human behavior or as representing different levels and temporal proximities of causation. Human behavior cannot be fully understood solely in terms of socio-structural factors or psychological factors. A full understanding requires an integrated causal system in which socio-structural influences operate through psychological mechanisms to produce behavioral effects. However, the self system is not merely a conduit for environmental influences. The self is socially constituted, but, by exercising personal and collective influence, human agency operates generatively and proactively on social systems, not just reactively. In short, social systems are the product of human activity.

In the theory of triadic reciprocal causation, socio-structural and personal determinants are treated as co-factors within a unified causal structure. For example, poverty is not a matter of multilayered or distal causation. Lacking the money to provide for the subsistence of one's family impinges pervasively on everyday life in a very proximal way. Economic conditions, socioeconomic status, and family structure affect behavior mainly through their impact on people's aspirations, sense of efficacy, and other self-regulatory factors rather than directly (Baldwin, Baldwin, Sameroff, & Seifer, 1989; Bandura, Barbaranelli, Caprara, & Pastorelli, 1996, 2001; Elder & Ardelt, 1992).

ADOLESCENT DEVELOPMENT

Each period of human development brings with it new competency requirements, challenges, and opportunities for personal growth. As an important transitional phase in the life course, adolescence presents a host of new challenges. Adolescents have to manage major biological, educational, and social role transitions concurrently. Learning how to deal with pubertal changes, emotionally invested partnerships, and the emergence of sexuality becomes a matter of considerable importance. Adolescents must manage not only pervasive physical changes but difficult educational transitions as well. The transition to middle-level schools involves a major environmental change that taxes personal efficacy.

In late adolescence, the roles of adulthood must begin to be addressed in almost every dimension of life. Adolescents must begin to consider seriously what they want to do with their lives occupationally. During this time, they have to master many new skills and the ways of adult society. They must do all this in a society that does not provide many preparatory roles for them.

Unlike childhood involvements, as adolescents expand the nature and scope of their activities into the larger social community, they have to assume increasing responsibility for conduct that plays a more decisive role in fostering or foreclosing various life courses. The way in which adolescents develop and exercise their personal efficacy during this transitional period can play a key role in setting the course their life paths take.

Adolescence has often been characterized as a period of psychosocial turmoil and discontinuity. While no period of life is ever free of problems, contrary to the stereotype of "storm and stress," most adolescents negotiate the important transitions of this period without inordinate disturbance or discord (Bandura, 1964; Petersen, 1988; Rutter, Graham, Chadwick, & Yule, 1976). Rather than construing adolescence as a time of turmoil and discontinuity, social cognitive theory emphasizes personal growth through mastery and other enabling experiences as the more normative developmental process.

Because of the salience of pubertal changes and their social impact, there is excessive attribution of changes in adolescence to perturbing sociobiological factors. The more histrionic theorizing depicts these factors as convulsive forces driven by raging pubertal hormones. Human functioning is embedded interdependently in changing social systems. Given the interdependent personal and cultural co-development, the changes that adolescents undergo cannot be fully understood disembodied from the evolving social systems through which they navigate. Some of the changes in adolescent functioning and well-being have more to do with how the social systems are structured than with intrapsychic and biological upheaval supposedly endemic to adolescence (Eccles et al., 1993).

ROLE OF EFFICACY BELIEFS IN FAMILY FUNCTIONING

Social cognitive theory assigns a prominent role to the perceived efficacy of families to manage the many aspects of familial relationships and the quality of family life (Bandura, 1997). To date, much of the self-efficacy research on family functioning has focused on dyadic parent-child relationships. These studies have added to our understanding of how parents' sense of efficacy contributes to children's development and reduces the stressfulness of parenthood.

Perceived parenting efficacy plays a key role in adaptation to parenthood. Mothers with strong beliefs in their parenting efficacy experience more positive emotional well-being and better adjustment to the parenting role, and they achieve a better marital relationship than do mothers who hold weaker beliefs about their parenting capabilities (Williams et al., 1987). The positive impact of parenting efficacy beliefs on their children's development is further verified in interventions designed to enhance a sense of parental efficacy. Mothers with difficult children, whose sense of parenting efficacy is raised, interact more positively with their children, experience lower familial stress and reductions in child behavior problems than mothers who did not have the benefit of the efficacy-enhancing program (Gross, Fogg, & Tucker, 1995; Sofronoff & Farbotko, 2002).

A strong sense of parenting efficacy also serves as an enabling and protective factor that reduces vulnerability to emotional distress and depression, which can weaken maternal attachment and impede the quality of parenting (Cutrona & Troutman, 1986; Elder, 1995; Olioff & Aboud, 1991; Silver, Bauman, & Ireys, 1995; Teti & Gelfand, 1991).

A strong sense of parental efficacy yields dividends not only in emotional well-being and quality of caretaking but in shaping children's developmental trajectories. Parents who believe in their efficacy to contribute to their children's development act on that belief in ways that cultivate their children's potential (Ardelt & Eccles, 2001). They build their children's sense of intellectual efficacy and aspirations which, in turn, contributes to their social relations, emotional well-being, academic development, and career choice and development (Bandura, Barbaranelli, Caprara, & Pastorelli, 1996, 2001). Moreover, self-efficacious parents are strong advocates for their children in interactions with social institutions that can have an important impact on their children during the formative period of their lives (Bandura, 1997).

Transactions within the parent-child dyad involve a bi-directionality of influence. In this reciprocal interplay, children are contributors to their development not just objects of unidirectional parental influence (Bandura, 1997; Kuczynski, 2003; Maccoby, 2003). There have been some preliminary efforts to examine prospectively the extent to which children's efficacy beliefs affect the outcomes of this dyadic subsystem (Caprara, Regalia, & Bandura, 2002; Caprara, Pastorelli, Regalia, Scabini, & Bandura, 2005). The stronger the children's beliefs in their efficacy to manage their parental relations regarding peer and family matters, the better their developmental outcomes. We shall examine later how adolescents' self-efficacy affects transactions with their parents.

The efficacy to manage the spousal relationship is another important dyad in the interlocking family system. Perceived spousal efficacy centers on the partners' perceived capability to communicate openly and confide in each other, provide mutual support to resolve marital relationship problems, and work through disagreements over child rearing and management of their finances. Spouses who approach challenges in their relationship beset with doubts about their ability to manage them are likely to favor avoidant rather than problem-solving strategies when they encounter difficulties. Lack of enabling and fulfilling reciprocity and unresolved marital discords can detract from the quality of family functioning and satisfaction with family life. There is some longitudinal evidence from families with dual careers that wives' perceived self-efficacy to enlist spousal aid in childcare improves their health and emotional life (Ozer, 1995). But otherwise, the spousal dyadic aspect of family efficacy has rarely been explored.

The family operates as a multilevel social system with interlocking relationships rather than simply as a collection of members. Both the parent-child and spousal subsystems are embedded in the network of interdependencies that constitute a family. In these multiple interlocking relationships, the roles of parent, spouse, and offspring carry different functional demands, developmental opportunities, constraints, and reciprocal obligations. There is a dynamic interplay among the dyadic relationships. For example, how well the spouses get along with each other can affect how they treat their children (Cox & Paley, 2003; Sameroff, 1995). Conversely, how well the parents get along with their children can strain or strengthen the marital relationship.

The perceived collective efficacy of a family is not simply the sum of the members' beliefs in their individual efficacies. Rather, it is a shared belief in their family's capability to work together to manage and improvise their lives. It is an emergent group belief because it incorporates the interactive dynamics of the family system operating collectively. The collective whole can be greater or lesser than the efficacy parts depending on whether the family transactions are mutually supportive and enabling or wrangling and debilitating.

Analyses of the interplay of perceived dyadic efficacy and collective efficacy within the family underscore the centrality of collective family efficacy in quality of family functioning and satisfaction with family life (Bandura, Caprara, Regalia, Scabini, & Barbaranelli, 2004). Perceived efficacy at the personal level contributes to a sense of collective family efficacy. Thus, spousal partners' efficacy to manage their marital relationship, parents' efficacy to guide their adolescents, and adolescents' efficacy to manage their relationship with their parents contribute to belief in collective family efficacy. Perceived collective family efficacy, in turn, fosters perceived efficacy to manage adolescent, parental, and spousal relationships.

Dyadic parent-child, spousal, and filial self-efficacy operates within the family almost entirely through collective family efficacy. For adolescents and parents alike, a high sense of collective family efficacy is accompanied by open family communication and enabling monitoring of adolescents' activities outside the home. Collective family efficacy contributes to parents' and adolescents' satisfaction with their family life both directly and through its impact on quality of family functioning.

SELF-EFFICACY IN EDUCATIONAL DEVELOPMENT

Educational systems have undergone fundamental changes during historical periods of cultural and technological change. Educational systems were originally designed to teach low-level skills in agricultural societies. When industrialization supplanted agriculture as the major economic enterprise, the educational system was adapted for the needs of heavy industry and manufacturing. Most of the occupational pursuits required rote performance without many cognitive skills. Increasing complexities in technologies, social systems, and the international economy present different realities demanding new types of competencies. These evolving new realities ushered in by the transition to the information era are placing a premium on the role of personal efficacy in educational self-development.

There are three main pathways through which efficacy beliefs play a key role in cognitive development and accomplishment: students' beliefs in their efficacy to regulate their learning activities and to master academic subjects, teachers' beliefs in the personal efficacy to motivate and promote learning in their students, and the faculties' collective sense of efficacy that their schools can accomplish significant academic progress. Considerable progress has been achieved in documenting the positive role of self-efficacy beliefs in students' academic interest, motivation, management of academic stressors, and growth of cognitive competencies (Bandura, 1997; Pajares & Schunk, 2001). Students can now exercise substantial control over their own learning. In the past, their educational development depended on the quality of the schools in which they were enrolled. Students now have the best libraries, museums, and multimedia instruction at their fingertips through the global Internet. They can educate themselves independently of time and place. This shift in locus of initiative involves a major reorientation in students' conception of education. They are agents of their own learning, not just recipients of information.

Adolescents need to commit themselves to goals that give them purpose and a sense of accomplishment. Without personal commitment to something worth doing, they are unmotivated, bored, or cynical. They become dependent on extrinsic sources of stimulation. A vision of a desired future helps to organize their lives, provides meaning to their activities, motivates them, and enables them to tolerate the hassles of getting there.

A major goal of formal education is to equip students with the intellectual tools, self-beliefs, and self-regulatory capabilities to educate themselves throughout their lifetime. The rapid pace of technological change and accelerated growth of knowledge are placing a premium on capability for self-directed learning. Metacognitive theorists view self-regulated learning largely in terms of the cognitive aspects. Training in metacognitive skills involves selecting appropriate strategies, testing one's comprehension and state of knowledge, correcting one's deficiencies, and recognizing the utility of cognitive strategies.

Zimmerman (1990) has been the leading proponent of an expanded model of academic self-regulation. Viewed within the framework of social cognitive theory, students must develop skills to regulate the motivational, emotional, and social determinants of their intellectual functioning, as well as the cognitive aspects. This requires bringing self-influence to bear on every aspect of their learning experiences. Efficacious self-regulators gain knowledge, skills, and intrinsic interests in intellectual matters. Weak self-regulators achieve limited self-development.

It is not enough to have self-management skills. They will contribute little if students cannot get themselves to apply those skills persistently in the face of difficulties, stressors, and competing attractions. Firm belief in one's self-management efficacy provides the staying power. The stronger the students' perceived efficacy to manage their own learning, the higher their aspirations and accomplishments (Zimmerman & Bandura, 1994; Zimmerman, Bandura & Martinez-Pons, 1992).

We are entering a new era in which the construction of knowledge will rely increasingly on electronic inquiry. At present, much information is available solely in electronic form. Before long, most information will be available only in this form. Those who lack Internet literacy will be cut off from critical information needed to manage their daily lives. Constructing knowledge through Internet inquiry involves complex self-management. Knowing how to access, process, and evaluate the glut of information is vital for knowledge construction and cognitive functioning. People who doubt their efficacy to conduct productive inquiries and to manage the electronic technology quickly become overwhelmed by the informational overload. In research on self-instruction through the Internet, students with high self-efficacy for self-regulated learning make the best use of Internet-based instruction (Joo, Bong, & Choi, 2000). Social cognitive theory provides guides for building the personal efficacy and cognitive skills needed to use the Internet productively and creatively (Debowski, Wood, & Bandura, 2001).

The task of creating productive learning environments rests heavily on the talents and efficacy of teachers. Teachers' beliefs in their instructional efficacy partly determine how they structure academic activities in their classrooms. This affects students' academic development and judgment of their intellectual capabilities. Teachers with high self-efficacy create mastery experiences for their students. Those beset by self-doubts construct classroom environments that are likely to undermine students' judgments of their abilities and their cognitive development (Gibson & Dembo, 1984; Woolfolk, Rosoff, & Hoy, 1990). Ashton and Webb (1996) showed that students learn much more from teachers who feel efficacious to manage educational demands than from those beset with self-doubts.

Adolescents must manage a difficult educational transition to middle-level schools. This involves a major environmental change that taxes personal efficacy. Adolescents move from a personalized school environment of familiar peers to an impersonal, departmentalized one with curricular tracking into college preparatory, general, or vocational paths. Under these new social structural arrangements, they have to reestablish their sense of efficacy, social connectedness, and status within an enlarged heterogeneous network of new peers and with multiple teachers in rotating class sessions. During this adaptational period, young adolescents sense some loss of personal control, become less confident in themselves, are more sensitive to social evaluation, and suffer some decline in self-motivation (Eccles & Midgley, 1989).

But these initial adverse effects are neither universal nor enduring for every adolescent. Like other new demands and challenges, school transitions can be detrimental or beneficial to the growth of personal efficacy. For example, adolescents who have a high sense of efficacy weather inefficacious teachers in the move to junior high school, whereas inefficacious students become even more self-doubting of their capabilities (Midgley, Feldlaufer, & Eccles, 1989).

The school operates as a multilevel social system with interlocking relationships. Teachers' shared beliefs in their collective power to motivate and educate students create school cultures conducive to educational development. Perceived efficacy explains differences in school achievement after controlling for student characteristics, enrollment stability, teachers' experience, and prior school achievement (Bandura, 1997).

SELF-EFFICACY BELIEFS AS SHAPERS OF CAREER ASPIRATIONS AND TRAJECTORIES

A major part of people's daily life is spent in occupational activities. These pursuits do more than simply provide income for one's livelihood. Occupations structure a large part of people's everyday reality and serve as a major source of personal identity and self-evaluation. As an interdependent activity, occupational pursuits also structure a good part of people's daily social relations. Moreover, experiences in the work life have considerable repercussions on family life and psychosocial well-being.

The choices made during formative periods of development shape the course of lives. Such choices determine which aspects of their potentialities people cultivate and which they leave undeveloped. The self-development during formative periods forecloses some types of options and makes others realizable. Among the choices that affect life paths, those that center on career choice and development are of special import for the reasons given. Although occupationally relevant choices play a key role in setting the course of lifestyle trajectories with diverse impact across the life span, this area of personal development has received surprisingly little attention in developmental psychology.

Research with young adults confirms that beliefs of personal efficacy play a key role in occupational development and pursuits (Bandura, 1997; Betz & Hackett, 1986; Hackett, 1995; Lent, Brown, & Hackett, 1994). The higher the students' perceived efficacy to fulfill educational requirements and occupational roles, the wider the career options they seriously consider pursuing, the greater the interest they have in them, the better they prepare themselves educationally for different occupational careers, and the greater their staying power in challenging career pursuits. People simply eliminate from consideration occupations they believe to be beyond their capabilities, however attractive the occupations may be. Efficacy beliefs predict occupational choices and level of mastery of educational requirements for those pursuits when variations in actual ability, prior level of academic achievement, scholastic aptitude, and vocational interests are controlled (Brown, Lent, & Larkin, 1989; Lent, Brown, & Larkin, 1984, 1986, 1987; Lent, Lopez, & Bieschke, 1993).

The task of choosing what lifework to pursue looms large in later adolescence. The preparatory choices in this realm play a key role in shaping the pathways that adolescents follow into adulthood and the course their lives will take. Research conducted within the framework of social cognitive theory is adding to our understanding of how efficacy beliefs operate in concert with socioeconomic and familial influences in shaping occupational aspirations and considerations of career pursuits (Bandura, Barbaranelli, et al., 2001).

Familial socioeconomic status is linked to adolescents occupational trajectories only indirectly by raising parental educational aspirations and belief in their efficacy to promote their children's academic development. The more strongly parents believe that they can play a part in their children's scholastic development, the higher the educational aspirations they hold for them. Aspiring parents act in ways that build their children's academic, social, and self-regulatory efficacy, raise their aspirations, and promote their scholastic achievements.

The patterning of children's perceived academic, social, and self-regulatory efficacy influences the types of occupational activities for which they judge themselves to be efficacious both directly and through its impact on academic aspirations. Perceived occupational self-efficacy gives direction to the kinds of career pursuits children seriously consider, or disfavor, for their life's work.

There are gender differences in perceived occupational efficacy, career choice, and preparatory development. The differences usually follow the stereotypic courses, with boys judging themselves more efficacious for careers in science and technology and girls reporting a higher sense of efficacy for social, educational, and health services. These differences in perceived occupational self-efficacy and choice are all the more telling because girls perform academically as well as do boys. Girls are catching up with boys in coursework in math and science in high school, but girls are still shunning careers in scientific and technical fields (Betz, 1994;

Lewin, 1998). Such findings suggest that the foreclosure of career options may rest more heavily on perceived inefficacy and societal impediments than on background preparation. There are a number of societal practices that undermine women's sense of efficacy in quantitative academic domains critical to career choice and development (Bandura, 1997; Bussey & Bandura, 1999; Hackett & Betz, 1981). The gender-linked biases operate in familial, educational, mass media, organizational, and societal systems.

Given that children's career trajectories become crystallized early in the developmental process, efforts to reduce biases that constrict women's career development require early intervention. Modeling supplemented with guided mastery experiences provides an especially effective vehicle for building resilient self-efficacy. In efforts to reduce gender disparities arising from constraining self-beliefs, this approach instills a strong sense of efficacy and skill in domains of educational and occupational activities in which many women are beset with self-doubt (Betz & Schifano, 2000; Gist, Schwoerer, & Rosen, 1989; Schunk & Lilly, 1984).

In acknowledging the influential role of perceived self-efficacy in gender differences in career aspirations and pursuits, one should not lose sight of the fact that inequitable educational practices, cultural constraints, disparate incentive systems, and truncated opportunity structures are important contributors to women's career development. It should also be noted that there is substantial diversity within sexes. Neither boys nor girls are a uniform group. Therefore, modal gender characteristics in perceived self-efficacy should not be imputed to all members within each sex group. Indeed, women who take a more egalitarian view toward the roles of women display a higher sense of efficacy for traditionally male occupations and pursue such careers more often (Hackett, 1985). They construct different identities and futures for themselves.

Preparing for a productive occupational career poses a major transitional challenge in late adolescence. The youth who pursue careers via higher education follow a structured pathway. They are counseled, informed about college entry requirements, adequately prepared in the requisite academic subjects, and financially supported in one way or another during their schooling. They have the benefit of advanced academic preparation, which not only expands career options but provides them access to opportunities through informal social networks and established institutional linkages.

The transition from school to occupational career is a much more difficult problem for the non-college-bound youth, especially in the U.S. educational system. Schools offer these young people little occupational counseling or help in vocational placement. Many are inadequately prepared in the basic skills required for the technologies of the modern workplace. Some prefer a period of freedom to explore things before set-tling on a particular vocational pursuit. The vast majority, however, find themselves in a marginal work status by exclusion from the primary labor market rather than by choice.

The problem does not reside solely in the deficiencies of youth. Orga-nizational hiring practices and the lack of functional linkages between schools and the workplace create institutional impediments to employ-ability. Employers come to regard recent school graduates as too imma-ture and unreliable to invest the time and effort to develop their vocational competencies. They prefer older applicants who have already passed through the presumed probationary period of instability and are ready to settle down to a stable vocational career. So after they leave school, many youth find themselves in a moratorium status, drifting between short-term jobs that require few skills and offer little future (Osterman, 1980).

Successful school performance reflects a constellation of personal com-petencies, including motivational and self-management capabilities as well as cognitive skills. Hence, academic achievement is a good predictor of vocational productivity at the outset and in the long term, but employ-ers do not use this information in their hiring decisions (Bishop, 1989). Because of the long delay between leaving school and being seriously con-sidered for permanent employment, employers ignore the academic pre-dictors of vocational success. Doing well in high school does not bring a better job and higher pay. These hiring practices remove the functional value of academic performance for non-college-bound youth.

Other societies create more formal social mechanisms for getting non-college-bound youth started early on valued occupational careers. These systems provide them with incentives to develop their intellectual compe-tencies. Many of these educational systems provide high-level occupa-tional routes through apprenticeship systems (Hamilton, 1987). Industry and schools share responsibility for occupational development and link educational programs to occupational career lines by combining aca-demic instruction with intensive apprenticeships at work sites that lead to skilled employment (Hamilton, 1987). Academic achievement is rewarded with preferred apprenticeships. These intensive apprentice-ships are held in high status and serve as good means for career advance-ment.

In other systems, schools and employers form close partnerships, with a mutual commitment of schools to educate their students well and busi-nesses to provide occupational career paths for them upon graduation (Rosenbaum & Kariya, 1989). The close partnership not only provides transition routes but also restores the functional value of educational development for non-college youth. Just as selective colleges foster mastery of academic competencies through their admission standards, business hiring standards do so by rewarding educational attainments with better occupational options.

ROLE OF SELF-EFFICACY IN HEALTH PROMOTION

The quality of health is heavily influenced by lifestyle habits. This enables individuals to exercise some control over their vitality and health. By managing their health habits, individuals can live healthier and reduce the risk of disease. To stay healthy they should exercise, reduce dietary fat, refrain from smoking, control substance abuse, and develop effective ways of managing stressors. Self-management is good medicine. If the huge health benefits of these few habits were put into a pill, it would be declared a scientific milestone in the field of medicine.

Many of the habits that build the foundation for a healthful life or jeopardize it are formed during childhood and adolescence. For example, unless youngsters take up the smoking habit in their teens, they rarely become smokers in adulthood. Adolescence is a time of experimentation with activities that can compromise the adolescent's future health. It is easier to prevent detrimental health habits than to try to change them after they become deeply entrenched as part of a lifestyle. However, adolescent development in the health domain is concerned not only with risk management, but with promotion of a healthful lifestyle.

Despite the heavy focus on the medical aspects of the adverse physical effects of unhealthful habits, we are witnessing a shift from the disease model to a health model. It is just as meaningful to speak of levels of vitality and healthfulness as of degrees of impairment and debility. People's beliefs that they can motivate themselves and regulate their health habits affect every phase of personal change-initiation, adoption, and maintenance (Bandura, 1997, 2004). Efficacy beliefs influence whether individuals consider changing detrimental health habits. They see little point in even trying if they believe they do not have what it takes to succeed. Among those who change detrimental health habits on their own, the successful ones have stronger perceived self-efficacy at the outset than do non-changers and subsequent relapsers (Carey & Carey, 1993). For those who try to do so, their sense of efficacy provides the staying power in the face of difficulties and setbacks during the adoption of health promoting behaviors.

Effective self-regulation is not achieved through an act of will. It requires development of self-regulatory skills. To build people's sense of efficacy, they must learn how to monitor their health behavior and the social and cognitive conditions under which they engage in it, set attainable sub-goals to motivate and guide their efforts, draw from an array of coping strategies rather than rely on a single technique, enlist self-motivating incentives and social supports to sustain the effort needed to succeed, and apply multiple self-influence consistently and persistently (Perri, 1985).

It is one thing to get people to adopt beneficial health habits. It is another thing to get them to stick to them. Maintenance of habit change relies heavily on self-regulatory capabilities and the functional value of the behavior. Development of self-management requires instilling a resilient sense of efficacy as well as imparting skills. Experiences in exercising control over troublesome situations serve as efficacy builders (Bandura, 1997; Marlatt, Baer, & Quigley, 1995). To strengthen resilience, people need to develop coping strategies not only to manage common precipitants of breakdown but to reinstate control after setbacks. This involves training in how to manage failure.

Health habits are rooted in familial practices. But schools have an important role to play in promoting the health of a nation. This is the only place where all children can be easily reached. It is a natural setting for promoting healthful eating and exercise habits, discouraging smoking and other types of substance abuse plied by peers, and building generic self-management skills.

An effective preventative program includes four major components (Bandura, 2004). The first component is informational. It informs children of the health risks and benefits of different lifestyle habits. The second component develops the social and self-management skills for translating informed concerns into effective preventative practices. The third component builds a resilient sense of efficacy to support the exercise of control in the face of difficulties and setbacks that inevitably arise. The final component enlists and creates social supports for desired personal changes. Educational efforts to promote the health of youths usually produce weak results. They provide factual information about health. But they usually do little to equip children with the skills and efficacy beliefs that enable them to manage the emotional and social pressures to adopt detrimental health habits.

Managing health habits involves managing social relationships, not just targeting a specific health behavior for change. Health promotion programs that include the essential elements of the self-management mastery model prevent or reduce injurious health habits. Health knowledge can be conveyed readily, but changes in values, self-efficacy, and health habits require greater effort. The more behavioral mastery experiences provided, the greater the beneficial effect (Murray, Pirie, Luepker, & Pallonen, 1989). The more intensive the program, and the better the implementation, the stronger the impact (Connell, Turner, & Mason, 1985).

Comprehensive approaches that integrate guided mastery health programs with family and community efforts are more successful in promoting health and in preventing detrimental habits than are programs in which the schools try to do it alone (Perry, Kelder, Murray, & Klepp, 1992). Alcohol, drug abuse, and other health-related habits can also be changed by self-management programs (Botvin & Dusenbury, 1992; Gilchrist, Schinke, Trimble, & Cvetkovich, 1987; Killen et al., 1989).

Schools are inadequately equipped with the resources, training, and incentives to undertake health promotion and early modification of habits that jeopardize health. As in other social systems, teachers focus on areas in which they are evaluated. They are not graded for health promotion. When preventive programs are grudgingly allowed in schools, they try to do too much, with too little, in too short a time, with fitful quality of implementations to achieve much. Such efforts often do more to discredit psychosocial approaches through deficient implementation than to advance the health of youths.

Health promotion must be structured as a part of a societal commitment that makes the health of its youth a matter of high priority. A serious commitment must provide the personnel, incentives, resources, and the operational control needed to do the job well. The programs should be *in* the school, but not *of* the school. New school-based models of health promotion should operate together with the home, the community, and the society at large.

Schools' health-related practices need changing as well. Schools that are provided with a brief health promotion curriculum and encouraged to lower the fat content of their lunch offerings and enhance their physical activity offerings produce lasting improvements in children's eating and exercise habits (Luepker et al., 1996).

Psychosocial programs for health promotion will be increasingly implemented via interactive internet-based systems. They provide a convenient, individualized means for informing, enabling, motivating, and guiding individuals in their efforts to make lifestyle changes. The personalized feedback can be adjusted to participants' self-efficacy level, the unique impediments in their lives, and the progress they are making. Adolescents at risk for health problems typically refuse preventative or remedial health services. But they will pursue online individualized guidance. For example, adolescents at high risk of eating disorders resist seeking help. But they use interactive Internet-delivered guidance because it is readily accessible, convenient, and provides a feeling of anonymity (Taylor, Winzelberg, & Celio, 2001). Adolescents reduce dissatisfaction with their weight and body shape, and they alter dysfunctional attitudes and disordered eating behavior by this means.

The quality of health of a nation's youth is a social matter, not just a personal one. It requires changing the practices of social systems that impair health rather than just changing the habits of individuals. It is the height of irony to strive to promote healthful habits in school children while schools promote in their lunch program fast foods, house vending machines that dispense soft drinks and candy, and advertise brand-name fast foods in return for substantial payments to schools by fast food corporations. Through efficacious collective action, parents in some school districts have banned these practices. Given the soaring rates of child and adolescent obesity, using schools to promote unhealthy diets should be banned legislatively nationwide.

SELF-EFFICACY IN AFFECT REGULATION

The recent years have witnessed a growing interest in the quality and function of people's emotional lives. To the extent that affect was addressed, it was usually treated as an effect of situational incitements rather than as determinants of psychosocial functioning. Affect has important intrapersonal, communicative, and behavioral functional value (Bandura, 1986; Caprara, 2002; Larsen, 2000). Affect is often the basis of social ties and their durability that influences the course of lives (Bandura, 1986). Emotional competence, as reflected in the ability to discern emotions, to understand the social consequences of one's emotionally expressive behavior, and to manage one's emotional states, is essential for successful interpersonal transactions in everyday life (Mayer & Salovey, 1997; Saarni, 1999). Moreover, positive affect enhances cognitive functioning, helps buffer the perturbing effects of aversive experiences, and facilitates adaptive coping (Folkman & Moskowitz, 2000; Fredrickson, 1998). Failures in affect regulation give rise to emotional and psychosocial dysfunctions (Gross & Munoz, 1995; Larsen, 2000).

Affective states are often depicted as operating directly on psychosocial functioning. Positive affect does good things. Negative affect does bad things. Actually, adaptive functioning requires discriminative regulation of affect. People would get into deep trouble if they vented their wrath every time they felt angry. Their lives would be severely constricted if fear automatically triggered immobility and avoidant behavior, because most important pursuits involve risks and fear-arousing threats. Nor can they go around expressing affection, liking, and joyfulness indiscriminately. The impact of affect on behavior operates largely through self-regulatory mechanisms. Thus, negative affect precipitates problem behavior in those of low self-regulatory efficacy but infrequently in those of high self-efficacy.

Adolescence is a time of involvement in intimate relationships, formation of emotionally-charged partnerships, and accompanying emotional ups and downs. Learning how to manage emotionally invested relationships becomes a matter of considerable importance. It is one thing to possess self-regulatory skills but another to be able to adhere to them in taxing and perturbing situations. A resilient sense of efficacy is needed to overrule emotional and psychosocial subverters of self-regulative efforts. Adolescents' sense of efficacy to manage their positive and negative emotional life contributes to their perceived self-efficacy to take charge of their academic life, to ward off peer pressures for transgressive behavior, and to feel empathy for the experiences of others (Bandura, Caprara, Barbaranelli, Gerbino, & Pastorelli, 2003). These forms of personal efficacy foster pro-socialness, deter engagement in antisocial activities and substance abuse, and enable adolescents to manage negative life events without suffering lingering bouts of despondency.

MANAGEMENT OF SEXUALITY

With achievement of reproductive maturity, which is occurring earlier than it did in the past, adolescents must learn how to manage their sexuality long before they are ready to take on the functions of parenthood. While the mass media serve up a heavy dose of sprightly sexual activity, mainly by unmarried partners in uncommitted relationships, societal practices largely foster sexual ignorance and unpreparedness (Brown, Childers, & Waszak, 1990). Unlike most other activities, sexual unpreparedness does not dissuade sexual ventures. Teenagers engage in a high rate of sexual activity and are initiating it at a younger age (Brooks-Gunn & Furstenberg, 1989). Early sexual activity is more prevalent among adolescents from disadvantaged backgrounds and those who have low educational aspirations.

Our society has always had difficulty providing comprehensive sex education and contraceptive services for its youth. Nor is much sexual guidance provided in the home (Koch, 1991). Because many parents do a poor job of it, most youngsters pick up their sex information and a good deal of misinformation late in their development primarily from peers and, to a lesser extent, from the media and from the adverse consequences of uninformed sexual experimentation. Moreover, socially oriented efforts at sex education are often thwarted by sectors of the society that lobby actively for maintaining a veil of silence regarding protective sexual practices in the belief that such information will promote indiscriminate sexuality. They vigorously oppose sex education programs in the schools that talk about contraceptive methods. Even adults who view sexual development more open-mindedly are uneasy talking frankly about sexual matters with their children and evade the subject as much as possible. They have learned to talk a good line, but they convey anxious attitudes about sexual relations. Many impart sexual information to their children only after they suspect their children have already learned "too much" from other sources (Bandura & Walters, 1959).

Because of anxious evasion and moral opposition, efforts at sex education are usually couched in desexualized generalities about reproduction processes that leave much ignorance in their wake. The net result is that teenagers in our society are more sexually ignorant and are getting pregnant at higher rates than in other societies that address the informational, attitudinal, and interpersonal aspects of sexual development openly and provide ready access to contraceptive services.

Most efforts to prevent the adverse consequences of early sexual activity center on educating teenagers about sexual matters and contraceptive use, encouraging them to postpone sexual intercourse, and providing the sexually active ones with contraceptive services. It is widely assumed that if teenagers are adequately informed about sexuality they will take appropriate self-protective action. Heightened awareness and knowledge of risks are important preconditions for self-directed change. Unfortunately, information alone does not necessarily exert much influence on sexual behavior. Translating sexual knowledge into effective self-management of sexuality requires social and self-regulative skills and personal efficacy to exercise control over sexual situations. As Gagnon and Simon (1973) have correctly observed, managing sexuality involves managing interpersonal relationships.

Sexual risk reduction calls for enhancing efficacy rather than simply targeting a specific behavior for change (Bandura, 1994). The major challenge is not teaching teenagers sex guidelines, which is easily achievable, but equipping them with skills that enable them to put the guidelines into practice consistently in the face of counteracting social pressures. Difficulties arise because knowledge and intentions often conflict with interpersonal pressures and sentiments. In these interpersonal predicaments, the sway of allurements, heightened sexual arousal, desire for social acceptance, coercive pressures, situational constraints, fear of rejection, and personal embarrassment can override the influence of the best informed judgment. The weaker the perceived self-efficacy to exercise personal control, the more such social and emotional influences can increase the likelihood of early or risky sexual behavior.

In managing sexuality, people have to exercise influence over themselves as well as over others. This requires self-regulative skills in guiding and motivating one's behavior. Self-regulation operates through internal standards, evaluative reactions to one's conduct, use of motivating self-incentives, and other forms of cognitive self-guidance. Self-regulative skills thus form an integral part of sexual self-management. They partly determine the social situations into which people get themselves, how well they navigate through them, and how effectively they can resist social inducements to risky sexual behavior. It is easier to wield control over preliminary choice behavior that may lead to difficult social predicaments than to try to extricate oneself from such situations while enmeshed in them. This is because the beginning phase involves mainly anticipatory motivators that are amenable to cognitive control. The entanglement phase includes stronger social inducements to engage in unprotected sexual behavior, which are less easily manageable.

The influential role played by efficacy beliefs in the management of sexual activities is documented in studies of contraceptive use by teenage women at high risk for unwanted pregnancy because they often engage in unprotected intercourse (Kasen, Vaughan, & Walter, 1992; Longmore, Manning, Giordino, & Rudolph, 2003). Such research shows that perceived efficacy to manage sexual relationships is associated with more effective use of contraceptives. The predictive relationship remains when controls are applied for demographic factors, knowledge, and sexual experience. Favorable attitudes toward contraceptives increases intentions to use them, but efficacy beliefs determine whether those intentions are put into practice (Basen-Engquist & Parcel, 1992). Even women who are sexually experienced, knowledgeable about contraception, and highly motivated to prevent pregnancy because it would jeopardize career plans fail to use contraceptives consistently and effectively if they lack a sense of personal efficacy (Heinrich, 1993). Drugs and alcohol lower perceived efficacy to adhere to safer sex practices, which increases the likelihood of unprotected sex (Kasen et al., 1992). Experiences of forced unwanted intercourse, which are not uncommon, also lower women's sense of efficacy to exercise control over contraceptive practices (Heinrich, 1993).

A low sense of self-regulatory efficacy in the presence of social pressures promoting risky sexual practices spells trouble. Indeed, the psychosocial profile of teenagers who engage in unprotected intercourse includes a low sense of efficacy to exercise self-protective control in sexual involvements, association with peers who sanction intercourse and are risky in their own sexual behavior, and misconceptions about the prevalence of unprotected intercourse among students their age (Walter et al., 1992). This combination of psychosocial influences overrides beliefs about personal susceptibility to sexually transmitted diseases (STDs) and about their severity. Perceived efficacy and peer influence similarly predict whether or not teenagers intend to become sexually active in the next year, have multiple partners, and use condoms (Walter et al., 1993). Values about sexual involvement at their age also affect behavioral intentions. Whether sexual values and standards determine peer affiliations or affiliations shape sexual standards remains to be determined. There is every indication that these types of influences operate bidirectionally (Bandura & Walters, 1959).

Gilchrist and Schinke (1983) applied the main features of the generic self-regulative model of personal change to teach teenagers how to exercise self-protective control over sexual situations. They received essential factual information about high-risk sexual behavior and self-protective measures. Through modeling, they were taught how to communicate frankly about sexual matters and contraceptives, how to deal with conflicts regarding sexual activities, and how to resist unwanted sexual advances. They practiced applying these social skills by role-playing in simulated situations and received enabling feedback. The self-regulative program significantly enhanced perceived efficacy and skill in managing sexuality. Botvin and his associates provide a comprehensive school-based program that teaches generic self-regulative skills for managing sexual activities and social pressures for alcohol and drug use (Botvin & Dusenbury, 1992). These personal and social life skills include, in addition to strategies for resisting coercions for detrimental conduct, skills in problem solving, decision making, self-guidance, and stress management. Educational aspirations delay initiation into sexual activity. Therefore, efforts to reduce early childbearing should also be directed at promoting educational self-development and aspiration.

Many adolescents engage in unprotected sex with multiple partners, which puts them at risk of STDs, including human immunodeficiency virus (HIV) infection. Change programs incorporating elements of the self-regulative model produce significant reductions in risky sexual behavior in male and female adolescents alike (Jemmott, Jemmott, & Fong, 1992; Jemmott, Jemmott, Spears, Hewitt, & Cruz-Collins, 1992). Those who had the benefit of the program were more knowledgeable about infective risks and more likely to use contraceptives to protect themselves against STDs and unwanted pregnancies than were those who received no instructive guidance or were only given detailed information on the causes, transmission, and prevention of STDs. The findings of these studies indicate that simply imparting sexual information without developing the self-regulative skills and sense of efficacy needed to exercise personal control over sexual relationships has little impact on patterns of sexual behavior.

MANAGEMENT OF HIGH-RISK ACTIVITIES

With growing independence during the passage out of childhood status, some experimentation with risky activities is not all that uncommon (Jessor, 1986). These activities include alcohol and marijuana use, smoking, tooling around in automobiles, and early sexual activity. Adolescents expand and strengthen their sense of efficacy by learning how to deal successfully with potentially troublesome situations in which they are unpracticed, as well as with advantageous life events. The strengthening of self-efficacy is best achieved through guided mastery experiences that provide the knowledge and skills needed to exercise adequate control over situations that place one at risk (Bandura, 1986). Development of resilient self-efficacy requires some experience in mastering difficulties through perseverant effort. Success in managing problem situations instills a strong belief in one's capabilities that provides staying power in the face of difficulties. Adolescents who have been sheltered and left ill-prepared in coping skills are vulnerable to distress and behavioral problems when they encounter difficult interpersonal predicaments that are not completely avoidable.

Most adolescents who experiment with hazardous behaviors quit them after a while, but some become deeply and chronically engaged in them. Activities rarely occur in isolation. Rather, they are clustered by social and normative influences. Sets of behaviors that are blended by social custom create separate clusters of activities, such as drinking goes with partying. Incompatible demands such as heavy partying detract from serious studying. Distinctive patterns of activities are also structured by socioeconomic status, sex, and age-graded practices.

Whatever the sources of the activity patterning may be, frequent engagement in some problem behaviors leads to involvement in other ones that form a high-risk lifestyle. Such behavior usually includes a constellation of activities such as heavy drinking, drug use, transgressive conduct, early sexual activity, and disengagement from academic pursuits (Donovan & Jessor, 1985; Elliott, 1993). Such a lifestyle often has reverberating consequences that jeopardize physical health and self-development. Some of the detrimental effects produce irretrievable losses of life options.

The development and exercise of self-regulatory efficacy is rooted in familial practices. As children increase in maturity and development, family management practices change in form and locus of guidance (Bandura, 1997). In childhood, the interactions are centered heavily within the family. This enables parents to influence directly the course of their children's development. As previously noted, in earlier phases of child development, parents contribute to acquisition of self-regulatory efficacy (Bandura et al., 1996). As adolescents move increasingly into the larger social world outside the home, parents cannot be present to guide their behavior. They rely on their children's personal standards and self-regulatory capabilities to serve as guides and deterrents in nonfamilial contexts. To provide further guidance and support to adolescents, parents need to know what activities these young people are engaging in and their choice of associates outside the home. Parents have to depend largely on the adolescents themselves to tell them what they are doing when they are on their own. Adolescents, therefore, play a major agentic role in this distal guidance process.

Adolescents' perceived efficacy to resist peer pressure to engage in troublesome activities counteracts involvement in delinquent conduct and substance abuse (Caprara et al., 1998, 2002). It does so both directly and by fostering open communication with parents. By acting on beliefs that they can manage peer pressure, adolescents reduce the likelihood of engaging in substance abuse and antisocial activities. Moreover, adolescents who feel efficacious to withstand peer pressure discuss with their parents the predicaments they face. Open familial communication enables parents to provide guidance and social support, and it identifies potential problem situations that may warrant some monitoring. Supportive and enabling parental communication and monitoring, in turn, operate as social safeguards against detrimental involvement in risky activities. Adolescents who have low efficacy to resist peer pressure for risky activities do not talk with their parents about what they are doing outside the home. This shuts out a source of assistance on how to manage an expanding social world centered heavily around peers, some of whom get themselves into highly risky situations.

In much of the theorizing about adolescents, the peer group is portrayed as a ruling force in their lives. Peers are an influential socializing agency, but as shown in the child-parent linkage in the management of high-risk activities, peer affiliation does not disembody adolescents from their families. Moreover, adolescents function agentically rather than just reactively in their transactions with peers.

Social cognitive theory specifies a number of factors that determine the depth of involvement in high-risk activities and the ease of disengagement from them (Bandura, 1997). As noted above, among these factors is the amount of social guidance and development of self-regulatory capabilities to manage potentially risky situations and to extricate oneself from detrimental ones. A secure sense of self-regulatory efficacy and supportive familial communication enable adolescents to elude hazardous and detrimental pathways. Other factors include the intensity of early involvement and the reversibility of effects. Heavy early use of habit-forming substances can create dependencies and lifelong personal vulnerabilities that make it hard to give them up. Experimentations that have benign effects are a different matter from those that place one at danger of injurious consequences or produce irreversible outcomes that shape life courses. For example, drunken driving that leaves one a paraplegic is a tragic event that has lifelong consequences. Good guidance can turn beginning involvement in potentially troublesome activities into opportunities to develop self-regulatory skills to avoid future problems.

The impact of engagement in risky activities on association networks is another predictor. Experimentations within prosocial peer networks carry much less risk than do those that inaugurate one into peer networks deeply enmeshed in a deviant lifestyle. Adolescents vary widely in their perceptions of the extent of peer involvement in problem behavior. Perceived normativeness of risky behavior comes into play. Adolescents who have an exaggerated view of peer involvement are more likely to continue risky activities than are those who believe that such involvement is less widespread. The final consideration is the degree of intrusion of risky activities into prosocial development. The more the problem behavior competes with and impairs prosocial development, the more it jeopardizes successful trajectories. Competitive intrusion on intellectual development is of special importance because intellectual development provides a major means for successful pursuit of prosocial lifestyles.

Detrimental behavior is better deterred by fostering satisfying prosocial options than by efforts to curtail detrimental ones that provide some rewards but at cumulative personal and social costs. Other forms of self-efficacy come into play in enablement for prosocial lifestyles sufficiently attractive to supplant detrimental ones. Thus, for example, a high sense of academic self-efficacy, social self-efficacy, and empathic efficacy are accompanied by low involvement in transgressive activities and substance abuse (Bandura, Caprara, Barbaranelli, Pastorelli, & Regalia, 2001; Bandura et al., 2003).

Thus, whether adolescents forsake risky activities or become chronically enmeshed in them is determined, in large part, by the interplay of personal competencies, self-regulatory capabilities, and the nature of the prevailing social influences in their lives. Those who adopt the hazardous pathway generally place low value on academic self-development and are heavily influenced by peers who model and approve engagement in problem behaviors (Jessor, 1986). Both academic self-development and management of peer pressures for risky activities rest partly on a firm sense of self-regulatory efficacy. Thus, adolescents who are insecure in their efficacy are less able to avoid or curtail involvement in drugs, unprotected sexual activity, and delinquent conduct that jeopardize beneficial life courses than are those who have a strong sense of self-regulatory efficacy (Allen, Leadbeater, & Aber, 1990).

Substance abuse weakens perceived efficacy to resist interpersonal pressures that lead to drug use, thus creating a self-debilitating cycle (Pentz, 1985). Impoverished, hazardous environments present harsh realities with minimal resources, models, and social supports for culturally valued pursuits. But they provide extensive modeling, incentives, social supports, and opportunity structures for antisocial pursuits. Such environments severely tax the coping efficacy of youth embedded in them to make it through adolescence in ways that do not irreversibly foreclose many beneficial life paths. Education provides the best escape from poverty, crime, and substance abuse. Adolescents living under these bleak circumstances need enablement programs that cultivate competencies that help to structure their lives and give meaning and purpose to them.

For adolescents who are drug users or at risk for taking up the habit, Gilchrist and Schinke (1985) developed a self-regulatory program that has been successful in preventing and reducing drug abuse by adolescents. This type of program informs adolescents about drug effects, provides them with interpersonal skills for managing personal and social pressures to use drugs, lowers drug use, and fosters a self-conception as a nonuser (Gilchrist et al., 1987). These findings are all the more interesting because they were achieved with ethnic and minority youth who have to contend with repeated inducements to use alcohol and drugs. Regarding oneself as a nonuser can produce important lifestyle changes by restructuring peer relations and the kinds of activities in which one gets involved (Stall & Biernacki, 1986).

Most of our theories greatly over-predict the incidence of psychosocial pathology under adversity. This is because they favor a *reactive risk* model rather than a *proactive mastery* model. For example, families in our inner cities are living under dismal conditions of poverty, physical decay, social disorganization, and inadequate human services. These environments provide few prosocial opportunities but many antisocial ones. Our theories would lead one to expect that most of the children living in these impoverished, risky environments would be heavily involved in crime, addicted to drugs, or too psychically impaired for a normal life. Adversity does not preordain pathology. Although some youths in high-risk environments are defeated by their pernicious circumstances, remarkably, most manage to make it through the developmental hazards. In adulthood, they support themselves through legitimate jobs, form partnerships, and stay clear of criminal activities.

Families achieve these results through self-sacrifice and perseverant effort that promote their children's development and protect them from dangerous neighborhood activities (Furstenberg, Eccles, Elder, Cook, & Sameroff, 1999). They carve out functional sub-communities through active involvement in church and other social organizations. These affiliations link their children to positive models, constructive activities, supportive social networks and values and social norms that parents hold dear. The social ties compensate for meager neighborhood resources. By exercising their sense of efficacy, the parents do not let their dismal environment defeat them. That most adolescents in hazardous environments manage to overcome their adverse circumstances without serious involvement in self-ruinous pursuits is testimony to their resilience and to the efficacy of their caretakers. But it places a heavy burden on personal efficacy to socially structure beneficial life paths under such conditions.

Such findings dispute the gloomy over-predictions by theories that are more preoccupied with how people are defeated by inimical life circumstances than with how they transcend them. Focusing solely on life risks fails to explain success under adversity. This is because enablement factors, which equip people with the skills and resilient self-beliefs to exert control over their lives, can override the negative effects of risk factors. When enabling factors are considered, as in resilience, they are depicted in static, epidemiological terms as protective factors.

Social cognitive theory construes the positive contributors to adaptation within an agentic perspective as *enablement* factors rather than as *protective* or sheltering factors. Protectiveness shields individuals from harsh realities or may weaken their impact. Enablement equips them with the personal resources to select and structure their environments in ways that set a successful course for their lives. This is the difference between proactive recruitment of sources of positive guidance and support and reactive adaptation to life circumstances. An agentic view of resilience also differs from the dualistic diathesis-stress model in which external stressors act upon personal vulnerabilities. Individuals play a proactive role in their adaptation rather than simply undergo happenings in which environments act upon their personal endowments.

The success with which the risks and challenges of adolescence are managed depends, in no small measure, on the strength of personal efficacy built up through prior mastery experiences. Youngsters who enter adolescence with a sense of efficacy manage the transitional stressors in ways that sustain or increase their sense of personal competence (Nottelmann, 1987). Those beset by a disabling sense of inefficacy transport their vulnerability to stress and dysfunction to the new environmental demands and to the pervasive biopsychosocial changes they find themselves undergoing.

POLITICAL PARTICIPATION AND SOCIAL COMMITMENT

The quality of life in a society rests partly on its political culture and institutional practices. Because of increasing complexity in the economic, technological, and social realities of life, governmental agencies perform many functions that were formerly carried out by familial and other social systems. Therefore, if people are to have some command of their lives, they must exercise influence over the political process. The politically uninvolved become accomplices to their own marginalization by relinquishing control to those who are more than happy to use the governmental system as an agency to advance their parochial interests.

There are two aspects to the exercise of control that are especially relevant to social change through political effort (Bandura, 1997; Gurin & Brim, 1984). The first is a sense of political efficacy that one can have a hand in effecting social change through political activity. The second is the changeableness of the sociopolitical system and its responsiveness to public interest and action. Those who wield power and influence build their privileges into legislative statutes, processes, and institutional structures (Bandura, 1997; Gardner, 1972). They do not relinquish privileges in acts of charity. Effecting social change requires perseverant, collective action in common cause. In the words of John Gardner, social change is not for the short winded.

The joint influence of collective political efficacy and trust in the sociopolitical system predicts the form and level of engagement in political activity (Wolfsfeld, 1986). People who believe they can achieve desired changes through their collective voice and view their governmental systems as trustworthy participate actively in conventional forms of political activities. Those who believe they can accomplish social changes by perseverant collective action but view the governing system and officeholders as untrustworthy favor more confrontive and coercive tactics. The politically apathetic have little faith that they can influence governmental functioning through collective initiatives and are disaffected from the political system.

The development of beliefs about efficacy to influence the political system and the responsiveness, character, and trustworthiness of governmental institutions and officeholders starts early in life. Children neither have much political knowledge nor participate in political activities. Some of their beliefs about the realities of political life are acquired through vicarious rather than direct experience. Children observe the animated political debates by adults around them and in the mass media about the ability to influence the political system and the character and trustworthiness of elected officials. In the vicarious source of political efficacy, the successes and failures of others instill beliefs in the utility and disutility of collective action (Muller, 1972). Children's beliefs about their efficacy to influence governmental practices may also be partially generalized from their experiences in trying to influence adults in educational and other institutional settings with which they must deal. Institutional practices that imbue children with a sense of efficacy that they can play a part in influencing their situations are more likely to instill a belief that political systems are also responsive and influenceable than are practices that breed a sense of futility that one can do much to affect authorities.

From elementary to high school, children's beliefs in their efficacy for political action increases, but their cynicism about government and those who run it also increases. The findings generally show that African American youths have a lower sense of political efficacy and higher political cynicism than do White youths (Lyons, 1970; Rodgers, 1974). But this reflects mainly differences in socioeconomic status. Youths of low socioeconomic status feel politically inefficacious and disaffected from the political system regardless of race. The racial differences emerge at the high socioeconomic level where African American youths express lower political efficacy and greater cynicism than do their White counterparts. This is especially true for perceived efficacy to affect the political process.

Group averages must be interpreted with caution, however, because they mask substantial diversity within ethnic and racial groupings. Thus, for high achievers, racial differences disappear in perceived efficacy for political action but remain in political cynicism. The more minority youths learn about the political system academically, the more cynical they become about it. Knowing how the system is supposed to work in the interests of the public only reinforces dissatisfaction with how it actually functions. Nor do the machinations of political life aired daily on the broadcast news media inspire faith in the integrity of governmental operations. Although heavy use of the news media raises personal political efficacy, it breeds disaffection with the political system (Newhagen, 1994a).

Social impediments and socialization practices may also be important contributors to differences in perceived political efficacy. No such differences are observed in childhood, but with increasing age, females feel less politically efficacious than do males (Campbell, Gurin, & Miller, 1954; Easton & Dennis, 1967). Studies of currently held efficacy beliefs are needed to determine whether the increased participation of women in political and legislative activities is reducing the gender gap in perceived efficacy to influence the political system. However, recent assessments reveal that the gender gap in perceived political efficacy is still with us (Fernández-Ballesteros, Díez-Nicolás, Caprara, Barbaranelli, & Bandura, 2002). The gender variability in political efficacy is, in many respects, more informative than faceless group averages. The suffragists were unshakable in their efficacy and unfazed by public ridicule and vigorous attacks on their efforts to secure voting rights for women. The members of the League of Women Voters, of which there are large numbers nationwide, are exceedingly well informed, highly self-efficacious, and politically active. Increasing numbers of women are becoming legislators, political leaders, and policymakers. In the words of the popular ballad, the times they are a'changing.

The evolving advances in Internet technology enable people to bring their voices to bear on social and political matters of concern in ways they could not do before. The Internet is swift, wide-reaching, and free of institutional controls. It provides an easily accessible forum unimpeded by gatekeepers who command power over the broadcast media. The Internet is not only a ready means for mobilizing grassroots activity to promote desired changes in social practices and policies. It can connect disparate groups to one another in pursuit of common cause. By coordinating and mobilizing decentralized self-organizing groups, participants can meld local networks into widespread collective action.

Political contests are shifting to the cyber-world. The unfettered, pluralistic nature of the Internet is also changing the locus of power of the news media. The cyber-world contains a multiplicity of voices. Online journalistic enterprises, serving diverse ideologies and vested interests, may eventually supplant old-line broadcast networks as the main purveyors of social and political information. Adolescents in this electronic era can now be active players in the sociopolitical arena, rather than just observers of its machinations. The Internet permits ready civic engagement by adolescents in the political process.

The Internet technology distributes the capacity to communicate throughout society and across national borders. But it does not determine the quality of online communities and what gets communicated. Moreover, easy access to communication technologies does not necessarily enlist active participation unless individuals believe that they can achieve desired results by this means. Strong personal and collective efficacy determines whether people make their voices heard in cyber-world politicking and whether they play an active part in bringing about meaningful changes in their lives (Newhagen, 1994a, 1994b). Differential use of this political vehicle may further widen the disparity in perceived political efficacy across gender, race, and ethnicity.

SOCIAL COGNITIVE THEORY IN CULTURAL CONTEXT

A contentious dualism pervades the field of cultural psychology pitting autonomy against interdependence, individualism against collectivism, and human agency against social structure reified as an entity disembodied from the behavior of individuals. It is widely claimed that Western theories lack generalizability to non-Western cultures. The blend of individual, proxy, and collective agency varies cross-culturally. But one needs all forms of agency to make it through the day, wherever one lives.

Most of our cultural psychology is based on territorial culturalism. Nations are used as proxies for psychosocial orientations. For example, residents of Japan get categorized as collectivists and those in the United States as individualists. Cultures are dynamic and internally diverse systems not static monoliths. There is substantial diversity among societies placed in the same category. For example, collectivistic systems founded on Confucianism, Buddhism, and Marxism favor a communal ethic. But they differ in values, meanings, and the customs they promote (Kim, Triandis, Kâitçibasi, Choi, & Yoon, 1994). Nor are so-called individualistic cultures a uniform lot. Americans, Italians, Germans, French, and the British differ in their brands of individualism. There is also diversity across regions within the same country. The Northeast brand of individualism is quite different from the Midwestern and Western versions, which differ from that of the Deep South (Vandello & Cohen, 1999).

There are even greater individual differences among members within cultures (Matsumoto, Kudoh, & Takeuchi, 1996). For example, there are generational and socioeconomic differences in communality in collectivistic cultures. The younger, higher educated, and more affluent members are adopting individualistic orientations. Analyses across activity domains and classes of social relationships reveal that people behave communally in some aspects of their lives and individualistically in many other aspects. They express their cultural orientations conditionally rather than invariantly depending on incentive conditions (Yamagishi, 1988). Thus, members of a collectivistically-oriented society are active contributors to collective effort with in-group members, but slacken their effort in groups composed of out-group members. But when negative sanctions against free riders are instituted they become as communal with outsiders as do people in individualistic cultures.

Freeman and Bordia (2001) further confirm that people vary in individualistic and collectivistic social orientations depending on whether the reference group is familial, peer, academic, or national. Cultural trait measures cast in terms of faceless others and disembodied from domains of activity, social contexts, and incentive conditions mask this diversity upon which human adaptation is conditional. Intra-cultural and inter-domain variability and changeability of cultural orientations as a function of incentive conditions underscores the conceptual and empirical problems of using nations as proxies for culture and then ascribing global traits to the nations and all its members as though they all believed and behaved alike (Gjerde & Onishi, 2000). Moreover, much of the cross-cultural research relies on bicultural contrasts. Members of a single collectivist culture are typically compared to those of a single individualistic one. Given the notable diversity, the dichotomizing approach can spawn a lot of misleading generalizations.

Not only are cultures not monolithic entities, but they are no longer insular. Global connectivity is shrinking cross-cultural uniqueness. Transnational interdependencies and global market forces are restructuring national economies and shaping the political and social life of societies. Advanced telecommunications technologies are disseminating ideas, values, and styles of behavior transnationally at an unprecedented rate. The symbolic environment, feeding off communication satellites, is altering national cultures and producing intercultural commonalities in some lifestyles. The growing role of electronic acculturation will foster a more extensive globalization of culture. People worldwide are becoming increasingly enmeshed in a cyber-world that transcends time, distance, place, and national borders. In addition, mass migrations of people and high global mobility of entertainers, athletes, journalists, academics, and employees of multinational corporations are changing cultural landscapes. This intermixing creates new hybrid cultural forms, blending elements from different ethnicities. Growing ethnic diversity within societies accords functional value to bicultural efficacy to navigate the demands of both one's ethnic subculture and that of the larger society.

These social forces are homogenizing some aspects of life, polarizing other aspects, and fostering a lot of cultural hybridization. The new realities call for broadening the scope of cross-cultural research beyond the focus on the social forces operating within given societies. The lives of contemporary adolescents in this boundless cyber-world are markedly different from the more insular experiences of the adolescents of yesteryear. Recall the earlier discussion of the mobile communication subculture of present-day adolescents.

One must distinguish between inherent capacities and how culture shapes these potentialities into diverse forms. For example, observational learning figures prominently in social cognitive theory. Humans have evolved an advanced capacity for observational learning. It is essential for their self-development and functioning regardless of the culture in which they reside. Indeed, in many cultures, the word for "*learning*" is the word for "*show*" (Reichard, 1938). Modeling is a universalized human capacity. But what is modeled, how modeling influences are socially structured, and the purposes they serve varies in different cultural milieus (Bandura & Walters, 1963).

A growing body of research similarly shows that a resilient sense of efficacy has generalized functional value regardless of whether one resides in an individualistically-oriented culture or a collectivistically-oriented one

(Earley, 1993, 1994; Gibson, 1995). Being immobilized by self-doubt and perceived futility of effort has little evolutionary value. But how efficacy beliefs are developed and structured, the ways in which they are exercised, and the purposes to which they are put vary cross-culturally. In short, there is a commonality in basic agentic capacities and mechanisms of operation, but diversity in the culturing of these inherent capacities.

Research testifies to the cross-cultural generalizability of self-efficacy theory. The factor structure of adolescents' self-efficacy beliefs is essentially the same in different cultural systems (Pastorelli et al., 2001). Not only is the structure of self-efficacy beliefs comparable cross-culturally, but so are their functional properties. Regardless of whether the cultures are American, Italian, Korean, or Chinese, the stronger the perceived self-efficacy, the higher the performance attainments (Bandura et al., 1996; Bong, 2001; Joo et al., 2000). The cross-cultural comparability of function is evident as well in the impact of efficacy beliefs on perceived occupational efficacy and career choice and development (Bandura, Barbarinelli, Caprara, & Pastorelli, 2001; Lent, Brown, Nota, & Soresi, 1987; Lent et al., 2001).

Even the mechanisms through which self-efficacy beliefs affect performance are replicated cross-culturally. For example, social support has been shown to enhance psychosocial functioning. However, mediational analysis across diverse spheres of functioning reveal that it does so only indirectly to the extent that it raises perceived self-efficacy to manage environmental demands (Bandura, 2002). Park and her associates (Park et al., 2000) examined the causal structure involving different sources of social support, perceived academic self-efficacy, life satisfaction, and academic achievement in Korean children at different age levels. In accord with the functional relations reported in studies in the American and Chinese milieu, the impact of social support on academic achievement is entirely mediated through perceived self-efficacy. Social support raises perceived efficacy, which, in turn, raises academic achievement and satisfaction with one's home and school life. Similarly, the impact of social support on anxiety and depression in Chinese students and on Italian students' career preferences is entirely mediated through perceived self-efficacy (Cheung & Sun, 2000; Lent et al., 2003).

SELF-EFFICACY IN SOCIAL COGNITIVE THEORY

It should be noted that the efficacy belief system operates as a component within the broader conceptual framework of social cognitive theory (Bandura, 1986, 2001). Personal and collective efficacy beliefs work in concert with other determinants in the theory to govern human thought, affect, motivation, and action. These various determinants, which fall beyond the scope of this volume, are reviewed in some detail elsewhere (Bandura, 1986). However, the efficacy belief system occupies a pivotal role in causal structures because it provides the foundation for many of the other classes of determinants in this agentic theoretical perspective.

REFERENCES

Allen, J. P., Leadbeater, B. J., & Aber, J. L. (1990). The relationship of adolescents' expectations and values to delinquency, hard drug use and unprotected sexual intercourse. *Development and Psychopathology, 2,* 85-98.

Ardelt, M., & Eccles, J. S. (2001). Effects of mothers' parental efficacy beliefs and promotive parenting strategies on inner-city youth. *Journal of Family Issues, 22,* 944-972.

Ashton, P. T., & Webb, R. B. (1986). *Making a difference: Teachers' sense of efficacy and student achievement.* White Plains, NY: Longman.

Baldwin, C., Baldwin, A., Sameroff, A., & Seifer, R. (1989, April). *The role of family interaction in the prediction of adolescent competence.* Paper presented at the biennial meeting of the Society for Research in Child Development, Kansas City, MO.

Baltes, M. M. (1996). *The many faces of dependency in old age.* New York: Cambridge University Press.

Baltes, P. B. (1983). Life-span developmental psychology: Observations on history and theory revisited. In R. M. Lerner (Ed.), *Developmental psychology: Historical and philosophical perspectives* (pp. 79-111). Hillsdale, NJ: Lawrence Erlbaum.

Bandura, A. (1964). The stormy decade: Fact or fiction? *Psychology in the Schools, 1,* 224-231.

Bandura, A. (1982). The psychology of chance encounters and life paths. *American Psychologist, 37,* 747-755.

Bandura, A. (1986). *Social foundations of thought and action: A social cognitive theory.* Englewood Cliffs, NJ: Prentice-Hall.

Bandura, A. (1994). Social cognitive theory and exercise of control over HIV infection. In R. J. DiClemente & J. L. Peterson (Eds.), *Preventing AIDS: Theories and methods of behavioral interventions* (pp. 25-59). New York: Plenum.

Bandura, A. (1997). *Self-efficacy: The exercise of control.* New York: Freeman.

Bandura, A. (1998). Exploration of fortuitous determinants of life paths. *Psychological Inquiry, 9,* 95-99.

Bandura, A. (2000). Exercise of human agency through collective efficacy. *Current Directions in Psychological Science, 9,* 75-78.

Bandura, A. (2001). Social cognitive theory: An agentic perspective. *Annual review of psychology* (Vol. 52, pp. 1-26). Palo Alto, CA: Annual Reviews.

Bandura, A. (2002). Social cognitive theory in cultural context. *Journal of Applied Psychology: An International Review, 51,* 269-290.

Bandura, A. (2004). Health promotion by social cognitive means. *Health Education & Behavior, 31,* 143-164.

Bandura, A., Barbaranelli, C., Caprara, G. V., & Pastorelli, C. (1996). Multifacted impact of self-efficacy beliefs on academic functioning. *Child Development, 67,* 1206-1222.

Bandura, A., Barbaranelli, C., Caprara, G. V., & Pastorelli, C. (2001). Self-efficacy beliefs as shapers of children's aspirations and career trajectories. *Child Development, 72,* 187-206.

Bandura, A., Caprara, G. V., Barbaranelli, C., Gerbino, M., & Pastorelli, C. (2001). Role of affective self-regulatory efficacy in diverse spheres of psychosocial functioning. *Child Development, 74,* 769-782.

Bandura, A., Caprara, G. V., Barbaranelli, C., Gerbino, M., & Pastorelli, C. (2003). Impact of affective self regulatory efficacy on diverse spheres of functioning. *Child Development, 74,* 1-14.

Bandura, A., Caprara, G. V., Barbaranelli, C., Pastorelli, C., & Regalia, C. (2001). Sociocognitive self-regulatory mechanisms governing transgressive behavior. *Journal of Personality and Social Psychology, 80,* 125-135.

Bandura, A., Caprara G. V., Regalia, C., Scabini, E., & Barbaranelli, C. (2004). *Impact of family efficacy beliefs on quality of family functioning and satisfaction with family life.* Manuscript submitted for publication.

Bandura, A., & Walters, R. H. (1959). *Adolescent aggression.* New York: Ronald Press.

Bandura, A., & Walters, R. H. (1963). *Social learning and personality development.* New York: Holt, Rinehart & Winston.

Basen-Engquist, K., & Parcel, G. S. (1992). Attitudes, norms and self-efficacy: A model of adolescents' HIV-related sexual risk behavior. *Health Education Quarterly, 19,* 263-277.

Betz, N. E. (1994). Career counseling for women in the sciences. In W. B. Walsh & S. H. Osipow (Eds.), *Career counseling for women* (pp. 237-262). Hillsdale, NJ: Erlbaum.

Betz, N. E., & Hackett, G. (1986). Applications of self-efficacy theory to understanding career choice behavior. *Journal of Social and Clinical Psychology, 4,* 279-289.

Betz, N. E., & Schifano, R. S. (2000). Evaluation of an intervention to increase realistic self-efficacy and interests in college women. *Journal of Vocational Behavior, 56,* 35-52.

Bishop, J. H. (1989). Why the apathy in American high schools? *Educational Researcher, 18,* 6-10.

Bong, M. (2001). Between- and within-domain relations of academic motivation among middle and high school students: Self-efficacy, task-value, and achievement goals. *Journal of Educational Psychology, 93,* 23-34.

Botvin, G. J., & Dusenbury, L. (1992). Substance abuse prevention: Implications for reducing risk of HIV infection. *Psychology of Addictive Behaviors, 6,* 70-80.

Brandstädter, J. (1992). Personal control over development: Implications of self-efficacy. In R. Schwarzer (Ed.), *Self-efficacy: Thought control of action* (pp. 127-145). Washington, DC: Hemisphere.

Brooks-Gunn, J., & Furstenberg, F. F., Jr. (1989). Adolescent sexual behavior. *American Psychologist, 44,* 249-257.

Brown, J. D., Childers, K. W., & Waszak, C. S. (1990). Television and adolescent sexuality. *Journal of Adolescent Health Care, 11*, 62-70.

Brown, S. D., Lent, R. D., & Larkin, K. C. (1989). Self-efficacy as a moderator of scholastic aptitude-academic performance relationships. *Journal of Vocational Behavior, 35*, 64-75.

Bussey, K., & Bandura, A. (1999). Social cognitive theory of gender development and differentiation. *Psychological Review, 106*, 676-713.

Campbell, A., Gurin, G., & Miller, W. E. (1954). *The voter decides.* Evanston, IL: Row, Peterson.

Caprara, G. V. (2002). Personality: Filling the gap between basic processes and molar functioning. In C. von Hofsten & L. Bäckman (Eds.), *Psychology at the turn of the Millennium: Vol. 2. Social, development, and clinical perspective* (pp. 201-224). Brighton, UK: Psychology Press.

Caprara, G. V., Pastorelli, C., Regalia, C., Scabini, E., & Bandura, A. (2005). Impact of adolescents' filial self-efficacy on family functioning and satisfaction. *Journal of Research on Adolescence, 15*, 71-97.

Caprara, G. V., Regalia, C., & Bandura, A. (2002). Longitudinal impact of perceived self-regulatory efficacy on violent conduct. *European Psychologist, 7*, 63-69.

Caprara, G. V., Scabini, E., Barbaranelli, C., Pastorelli, C., Regalia, C., & Bandura, A. (1998). Impact of adolescents' perceived self-regulatory efficacy on familial communication and antisocial conduct. *European Psychologist, 3*, 125-132.

Carey, K. B., & Carey, M. P. (1993). Changes in self-efficacy resulting from unaided attempts to quit smoking. *Psychology of Addictive Behaviors, 7*, 219-224.

Cheung, S., & Sun, S. Y. K. (2000). Effects of self-efficacy and social support on the mental health conditions of mutual-aid organization members. *Social Behavior and Personality, 28*, 413-422.

Connell, D. B., Turner, R. R., & Mason, E. F. (1985). Summary of findings of the school health education evaluation: Health promotion effectiveness, implementation, and costs. *Journal of School Health, 55*, 316-321.

Cox, M. J., & Paley, B. (2003). Understanding families as systems. *Current Directions in Psychological Science, 12*, 193-196.

Cutrona, C. E., & Troutman, B. R. (1986). Social support, infant temperament, and parenting self-efficacy: A mediational model of postpartum depression. *Child Development, 57*, 1507-1518.

Debowski, S., Wood, R., & Bandura, A. (2001). Impact of guided exploration and enactive exploration on self-regulatory mechanisms and information acquisition through electronic search. *Journal of Applied Psychology. 6*, 1129-11.

Donovan, J. E., & Jessor, R. (1985). Structure of problem behavior in adolescence and young adulthood. *Journal of Consulting and Clinical Psychology, 53*, 890-904.

Earley, P. C. (1993). East meets West meets Mideast: Further explorations of collectivistic and individualistic work groups. *Academy of Management Journal, 36*, 319-348.

Earley, P. C. (1994). Self or group? Cultural effects of training on self-efficacy and performance. *Administrative Science Quarterly, 39*, 89-117.

Easton, D., & Dennis, J. (1967). The child's acquisition of regime norms: Political efficacy. *The American Political Science Review, 35*, 25-38.

Eccles, J. S., & Midgley, C. (1989). Stage-environment fit: Developmentally appropriate classrooms for young adolescents. In C. Ames & R. Ames (Eds.), *Research on motivation in education* (Vol. 3, pp. 139-186). San Diego: Academic Press.

Eccles, J. S., Midgley, C., Wigfield, A., Buchanan, D. R., Flanagan, C., & Mac Iver, D. (1993). The impact of stage-environment fit on young adolescents' experiences in schools and families. *American Psychologist, 48*, 90-101.

Elder, G. H., Jr. (1981). History and the life course. In D. Bertaux (Ed.), *Biography and society: The life history approach in the social sciences* (pp. 77-115). Beverly Hills, CA: Sage.

Elder, G. H., Jr. (1994). Time, human agency, and social change: Perspectives on the life course. *Social Psychology Quarterly, 57*, 4-15.

Elder, G. H., Jr. (1995). Life trajectories in changing societies. In A. Bandura (Ed.), *Self-efficacy in changing societies* (pp. 46-68). New York: Cambridge University Press.

Elder, G. H., & Ardelt, M. (1992, March). *Families adapting to economic pressure: Some consequences for parents and adolescents.* Paper presented at the Society for Research on Adolescence, Washington, DC.

Elliott, D. S. (1993). Health-enhancing and health compromising lifestyles. In S. G. Millstein, A. C. Petersen, & E. O. Nightingale (Eds.), *Promoting the health of adolescents: New directions for the twenty-first century* (pp. 119-145). New York: Oxford University Press.

Fernández-Ballesteros, R., Díez-Nicolás, J., Caprara, G. V., Barbaranelli, C., & Bandura, A. (2002). Structural relation of perceived personal efficacy to perceived collective efficacy. *Applied Psychology: An International Review, 51*, 107-125.

Folkman, S., & Moskowitz, J. T. (2000). Positive affect and the other side of coping. *American Psychologist, 55*, 647-654.

Freeman, M. A., & Bordia, P. (2001). The structure of individualism-collectivism: An integrative review and confirmatory factor analysis. *European Journal of Personality, 15*, 105-121.

Fredrickson, B. L. (1998). What good are positive emotions? *Review of General Psychology, 2*, 300-319.

Furstenberg, F. F., Eccles, J., Elder, G. H., Jr., Cook, T., & Sameroff, A. (1999). *Adolescent development in urban communities: How families manage risk and opportunity.* Chicago: University of Chicago Press.

Gagnon, J., & Simon, W. (1973). *Sexual conduct, the social sources of human sexuality.* Chicago: Aldine.

Gardner, J. W. (1972). *In common cause.* New York: W. W. Norton.

Gibson, C. B. (1995). *Determinants and consequences of group-efficacy beliefs in work organizations in U.S., Hong Kong, and Indonesia.* Unpublished doctoral dissertation, University of California, Irvine, CA.

Gibson, S., & Dembo, M. (1984). Teacher efficacy: A construct validation. *Journal of Educational Psychology, 76*, 569-582.

Giddens, A. (1984). *The constitution of society: Outline of the theory of structuration.* Berkeley, CA: University of California Press.

Gilchrist, L. D., & Schinke, S. P. (1983). Coping with contraception: Cognitive and behavioral methods with adolescents. *Cognitive Therapy and Research, 7,* 379-388.

Gilchrist, L. D., & Schinke, S. P. (Eds.). (1985). *Preventing social and health problems through life skills training.* Seattle, WA: University of Washington.

Gilchrist, L. D., Schinke, S. P., Trimble, J. E., & Cvetkovich, G. T. (1987). Skills enhancement to prevent substance abuse among American Indian adolescents. *International Journal of the Addictions, 22,* 869-879.

Gist, M. E., Schwoerer, C., & Rosen, B. (1989). Effects of alternative training methods on self-efficacy and performance in computer software training. *Journal of Applied Psychology, 74,* 884-891.

Gjerde, P. F., & Onishi, M. (2000). Selves, cultures, and nations: The psychological imagination of the Japanese in the era of globalization. *Human Development, 43,* 216-226.

Gross, D., Fogg, L., & Tucker, S. (1995). The efficacy of parent training for promoting positive parent-toddler relationships. *Research in Nursing & Health, 18,* 489-499.

Gross, J. J., & Munoz, R. F. (1995). Emotion regulation and mental health. *Clinical Psychology: Science and Practice, 2,* 151-164.

Gurin, P., & Brim, O. G., Jr. (1984). Change in self in adulthood: The example of sense of control. In P. B. Baltes & O. G. Brim, Jr. (Eds.), *Life-span development and behavior* (Vol. 6, pp. 281-334). New York: Academic Press.

Hackett, G. (1985). The role of mathematics self-efficacy in the choice of math-related majors of college women and men: A path analysis. *Journal of Counseling Psychology, 32,* 47-56.

Hackett, G. (1995). Self-efficacy in career choice and development. In A. Bandura (Ed.), *Self-efficacy in changing societies* (pp. 232-258). New York: Cambridge University Press.

Hackett, G., & Betz, N. E. (1981). A self-efficacy approach to the career development of women. *Journal of Vocational Behavior, 18,* 326-339.

Hamilton, S. F. (1987). Apprenticeship as a transition to adulthood in West Germany. *American Journal of Education, 95,* 314-345.

Heinrich, L. B. (1993). Contraceptive self-efficacy in college women. *Journal of Adolescent Health, 14,* 269-276.

Hultsch, D. F., & Plemons, J. K. (1979). Life events and life-span development. In P. B. Bates & O. G. Brim, Jr. (Eds.), *Life-span development and behavior* (Vol. 2, pp. 1-36). New York: Academic Press.

Jemmott, J. B., III, Jemmott, L. S., & Fong, G. T. (1992). Reductions in HIV risk-associated sexual behaviors among black male adolescents: Effects of an AIDS prevention intervention. *American Journal of Public Health, 82,* 372-377.

Jemmott, J. B., III, Jemmott, L. S., Spears, H., Hewitt, N., & Cruz-Collins, M. (1992). Self-efficacy, hedonistic expectancies, and condom-use intentions among inner-city black adolescent women: A social cognitive approach to AIDS risk behavior. *Journal of Adolescent Health, 13,* 512-519.

Jessor, R. (1986). Adolescent problem drinking: Psychosocial aspects and developmental outcomes. In R. K. Silbereisen, K. Eyferth, & G, Rudinger (Eds.), *Development as action in context* (pp. 241-264). Berlin: Springer-Verlag.

Joo, Y. J., Bong, M., & Choi, H. J. (2000). Self-efficacy for self-regulated learning, academic self-efficacy, and internet self-efficacy in web-based instruction. *Educational Technology Research and Development, 48*, 5-17.

Kasen, S., Vaughan, R. D., & Walter, H. J. (1992). Self-efficacy for AIDS preventive behaviors among tenth grade students. *Health Education Quarterly, 19*, 187-202.

Killen, J. D., Robinson, T. N., Telch, M. J., Saylor, K. E., Maron, D. J., Rich, T., et al. (1989). The Stanford adolescent heart health program. *Health Education Quarterly, 16*, 263-283.

Kim, U., Triandis, H. D., Kâitçibasi, C., Choi, S., & Yoon, G. (1994). *Individualism and collectivism: Theory, method, and applications.* Thousand Oaks, CA: Sage.

Koch, P. B. (1991). Sex education. In R. M. Lerner, A. C. Petersen, & J. Brooks-Gunn (Eds.), *Encyclopedia of adolescence* (Vol. 2, pp. 1004-1006). New York: Garland.

Kuczynski, L. (2003). *Handbook of dynamics in parent-child relations.* Thousand Oaks, CA: Sage.

Larsen, R. J. (2000). Toward a science of mood regulation. *Psychological Inquiry, 11*, 129-141.

Lent, R. W., Brown, S. D., Brenner, B., Batra Chopra, S., Davis, T., Talleyrand, R., et al. (2001). The role of contextual supports and barriers in the choice of math/science educational options: A test of social cognitive hypotheses. *Journal of Counseling Psychology, 48*, 474-483.

Lent, R. W., Brown, S. D., & Hackett, G. (1994). Toward a unifying social cognitive theory of career and academic interest, choice, and performance. *Journal of Vocational Behavior, 45*, 79-122.

Lent, R. W., Brown, S. D., & Larkin, K. C. (1984). Relation of self-efficacy expectations to academic achievement and persistence. *Journal of Counseling Psychology, 31*, 356-362.

Lent, R. W., Brown, S. D., & Larkin, K. C. (1986). Self-efficacy in the prediction of academic performance and perceived career options. *Journal of Counseling Psychology, 33*, 265-269.

Lent, R. W., Brown, S. D., & Larkin, K. C. (1987). Comparison of three theoretically derived variables in predicting career and academic behavior: Self-efficacy, interest congruence, and consequence thinking. *Journal of Counseling Psychology, 34*, 293-298.

Lent, R. W., Brown, S. D., Nota, L., & Soresi, S. (2003). Testing social cognitive interest and choice hypotheses across Holland types in Italian high school students. *Journal of Vocational Behavior, 62*, 101-118.

Lent, R. W., Lopez, F. G., & Bieschke, K. J. (1993). Predicting mathematics-related choice and success behaviors: Test of an expanded social cognitive model. *Journal of Vocational Behavior, 42*, 223-236.

Lewin, T. (1998, October 4). "How Boys Lost Out to Girl Power." *New York Times*, p. A21.

Longmore, M. A., Manning, W. D., Giordano, P. C., & Rudolph, J. L. (2003). Contraceptive self-effiacy: Does it influence adolescents' contraceptive use? *Journal of Health and Social Behavior, 44*, 45-60.

Luepker, R. V., Perry, C. L., McKinlay, S. M., Nader, P. R., Parcel, G. S., Stone, E. J., et al. (1996). Outcomes of a field trial to improve children's dietary patterns and physical activity: The child and adolescent trial for cardiovascular health (CATCH). *Journal of the American Medical Association, 275*, 768-776.

Lyons, S. R. (1970). The political socialization of ghetto children: Efficacy and cynicism. *Journal of Politics, 32*, 288-304.

Maccoby, E. (2003). Dynamic viewpoints on parent-child relations: Their implications for socialization processes. In L. Kuczynski (Ed.). *Handbook of dynamics in parent-child relations* (pp. 439-452). Thousand Oaks, CA: Sage.

Marlatt, G. A., Baer, J. S., & Quigley, L. A. (1995). Self-efficacy and addictive behavior. In A. Bandura (Ed.), *Self-efficacy in changing societies* (pp. 289-315). New York: Cambridge University Press.

Matsumoto, D., Kudoh, T., & Takeuchi, S. (1996). Changing patterns of individualism and collectivism in the United States and Japan. *Culture & Psychology, 2*, 77-107.

Mayer, J. D., & Salovey, P. (1997). What is emotional intelligence? In P. Salovey & D. Sluyter (Eds.), *Emotional development and emotional intelligence: Implications for educators* (pp. 3-31). New York: Basic Books.

Midgley, C., Feldlaufer, H., & Eccles, J. S. (1989). Change in teacher efficacy and student self- and task-related beliefs in mathematics during the transition to junior high school. *Journal of Educational Psychology, 81*, 247-258.

Muller, E. N. (1972). A test of a partial theory of potential for political violence. *The American Political Science Review, 66*, 928-959.

Murray, D. M., Pirie, P., Luepker, R. V., & Pallonen, U. (1989). Five-and six-year follow-up results from four seventh-grade smoking prevention strategies. *Journal of Behavioral Medicine, 12*, 207-218.

Newhagen, J. E. (1994a). Self-efficacy and call-in political television show use. *Communication Research, 21*, 366- 379.

Newhagen, J. E. (1994b). Media use and political efficacy: The suburbanization of race and class. *Journal of the American Society for Information Science, 45*, 386-394.

Nottelmann, E. D. (1987). Competence and self-esteem during transition from childhood to adolescence. *Developmental Psychology, 23*, 441-450.

Oksman, V., & Turtiainen, J. (2004). Mobile communication as a social stage: Meanings of mobile communication in everyday life among teenagers in Finland. *New Media & Society, 6*, 319-339.

Olioff, M., & Aboud, F. E. (1991). Predicting postpartum dysphoria in primiparous mothers: Roles of perceived parenting self-efficacy and self-esteem. *Journal of Cognitive Psychotherapy, 5*, 3-14.

Osterman, P. (1980). *Getting started: The youth labor market*. Cambridge, MA: MIT Press.

Ozer, E. M. (1995). The impact of childcare responsibility and self-efficacy on the psychological health of working mothers. *Psychology of Women Quarterly, 19*, 315-336.

Pajares, F., & Schunk, D. H. (2001). Self-beliefs and school success: Self-efficacy, self-concept, and school achievement. In R. J. Riding & S. G. Rayner (Eds.), *International perspectives on individual differences, Vol 2: Self perception* (pp. 239-265). Westport, CT: Ablex.

Park, Y. S., Kim, U., Chung, K. S., Lee, S. M., Kwon, H. H., & Yang, K. M. (2000). Causes and consequences of life-satisfaction among primary, junior high, senior high school students. *Korean Journal of Health Psychology, 5*, 94-118.

Pastorelli, C., Caprara, G. V., Barbaranelli, C., Rola, J., Rozsa, S., & Bandura, A. (2001). Structure of children's perceived self-efficacy: A cross-national study. *European Journal of Psychological Assessment, 17*, 87-97.

Pentz, M. A. (1985). Social competence and self-efficacy as determinants of substance abuse in adolescence. In T. A. Wills & S. Shiffman (Eds.), *Coping and substance use* (pp. 117-142). New York: Academic Press.

Perri, M. G. (1985). Self-change strategies for the control of smoking, obesity, and problem drinking. In T. A. Wills & S. Shiffman (Eds.), *Coping and substance use* (pp. 295-317). New York: Academic Press.

Perry, C. L., Kelder, S. H., Murray, D. M., & Klepp, K. (1992). Communitywide smoking prevention: Long-term outcomes of the Minnesota heart health program and the class of 1989 study. *American Journal of Public Health, 82*, 1210-1216.

Petersen, A. C. (1988). Adolescent development. In M. R. Rosenzweig & L. W. Porter (Eds.), *Annual Review of Psychology* (pp. 583-607). Palo Alto, CA: Annual Reviews.

Reichard, G. A. (1938). Social life. In F. Boas (Ed.), *General anthropology* (pp. 409-486). Boston: D. C. Heath.

Rodgers, H. R. (1974). Toward explanation of the political efficacy and political cynicism of black adolescents: An exploratory study. *American Journal of Political Science, 18*, 257-282.

Rosenbaum, J. E., & Kariya, T. (1989). From high school to work: Market and institutional mechanisms in Japan. *American Journal of Sociology, 94*, 1334-1365.

Rutter, M., Graham, P., Chadwick, O. F. D., & Yule, W. (1976). Adolescent turmoil: Fact or fiction? *Journal of Child Psychology and Psychiatry, 17*, 35-56.

Saarni, C. (1999) *The development of emotional competence.* New York: Guilford.

Sameroff, A. J. (1995). General systems theory and developmental psychopathology. In D. Cicchetti & D. J. Cohen (Eds.), *Developmental psychopathology* (Vol. 1, pp. 659-695). New York: Wiley.

Schunk, D. H., & Lilly, M. W. (1984). Sex differences in self-efficacy and attributions: Influence of performance feedback. *Journal of Early Adolescence, 4*, 203-213.

Silver, E. J., Bauman, L. J., & Ireys, H. T. (1995). Relationships of self-esteem and efficacy to psychological distress in mothers of children with chronic physical illnesses. *Health Psychology, 14*, 333-340.

Sofronoff, K., & Farbotko, M. (2002). The effectiveness of parent management training to increase self-efficacy in parents of children with Asperger syndrome. *Autism, 6*, 271-286.

Stall, R., & Biernacki, P. (1986). Spontaneous remission from the problematic use of substances: An inductive model derived from a comparative analysis of the alcohol, opiate, tobacco, and food/obesity literatures. *The International Journal of the Addictions, 21*, 1-23.

Taylor C. B., Winzelberg, A., & Celio, A. (2001). Use of interactive media to prevent eating disorders. In R. Striegel-Moor & L. J. Smolak (Eds.), *Eating disorders: New direction for research and practice* (pp. 255-270). Washington, DC: American Psychological Association.

Teti, D. M., & Gelfand, D. M. (1991). Behavioral competence among mothers of infants in the first year: The mediational role of maternal self-efficacy. *Child Development, 62*, 918-929.

Vandello, J. A. & Cohen, D. (1999). Patterns of individualism and collectivism across the United States. *Journal of Personality and Social Psychology, 77*, 279-292.

Walter, H., Vaughn, R., Gladis, M., Ragin, D., Kasen, S., & Cohall, A. (1992). Factors associated with AIDS risk behaviors among high school students in an AIDS epicenter. *American Journal of Public Health, 82*, 528-532.

Walter, H., Vaughn, R., Gladis, M., Ragin, D., Kasen, S., & Cohall, A. (1993). Factors associated with AIDS-related behavioral intentions among high school students in an AIDS epicenter. *Health Education Quarterly, 20*, 409-420.

Williams, T. M., Joy, L. A., Travis, L., Gotowiec, A., Blum-Steele, M., Aiken, L. S., et al. (1987). Transition to motherhood: A longitudinal study. *Infant Mental Health Journal, 8*, 251-265.

Wolfsfeld, G. (1986). Evaluational origins of political action: The case of Israel. *Political Psychology, 7*, 767-788.

Woolfolk, A. E., Rosoff, B., & Hoy, W. K. (1990). Teachers' sense of efficacy and their beliefs about managing students. *Teaching & Teacher Education, 6*, 137-148.

Yamagishi, T. (1988). The provision of a sanctioning system in the United States and Japan. *Social Psychology Quarterly, 51*, 265-271.

Zimmerman, B. J. (1990). Self-regulating academic learning and achievement: The emergence of a social cognitive perspective. *Educational Psychology Review, 2*, 173-201.

Zimmerman, B. J., & Bandura, A. (1994). Impact of self-regulatory influences on writing course attainment. *American Educational Research Journal, 31*, 845–862.

Zimmerman, B. J., Bandura, A., & Martinez-Pons, M. (1992). Self-motivation for academic attainment: The role of self-efficacy beliefs and personal goal setting. *American Educational Research Journal, 29*, 663–676.

CHAPTER 2

ADOLESCENTS' DEVELOPMENT OF PERSONAL AGENCY

The Role of Self-Efficacy Beliefs and Self-Regulatory Skill

Barry J. Zimmerman and Timothy J. Cleary

Adolescence is often a stressful period during development because it involves a pivotal transition from childhood dependency to adulthood independence and self-sufficiency (Smith, Cowie, & Blades, 1998). One major challenge that adolescents encounter during their teenage years involves acquiring a sense of personal agency in what often seems to be a recalcitrant world. Personal agency refers to one's capability to originate and direct actions for given purposes. It is influenced by the belief in one's effectiveness in performing specific tasks, which is termed *self-efficacy,* as well as by one's actual skill. In this chapter, we trace the development of personal agency during adolescence as well as the defining and distinctive features of adolescent students' self-efficacy beliefs. We then contrast self-efficacy with alternative self-related con-

Self-Efficacy Beliefs of Adolescents, 45–69
Copyright © 2006 by Information Age Publishing

structs, and we examine its causal role in adolescents' motivation, achievement, and academic development. Finally, we describe the interdependence of adolescents' academic self-efficacy beliefs and their use of self-regulatory processes, and we consider the implications of this research for designing training interventions to enhance students' academic agency.

ADOLESCENCE AND THE DEVELOPMENT OF PERSONAL AGENCY

In both the schools and the larger society, the onset of adolescence marks a profound shift in expectations regarding students' ability to assume responsibility for their functioning. When students enter middle or junior high schools, they are no longer under the direct control of a single teacher but instead are taught by a number of teachers in different classrooms, often with different classmates. These adolescents are expected to personally manage these diverse requirements for learning in class or to seek out help when it is needed, especially from their teachers. At this middle level of schooling, a significant part of students' academic work is completed outside of class, including reading assigned texts, writing papers, and preparing for tests. Adolescents' success in making this developmental transition is complicated by a major increase in the difficulty of the academic work that is assigned in middle or junior high schools (Wigfield, Eccles, & Pintrich, 1996). If adolescents fail to regulate this demanding academic environment effectively, their academic grades will likely decline—often leading to a loss of self-efficacy about succeeding in school. As their self-efficacy diminishes, adolescents can become embedded in a downward cycle of academic achievement that may involve aligning themselves with peers who possess unfavorable views about the value and importance of school (Steinberg, Brown, & Dornbusch, 1996). Conversely, adolescents with a strong sense of efficacy for learning are more resilient and better able to resist the adverse academic influences of low-achieving peers than are those with a weak sense of efficacy (Bandura, Barbaranelli, Caprara, & Pastorelli, 1996).

To succeed in school, adolescents develop diverse self-regulatory skills, such as goal setting, self-monitoring, time management, and self-evaluation. Homework assignments must be transformed into personal goals; study time needs to be allocated prudently; and completion of the goals needs to be self-monitored closely. Adolescents also must learn powerful strategies to enhance various forms of learning, such as note-taking, help-seeking, storing and recalling information, reading, writing, and test preparation (Zimmerman, Bonner, & Kovach, 1996). Strategies are also beneficial in assisting them to manage out-of-school extracurricular activities, such as music or sports (Cleary & Zimmerman, 2001; McPherson & Zimmerman, 2002). Unfortunately, adolescents are often poor at setting goals and anticipating the consequences of various courses of action. As a result, they fail to employ effective task-specific strategies such as preparing for tests. Later in this chapter, we will discuss how effective strategies can be learned through observation of successful models and from personal experiences with success and failure. We will also describe how self-regulated students cope with failure in a sequence of cyclical self-processes without experiencing a loss of self-efficacy and how this resilient sense of self-efficacy can sustain their efforts to learn in a self-directed way. This belief in one's self-regulative capability to attain goals is the core of a resolute sense of personal agency.

WHAT IS SELF-EFFICACY AND HOW ARE THESE BELIEFS DISTINCTIVE?

Self-efficacy refers to subjective judgments of one's capabilities to organize and execute courses of action to attain designated goals (Bandura, 1977, 1997). It is a belief about what a person *can* do rather than personal judgments about one's physical or personality attributes. It is also context-specific and varies across several dimensions, such as level, generality, and strength. The *level* of self-efficacy refers to its dependence on the difficultly level of a particular task, such as math addition problems of increasing difficulty; *generality* of self-efficacy beliefs refers to the transferability of one's efficacy judgments across different tasks or activities, such as different academic subjects; *strength* of efficacy judgments pertains to the certainty with which one can perform a specific task (Zimmerman, 1995).

The construct of self-efficacy has a variety of distinctive characteristics. These features are important because they provide a point of comparison with other constructs and have implications for how self-efficacy perceptions should be measured. First, self-efficacy judgments focus on perceived capabilities to perform an activity rather than on personality or psychological traits or characteristics (Zimmerman, 1995). In other words, self-efficacy addresses "how well can I do something?" rather than "what am I like?" Second, self-efficacy percepts are distinctive because they are not only domain-specific but are also context- and task-specific. In terms of context-specificity, a student may express a lower sense of efficacy to learn mathematics in competitive classroom structures than in cooperative ones. However, self-efficacy measures are also multi-dimensional in nature in that they vary across specific tasks or activities within a particular domain. For example, one may report feeling capable of performing addition and multiplication problems but may have low efficacy perceptions for solving subtraction and division problems. This multi-dimensional level of analysis is a hallmark feature of microanalytic, self-efficacy assessment (Bandura, 1997; Cleary & Zimmerman, 2004).

A third feature of self-efficacy is its dependence on a mastery criterion of performance rather than on normative or other criteria. For example, students rate how well they can write an essay at a specific level of performance rather than how much better they can write than their peers. Finally, self-efficacy beliefs are typically assessed prior to engaging in a particular task or activity. This antecedent property provides the temporal ordering necessary for assessing the role of efficacy percepts in causal structures. As a result, self-efficacy has been conceptualized as a forethought process within self-regulation models because of its proactive impact on performance and self-evaluative processes following performance (Zimmerman, 2000).

HOW IS SELF-EFFICACY DIFFERENT FROM OTHER TYPES OF SELF-BELIEFS?

Expectancy-Related Constructs

Constructs often confused with self-efficacy pertain to individuals' self-perceptions regarding their personal qualities, characteristics, and/ or competencies. These include self-concept, self-esteem, outcome expectations, and locus of control. Although these terms are often mistakenly used interchangeably by laypersons, they represent quite distinct constructs.

Self-Concept

Although the conceptual distinction between self-efficacy and self-concept beliefs may appear minimal at first glance, the two constructs represent different phenomena (Bandura, 1986). Self-concept refers to a generalized self-assessment incorporating a variety of self-reactions and beliefs such as feelings of self-worth and general beliefs of competence. In contrast, self-efficacy beliefs are context-specific judgments of personal capability to organize and execute a course of action to attain a set goal. Self-efficacy focuses more specifically on the tasks or activities that an individual feels capable of performing rather than a more global assessment of "how good you are at something" as provided in assessments of self-concept. It should be noted that measures of self-concept may include self-efficacy items but also incorporate items pertaining to self-esteem and global perceptions of competence.

The distinction between these two self-perceptions has been established empirically by a number of researchers (see Bong & Skaalvik, 2003). For example, Pajares and Miller (1994) used path analysis to examine the predictive and mediational roles of self-efficacy in the mathematical problem-solving skills of college students. The researchers developed a model incorporating variables such as self-efficacy, self-concept, perceived usefulness, prior mathematics experience, and mathematics problem-solving. Self-efficacy was a better predictor of math performance than was self-concept and also exerted an indirect impact on performance through self-concept. Thus, self-efficacy enhances academic performance directly as well as indirectly through its influence on a student's self-concept.

Self-Esteem

Self-esteem has been defined as a type of belief involving judgments of self-worth. It is an *affective* reaction indicating how a person feels about him- or herself. This is quite distinct from self-efficacy perceptions, which involve *cognitive* judgments of personal capability (Pintrich & Schunk, 2002). Perceptions of worth or self-esteem may develop from a person's global self-perception (i.e., self-concept) as well as from a variety of other sources, such as possession of attributes that are either valued or de-valued by society (Bandura, 1997). Thus, a person may establish feelings of worth or think "I am a good person" if she perceives herself as being competent in particular domains or as possessing socially-important characteristics, such as altruism and empathy.

Although positive self-esteem is desirable and even necessary for adaptive functioning, the key issues are whether self-esteem is related to self-efficacy perceptions and whether it is a distinctive predictor of academic performance from self-efficacy. The comparative effects of self-efficacy and self-esteem have been investigated by Mone, Baker, and Jeffries (1995), who studied the validity of self-efficacy and self-esteem for predicting the personal goals and performance of college students. Students were given these measures prior to three exams throughout the semester. Self-efficacy accounted for almost half of the variance in the prediction of goals and between 6% and 14% of the variance in the prediction of performance. Self-esteem was not predictive of either outcome. Clearly, self-efficacy is a distinctive predictor of academic outcomes compared to self-esteem. These findings lend support for the contention that the predictiveness of self-perception measures increase as the task-specificity of the items increase.

Outcome Expectations

Although it has been argued that outcome expectations are distinctive and important for understanding behavior (Bandura, 1997), research has shown that self-efficacy beliefs are usually better predictors of behavior than are outcome expectations (Schunk & Miller, 2002). Shell, Murphy, and Bruning (1989) examined the predictive power of self-efficacy and outcome expectations on reading and writing achievement. Self-efficacy was assessed as a student's perceived capability to perform various reading and writing tasks, whereas outcome expectations were students' ratings of the importance of reading and writing skills in attaining various outcomes in employment, social endeavors, family life, and education. Although self-efficacy and outcome expectations accounted for 32% of the variance in reading achievement, self-efficacy accounted for most of that variance (28%).

Perceived Control

The construct of perceived control, which emerged from earlier research on locus of control (Rotter, 1966), is concerned with general expectancies that outcomes are controlled by either one's behavior or by external events. This dualistic view of control suggests that an internal locus of control promotes self-directed behavior, whereas external locus of control inhibits one's agentic abilities. Perceptions of control and perceived self-efficacy are similar in that they both deal with how individuals can act in agentic ways on their environment. Self-efficacious individuals and those with an internal locus of control will exhibit more self-directed behavior than will low self-efficacious individuals or those with an external locus of control. However, similar to the distinction between outcome expectations and self-efficacy, perceived control does not take into account how confident an individual feels about performing specific tasks within a particular context. In addition, Bandura (1986, 1997) questioned the value of de-contextualized perceptions of control. In support of this conclusion, Smith (1989) found that locus of control did not predict improvement in academic performance and did not reduce the anxiety of anxious students who underwent coping skills training. Self-efficacy, however, did predict such improvements. In essence, self-efficacy judgments differ from other expectancy constructs because they are task- and context-specific and focus exclusively on one's perceptions of capability.

HOW DO SELF-EFFICACY BELIEFS AFFECT ADOLESCENTS' SCHOOL-RELATED FUNCTIONING?

One might argue that assessing adolescents' self-beliefs and perceptions of capability is important because it can help parents and teachers empathize with or at least better understand how adolescents interpret and perceive the world in which they live. Although enhanced parental and teacher understanding is beneficial, the key issue for educators involves whether self-efficacy has a significant impact on adolescents' ability to succeed in school. In this section, we discuss the relationship between self-efficacy and three important variables related to school functioning: academic motivation, academic achievement, and academic and personal development. The causal influence of self-efficacy on these variables will be emphasized.

Academic Motivation

Motivation has been defined by social cognitive researchers as a process in which goal-directed behavior is instigated and sustained (Pintrich & Schunk, 2002). It is an important variable because it has been consistently associated with academic competence (Linnenbrink & Pintrich, 2002) and is often the subject of teacher concerns about students struggling in school. Motivation can manifest itself in various forms such as effort, persistence, and choice of activities—indexes that are hypothesized to be influenced by students' self-efficacy (Bandura, 1977). This hypothesis has been consistently confirmed by researchers over the past few decades (Bandura, 1997; Pajares, 1996; Schunk, 1981; Schunk & Hanson, 1985). That is, when students believe that they can perform a task in a proficient manner, they will become more engaged in the activity, work harder, and sustain high levels of effort even when obstacles are encountered.

In terms of effort, two measures have typically been employed in research: rate of performance and expenditure of energy (Zimmerman, 1995). There is supporting evidence for the association between self-efficacy and both indexes. Schunk and his colleagues showed that students' perceived self-efficacy for learning correlates positively with their rate of solution of arithmetic problems (Schunk, 1981; Schunk & Hanson, 1985). In addition, Salomon (1984) examined the relationship between sixth grade students' self-efficacy for learning from text and both mental effort and achievement. The self-efficacy of students who were exposed to the print material were positively associated with mental effort and achievement. That is, as students' confidence in their ability to learn from the print material increased, so did their perceived mental effort to complete the task.

Self-efficacy has also been consistently associated with levels of persistence (Bouffard-Bouchard, Parent, & Larivée, 1991; Multon, Brown, & Lent, 1991; Schunk, 1981). When they view a task as difficult, students with higher self-efficacy tend to be more persistent than are students with lower self-efficacy. Zimmerman and Ringle (1981) assigned children to either an optimistic or a pessimistic model condition, wherein the children observed an adult attempt the solution of an unsolvable wire puzzle. The optimistic model expressed confidence about solving the puzzle (e.g., "I am sure I can separate these wires; I just have to keep trying different ways, and then I will find the right one") whereas the pessimistic model expressed concern about solving it (e.g., "I don't think I can separate these wires; I have tried many different ways and nothing seems to work"). Students in the optimistic condition felt more efficacious about being able to solve a similar puzzle and persisted longer than did students in the pessimistic group during an opportunity to solve the problem. The optimistic students also persisted longer in solving an embedded word problem. This study demonstrated that vicariously-induced self-efficacy not only enhanced persistence on a similar motoric puzzle but also facilitated transfer in persistence to a verbal puzzle within the same experimental context. In addition to its effects on persistence, self-efficacy has been shown to be predictive of students' choice of activities (Bandura & Schunk, 1981; Zimmerman & Kitsantas, 1999).

Academic Achievement

Although student motivation is an important issue, the bottom line often entails improving students' academic skills and maximizing their overall performance in school. It is widely accepted that students' academic success is influenced primarily by their cognitive abilities. That is, students with great intellectual potential will often succeed at a higher level than will students with lower ability. However, given that the correlation between IQ and achievement is typically only in the moderate range, it seems reasonable to suggest that cognitive potential does not always translate into attained success. Just as there are intellectually gifted individuals who do not perform well, there exist many lower ability students who perform at or above age or grade expectations. Although it is clear that many variables interact to produce this phenomenon, we will consider the role that self-efficacy perceptions play in determining how well individuals perform academically.

Merely possessing knowledge and skills does not mean that one will use them effectively under difficult conditions (Bandura, 1993). Students often encounter obstacles during learning. These can include noisy study environments, disruptive thoughts, negative emotional reactions, and poor organization skills. Those who are more self-efficacious about being able to effectively manage and cope with these circumstances are expected to have a higher probability of succeeding, even if others have the same inherent ability or skill level. Collins (1982) studied students of high or low perceived math self-efficacy within each of three levels of math ability: high, intermediate, and low. At each level of math ability, students who were assured of their self-efficacy discarded faulty solution strategies more quickly, reworked more failed problems, and achieved higher math performance than did students who were low in their sense of self-efficacy. Thus, self-efficacy was a better predictor of positive attitudes to mathematics than was actual ability. Similar results were reported by Bouffard-Bouchard (1990) who experimentally increased the self-efficacy of students at two levels of ability on a novel problem-solving task. The students' self-efficacy was varied through arbitrary feedback. Regardless of their pretest level of ability, students whose self-efficacy was raised used more effective strategies and were more successful in their problem solving than students whose self-efficacy was lowered. These studies revealed that students' self-efficacy beliefs contribute to academic performance over and above the effects of their ability (Bandura, 1993).

There is much evidence documenting the significant relation between self-efficacy beliefs and achievement in academic settings (Bandura, 1997; Multon et al., 1991; Schunk, 1981; Schunk & Miller, 2002), athletics (Zimmerman & Kitsantas, 1996), health-promoting behavior, and coping skills. In the academic domain, Multon et al. (1991) meta-analyzed results of studies conducted between 1977 and 1988 to examine the effect of efficacy beliefs on academic achievement. The studies assessed academic performance in a variety of ways, including basic cognitive skills, academic course work, and standardized tests, and they were diverse in terms of sample and experimental design. Multon et al. reported an overall effect size of 0.38, indicating that self-efficacy accounted for approximately 14% of the variance in students' academic performance. Self-efficacy was most predictive of academic accomplishments when posttreatment efficacy beliefs were used as predictors. Thus, assessing students' efficacy prior to instruction, although important, will not be as predictive of academic achievement as measuring these beliefs following instruction or modeling experiences.

Path analytic studies have shown that self-efficacy has a direct effect on students' academic performance across academic domains such as writing and mathematics (Pajares & Miller, 1994; Schunk, 1981; Zimmerman & Bandura, 1994). For example, Pajares and Kranzler (1995) investigated the impact of mathematics self-efficacy and general aptitude on the mathematics problem-solving skills of high school students. The researchers wanted to assess the unique contribution made by self-efficacy to the prediction of academic achievement when a measure of general intelligence, or g, was included in the model. The path model included mathematics self-efficacy, general mental ability, math anxiety, high school math level, and gender. Although it is widely recognized that the g factor is a strong predictor of academic performance, results revealed that self-efficacy and general mental ability had comparable direct effects on students' math problem-solving skills. Thus, even when the effects of general cognitive ability are controlled, adolescents' perceptions of efficacy are able to account for unique variance in an academic outcome. Self-efficacy also mediated the effects of general cognitive ability and math anxiety on overall math performance.

Academic and Personal Development

To understand the role of self-efficacy perceptions on adolescents' academic and personal development, Bandura and his colleagues at the University of Rome have undertaken a series of ecological studies (e.g., Bandura, Barbaranelli, Caprara, & Pastorelli, 1996, 2001). The studies have included a wide network of parent, student, and teacher measures. Bandura (1997) cautioned against adopting narrow measures of either self-efficacy or personal functioning when broad developmental issues are of interest. From a social cognitive perspective, students' academic functioning is influenced by a number of nonacademic but school-related context variables as well as by academic variables. For example, students who cannot form and maintain positive social relationships with classmates or who have trouble self-regulating their behavior will often suffer academically as well as socially and personally. Three general types of students' efficacy beliefs were investigated: social functioning (e.g., forming and maintaining peer relationships), personal self-regulatory functioning (e.g., resisting peer pressure to engage in high risk activities like drugs and alcohol), and academic functioning (e.g., self-regulating learning and mastering various types of subject matter). Also included were a wide range of nonacademic measures of adolescent functioning (e.g., depression, problem behaviors, moral disengagement, prosocial behavior, and peer preferences) as well as academic achievement measures. In addition to these student measures, parental self-efficacy measures (e.g., ability to influence their children's development) and parental academic aspirations for their children (e.g., expected performance and amount of schooling) were included in the research design.

Using a path analysis, Bandura et al. (1996) found that the influence of the families' socioeconomic status was entirely mediated through parents' academic aspirations and children's prosocial behavior, such that the higher the status of the family, the higher the parents' academic aspirations for their children and the greater their children's pro-social behavior. All three forms of children's self-efficacy contributed to academic achievement, but through different paths of mediating variables. For example, children's self-regulatory efficacy influenced achievement directly and by reducing problem behaviors. Although children's academic self-efficacy directly enhanced academic achievement, it also influenced this achievement indirectly via reductions in depression, increases in pro-social behavior, and increases in the children's academic aspirations. The children's academic aspirations were also influenced directly by their parents' academic aspirations. A high degree of pro-social behavior influenced the children's peer preferences and prevented them from disengaging their moral standards or engaging in problem behaviors. The combined variables in this path model accounted for 58% of the variance in the children's academic achievement. This ecological account of children's academic development reveals that children who doubt their efficacy reduce their academic aspirations, experience greater depression, and develop less prosocial and more problem behavior. Over time, students' growing doubts about their intellectual capabilities and the resulting deficiencies in academic skill are likely to foreclose occupational avenues for them.

In a subsequent study of these children's career choices, Bandura et al. (2001) studied the influence of the children's three general types of self-efficacy, academic aspirations, and academic achievement on their efficacy perceptions regarding six specific career paths (science-technology, education-medical, literary-art, social service, military-police, and agricultural-horticultural). These types of occupational self-efficacy proved to be key determinants of the children's career choices. Interestingly, students' academic achievements did not directly predict their career choice but rather were mediated via their occupational self-efficacy beliefs. Clearly self-efficacy play a major role in students' academic and career development.

DOES ENHANCING SELF-EFFICACY EMPOWER STUDENTS TO BECOME MORE SELF-DIRECTED, INDEPENDENT LEARNERS?

The primary goals of secondary education are to teach students content knowledge in a particular subject area and to build students' reading, writing, and arithmetic skills. Given the proliferation of federal mandates for establishing minimum academic proficiency levels and statewide tests for assessing students' academic skills, it is understandable that education focus intensely in these areas. However, a broader, more long-term goal of secondary education should involve empowering students to become independent, self-regulated learners. When students graduate from high school and go on to college or enter the workforce, one hopes they feel a sense of personal agency for effectively and responsibly managing their own behavior and acting on the world in which they live. Individuals who seek to proactively and efficiently manage their lives to achieve self-set goals are often called self-regulated learners. Self-regulated individuals naturally feel empowered because of their adaptive self-motivational beliefs, particularly with regard to their perceptions of personal capability. In this section, we will explore the reciprocal links between students' self-efficacy and their self-regulated behaviors.

From a social cognitive perspective, self-regulation has been defined as self-generated thoughts, feelings, and actions that are planned and cyclically adapted based on performance feedback to attain self-set goals (Zimmerman, 2000). It is a complex, multi-faceted process that integrates several motivational and self-processes (see Figure 2.1). These motivational and self-processes are hypothesized to operate in a cyclical feedback loop, whereby a learner gathers and uses feedback information to make adjustments during current and future learning attempts (Zimmerman, 2000). This cyclical loop includes three general phases: forethought (processes that precede efforts to act), performance control (processes that occur during learning) and self-reflection (processes that occur after performance). It is hypothesized that forethought processes influence performance control phase processes, which in turn influence self-reflection phase processes. A cycle is complete when the self-reflection processes influence forethought processes during a subsequent learning attempt. Self-efficacy beliefs exist within this system of self-regulatory beliefs and processes. These beliefs are critical to the forethought phase process because it can sustain high levels of motivation and resiliency in learners when they encounter obstacles or difficulties in learning. It should be noted that, although self-efficacy is presented as a forethought process, it has direct influences on many of the self-regulation processes throughout the entire cyclical feedback loop. We will review the relationship between students' self-efficacy and key forethought phase processes (e.g., goal setting, strategic planning, self-motivational beliefs), performance control phase processes (e.g., self-observation, strategy use) and self-reflection phase processes (e.g., self-evaluative standards, attributions).

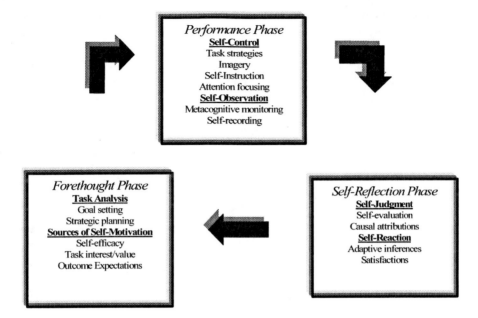

Figure 2.1   Phases and subprocesses of self-regulation.

Forethought Phase Processes

Goal-Setting

Goal-setting has been defined as deciding on specific outcomes of learning or performance, such as learning the steps of a writing strategy or achieving a grade of 100 on a science test (Locke & Latham, 1990). Beliefs of personal capabilities affect the type of goals that individuals select and their commitment to them (Zimmerman, 1995). For example, when individuals feel capable of performing a particular task, they are more likely to set challenging and specific goals (Bandura, 1986; Zimmerman, Bandura, & Martinez-Pons, 1992). In a study with adolescent basketball players, Cleary and Zimmerman (2001) investigated self-efficacy differences between expert, non-expert, and novice players as well as the relationship between self-efficacy and other self-regulatory processes. Participants were asked to rate their self-efficacy for making two free-throw shots in a row as well as to identify any goals they had before practicing their free-throws. Individuals who were highly confident about making the free-throws tended to set more *specific* outcome goals (e.g., "to make 10 out of 10 shots"), whereas those who were not confident tended to set vague outcome goals (e.g., "to make baskets"). Specific goals are advantageous because they enable one to evaluate personal progress more effectively.

Other studies have examined the causal effect of self-efficacy on goal-setting and academic achievement (Zimmerman & Bandura, 1994). Zimmerman et al. (1992) performed a path analysis to analyze the causal effects of several variables, such as prior grades, parent grade goals, student grade goals, self-efficacy for self-regulated learning, and self-efficacy for academic achievement on high school students' grades in social studies. Although self-efficacy for academic achievement directly predicted students' social studies grades, it also had a direct effect on the goals that students set for themselves. That is, individuals who were highly confident in their ability to earn a high grade were more likely to set *challenging* academic goals. These studies are important because they suggest that, as perceptions of capability increase, one will likely set more specific, challenging goals, the types of goals that lead to the most positive outcomes (Locke & Latham, 1990).

Although self-efficacy beliefs can influence self-regulation processes, this relationship is reciprocal in that manipulating self-regulation processes can also produce changes in one's self-perceptions. Goal-setting influences self-efficacy perceptions because it enables learners to evaluate goal progress and personal mastery over tasks (Schunk & Miller, 2002). Several experimental studies using academic and athletic tasks have shown that the types of goals students set for themselves directly influence their self-efficacy and achievement (Schunk & Rice, 1989, 1991). Schunk and Swartz (1993) conducted one of the first studies to assess how process goals influenced student writing skills and self-efficacy perceptions. Grade 5 students were randomly assigned to different writing strategy instructional groups based on type of goal (process, product, or general goals). Students who set process goals (i.e., focus on executing the writing strategy) exhibited higher perceptions of writing self-efficacy than did students who set general goals (i.e., do your best). When a progress feedback condition was given to some of the students in the process goal group, they exhibited more adaptive efficacy beliefs than did students in either the product goal or general goal conditions.

In a study of athletic functioning in adolescent girls, Zimmerman and Kitsantas (1996) compared the effects of process and outcome goals on the dart skill, self-efficacy, and level of satisfaction of the novice dart-throwers. Girls were randomly assigned to one of four conditions based on type of goals (process or outcome) and self-recording (present or absent). All participants received identical throwing instructions, but the process goal group was instructed to focus on the dart-throwing strategy while practicing. In reference to the goal-setting effects, girls who were in the process goal group had higher dart-throwing scores and self-efficacy perceptions than did the girls who set outcome goals (i.e., to obtain the highest score).

These studies suggest that encouraging adolescent students to set process goals will have both achievement and motivational advantages because it directs attention to executing the essential aspects of a particular task. Process goals encourage learners to keep track of how well they perform a strategy, evaluate goal progress, and judge perceptions of competence.

Strategic Planning

Before students can engage in academic pursuits, they must learn methods that are appropriate for a particular task within a specific context (Zimmerman, 2000). Strategies can be thought of as purposive personal processes and actions directed at acquiring knowledge or skills. They are important because they represent the tools with which individuals learn and improve their performance and level of skill. A variety of descriptive studies have investigated the relationship between use of learning strategies and self-efficacy perceptions. Zimmerman and Martinez-Pons (1990) investigated this with students in Grades 5, 8, and 11. They hypothesized that measures of self-efficacy would be predictive of students' use of self-regulated learning strategies. Verbal self-efficacy accounted for 18% of the variance in strategy use and was predictive of using several different types of strategies.

In the study of athletes earlier discussed, Cleary and Zimmerman (2001) showed that the self-efficacy beliefs of adolescent basketball players were not just predictive of whether one will use a strategy, but also of the quality and type of strategy used. Participants were asked to rate their self-efficacy as well as the strategy that they would use to achieve a shooting goal during a practice session. Given that the self-efficacy question was asked prior to the strategy question, the resulting correlation reflected self-efficacy predicting strategy use. Individuals who were highly self-efficacious usually selected technique-specific strategies (e.g., "bend my knees correctly") to achieve their goals, whereas those who doubted their capabilities rarely endorsed this type of strategy. The use of these technique-oriented strategies was important because they directly corresponded to the correct shooting form, thus focusing the individual's attention on important shooting form processes rather than on other external or distracting factors. Although this study does not imply causation between self-efficacy and strategy use, it does suggest that confident individuals may tend to use strategies that are specific to the task at hand.

Some experimental studies have established a causal link between self-efficacy and strategy use (e.g., Schunk & Rice, 1991). Schunk and Swartz (1993) found that students whose self-efficacy increased as a result of goal-setting and progress feedback were more likely to continue to use the writing strategies effectively in follow-up assessments.

Sources of Self-Motivation

Zimmerman's model of self-regulation incorporates various motivational processes such as self-efficacy, outcome expectations, and task interest or valuing. The model predicts that self-efficacy, being the key motivational process, will be related to the other motivational processes. A series of studies conducted with expert and novice athletes (Cleary & Zimmerman, 2001; Kitsantas & Zimmerman, 2002; Zimmerman & Kitsantas, 1996, 1997) support these predictions. In most of the studies, students' level of self-efficacy is typically predictive of task interest and of value for accomplishing future goals (a form of outcome expectations). Pajares and Miller (1994) used path analysis to study the predictive and mediational role of college students' mathematics self-efficacy beliefs. They reported that self-efficacy beliefs had a direct effect on students' perceived usefulness of mathematics for achieving various life goals. That is, when individuals were more confident in their personal capabilities in mathematics, they were more likely to perceive mathematics as being valuable and important. Although these findings support the premise that different motivational beliefs are related to each other, at this point the precise nature of this relationship is not well understood. It is important for future research to examine the effects of different thresholds of self-efficacy on other motivational beliefs.

Performance Control Phase Processes

Self-Observation

Self-observation (also called self-monitoring) is a performance control phase process that involves selectively attending to particular aspects of one's behavior or performance (Schunk, 1983; Zimmerman & Paulsen, 1995). It is an important process because it helps learners discriminate between effective and ineffective performances and helps to isolate the source of error or confusion when one is performing poorly. Similar to the relationship between self-efficacy and other self-regulation processes, there is a reciprocal relation between efficacy judgments and self-monitoring behaviors. Individuals with high self-efficacy will often be motivated to self-monitor and will be more proficient at monitoring their behaviors during an academic activity (Schunk, 1983; Zimmerman & Paulsen, 1995). Bouffard-Bouchard et al. (1991) examined the effects of efficacy beliefs on self-monitoring during a learning activity with junior high and high school students and reported that students with higher self-efficacy were better at monitoring their working time, were more persistent, and were less likely to reject correct hypotheses prematurely than were those who did not feel as capable.

There is also evidence for self-monitoring processes directly influencing one's self-efficacy beliefs. In a classic self-monitoring study, Schunk (1983) examined whether self-monitoring would influence elementary school students' subtraction skills and self-efficacy to solve subtraction problems. All students received 30-minute training sessions that involved instruction and individual practice sessions. In addition, some were taught to self-monitor the number of pages they completed during each session. The self-monitoring group reported higher self-efficacy for solving problems and had higher scores on a skills test than did the group who did not self-monitor. The effects of self-monitoring on self-efficacy have also been demonstrated in a training study of writing revision (Zimmerman & Kitsantas, 1999). Adolescent girls who were required to record specific steps of a text revision strategy exhibited higher levels of writing skill and self-efficacy than did girls who learned without self-recording.

Self-Reflection Processes

Self-Evaluation

Self-efficacy beliefs not only influence the goals students set for themselves but also their evaluative reactions of goal progress. The role of self-efficacy beliefs concerning the academic attainment and regulation of writing, academic goals, and self-standards in the development of writing proficiency was studied with college freshmen using path analysis (Zimmerman & Bandura, 1994). Two scales were developed to measure self-efficacy. The first assessed beliefs about personal capability to regulate writing activities (e.g., "I can rewrite my wordy or confusing sentences clearly"), and the second asked students to rate the strength of their belief that they could attain particular achievement outcomes (e.g., an A- in the course). Students' self-evaluative standards were assessed in terms of their level of satisfaction and dissatisfaction for different writing grades. The key result was the causal link between the students' self-regulatory self-efficacy for writing with their personal standards of performance. Students who felt more confident in their ability to regulate the writing process set high personal standards for the quality of their writing and thus were more easily dissatisfied than were students who possessed low self-efficacy.

Conversely, the process of self-evaluating one's abilities or one's progress in strategy or skill acquisition is important for cultivating strong self-efficacy (Schunk, 2003). It is the cognitive appraisal of one's personal improvement or progress that will ultimately lead to fluctuations in one's capability judgments. For example, if a student is not satisfied with her performance on a math test but believes that her future performance could be improved by adjusting ineffective strategies, then her self-efficacy beliefs will not diminish. This phenomenon has been demonstrated in experimental studies involving the use of self-monitored information about performance processes to evaluate one's skill on a particular task (Zimmerman & Kitsantas, 1999).

Attributions

Efficacy beliefs are influenced by a variety of factors such as prior accomplishments and vicarious experiences. Although mastery experiences are the strongest source of self-efficacy, cognitive analysis of one's performance experiences is a key mediating factor for changing capability judgments. From a self-regulatory perspective, after students perform a task or an activity, they will often evaluate or reflect cognitively on the perceived causes of that performance. These causes are termed causal attributions (Zimmerman, 2000). Attribution theorists contend that students' perceptions of the causes of their academic successes and failures determine their expectancies for future performance (Weiner, 1986). For example, Jen's motivation would be heightened if she attributed her poor performance in math to internal, controllable factors such as effort and strategy use, but it would decrease if she attributed it to uncontrollable factors such as luck or ability (Cleary & Zimmerman, 2001; Clifford, 1986).

As with most self-regulatory processes, there is empirical evidence showing a reciprocal relationship between students' causal attributions and their perceptions of personal efficacy. That is, highly efficacious students believe performance outcomes to be personally controllable (Bandura, 1997), so they tend to attribute failure to factors that they can change. Conversely, students with low self-efficacy attribute failure to uncontrollable factors, thereby increasing feelings of despair and helplessness (Silver, Mitchell, & Gist, 1989). These types of attributions are particularly important because they encourage students to make *adaptive* changes or self-adjustments to their learning methods following failure or poor performances. In addition, students who are provided strategy or effort feedback following performance on academic tasks often experience increases in their personal efficacy (Pintrich & Schunk, 2002; Schunk & Rice, 1991). In the following section, we consider the role of attribution as well as other forms of self-regulatory training on students' self-efficacy and academic performance.

HOW CAN WE ENHANCE ADOLESCENT STUDENTS' SELF-EFFICACY PERCEPTIONS?

Although it is important for parents and educators to understand the nature and role of self-efficacy in children's and adolescents' academic functioning, the ultimate question is how to cultivate or enhance students' perceptions of personal agency. The previous section on the reciprocal relationship between self-efficacy beliefs and self-regulatory processes showed that training students in self-regulation processes such as goal setting, self-monitoring, and strategic planning can increase their confidence levels to perform specific tasks in school. These interventions can be loosely categorized under one of the four sources of self-efficacy as identified by Bandura (1986). He argued that an individual's self-efficacy perceptions are influenced by one's prior accomplishments/mastery, physiological reactions, vicarious experiences, and forms of persuasion.

Personal mastery experiences, which involve one's accomplishments, are the strongest source of enhancing perceptions of personal efficacy (Bandura, 1997; Schunk, 2003). There are numerous studies showing that as one's mastery or proficiency at an activity increases, so does one's self-efficacy (Schunk, 1981; Schunk & Schwartz, 1993; Zimmerman & Kitsantas, 1996). In general, frequent successes lead to higher self-efficacy, and consistent failure experiences usually lower it. However, this general rule of thumb requires qualification. Accomplishments are interpreted in light of one's self-regulatory processes, such as self-evaluations, attributions, strategy use, and goal setting. For example, self-efficacy percepts depend on how an individual evaluates the circumstances and factors surrounding the accomplishments (Bandura, 1986; Schunk & Pajares, 2004). If a student receives a 95% on a math test but perceives the test to be easier than typical math tests, it is unlikely that her efficacy judgments will change. Conversely, failing her next math test may not adversely affect her self-efficacy if she believes that an external factor, such as a family emergency, prevented her from studying and caused her to fail. Similarly, students who select a strategy to revise an essay and use the strategy as a process goal to guide and self-monitor learning are less likely to attribute poor results to fixed abilities and more likely to sustain their self-efficacy to ultimately master the task (Zimmerman & Kitsantas, 1999). The second source of self-efficacy, physiological reactions, can also influence how an individual makes an efficacy judgment. If a student gets extremely anxious during math activities, she may interpret her rapid heart rate or sweating palms as indicators of personal ineffectiveness.

An important aspect of social cognitive theory is its assumption that an individual's social milieu is a primary determinant of his or her functioning, attitudes, and beliefs (Bandura, 1986). Adolescent students do not have to act or engage in an activity to learn or to feel confident in their abilities. Rather, their sense of efficacy can be either enhanced or lowered by the behaviors and/or feedback given by important individuals in their lives such as parents, teachers, counselors, and peers. Social agents promote positive perceptions of efficacy in adolescents by either using various forms of verbal persuasion (e.g., encouragement, progress feedback) or by modeling specific strategies, behaviors, or thoughts.

Adolescents will often judge their level of self-efficacy through vicarious experiences, most notably modeling, which has been defined as the behavioral, cognitive, and affective changes resulting from observing other individuals perform a behavior (Pintrich & Schunk, 2002). Modeling is one of the most important ways to promote learning and self-efficacy (Schunk, 1981, 2003; Schunk & Hanson, 1985). The impact of a model on self-efficacy beliefs will be strongest when observers believe that they can be successful if they follow the model's behaviors and if they believe they are similar to the model in terms of age, ability, and gender (Schunk, 1987; Schunk, Hanson, & Cox, 1987). It should also be noted that models can be different types of individuals (e.g., peers and adults), can take various forms (e.g., live models and symbolic models), and can be used in different formats (e.g., coping and mastery models). Coping models, who display confidence and adaptation when confronting errors in learning are significantly more effective in sustaining students' perceptions of self-efficacy than are mastery models who perform without errors (Kitsantas, Zimmerman, & Cleary, 2000; Schunk et al., 1987; Schunk & Hanson, 1985; Zimmerman & Kitsantas, 2002).

Social persuasion is another source of information that adolescents use to shape and form perceptions of personal capability. Although encouraging comments (e.g., "I know you can do it") and reassuring statements from a parent or teacher (e.g., "You will do better next time") may help struggling students sustain their motivation in the short-term, the effects of such statements will be short-lived if the student is consistently unable to attain perceived successes. However, social agents can play a key role in cultivating more long-lasting changes in adolescents' self-efficacy beliefs for academic tasks by providing them with feedback linking performance progress with *strategy use* (Cleary & Zimmerman, 2004, Schunk & Rice, 1991; Schunk & Swartz, 1993). Social feedback is important not only for its impact on self-efficacy beliefs but also because it focuses a student's attention on important learning processes. It also enables students to make adaptive self-reflections, such as evaluating their performance in relation to mastery goals and attributing poor performances to ineffective strategy use (Cleary & Zimmerman, 2004; Zimmerman, 2000). Thinking in the "language of strategies" motivates adolescents because they begin to view success and failures in terms of successfully using "controllable" strategies rather than innate, unchangeable factors such as ability.

CONCLUSION

Adolescents' perceptions of efficacy play a major role in their transition from childhood dependency to adulthood self-sufficiency. Ecologically-oriented research has shown that adolescents' self-efficacy beliefs emerge from a rich and complex interplay of forces in which these beliefs are both causes and effects of personal and academic functioning as well as future occupational choices. Bandura (1997) hypothesized that self-efficacy beliefs interact with many other determinants of academic functioning—personal, contextual, and behavioral. For this reason, self-efficacy measures are designed to reveal the task-, condition-, and context-specificity of personal competence beliefs and to be sensitive to changes in functioning. Although the importance of self-efficacy is now well established, the magnitude of its effect varies considerably depending on other variables. Adolescents' sense of personal efficacy is especially influenced by their capability to self-regulate their functioning, such as setting optimal goals, implementing effective strategies, self-monitoring accurately, self-evaluating using appropriate criteria, and attributing causation to adaptable processes. When training interventions are designed to enhance these and other academic self-regulatory functions, adolescents are significantly empowered to make this vital developmental transition.

ACKNOWLEDGMENT

We would like to thank Frank Pajares and Tim Urdan for their helpful comments on an earlier draft of this chapter.

REFERENCES

Bandura, A. (1977). Self-efficacy: Toward a unifying theory of behavior change. *Psychological Review, 84,* 191-215.

Bandura, A. (1986). *Social foundations of thought and action: A social cognitive theory.* Englewood Cliffs, NJ: Prentice-Hall.

Bandura, A. (1993). Perceived self-efficacy in cognitive development and functioning. *Educational Psychologist, 28,* 117-148.

Bandura, A. (1997). *Self-efficacy: The exercise of self-control.* New York: W.H. Freeman and Company.

Bandura, A., Barbaranelli, C., Caprara, G. V., & Pastorelli, C. (1996). Multifaceted impact of self-efficacy beliefs on academic functioning. *Child Development, 67,* 1206-1222.

Bandura, A., Barbaranelli, C., Caprara, G. V., & Pastorelli, C. (2001). Self-efficacy beliefs as shapers of children's aspirations and career trajectories. *Child Development, 72,* 187-206.

Bandura, A., & Schunk, D. H. (1981). Cultivating competence, self-efficacy, and intrinsic interest through proximal self-motivation. *Journal of Personality and Social Psychology, 41,* 586-598.

Bong, M., & Skaalvik, E. M. (2003). Academic self-concept and self-efficacy: How different are they really? *Educational Psychology Review, 15,* 1-40.

Bouffard-Bouchard, T. (1990). Influence of self-efficacy on performance in a cognitive task. *Journal of Social Psychology, 130,* 353-363.

Bouffard-Bouchard, T., Parent, S., & Larivee, S. (1991). Influence of self-efficacy on self-regulation and performance among junior and senior high-school age students. *International Journal of Behavioral Development, 14,* 153-164.

Cleary, T. J., & Zimmerman, B. J. (2001). Self-regulation differences during athletic practice by experts, non-experts, and novices. *Journal of Applied Sport Psychology, 13,* 185-206.

Cleary, T. J., & Zimmerman, B. J. (2004). Self-regulation empowerment program: A school-based program to enhance self-regulated and self-motivated cycles of student learning. *Psychology in the Schools, 41,* 537-550.

Clifford, M. (1986). Comparative effects of strategy and effort attributions. *British Journal of Educational Psychology, 56,* 75-83.

Collins, J. L. (1982, March). *Self-efficacy and ability in achievement behavior.* Paper presented at the annual meeting of the American Educational Research Association, New York.

Kitsantas, A., & Zimmerman, B. J. (2002). Comparing self-regulatory processes among novice, non-expert, and expert volleyball players: A microanalytic study. *Journal of Applied Sport Psychology, 14,* 91-105.

Kitsantas, A., Zimmerman, B. J., & Cleary, T. (2000). The role of observation and emulation in the development of athletic self-regulation. *Journal of Educational Psychology, 91,* 241-250.

Linnenbrink, E. A., & Pintrich, P. R. (2002). Motivation as an enabler for academic success. *School Psychology Review, 31,* 313-327.

Locke, E. A., & Latham, G. P. (1990). *A theory of goal setting and task performance.* Englewood Cliffs, NJ: Prentice-Hall.

McPherson, G. E., & Zimmerman, B. J. (2002). Self-regulation of musical learning: A social cognitive perspective. In R. Colwell & C. Richardson (Eds.), *The new handbook of research on music teaching and learning* (pp. 327-347). New York: Oxford University Press.

Mone, M. A., Baker, D. D., & Jeffries, F. (1995). Predictive validity and time dependency of self-efficacy, self-esteem, personal goals, and academic performance. *Educational and Psychological Measurement, 55,* 716-727.

Multon, K. D., Brown, S. D., & Lent, R. W. (1991). Relation of self-efficacy beliefs to academic outcomes: A meta-analytic investigation. *Journal of Counseling Psychology, 18,* 30-38.

Pajares, F. (1996). Self-efficacy beliefs in academic settings. *Review of Educational Research, 66,* 543-578.

Pajares, F., & Kranzler, J. (1995). Self-efficacy beliefs and general mental ability in mathematical problem-solving. *Contemporary Educational Psychology, 20,* 426-443.

Pajares, F., & Miller, M. D. (1994). The role of self-efficacy and self-concept beliefs in mathematical problem-solving: A path analysis. *Journal of Educational Psychology, 86,* 193-203.

Pintrich, P. R., & Schunk, D. H. (2002). *Motivation in education: Theory, research, and Applications* (2nd ed.). Upper Saddle, NJ: Prentice-Hall, Inc.

Rotter, J. B. (1966). Generalized expectations for internal versus external control of reinforcement. *Psychological Monographs, 80* (1, Whole No. 609).

Salomon, G. (1984). Television is "easy" and print is "tough": The differential investment of mental effort in learning as a function of perceptions and attributions. *Journal of Educational Psychology, 76,* 647-658.

Schunk, D. H. (1981). Modeling and attributional effects on children achievement: A self-efficacy analysis. *Journal of Educational Psychology, 73,* 93-105.

Schunk, D. H. (1983). Progress self-monitoring: Effects on children's self-efficacy and achievement. *Journal of Experimental Education, 51,* 89-93.

Schunk, D. H. (1987). Peer models and children's behavioral change. *Review of Educational Research, 57,* 149-174.

Schunk, D. H. (2003). Self-efficacy for reading and writing: Influence of modeling, goal-setting, and self-evaluation. *Reading and Writing Quarterly, 19,* 159-172.

Schunk, D. H., & Hanson, A. R. (1985). Peer models: Influence on children's self-efficacy and achievement. *Journal of Educational Psychology, 81,* 201-209.

Schunk, D. H., Hanson, A. R., & Cox, P. D. (1987). Peer-model attributes and children's achievement behaviors. *Journal of Educational Psychology, 79,* 54-61.

Schunk, D. H., & Miller, S. D. (2002). Self-efficacy and adolescents' motivation. In F. Pajares & T. Urdan (Eds.), *Academic motivation of adolescents* (pp. 29-52). Greenwich, CT: Information Age.

Schunk, D. H., & Pajares, F. (2004). Self-efficacy in education revisited: Empirical and applied evidence. In D. M. McInerney & S. Van Etten (Eds.), *Big theories revisited* (pp. 115-138). Greenwich, CT: Information Age.

Schunk, D. H., & Rice, J. M. (1989). Learning goals and children's reading comprehension. *Journal of Reading Behavior, 21,* 279-293.

Schunk, D. H., & Rice, J. M. (1991). Learning goals and progress feedback during reading comprehension instruction. *Journal of Reading Behavior, 23,* 351-364.

Schunk, D. H., & Swartz, C. W. (1993). Goals and progressive feedback: Effects on self-efficacy and writing achievement. *Contemporary Educational Psychology, 18,* 337-354.

Shell, D. F., Murphy, C. C., & Bruning, R. H. (1989). Self-efficacy and outcome expectancy mechanisms in reading and writing achievement. *Journal of Educational Psychology, 81,* 91-100.

Silver, W. S., Mitchell, T. R., & Gist, M. E. (1995). Responses to successful and unsuccessful performance: The moderating effect of self-efficacy on the relationship between performance and attributions. *Organizational Behavior and Human Decision Processes, 62,* 286-299.

Smith, P. K., Cowie, H., & Blades, M. (1998). *Understanding children's development* (3rd ed.). Massachusetts: Blackwell Publishers.

Smith, R. E. (1989). Effects of coping skills training on generalized self-efficacy and locus of control. *Journal of Personality and Social Psychology, 56,* 228-233.

Steinberg, L., Brown, B. B., & Dornbusch, S. M. (1996). *Beyond the classroom.* New York: Simon &Schuster.

Weiner, B. (1986). *An attribution theory of motivation and emotion.* New York: Springer-Verlag.

Wigfield, A., Eccles, J., & Pintrich, P. R. (1996). Development between the ages 11 and 25. In D. Berliner & R. Calfee (Eds.), *Handbook of educational psychology* (pp. 148-185). New York: Macmillan.

Zimmerman, B. J. (1995). Self-efficacy and educational development. In A. Bandura (Ed.), *Self-efficacy in changing societies* (pp. 202-231). New York: Cambridge University Press.

Zimmerman, B. J. (2000). Attaining self-regulation: A social-cognitive perspective. In M. Boekaerts, P. R. Pintrich, & M. Zeidner (Eds.), *Handbook of self-regulation* (pp. 13-39). San Diego, CA: Academic Press.

Zimmerman, B. J., & Bandura, A. (1994). Impact of self-regulatory influences on writing course attainment. *American Educational Research Journal, 31,* 845-862.

Zimmerman, B. J., & Bandura, A., & Martinez-Pons, M. (1992). Self-motivation for academic attainment. *American Educational Research Journal, 31,* 845-862.

Zimmerman, B. J., Bonner, S., & Kovach, R. (1996). *Developing self-regulated learners: Beyond achievement to self-efficacy.* Washington, DC: American Psychological Association.

Zimmerman, B. J., & Kitsantas, A. (1996). Self-regulated learning of a motoric skill: The role of goal-setting and self-monitoring. *Journal of Applied Sport Psychology, 8,* 60-75.

Zimmerman, B. J., & Kitsantas, A. (1997). Developmental phases in self-regulation: Shifting from process to outcome goals. *Journal of Educational Psychology, 89,* 29-36.

Zimmerman, B. J., & Kitsantas, A. (1999). Acquiring writing revision skill: Shifting from process to outcome self-regulatory goals. *Journal of Educational Psychology, 91,* 1-10.

Zimmerman, B. J., & Kitsantas, A. (2002). Acquiring writing revision and self-regulatory skill through observation and emulation. *Journal of Educational Psychology, 94,* 660-668.

Zimmerman, B. J., & Martinez-Pons, M. (1990). Student differences in self-regulated learning: Relating grade, sex, and giftedness to self-efficacy and strategy use. *Journal of Educational Psychology, 82,* 51-59.

Zimmerman, B. J., & Paulsen, A. S. (1995). Self-monitoring during collegiate studying: An invaluable tool for academic self-regulation. In P. Pintrich (Ed.), *New directions in college teaching and learning* (pp. 13-28). San Francisco, CA: Jossey-Bass.

Zimmerman, B. J., & Ringle, J. (1981). Effects of model persistence and statements of confidence on children's efficacy and problem-solving. *Journal of Educational Psychology, 73,* 485-493.

CHAPTER 3

SELF-EFFICACY DEVELOPMENT IN ADOLESCENCE

Dale H. Schunk and Judith L. Meece

Stacie and Meg—juniors at Atlas High School—soon must submit their course requests for next year. They have completed 3 years of science as mandated by the school system and must decide whether to take additional courses. Physics is an option, and although it is not required they believe that taking it may help with college admission. To date they have received similar grades (As and Bs) in science courses. The night before the class sign-up date they discuss the situation with their parents. Meg's dad feels that she should take physics since it will help her understand how the world works. Meg notes that Ms. Blakely (the physics teacher) is not very good. After further discussion, however, Meg concludes that she feels confident about learning physics because she always has been able to learn science in the past and that if she does not understand something she will ask the teacher. So Meg decides to sign up for it. Stacie, on the other hand, tells her parents that she just does not feel smart enough to learn or do well in physics and that because Ms. Blakely is not a good teacher Stacie would not receive much help from her. Stacie also tells her parents that few girls take the course. Under no pressure from her parents, Stacie decides she will not sign up for physics.

Self-Efficacy Beliefs of Adolescents, 71–96
Copyright © 2006 by Information Age Publishing
All rights of reproduction in any form reserved.

Adolescence is the period of time stretching from puberty to the early 20s. It is a time of great changes—physical, cognitive, social, and emotional. Adolescents also experience significant changes in their family relations, school environments, and peer group affiliations, and these changes can have profound effects on adolescents' motivation and learning.

In this chapter, we focus on the development of one type of cognitive factor—*self-efficacy*, defined as one's perceived capabilities for learning or performing actions at designated levels (Bandura, 1997). The manifestation of self-efficacy is evident in the opening scenario. Whereas Stacie professes self-doubts about her capability to learn and achieve well in physics, Meg expresses higher self-efficacy and believes that she can learn with the aid of her teacher. It is not surprising that Meg will take physics and Stacie will avoid it.

Although self-efficacy is a type of cognition, theory and research support the idea that it can affect other facets of development (e.g., social, emotional, behavioral) and that it is influenced by various personal, social, and contextual variables (Bandura, 1997). Self-efficacy affected Stacie's and Meg's decisions about physics, and their self-efficacy undoubtedly was influenced by many factors including their perceptions of the teacher and of girls who take physics. The changes in self-efficacy as adolescents develop have important implications for their school performances, friendships, and career and vocational choices.

The next section provides a theoretical background of self-efficacy framed within the context of social cognitive theory (Bandura, 1986). The sources of self-efficacy information and the consequences of self-efficacy are described. We also discuss methods of assessing self-efficacy. Research on the development of self-efficacy and related constructs (e.g., perceived ability and perceptions of competence) is summarized. We address self-efficacy development stemming from three influences: families, schooling, and peers. The implications of the theory and research findings for teaching and parenting are discussed and we suggest ways of helping adolescents develop self-efficacy in important areas of their lives.

THEORETICAL BACKGROUND

Social Cognitive Theory

Self-efficacy is grounded in the larger theoretical framework of *social cognitive theory*. This theory postulates that human functioning results from interactions among personal factors (e.g., cognitions, emotions), behaviors, and environmental conditions (Bandura, 1986, 1997). From this perspective, self-efficacy affects one's behaviors and the environments with which one interacts, and is influenced by one's actions and conditions in the environment.

Self-efficacy is hypothesized to affect individuals' task choices, effort, persistence, and achievement (Bandura, 1997; Schunk, 1995). Compared with learners who doubt their capabilities, those who feel self-efficacious about learning or performing a task competently are apt to participate more readily, work harder, persist longer when they encounter difficulties, and achieve at higher levels.

Information used to appraise self-efficacy is acquired from four primary sources: actual performances, vicarious experiences, forms of persuasion, and physiological reactions. Students' own performances offer the most reliable guides for gauging self-efficacy; effects of the other sources are more variable. In general, successes raise and failures lower self-efficacy, although an occasional failure (success) after some successes (failures) is unlikely to have much impact.

Learners acquire self-efficacy information from knowledge of others' performances through social comparisons. Similar others offer the best basis for comparison. Students who observe similar peers learn a task may also believe that they can learn it. Such vicarious information typically has a weaker effect than actual performance because vicariously-induced self-efficacy can be negated by subsequent performance failure.

Persuasive information, as in verbal encouragement from others (e.g., "You can do it!"), can raise self-efficacy, but its effects can be transitory if subsequent performance turns out differently. Learners also acquire self-efficacy information from physiological indicators (e.g., heart rate, feelings of anxiety). Such symptoms can signal that one lacks skills; conversely, when learners experience fewer emotional symptoms they may feel more self-efficacious.

The effects of information acquired from these sources on self-efficacy do not occur automatically; rather, information must be cognitively weighed and appraised. Learners typically use multiple factors such as perceptions of their abilities, prior successes, perceived task difficulty, amount of effort expended, time persisted, amount of help received, perceived similarity to models, credibility of persuaders, and type and intensity of emotional symptoms (Schunk, 1995).

Self-efficacy is not the only influence on learning and achievement, nor is it necessarily the most important one. No amount of self-efficacy will produce a competent performance if requisite *knowledge and skills* are lacking. *Outcome expectations*, or beliefs about the anticipated consequences of actions, also are critical. Students are apt to engage in activities that they believe will result in favorable outcomes and avoid those with perceived negative consequences. *Values* also are important; learners will engage in activities that they believe are important or which have desired outcomes

(Eccles et al., 1983; Meece, Wigfield, & Eccles, 1990; Wigfield & Eccles, 1992). Students may engage in an activity because they value it or its outcomes even if they do not feel highly self-efficacious about succeeding.

Contextual Factors Affecting Adolescents' Self-Efficacy

Development takes place in many different social contexts. During adolescence there are important changes in young people's family, school, and peer environments. Influences associated with each of these social contexts may have profound effects on adolescents' beliefs about their capabilities of succeeding in and out of school.

Beginning in infancy, *families* provide experiences that influence children's self-efficacy. Families differ in *capital*, such as financial or material resources (e.g., income), human or nonmaterial resources (e.g., education), and social resources (e.g., social networks and connections) (Bradley & Corwyn, 2002; Putnam, 2000). In general, families with greater capital provide richer experiences that raise children's self-efficacy. Families also differ in the types of trajectories onto which they launch their children, such as by enrolling them in classes or camps where they receive academic and social benefits and by shaping children's perceptions of their ability to succeed in school. Families differ in how well they motivate their children to attempt challenges and to achieve, the types of models available to children, and the extent to which they teach children strategies to cope with difficulties. Self-efficacy will be enhanced when children are motivated to achieve, when they are exposed to positive academic and social models, and when they are taught strategies that they can use to overcome challenges.

Schooling contains many potential influences on adolescents' self-efficacy including how instruction is structured, the ease or difficulty of learning, feedback about performance, competition, grading practices, amount and type of teacher attention, and school transitions. For example, rigid instructional sequences frustrate some students who have difficulty learning and increasingly fall behind. Learning difficulty signals that one may lack ability, which decreases self-efficacy. Performance feedback that conveys to students their progress can raise self-efficacy but may lower self-efficacy when it indicates how far behind they are. Classrooms with much competition and social comparison can decrease self-efficacy among students who feel they are deficient. Teacher assistance can aid learning, but when teachers provide too much help students may believe that the teachers think they lack the ability to learn, which lowers self-efficacy. School transitions (e.g., middle to high school) bring many changes in teacher relations, peer groups, classes, and grading practices—any of which can affect self-efficacy.

The influence of *peers* is especially potent among adolescents because peers contribute significantly to their socialization and views of themselves. With development peers assume much of the socialization function formerly carried out by parents and caregivers. Peer influence operates extensively through *peer networks,* or large groups of peers with whom students associate. Students in networks tend to be similar in many ways (Cairns, Cairns, & Neckerman, 1989; Hamm, 2000; Ryan, 2000), and perceived similarity enhances peer influence. Peer influence on self-efficacy also occurs because adolescents are unfamiliar with many tasks and have little information other than their friends' behaviors with which to gauge their own self-efficacy.

Assessment of Self-Efficacy

Self-efficacy beliefs are domain specific and refer to perceptions of capabilities to learn or perform given tasks within specified domains (Pajares, 1996a). Some examples are self-efficacy for performing operations on different types of radical expressions, self-efficacy for comprehending reading passages of varying levels of difficulty, self-efficacy for swimming 100 meters in different times, self-efficacy for safely driving an automobile under different conditions, self-efficacy for learning technical terms in biology, and self-efficacy for performing various household chores.

In gauging their self-efficacy, people assess their skills and capabilities to translate those skills into actions. Possessing skill can raise self-efficacy, which in turn can lead to further skill acquisition, but skill and self-efficacy are not synonymous in meaning. How people act can often be predicted better by their self-efficacy (i.e., the beliefs about their capabilities) than by their actual skills (Bandura, 1986).

Self-efficacy also depends on students' intelligence and abilities. In general, high-ability students feel more efficacious about performing well than do low-ability students, but self-efficacy is not a direct reflection of students' intelligence and abilities. Collins (1982) identified high-, average-, and low-ability students in mathematics; within each level she found students with high and low mathematical self-efficacy. She tested students on mathematical achievement. Although ability level related positively to achievement, regardless of ability level students with high self-efficacy demonstrated higher achievement and persistence on difficult problems.

Although self-efficacy differs from outcome expectations, the two are often related. Students with high self-efficacy expect—and usually receive—positive outcomes for their actions. But there is no automatic relation. Students can expect positive outcomes from an action (e.g., a high grade for an excellent term paper) but doubt their self-efficacy to produce the excellent term paper.

Self-efficacy beliefs are sensitive to differences in contextual factors (e.g., changing environmental conditions) and personal factors (e.g., level of motivation, affective states). As such, self-efficacy differs from many other expectancy beliefs in that self-efficacy is both more task- and situation-specific and individuals make use of self-efficacy beliefs in reference to some type of goal (Pajares, 1997; Schunk & Pajares, 2002). Self-efficacy generally is assessed at a more situationally-specific level than are other expectancy constructs (e.g., self-concept), which form more global and general self-perceptions. For example, researchers might assess self-efficacy for successfully long jumping various distances, solving different types of algebra problems, and interacting in various types of social situations. Due to their greater specificity, self-efficacy beliefs often are stronger predictors of achievement outcomes when compared with other competence-related perceptions (Bandura, 1997; Bong & Clark, 1999; Pajares, 1996a; Valentine, DuBois, & Cooper, 2004).

Much self-efficacy research has followed Bandura's original model of identifying tasks in a domain, ordering them in terms of difficulty, having individuals judge their self-efficacy for learning or performing these tasks, and then asking them to perform the same or similar tasks. Self-efficacy judgments then can be used to predict subsequent behaviors reflecting motivation, learning, and performance. Educational researchers have modified the original methodology somewhat, but self-efficacy usually is assessed at a level of specificity that corresponds to the criterion task within the domain of functioning being analyzed (Schunk & Pajares, 2004).

Although it might seem that motivation and learning benefit from a realistic sense of self-efficacy, Bandura (1986, 1997) contends that the most functional self-efficacy judgments are those that slightly exceed what one actually can do. This slight overestimation raises motivation and achievement. A challenge for educators is to facilitate optimism in students while ensuring that they have the skills to be successful.

RESEARCH ON SELF-EFFICACY IN ADOLESCENCE

In this section, we discuss correlational and experimental research on self-efficacy during adolescence in five areas: developmental changes, group differences, schooling, peers, and families (Table 3.1). Although adolescence extends beyond age 18, we focus our discussion on the changes that occur during the middle and high school years. Much developmental

**Table 3.1.   Key Areas of Research on
Adolescents' Self-Efficacy and Related Constructs**

- Developmental changes
- Group differences
- Schooling
- Peers
- Families

research has not employed self-efficacy per se but rather variables that are conceptually similar to self-efficacy, such as perceived competence and perceptions of abilities. Accordingly, our discussion includes research that examined the roles of these conceptually similar constructs.

Developmental Changes

The cognitive, physical, and social changes associated with adolescence have important implications for how young people view their capabilities. Research has shown that adolescents' self-descriptions tend to be more abstract, multidimensional, and hierarchical. These changes are believed to be due in part to adolescents' increased abilities for cognitive abstraction, reflection, and social comparison (Harter, 1998). As teens become more skilled at coordinating conflicting information and expectations, they form more stable and integrated views of their capabilities, values, and attributes.

Researchers have documented several interesting changes in young people's competence and efficacy beliefs during adolescence. Research using academic or domain-specific measures of competence shows that self-perceptions of competence begin to decline in Grade 7 or earlier (Eccles, Wigfield, & Schiefele, 1998; Wigfield et al., 1997). Declines in competence beliefs are particularly evident at the transition to middle school—especially in mathematics—and continue into high school (Jacobs, Lanza, Osgood, Eccles, & Wigfield, 2002).

In contrast, research using measures of self-efficacy have shown mixed results. Some studies also show this decline in efficacy beliefs (Anderman, Maehr, & Midgley, 1999; Pajares & Valiante, 1999; Urdan & Midgley, 2003), whereas others have found an increase in language and mathematics self-efficacy with development (Shell, Colvin, & Bruning, 1995; Zimmerman & Martinez-Pons, 1990). The inconsistency of findings across developmental studies may be due to differences in the specificity of self-efficacy and competence measures. Also, most competence measures include a social comparison component. Competence perceptions may be more dependent on an adolescent's relative standing with peers, rather than his or her prior experience with a particular course or task (Bong & Clark, 1999).

Group Differences

Adolescence is an important time for identity formation (Erikson, 1968; Waterman, 1999). As part of this process, adolescents—with their increased cognitive abilities and social experiences—begin to consider cultural expectations and standards for behavior. During early and middle adolescence young people are vulnerable to social standards for behavior (Harter, 1999) and strongly influenced by cultural stereotypes about the capabilities and traits of different social groups. Although social stereotypes in the United States are changing, they continue to portray women and non-White minorities as less skilled and academically oriented than White men, especially with regard to mathematics, science, and technology (Meece & Scantlebury, in press). If endorsed, these social stereotypes can shape adolescents' identities as learners.

Most research on group differences in self-efficacy has focused on gender and ability, whereas only a few studies have examined the role of socioeconomic or ethnic background. With regard to gender, studies reveal mixed findings. Some researchers report gender differences in self-efficacy favoring adolescent boys (Anderman & Young, 1994; Meece & Jones, 1996; Pintrich & De Groot, 1990; Zimmerman & Martinez-Pons, 1990), some report differences favoring girls (Britner & Pajares, 2001), and others reveal no gender differences (Pajares, 1996b; Pajares & Graham, 1999; Roeser, Midgley, & Urdan, 1996; Smith, Sinclair, & Chapman, 2002). These findings differ from longitudinal studies of academic competence beliefs, which report gender differences in sex-typed domains such as mathematics and language arts during adolescence (Eccles et al., 1998; Jacobs et al., 2002; Marsh, 1989; Wigfield, Eccles, Mac Iver, Rueman, & Midgley, 1991). Gender differences may be more prevalent in measures that elicit group comparisons or evaluation of worth (e.g., "I am good at math"). In making these assessments, stereotypes or feedback from others may lead to biased assessments.

The few studies that have examined ethnic differences in adolescents' self-efficacy report mixed findings. Britner and Pajares (2001) report no significant differences between middle school African American and White adolescents' self-concepts and self-efficacy for regulating their learning in science. Roeser et al. (1996) found no significant ethnic differences in middle school students' academic self-efficacy. Other studies, however, show that African American adolescents have lower mathematics self-efficacy than do their White peers (Pajares & Kranzler, 1995), and Hispanic high school students report lower writing self-efficacy than do non-Hispanic students (Pajares & Johnson, 1996). Inconsistencies in findings may be due to the specificity of the self-efficacy beliefs assessed, as well as to students' abilities and socioeconomic backgrounds. In studying ethnic differences it is essential to separate race from other background characteristics that may influence self-efficacy (Graham, 1994). It also is important to move away from race comparative studies to examine the processes by which self-efficacy beliefs are formed and affect achievement outcomes.

Schooling

Adolescents' school experiences help shape their self-efficacy beliefs. With cognitive maturity, adolescents are better able to interpret and integrate multiple sources of information about their competencies, and they have a much more differentiated view of their abilities (Eccles et al., 1998). There often is a stronger relation between performance feedback and competence beliefs for adolescents than for younger children. Additionally, as identity processes unfold, adolescents tend to compare themselves with others to find their unique place within their peer group. When an adolescent is not performing as well as his or her peers within a specific academic or interpersonal domain, social comparisons can have a negative impact, especially when performance in this area is valued by the adolescent, peers, or family members.

Research supports the hypothesized relation of self-efficacy to academic motivation (effort, persistence) and achievement. Among students of different ages, significant and positive correlations have been obtained between self-efficacy for learning (assessed prior to instruction) and subsequent motivation during learning (Schunk, 1995). Self-efficacy for learning also correlates positively with post-instruction self-efficacy and skillful performance (Schunk, 1995). Studies across different content domains (e.g., reading, writing, mathematics) using children and adolescents have yielded significant and positive correlations between self-efficacy and academic achievement (Lent, Brown, & Larkin, 1986; Multon, Brown, & Lent, 1991; Pajares, 1996a; Schunk, 1995).

Bouffard-Bouchard, Parent, and Larivée (1991) found that high school students with high self-efficacy for problem solving demonstrated greater performance-monitoring and persistence than did students with lower self-efficacy. Among college students, Zimmerman and Bandura (1994) obtained evidence that self-efficacy for writing correlated positively with goals for course achievement, self-evaluative standards (satisfaction with potential grades), and actual achievement.

Periods of transition in schooling can cause changes in self-efficacy (Schunk & Pajares, 2002). Much research has investigated the transition from elementary to junior high/middle school with its many changes in teachers, peers, classes, and grading criteria (Eccles & Midgley, 1989; Eccles, Midgley, & Adler, 1984). Young adolescents often experience declines in their competence and efficacy beliefs as they make the transition from elementary to middle school (Anderman et al., 1999; Anderman & Midgley, 1997; Eccles et al., 1983; Harter, Whitesall, & Lowalski, 1992; Urdan & Midgley, 2003; Wigfield et al., 1991); however, negative changes in self-perceptions are not inevitable and may result from changes in the school environment.

Studies reveal that elementary and secondary classrooms tend to have different goal structures. Compared with elementary students, middle school students perceive their learning environment as less focused on learning and mastery and more focused on competition and ability differences (Anderman et al., 1999; Anderman & Midgley, 1997; Urdan & Midgley, 2003; Urdan, Midgley, & Anderman, 1998). When classroom environments emphasize competition and normative evaluation (performance goals) rather than individual mastery and self-improvement, adolescents can experience a decline in their self-efficacy. In contrast, classroom environments that emphasize the importance of effort, meaningful learning, self-improvement, collaboration, and student interests help adolescents maintain positive perceptions of their efficacy and competence (Anderman & Midgley, 1997; Anderman & Young, 1994; Greene, Miller, Crowson, Duke, & Akey, 2004; Meece, 1991, 1994; Meece, Herman, & McCombs, 2003; Roeser et al., 1996; Urdan & Midgley, 2003).

Research on the effects of different classroom environments is consistent with experimental studies designed to examine relations between instructional conditions and adolescents' self-efficacy beliefs. Social cognitive theory predicts that at the outset of an activity students differ in their self-efficacy for learning as a function of their prior experiences, personal qualities, and social supports (e.g., extent that parents and teachers encourage them, facilitate their access to learning resources, and teach them strategies for learning) (Schunk, 1995). As students engage in activities they are affected by personal (e.g., goals, cognitive processing) and situational influences (e.g., instruction, feedback). These factors provide students with cues about how well they are learning, which they then use to gauge self-efficacy for continued learning.

Some instructional conditions that have been shown to develop self-efficacy among adolescents are proximal and specific learning goals, instruction on learning strategies, social models, performance and attributional feedback indicating progress, and rewards contingent on improvement (Schunk, 1995). These processes are hypothesized to affect self-efficacy and motivation through the common mechanism of informing students of their progress in learning.

Schunk and Lilly (1984) gave middle school students instruction on a novel mathematical task. Prior to the instruction girls judged self-efficacy for learning lower than did boys. Following the instruction (which included performance feedback), girls and boys did not differ in achievement or self-efficacy for solving problems. There also were no differences in male and female students' problem solving during instruction. The performance feedback indicating that learners were successful overrode the girls' preconceptions about learning mathematics.

Zimmerman and Kitsantas (1996, 1997) found that providing learning (process) goals raised self-efficacy and self-regulation during dart throwing. High school girls were assigned to a process-goal condition and asked to focus on the steps in dart throwing; others were assigned to a product-goal condition and asked to concentrate on their scores. After each throw some girls self-recorded progress by writing down steps accomplished properly or the outcome. Process-goal girls demonstrated higher self-efficacy and performance than did product-goal girls (Zimmerman & Kitsantas, 1996), and self-recording enhanced these outcomes. Zimmerman and Kitsantas (1997) replicated these results and also included a shifting-goal group where girls pursued a process goal, but once they could perform the steps they switched to a product goal of attaining high scores. The shifting goal led to the highest self-efficacy and performance.

Schunk and Ertmer (1999) pretested students on self-efficacy and performance of computer applications and on how well and often they applied self-regulation strategies while learning computer skills (e.g., set goals, use appropriate manuals). Students were assigned to a process (learn the applications) or product (do the work) goal condition; within each condition half of the students evaluated their progress during the instruction on computer applications. The process goal, with or without self-evaluation, led to higher self-efficacy and strategy competence and frequency than did the product goal with no self-evaluation. Students who received the process goal with self-evaluation judged self-efficacy higher than did process-goal students who did not receive self-evaluation and product-goal students who self-evaluated. Among self-evaluation students, those who pursued process goals evaluated their learning progress better than did those who received product goals. These results corroborate those of Schunk (1996), who found with children that self-evaluation combined with process goals is beneficial for self-efficacy and self-regulation.

Taken together, classroom and experimental studies suggest that adolescents, as they are gaining new cognitive abilities, need classroom environments that help them set goals for their learning, support their goal progress, and focus on improvement and mastery. Other research emphasizes the importance of learning environments that are both intellectually challenging and supportive of adolescents' academic development (Anderman, Patrick, Hruda, & Linnenbrink, 2002; McCombs, 2003; Ryan & Patrick, 2001). Meece et al. (2003) found that middle and high school students reported more positive self-efficacy when their teachers used learner-centered instructional practices that promoted higher-order thinking, honored student voices, created supportive relations, and adapted instruction to individual and developmental needs.

Peers

Adolescence brings important changes in young people's peer relations. A growing body of research suggests that adolescents' self-efficacy is strongly influenced by peers (Schunk & Miller, 2002). Observations of peers accomplishing a task can raise observers' self-efficacy and lead them to believe that they also can perform the task. When peers are unsuccessful, observers' self-efficacy may decrease.

Vicarious effects are aided by perceived similarity in areas such as academic or athletic ability, grades, ease or difficulty in learning, background experiences, gender, ethnicity, and interests. Similarity exerts its greatest effects when observers are unfamiliar with the task or setting and must use non-performance sources of information to gauge self-efficacy. This commonly happens among adolescents who are exposed to new classes and content. School transitions that occur with development (e.g., middle to high school) and those caused by family moves create unfamiliarity.

Key social influences on adolescents' self-efficacy are friends and peer networks. Students tend to select their friends and peer groups on the basis of similarity (Ryan, 2000), which enhances the potential influence of modeling. In general, peer similarity is strongest for Asian American and European American adolescents; African American students choose friends who are less similar with respect to academic orientation (Hamm, 2000). Networks help to define students' opportunities for interactions and observations of peers' interactions. Conversations between friends influence their choices of activities, and friends often make similar choices (Berndt & Keefe, 1992).

Peer groups promote motivational socialization (Schunk & Miller, 2002). Kindermann (1993) and Kindermann, McCollam, and Gibson (1996) examined motivation in peer selection and socialization among children and adolescents. Adolescent peer networks were more complex than were those of children. Most children's networks were dyads, but adolescents tended to have several dyads and triads, as well as larger networks. Among children, networks tended to be same sex, but adolescent groups included members of both sexes. The researchers found a significant decline in academic motivation with development. This decline may be partly a function of the greater diversity of adolescents' peer groups, which increases the likelihood that adolescents will judge themselves negatively relative to some group members.

Among ninth graders, more academically-motivated students had larger peer networks. Changes in adolescents' motivational engagement across the school year were predicted by their peer group membership at the start of the year. Students affiliated with groups high in academic motivation changed positively, whereas those in less-motivated groups changed negatively. Students in highly motivated peer groups that contained members from across grades increased in motivation across the school year, whereas those in low-motivation peer networks that had little grade diversity tended to decrease in motivation. Although this research by Kindermann and colleagues is correlational and does not permit conclusions about causality, the results suggest that peer group socialization may influence the group's academic self-efficacy and motivation (Schunk & Pajares, 2002).

Ryan (2001) found that students end up in peer networks with motivational beliefs similar to theirs at the beginning of a school year. Over the course of the year the peer group influences the group's members, and they tend to become more similar. Altermatt and Pomerantz (2003) report similar findings for grades, competence perceptions, and motivation beliefs (e.g., standards for performance, importance of meeting standards, and preference for challenge). Peer influence was strongest during an academic year, and strongest for reciprocated, rather than unilateral, friendships. Friends also influenced young adolescents' attributions for failure as they moved to a new grade level, when they may be experiencing novel learning situations (Altermatt & Pomerantz, 2003).

Steinberg, Brown, and Dornbusch (1996) conducted a 10-year project that studied several thousand adolescents from when they entered high school until their senior year. These researchers found developmental patterns in the influence of peer pressure on academic motivation and performance. Peer pressure tends to rise during childhood and peaks around Grade 8 or 9 but declines somewhat through high school. A key period is between ages 12 and 16, a time during which parents' involvement in their children's activities often declines thereby enhancing the strength of peer influence. Steinberg et al. (1996) investigated whether adolescents who began high school with similar grades but who became affiliated with different peer groups remained academically similar. Adolescents in more academically oriented crowds achieved better during high school compared with those in less academically oriented crowds. Not surprisingly, delinquency rates also were associated with peer groups.

To what extent is the frequent decline in adolescents' self-efficacy or perceptions of competence due to peer influence? This is a complex question, and, unfortunately, research findings do not provide a simple answer (Wentzel, Barry, & Caldwell, 2004). Findings suggest that peer groups may contribute to a decline in self-efficacy, but they also may help to maintain self-efficacy or even increase it. Although peers and schooling are important, the academic influence of families also is critical.

Families

Adolescents acquire much self-efficacy information from their families and home environments (Schunk & Miller, 2002). Family influences that promote effective interactions with the environment enhance self-efficacy and competence beliefs. More specifically, parents and caregivers help children build a sense of competence when they provide an environment that offers some challenges, encourages, sets high but realistic aspirations, contains positive role models, provides and supports mastery experiences, and teaches how to deal with difficulties. These effects are reciprocal, because children who are curious and partake of new experiences promote parental responsiveness. Parents who are most successful in promoting positive competence perceptions are able to modify their expectations and demands according to the changing needs, abilities, and dispositions of children as they develop (Eccles et al., 1998).

Families differ in their capital (Putnam, 2000), which often is used to define *socioeconomic status* (Bradley & Corwyn, 2002). We must keep in mind that socioeconomic status is a descriptive rather than an explanatory variable. To say that adolescents from low socioeconomic status families generally have lower self-efficacy is not to explain it. Instead, one must look at the factors and processes that characterize families of different socioeconomic levels (Bronfenbrenner, 1986). Not all children from poor families hold low self-efficacy.

There is much correlational research showing that economic hardship and low parental education relate to difficulties in development and learning (Bradley & Corwyn, 2002; McLoyd, 1990). This seems intuitively plausible, because families with less education and less income cannot provide much capital that helps stimulate cognitive development (e.g., computers, books, travel, games, cultural experiences). Research also suggests that family income levels are positively associated with parents' expectations for their child's immediate and long-term educational success (Alexander & Entwisle, 1988). Due to a number of different factors, lower income children are more likely to experience learning problems early in school, which can result in lower self-efficacy for learning (Schunk & Miller, 2002). Socioeconomic status is one of the major predictors of early school dropout (Sherman, 1997).

A number of studies have examined the influence of parenting styles on adolescents' academic orientations and school achievement (Steinberg, 2001). Developmental researchers have identified four major types of parenting styles that differ in levels of warmth, responsiveness, and control (Baumrind, 1967; Maccoby & Martin, 1983). In general, an authoritative parenting style has the best combination of warmth, responsiveness, and control to support children and adolescents. It is associated with many positive developmental outcomes including school achievement. These positive effects generally are found across different ethnic groups in the United States, although European American and Hispanic American adolescents may benefit the most from authoritative parenting practices.

Other studies of family socialization processes have examined the influence of parental beliefs on children's self-perceptions of ability and efficacy. Eccles and her colleagues contend that parents serve as important socializers of competence beliefs (Eccles et al., 1983, 1998; Jacobs & Eccles, 1992). Research suggests that parents form perceptions of their children's academic abilities, which in turn affect their children's own competence beliefs. Parents' and children's ability perceptions are significantly related by first grade and grow in strength over the elementary years (Fredericks & Eccles, 2002). Considerable evidence also suggests that children's ability perceptions are more directly related to parental perceptions than to measures of performance or ability (Eccles et al., 1998).

In forming their beliefs, parents tend to rely heavily on objective feedback, such as school grades or performance. However, some evidence suggests that parents' perceptions may be shaped more by cultural stereotypes, especially with regards to the differential abilities of women and men (Frome & Eccles, 1998; Jacobs & Eccles, 1992). For example, studies suggest that parents are more likely to attribute success in mathematics to natural abilities for sons than for daughters, even when the children have equal abilities (Yee & Eccles, 1988). Parents communicate their beliefs through explicit statements about their child's ability, causal attributions for their child's performance, the types of learning activities they encourage or discourage, and their immediate and long-term expectations for their child (Eccles et al., 1998). Recent evidence suggests that parental ability perceptions not only have a strong impact on their children's self-perceptions of ability but also predict their career choices and educational plans 12 years later (Bleeker & Jacobs, 2004).

Another critical factor is parents' involvement in their children's education. During adolescence, when parents typically become less involved in children's activities, parents who stay involved can exert indirect influence on children's growth. For example, parents who offer their home as a place where friends are welcome continue the trajectory of steering their children in positive directions. Parents who want their children to be academically focused are apt to urge them to become involved in academic activities (e.g., French club), which can strengthen children's self-efficacy. Fan and Chen (2001) conducted a meta-analysis of research on the relation of parental involvement to children's academic attainments. The results showed that parents' expectations for their children's academic successes related positively to actual academic achievements. It is reasonable to assume that parents convey their expectations to children directly (e.g., verbally) and indirectly (e.g., involving children in academic activities, assisting with homework), which in turn affects children's expectations (self-efficacy) for themselves. The effects of parental expectations on children's achievement seem greatest when a high level of parent involvement exists in the neighborhood (Collins, Maccoby, Steinberg, Hetherington, & Bornstein, 2000). Miliotis, Sesma, and Masten (1999) found that after families left homeless shelters, high parent involvement in children's education predicted children's school success.

Other research shows that parent involvement can influence children's self-regulation, especially the type of instruction that parents provide. When parents give understandable metacognitive instruction children display greater classroom monitoring, participation, and metacognitive talk (Stright, Neitzel, Sears, & Hoke-Sinex, 2001). Such instruction is part of the parental socialization that can prepare children and adolescents for school success. Students who believe they possess the self-regulatory strategies to learn in school are apt to feel more self-efficacious about succeeding.

IMPLICATIONS FOR TEACHING AND PARENTING

Adolescence can be a difficult time for students and for those close to them. The many physical, cognitive, social, emotional, and environmental changes cause stress, and coping can prove difficult. Ideally adolescents will develop a sense of self-efficacy for being able to exert a good measure of control over their lives, or *agency* (Bandura, 2001). A resilient sense of self-efficacy that can overcome difficulties will serve them well during adolescence and beyond (Schunk & Miller, 2002).

Table 3.2.   Implications for Teaching and Parenting

- Understand the multiple influences on self-efficacy
- Structure curricular and social experiences
- Involve parents
- Ensure smooth transitions
- Create supportive home and classroom environments
- Teach effective life skills

The theory and research on the development of adolescents' self-efficacy provide suggestions for teachers and parents who want to be as helpful as possible. Some key implications are discussed below (Table 3.2).

Understand the Multiple Influences on Self-Efficacy

Self-efficacy is affected by one's actual performances, vicarious experiences, verbal persuasion, and emotional responses. Adolescents receive much information from these sources in schools, homes, and social environments. Actual performance is the most reliable source, but not the only one. Students weigh and combine information from many sources, and the process whereby they do this is not well understood.

The implication is that to help adolescents develop a resilient sense of self-efficacy teachers and parents should appeal to multiple sources. For example, students who believe that they are not smart enough to learn Algebra 2 may not be swayed much by parents telling them that they did well in Pre-Algebra and Algebra 1. The adolescents may know some peers who did well in the prerequisites but struggled with Algebra 2, and such social information may have an overwhelming effect on their self-efficacy for learning. It may take actual successes, encouragement, tutoring, and observing some similar peers succeeding in Algebra 2, to outweigh the preconception.

Structure Curricular and Social Experiences

Teachers and parents can structure curricular and social experiences to aid the development of adolescents' self-efficacy. With respect to the curriculum, students will feel more self-efficacious about learning when they understand how the new learning builds on what they know. Although self-efficacy is a domain-specific construct, it is plausible that self-efficacy for learning will generalize to other situations when students understand how the new learning relates to the old. Thus, students are apt to feel more efficacious about learning Algebra 2 content when they understand that it utilizes much of the content they have learned in previous courses.

Social experiences that are likely to enhance adolescents' self-efficacy can be planned. Many teachers use peer models to teach others skills. Low achievers' self-efficacy may not be aided much by observing highly-competent students demonstrate skills. Rather, models whom students believe are similar to themselves (i.e., similarly-achieving students who have mastered the new operations) are apt to exert better effects on observers' self-efficacy for learning.

Although parents and teachers cannot completely control their adolescents' choice of friends, they can steer their children in appropriate directions by enrolling them in activities with the desired type of friends. This helps to ensure that adolescents are exposed to peers whom they will view as similar, which helps to build their self-efficacy.

Involve Parents

Although parent involvement is high in some schools, in other parents are reluctant to participate. A good first step is to keep parents informed about school activities, such as by sending home frequent notes and e-mails. Where possible, school events can be scheduled at times that parents can attend. Parent involvement can be increased by scheduling field trips to places in the community—such as museums or businesses—and asking parents to serve as tour guides.

Parents also can help ensure that home influences are positive. Many students have difficulty studying because of poor planning or distracting home environments. Schools can schedule sessions in which students learn effective study strategies such as how to budget time, eliminate distractions, and monitor progress on homework and studying for tests.

Ensure Smooth Transitions

School personnel can ease the natural stress of transitions in several ways. Middle school students who will be transitioning to high school can be given tours of the high school and sessions with counselors on schedules and school life. Some schools set up buddy systems, where a current high school student is assigned to each incoming student to help the newcomer with the transition. Students are apt to have higher self-efficacy for succeeding in the new environment when they are familiar with it and believe that others are available to help them overcome difficulties.

Schools can help students establish good planning, organization, and other study skills before students make the transition. In middle schools, for example, students typically change classes and many schools require that students use planners. Good planning becomes essential as adolescents' lives become increasingly busy with school, activities, athletics, school events, studying, and time with friends. Students who believe they possess good planning, organization, and study skills, are apt to feel personally efficacious about performing well in school.

Create Supportive Home and Classroom Environments

Parents and teachers also can enhance young people's self-efficacy by creating supportive environments. Adolescents benefit the most from home environments that are characterized by warmth, fair and consistent standards for behavior, open communication, encouragement for self-reliance and autonomy, and effective monitoring of peer relations and social activities (Steinberg, 2001). Positive effects are found for a wide range of outcomes, including school adjustment and achievement (Wentzel, 2002).

Similarly, adolescents benefit from teachers who are caring and supportive. According to their students, these teachers recognize students' strengths and weaknesses, treat students as individuals, promote respectful interactions, and listen to students and show an interest in their concerns (Wentzel, 1997). Additionally, adolescents need learning environments that are intellectually challenging and supportive of individual progress and mastery. Adolescents report greater self-efficacy and engagement in learning when they believe that their teachers promote higher-order thinking and understanding, emphasize the importance of individual mastery and understanding, communicate high expectations for learning, honor student voices, create supportive social relations, and adapt instruction to students' needs and interests (Meece et al., 2003).

Teach Effective Life Skills

To successfully manage their lives adolescents need study skills and such other skills as self-control, conflict management, and decision making. Some high schools hold new student orientation programs prior to the start of school to help familiarize newcomers with the school building and procedures, and these types of skills can be included in such programs.

Many organizations offer workshops for parents on topics that concern adolescents. Schools can help keep parents informed of these opportunities. In school, teachers can promote the development of responsible adolescent behavior by using fewer lectures and drills and more activities that require collaborative decision making. These activities may help to alleviate common complaints of college counselors that many students come to college academically able but deficient in personal management and social skills.

CONCLUSION

Self-efficacy is a key cognitive process contributing to healthy human functioning. Factors associated with schooling, peers, and families affect self-efficacy development in adolescents. Adolescence is a challenging time and there are multiple ways that negative influences can lower students' self-efficacy. Theory and research suggest strategies that teachers and parents can use to help promote self-efficacy in adolescents. Individuals who develop a resilient sense of self-efficacy during adolescence are in a better position to withstand the normal challenges of development and are well positioned for learning into adulthood.

REFERENCES

Alexander, K., & Entwisle, D. (1988). Achievement in the first two years of school: Patterns and processes. *Monograph for Research in Child Development, 53*(2):1-157.

Altermatt, E. R., & Pomerantz, E. M. (2003). The development of competence-related and motivation beliefs: An investigation of similarity and influence among friends. *Journal of Educational Psychology, 95,* 111-125.

Anderman, E. M., Maehr, M. L., & Midgley, C. (1999). Declining motivation after the transition to middle school: Schools can make a difference. *Journal of Research and Development in Education, 32,* 131-147.

Anderman, E. M., & Midgley, C. (1997). Changes in personal achievement goals and the perceived goal structures across the transition to middle schools. *Contemporary Educational Psychology, 22,* 269-298.

Anderman, E. M., Patrick, H., Hruda, L. Z., & Linnenbrink, E. (2002). Observing classroom goal structures to clarify and expand goal theory. In C. Midgley (Ed.), *Goals, goal structures, and patterns of adaptive learning* (pp. 243-278). Mahwah, NJ: Erlbaum.

Anderman, E. M., & Young, A. J. (1994). Motivation and strategy use in science: Individual differences and classroom effects. *Journal of Research in Science Teaching, 31,* 811-831.

Bandura, A. (1986). *Social foundations of thought and action: A social cognitive theory.* Englewood Cliffs, NJ: Prentice Hall.

Bandura, A. (1997). *Self-efficacy: The exercise of control.* New York: Freeman.

Bandura, A. (2001). Social cognitive theory: An agentic perspective. *Annual Review of Psychology, 52,* 1-26.

Baumrind, D. (1967). Current patterns of parental authority. *Genetic Psychology Monographs, 75,* 43-88.

Berndt, T. J., & Keefe, K. (1992). Friends' influence on adolescents' perceptions of themselves at school. In D. H. Schunk & J. L. Meece (Eds.), *Student perceptions in the classroom* (pp. 51-73). Hillsdale, NJ: Erlbaum.

Bleeker, M. M., & Jacobs, J. E. (2004). Achievement in math and science: Do mothers' beliefs matter 12 years later? *Journal of Educational Psychology, 96,* 97-109.

Bong, M., & Clark, R. (1999). Comparison between self-concept and self-efficacy in academic motivation research. *Educational Psychologist, 34,* 139-153.

Bouffard-Bouchard, T., Parent, S., & Larivée, S. (1991). Influence of self-efficacy on self-regulation and performance among junior and senior high-school age students. *International Journal of Behavioral Development, 14,* 153-164.

Bradley, R. H., & Corwyn, R. F. (2002). Socioeconomic status and child development. *Annual Review of Psychology, 52,* 371-399.

Britner, S. L., & Pajares, F. (2001). Self-efficacy beliefs, motivation, race, and gender in middle school science. *Journal of Women and Minorities in Science and Engineering, 7,* 271-285.

Bronfenbrenner, U. (1986). Ecology of the family as a context for human development: Research perspectives. *Developmental Psychology, 22,* 723-742.

Cairns, R. B., Cairns, B. D., & Neckerman, J. J. (1989). Early school dropout: Configurations and determinants. *Child Development, 60,* 1437-1452.

Collins, J. L. (1982, March). *Self-efficacy and ability in achievement behavior.* Paper presented at the annual meeting of the American Educational Research Association, New York.

Collins, W. A., Maccoby, E. E., Steinberg, L., Hetherington, E. M., & Bornstein, M. H. (2000). Contemporary research on parenting: The case for nature and nurture. *American Psychologist, 55,* 218-232.

Eccles, J. S., Adler, T., Futterman, R., Goff, S. B., Kaczala, C., Meece, J. L., et al. (1983). Expectations, values, and academic behaviors. In J. T. Spence (Ed.), *Achievement and achievement motivation* (pp. 75-146). San Francisco: Freeman.

Eccles, J. S., & Midgley, C. (1989). Stage-environment fit: Developmentally appropriate classrooms for young adolescents. In C. Ames & R. Ames (Eds.), *Research on motivation in education* (Vol. 3, pp. 139-186). San Diego: Academic Press.

Eccles, J. S., Midgley, C., & Adler, T. F. (1984). Grade-related changes in the school environment: Effects on achievement motivation. In J. Nicholls (Ed.), *Advances in motivation and achievement* (Vol. 3, pp. 283-311). Greenwich, CT: JAI Press.

Eccles, J. S., Wigfield, A., & Schiefele, U. (1998). Motivation to succeed. In N. Eisenberg (Ed.), *Handbook of child psychology: Vol. 3. Social, emotional, and personality development* (5th ed., pp. 1017-1095). New York: Wiley.

Erikson, E. (1968). *Identity: Youth and crisis*. New York: Norton.

Fan, X., & Chen, M. (2001). Parental involvement and students' academic achievement: A meta-analysis. *Educational Psychology Review, 13*, 1-22.

Fredericks, J. A., & Eccles, J. S. (2002). Children's competence and value beliefs from childhood through adolescence: Growth trajectories in two male-sex-typed domains. *Developmental Psychology, 38*, 519-533.

Frome, P., & Eccles, J. S. (1998). Parents' influences on children's achievement-related perceptions. *Journal of Personality and Social Psychology, 74*, 435-452.

Graham, S. (1994). Motivation in African Americans. *Review of Educational Research, 64*, 55-117.

Greene, B., Miller, R., Crowson, H. M., Duke, B. L., & Akey, K. L. (2004). Predicting high school students' cognitive engagement and achievement: Contributions of classroom perceptions and motivation. *Contemporary Educational Psychology, 29*, 462-482.

Hamm, J. (2000). Do birds of a feather flock together? The variable bases for African American and European American adolescents' selection of similar friends. *Developmental Psychology, 36*, 209-219.

Harter, S. (1998). The development of self-representations. In N. Eisenberg (Ed.), *Handbook of child psychology* (Vol. 3, pp. 1017-1095). New York: Wiley.

Harter, S. (1999). *The construction of the self: A developmental perspective*. New York: Guilford Press.

Harter, S., Whitesall, N., & Lowalski, P. (1992). Individual differences in the effects of educational transitions on young adolescents' perceptions of competence and motivational orientation. *American Educational Research Journal, 29*, 77-87.

Jacobs, J. E., & Eccles, J. S. (1992). The impact of mothers' gender-role stereotypic beliefs on mothers' and children's ability perceptions. *Journal of Personality and Social Psychology, 63*, 932-944.

Jacobs, J. E., Lanza, S., Osgood, W., Eccles, J. S., & Wigfield, A. (2002). Changes in children's self-competence and values: Gender and domain differences across grades one through twelve. *Child Development, 73*, 509-527.

Kindermann, T. A. (1993). Natural peer groups as contexts for individual development: The case of children's motivation in school. *Developmental Psychology, 29*, 970-977.

Kindermann, T. A., McCollam, T. L., & Gibson, E., Jr. (1996). Peer networks and students' classroom engagement during childhood and adolescence. In J. Juvonen & K. R. Wentzel (Eds.), *Social motivation: Understanding children's school adjustment* (pp. 279-312). Cambridge, England: Cambridge University Press.

Lent, R. W., Brown, S. D., & Larkin, K. C. (1986). Self-efficacy in the prediction of academic performance and perceived career options. *Journal of Counseling Psychology, 33*, 265-269.

Maccoby, E. E., & Martin, J. (1983). Socialization in the context of the family: Parent-child interactions. In E. M. Hetherington (Ed.), *Handbook of child psychology* (Vol. 4, pp. 1-101). New York: Wiley.

Marsh, H. W. (1989). Age and sex effects in multiple dimensions of self-concept: Preadolescence to adulthood. *Journal of Educational Psychology, 81*, 417-430.

McCombs, B. (2003). Applying educational psychology knowledge base in educational reform: From research to application to policy. In W. M. Reynolds & G. E. Miller (Eds.), *Comprehensive handbook of psychology: Vol. 7. Educational psychology* (pp. 583-607). New York: Wiley.

McLoyd, V. (1990). The impact of economic hardship on black families and children: Psychological distress, parenting, and socioeconomic development. *Child Development, 61,* 311-346.

Meece, J. L. (1991). The classroom context and children's motivational goals. In M. L. Maehr & P. R. Pintrich (Eds.), *Advances in achievement motivation research* (Vol. 7, pp. 261-285). New York: Academic Press.

Meece, J. L. (1994). The role of motivation in self-regulation. In D. H. Schunk & B. J. Zimmerman (Eds.), *Self-regulation of learning and performance: Issues and educational applications* (pp. 25-44). Hillsdale, NJ: Erlbaum.

Meece, J. L., Herman, P., & McCombs, B. (2003). Relations of learner-centered teaching practices to adolescents' achievement goals. *International Journal of Educational Research, 39,* 457-475.

Meece, J. L., & Jones, G. (1996). Gender differences in motivation and strategy use in science: Are girls rote learners? *Journal of Research on Science Teaching, 33,* 407-431.

Meece, J. L., & Scantlebury, K. S. (in press). Gender and schooling. In J. Worell & C. Goodheart (Eds.), *Handbook of girls' and women's psychological health.* New York: Oxford Press.

Meece, J. L., Wigfield, A., & Eccles, J. S. (1990). Predictors of math anxiety and its consequences for young adolescents' course enrollment intentions and performance in mathematics. *Journal of Educational Psychology, 82,* 60-70.

Miliotis, D., Sesma, A., Jr., & Masten, A. S. (1999). Parenting as a protective process for school success in children from homeless families. *Early Education and Development, 10,* 111-133.

Multon, K. D., Brown, S. D., & Lent, R. W. (1991). Relation of self-efficacy beliefs to academic outcomes: A meta-analytic investigation. *Journal of Counseling Psychology, 38,* 30-38.

Pajares, F. (1996a). Self-efficacy beliefs in achievement settings. *Review of Educational Research, 66,* 543-578.

Pajares, F. (1996b). Self-efficacy beliefs and mathematical problem-solving of gifted students. *Contemporary Educational Psychology, 21,* 325-344.

Pajares, F. (1997). Current directions in self-efficacy research. In M. Maehr & P. R. Pintrich (Eds.), *Advances in motivation and achievement* (Vol. 10, pp. 1-49). Greenwich, CT: JAI Press.

Pajares, F., & Graham, L. (1999). Self-efficacy, motivation constructs, and mathematics performance of entering middle school students. *Contemporary Educational Psychology, 24,* 124-139.

Pajares, F., & Johnson, M. J. (1996). Self-efficacy beliefs in the writing of high school students: A path analysis. *Psychology in the Schools, 33,* 163-175.

Pajares, F., & Kranzler, J. (1995). Self-efficacy beliefs and general mental ability in mathematical problem-solving. *Contemporary Educational Psychology, 20,* 426-443.

Pajares, F., & Valiante, G. (1999). Grade level and gender differences in the writing self-beliefs of middle school students. *Contemporary Educational Psychology, 24,* 390-405.

Pintrich, P. R., & De Groot, E. V. (1990). Motivational and self-regulated learning components of classroom academic performance. *Journal of Educational Psychology, 82,* 33-40.

Putnam, R. D. (2000). *Bowling alone: The collapse and revival of American community.* New York: Simon & Schuster.

Roeser, R. W., Midgley, C., & Urdan, T. C. (1996). Perceptions of the school psychological environment and early adolescents' psychological and behavioral functioning in school: The mediating role of goals and belonging. *Journal of Educational Psychology, 88,* 408-422.

Ryan, A. (2000). Peer groups as a context for the socialization of adolescents' motivation, engagement, and achievement in school. *Educational Psychologist, 35,* 101-111.

Ryan, A. (2001). The peer group as a context for the development of young adolescent motivation and achievement. *Child Development, 72,* 1135-1150.

Ryan, A., & Patrick, H. (2001). The classroom social environment and changes in adolescents' motivation and engagement during middle school. *American Educational Research Journal, 38,* 437-460.

Schunk, D. H. (1995). Self-efficacy and education and instruction. In J. E.Maddux (Ed.), *Self-efficacy, adaptation, and adjustment: Theory, research, and applications* (pp. 281-303). New York: Plenum.

Schunk, D. H. (1996). Goal and self-evaluative influences during children's cognitive skill learning. *American Educational Research Journal, 33,* 359-382.

Schunk, D. H., & Ertmer, P. A. (1999). Self-regulatory processes during computer skill acquisition: Goal and self-evaluative influences. *Journal of Educational Psychology, 91,* 251-260.

Schunk, D. H., & Lilly, M. W. (1984). Sex differences in self-efficacy andattributions: Influence of performance feedback. *Journal of Early Adolescence, 4,* 203-213.

Schunk, D. H., & Miller, S. D. (2002). Self-efficacy and adolescents' motivation. In F. Pajares & T. Urdan (Eds.), *Academic motivation of adolescents* (pp. 29-52). Greenwich, CT: Information Age.

Schunk, D. H., & Pajares, F. (2002). The development of academic self-efficacy. In A. Wigfield & J. S. Eccles (Eds.), *Development of achievement motivation* (pp. 15-31). San Diego: Academic Press.

Schunk, D. H., & Pajares, F. (2004). Self-efficacy in education revisited: Empirical and applied evidence. In D. M. McInerney & S. Van Etten (Eds.), *Big theories revisited* (pp. 115-138). Greenwich, CT: Information Age.

Shell, D. F., Colvin, C., & Bruning, R. H. (1995). Self-efficacy, attributions, and outcome expectancy mechanisms in reading and writing achievement: Grade-level and achievement-level differences. *Journal of Educational Psychology, 87,* 386-398.

Sherman, A. (1997). *Poverty matters: The cost of child poverty in America.* Washington, DC: Children's Defense Fund.

Smith, L., Sinclair, K. E., & Chapman, E. S. (2002). Students' goals, self-efficacy, self-handicapping, and negative affective responses: An Australian senior school student study. *Contemporary Educational Psychology, 27*, 471-485.

Steinberg, L. (2001). We know some things: Parent-adolescent relationships in retrospect and prospect. *Journal of Research on Adolescence, 11*, 1-19.

Steinberg, L., Brown, B. B., & Dornbusch, S. M. (1996). *Beyond the classroom: Why school reform has failed and what parents need to do.* New York:Simon & Schuster.

Stright, A. D., Neitzel, C., Sears, K. G., & Hoke-Sinex, L. (2001). Instruction begins in the home: Relations between parental instruction and children's self-regulation in the classroom. *Journal of Educational Psychology, 93*, 456-466.

Urdan, T., & Midgley, C. (2003). Changes in the perceived classroom goal structure and pattern of adaptive learning during early adolescence. *Contemporary Educational Psychology, 28*, 524-551.

Urdan, T., Midgley, C., & Anderman, E. M. (1998). The role of the classroom goal structure in students' use of self-handicapping strategies. *American Educational Research Journal, 35*, 101-122.

Valentine, J. C., DuBois, D. L., & Cooper, H. (2004). The relation between self-beliefs and academic achievement: A meta-analytic review. *Educational Psychologist, 39*, 111-134.

Waterman, A. (1999). Identity, the identity statuses, and identity status development: A contemporary statement. *Developmental Psychology, 19*, 591-621.

Wentzel, K. (1997). Student motivation in middle school: The role of perceived pedagogical caring. *Journal of Educational Psychology, 89*, 411-419.

Wentzel, K. (2002). Are effective teachers like good parents? Teaching styles and student adjustment in early adolescence. *Child Development, 73*, 287-301.

Wentzel, K., Barry, C. B., & Caldwell, K. A. (2004). Friendships in middle school: Influences on motivation and school adjustment. *Journal of Educational Psychology, 96*, 195-203.

Wigfield, A., & Eccles, J. S. (1992). The development of achievement task values: A theoretical analysis. *Developmental Review, 12*, 265-310.

Wigfield, A., Eccles, J. S., Mac Iver, D., Reuman, D., & Midgley, C. (1991). Transitions at early adolescence: Changes in children's domain-specific self-perceptions and general self-esteem across the transition to junior high school. *Developmental Psychology, 27*, 552-565.

Wigfield, A., Eccles, J. S., Yoon, K. S., Harold, R. D., Arbreton, A. J. A., Freedman-Doan, C., et al. (1997). Change in children's competence beliefs and subjective task values across the elementary school years: A 3-year study. *Journal of Educational Psychology, 89*, 451-469.

Yee, D. K., & Eccles, J. S. (1988). Parental perceptions and attributions for children's math achievement. *Sex Roles, 19*, 317-333.

Zimmerman, B. J., & Bandura, A. (1994). Impact of self-regulatory influences onwriting course achievement. *American Educational Research Journal, 31*, 845-862.

Zimmerman, B. J., & Kitsantas, A. (1996). Self-regulated learning of a motoric skill: The role of goal setting and self-monitoring. *Journal of Applied Sport Psychology, 8*, 60-75.

Zimmerman, B. J., & Kitsantas, A. (1997). Developmental phases in self-regulation: Shifting from process goals to outcome goals. *Journal of Educational Psychology, 89*, 29-36.

Zimmerman, B. J., & Martinez-Pons, M. (1990). Student differences in self-regulated learning: Relating grade, sex, and giftedness to self-efficacy and strategy use. *Journal of Educational Psychology, 82*, 51-59.

CHAPTER 4

THE IMPACT OF PERCEIVED FAMILY EFFICACY BELIEFS ON ADOLESCENT DEVELOPMENT

Gian Vittorio Caprara, Eugenia Scabini, and Camillo Regalia

Self-efficacy beliefs play a pervasive influence in many contexts of an adolescent's life, including school, sport, career decisions, and health functioning. Indeed, these beliefs are at the root of human agency. Adolescents do not undertake tasks they feel are beyond their abilities, nor are they inclined to pursue ambitious goals and persevere in the face of difficulties unless they believe they can produce desired results. Instead, the more convinced they are that they can deal with situations effectively, the more they seize opportunities and the better they express their talents, thus increasing the probability of their success and well-being.

Adolescents' self-efficacy beliefs are not by themselves sufficient to ensure the achievement of goals that exceed individual talent. Instead, self-efficacy results from sharing knowledge and responsibility, multiple interconnections, mutual obligations, and concerted actions with others. In contexts calling on social interdependence, such as family, school, and teams, success depends on others' efficacy beliefs as well as on collective efficacy, namely, the practices of acting together efficaciously and the beliefs that sustain these practices.

Self-Efficacy Beliefs of Adolescents, 97–115

The family is a social system that exerts a profound influence on the development of an adolescent. The beliefs that parents and children hold about their capacity to meet reciprocal obligations and about the family's capacity to promote its members' well-being are critical to the family's smooth functioning. This is particularly true nowadays, as extended education and delayed financial independence prolong the time children live at home. The longer that children live with their parents and the more they expand their area of freedom within the family, the more their relationships with parents are continuously renegotiated.

The transition to adulthood represents a complex relational-intergenerational process. This is a joint developmental enterprise in which the capacity of the family and its members to face challenges is tested (Caprara, Scabini, & Sgritta, 2003). Since parents and adolescents should be capable of self-confidence and mutual acceptance, shared beliefs in family efficacy should protect parents and adolescents from feelings of inadequacy or despondency. In accordance with these premises, in this chapter we draw on findings from our research to provide insights about filial, parental, and collective family efficacy beliefs.

EFFICACY BELIEFS AND FAMILY FUNCTIONING

Throughout their lives, people face a variety of demands and challenges as part of family systems consisting of multiple interlocking relationships in which all members reciprocally influence one another. From the moment two people commit themselves to each other to the moment they decide to have children and throughout their development, family life consists of a sequence of transitions, each of which calls for unique tasks from family members (Caprara & Cervone, 2000; Scabini, 1995; Walsh, 1993). Under these conditions, family members must be able to change continuously in their ways of thinking, feeling, and behaving to fit different roles, meet different demands, and, ultimately, match their personal expectations with their social obligations.

Family life traditionally begins with the formation of a marital union, a process involving both intimacy and mutual commitment between partners. The quality of the union prepares the transition to parenthood and the quality of parent-child relationships (Erel & Burman, 1995; Hinde & Stevenson, 1988). Parenthood brings multiple challenges as it changes the relationship between the partners and their interactions with their relatives.

As children progress in their development, parents' family management practices change in form and locus of guidance (Bandura, 1997). Newborns mostly need caring. Parents too benefit from the caring provided by their spouses' support (Parke, 1988). Soon after, instilling norms becomes as important as caring in the socialization of children, who must acquire the capacities needed to interact effectively with others. Open communication, clarity, and consistency in setting rules can promote children's autonomy and competence. Throughout adolescence, the relationships between parents and children are continuously renegotiated along two axes of affect and control, with "optimal development taking place where there is a good stage environment fit between the needs of developing individuals and the opportunities afforded by their social environments" (Eccles, Midgley, Wigfield, & Buchanàn, 1993, p. 98). As direct parental control declines, parental guidance takes the form of advice, mutual confidence, and trust. To provide their guidance, parents must rely on their children's personal standards and self-regulatory capabilities to serve as guides and deterrents when their children are outside the home.

To benefit from parental advice, adolescents must disclose their experience to their parents. As adolescents move into the ranks of young adulthood while remaining at home, as frequently happens in most Western countries, they extend the nature and scope of their activities and assume increasing responsibilities in the social community. At this time, relationships between generations have to be renegotiated along the two axes of interdependence and respect. Familial relationships grounded on mutual respect promote autonomy while granting the emotional support needed to face new challenges and responsibilities and to weather stressors and adversities. The function of the husband-wife dyad changes as well in accordance with changes occurring in the parent-child dyads and the changes associated with the aging of spouses, their career progressions, and the links with other relatives. Grown-up children leave their parents' home, and their parents often have to take care of their own parents during old age.

At each moment in a family's transition, the various roles of spouses, parents, and children carry different opportunities, constraints, and reciprocal obligations. Each represents a domain in which the beliefs individuals hold concerning their capacity to deal effectively with their own role requirements may prove to be critical for the family's proper functioning. Although it may be desirable, it is unlikely that spouses, parents, and children feel equally confident in their capacities to behave efficaciously in the presence of the different tasks they face over the course of family life. Being a self-efficacious spouse rests on the capacity to deal with obligations that differ from those of being a self-efficacious parent. Similarly, parenting of infants, adolescents, and young adults requires self-efficacy for meeting demands specific to each group.

Self-efficacy research concerning various family roles is relatively sparse despite the growing recognition of the influence that efficacy beliefs exert in several contexts and domains of human functioning. Furthermore, much of the research on self-efficacy and family functioning has focused on dyadic relationships, either between spouses or between parents and their children. In particular, most research has focused on parental efficacy beliefs, namely, the beliefs that parents, mostly mothers, hold about their capacity to care and to promote their children's development. This research attests to the influence that parents' perceived competence exerts on earlier positive parenting, either directly or by mediating the effects of other important determinants of parenting quality, such as poverty, social support, parents' characteristics (experience with children, depression), and child characteristics (temperament, physical health). Perceived parenting efficacy fosters the transition to parenthood and plays a protective role in early child development. Mothers with strong beliefs in their caretaking efficacy, as measured before the birth of their first child, experience more positive emotional well-being, closer attachment to their baby, better adjustment to their parenting role during the postpartum phase, and less conflict over the parenting role. As children grow up, parenting self-efficacy is associated with the promotion of children's aspirations and competencies, with effective monitoring of their activities, and with active parental involvement in community organizations. The developmental benefits of parenting self-efficacy have been verified across different levels of socioeconomic status and family structure, under conditions of economic adversity, and in different cultural milieus (Bandura, Barbaranelli, Caprara, & Pastorelli, 1996, 2001; Coleman & Karraker, 1998, 2000; Cutrona & Troutman, 1986; Elder, Eccles, Ardelt, & Lord, 1995; Forkel & Silbereisen, 2003; Teti & Gelfand, 1991; Teti, O'Connell, & Reiner, 1996).

Parents who believe in their efficacy to contribute to their children's development act in ways that cultivate their potential (Ardelt & Eccles, 2001; Bandura, this volume). They build their children's aspirations and sense of intellectual efficacy, which, in turn, contribute to their social relations, emotional well-being, academic development, and career choices (Bandura et al., 1996, 2001; Pastorelli, Steca, Gerbino, & Vecchio, 2001).

Much less is known about the influence that filial and spousal efficacy beliefs exert on family members' relationships as well as on their well-being and development. Transactions within parent-child dyads involve reciprocal influences. Transactional models conceive development as a continual interplay between a changing individual and a changing environment, with child characteristics influencing parental practices that, in turn, affect children's behavior that, in turn, affects parental behavior (Halverson & Wampler, 1997). Social cognitive theorists emphasize how developing individuals influence directly (as agents) and indirectly (as targets of others' reactions and expectations) their own development and the family itself (Bandura, 1997; Bell & Harper, 1977; Kuczynski, 2003; Maccoby, 1988). Our own current research documents the extent to which children's filial efficacy beliefs affect their relationships with their parents and actively contribute to family well-functioning and to children's own development (Bandura, Caprara, Regalia, Scabini, & Barbaranelli, 2004; Caprara et al., 1998, 1999; Caprara, Pastorelli, Regalia, Scabini, & Bandura, 2005; Caprara, Regalia, & Bandura, 2002; Regalia, Barbaranelli, Pastorelli, & Mazzotti, 1999; Regalia, Pastorelli, Barbaranelli, & Gerbino, 2001).

Spousal relationship is another important dyad in the family interlocking system. One's perceived spousal self-efficacy centers on the partners' perceived capability to communicate with and confide in the other openly, provide mutual support, resolve marital relationship problems, and work through disagreements over child rearing, financial, and other family issues. The lack of enabling and fulfilling reciprocity and unresolved marital discord can detract from the quality of family functioning and satisfaction with family life, with the net result of jeopardizing the relationships with children and other relatives and negatively affecting each partner's subjective well-being. Only a few studies have explored the spousal dyadic aspects of family efficacy. In married women who pursue professional careers, perceived efficacy to manage dual homemaking and occupational demands contributes to personal well-being and health, rather than merely protecting against distress (Ozer, 1995). Furthermore, spousal efficacy also is associated with family satisfaction both directly and through collective efficacy (Bandura et al., 2004).

As in other domains, research and theory on human agency and family functioning has centered on personal agency exercised individually. This despite the fact that a family is a highly interdependent social system whose functioning largely reflects people's shared beliefs in their joint capabilities to operate in concert, to create synergies, and to achieve common goals. Indeed, recent research shows that spousal, parental, and filial efficacy beliefs mostly operate through perceived collective family efficacy (Bandura et al., 2004).

ASSESSMENT OF FAMILY EFFICACY BELIEFS

The lack of suitable analytic tools has been a major limitation to addressing the intricacy of family subsystems as they operate and change over the course of a family's life cycle. In the multiple interlocking relationships constituting a family, the roles of parents, spouses, and offspring carry different functional demands, opportunities, constraints, and reciprocal obligations. As members' beliefs in their efficacy to operate collaboratively within the family system are conditionally linked to functional roles and developmental status, one cannot expect to assess spousal, parental, filial, or family collective perceived efficacy as a stable trait and without regard to the differential demands that these individuals face at different moments in their life. Newborns impose different demands on their parents than do adolescents, aging parents impose different obligations on their children, and family collective efficacy rests on different capacities to communicate openly and constructively with one another, to operate in concert towards common accomplishments, and to promote one another's development and well-being.

To address these issues, we have developed a series of measures of beliefs in perceived marital, parental, filial, and family collective efficacy as part of a longitudinal project aimed at identifying the personal and social determinants of one's social adaptation and well-being from childhood, through adolescence, to adulthood (Caprara, Regalia, & Scabini, 2001; Caprara, Regalia, Scabini, Barbaranelli & Bandura, 2004). The various measures have been explicitly conceived to tap self- and collective efficacy beliefs related to the different roles of families with adolescents.

Filial self-efficacy refers to children's beliefs in their capability to establish and maintain good relationships with their parents while voicing their own opinions and negotiating their freedom. These capabilities are likely to include open communication with parents about personal problems even under difficult circumstances and the capacity to express positive feelings and to manage negative mood. They also include getting parents to see their children's side on contentious issues, manage stress arising from marital conflicts, and be able to influence constructively parental attitudes and social practices (Brannen, 1999; Demo & Acock, 1996; Noller, 1995; Scabini, 1995; Smetana, 1996).

Parental self-efficacy involves parents' beliefs about their capability to deal with their adolescent children, especially in terms of being able to combine affective closeness and disciplinary firmness and, thus, to promote monitoring, support, protection, guidance, and encouragement. These capabilities are likely to include the capacity of being able to maintain open communication with children, to support their efforts to gain self-reliance and manage new challenges, to achieve consensus on personal responsibilities, to firmly handle violations of rules and commitments, to prevent disagreements from escalating into open conflicts, and to make time for enjoyable activities (Barnes, Reifman, Farrell, & Dintcheff, 2000; Fisher & Feldman, 1998; Patterson, Reid, & Dishion, 1992; Scabini & Cigoli, 2000; Scabini, Lanz, & Marta, 1999; Steinberg, 2001).

Marital self-efficacy refers to spouses' beliefs in their capability to foster reciprocal care and satisfactory relationships. These capabilities include open communication, mutual confidence, and trust, even on contentious issues. In addition, marital self-efficacy includes spouses' beliefs in their capacity to share feelings, aspirations, and worries; to provide each other with emotional support; to cope jointly with marital problems; to work constructively through disagreements; to meet the competing demands of children, relatives, and the community at large; to operate in concert toward the achievements of common goals; and to enjoy common social relations and activities (Bodenmann, Kaiser, Hahlweg, & Fehm-Wolfsdorf, 1998; Olson & DeFrain, 2000; Scabini & Cigoli, 2000).

Family collective efficacy beliefs refer to the judgments family members make about the capacity of the family as a whole to accomplish tasks necessary for family functioning. Although the efficacy beliefs described above are mostly concerned with dyadic relationships (parent-child, husband-wife), family collective efficacy focuses on members' perceived capabilities of the family to operate as a whole. Beliefs in one's personal efficacy may not be sufficient alone to ensure the achievement of desired goals, nor can spouses, parents, and children fully meet their role requirements independently from other family members' feelings, expectations, and behaviors. In fact, many family outcomes are achievable only by the concerted action of all family members pooling their resources and efforts together. In the family, as in any other social system, perceived collective efficacy is likely to affect the sense or mission and purpose of the system, the strength of its members' commitment to what the system seeks to achieve, how well its members believe in their capacity to meet their mutual obligations, and the family's resilience in the face of adversities (Bandura, 1997, 2000). Thus, family collective efficacy includes the family's capabilities of achieving consensus in decision making and planning, of promoting reciprocal commitment, of providing emotional support in difficult times and in stressful situations, of keeping good relations with relatives and the community at large, and of enjoying being together. The family efficacy scales used thus far have proved to have good psychometric properties, and confirmatory factor analysis has corroborated their conceptual distinctiveness (Caprara et al., 2004).

STUDIES ON FILIAL, PARENTAL, AND FAMILY COLLECTIVE EFFICACY WITHIN FAMILIES WITH ADOLESCENTS

A vast literature underscores the importance of familial relationships in supporting adolescents' efforts to gain increasing independence and to manage the many challenges they face (Arnett, 1999, 2001; Caprara et al., 2003; Noller, 1995; Steinberg & Morris, 2000; Youniss & Smollar, 1985). Although the family continues to represent a context of secure belonging, adolescents are accorded new civic responsibilities, become involved in emotionally charged partnerships, and actively participate in making decisions affecting the life of all family members.

The transition to adulthood is thus a complex, relational, intergenerational process that brings significant changes, uncertainty, and challenges for everyone involved in the process. Although adolescents are in a condition of financial dependence on their parents, they should be capable of gradually moving toward a status of greater autonomy, new responsibilities, and important prospects with regard to their personal and professional achievements. On the other hand, parents should be capable of looking after their children in novel and flexible ways, of encouraging their autonomy, and of supporting their choices from a responsible distance while continuing to provide guidance toward social goals and ambitions. Likewise, spouses should be capable of facing the opportunities and challenges that come over time and with aging together while continuing to grant their support to their children and benefiting, in turn, from their children's support and advice. Finally, the family as a whole should represent for parents, children, and spouses a safe context in which different generations share experiences and operate in concert to promote each other's well-being and development. These premises led us to develop measures to investigate the influence that family members' personal and collective efficacy beliefs exert on various aspects of family functioning as well as on a variety of individual outcomes.

CORRELATES OF FAMILY EFFICACY BELIEFS

A first wave of studies examined the extent to which parents' and children's efficacy beliefs concerning their roles are interrelated. A number of studies have documented the different influence that mothers and fathers may exert on their adolescent girls and boys, as well as the influence that children, in their turn, may exert on their parents (Bell & Harper, 1977; Bussey & Bandura, 1999; Halverson & Wampler, 1997; Maccoby, 1998; Parke, 1996, 2004; Parke & Buriel, 1998; Scabini, 1995; Scabini & Cigoli, 2000). The correlations of adolescents' perceived filial and collective efficacy with their parents' marital, parental, and collective efficacy were all statistically significant. As expected, the correlations within same-sex dyads were generally greater than were the correlations within opposite-sex dyads.

A second wave of studies examined the impact that filial, parental, and collective efficacy exert on important dimensions of family functioning, such as marital support, involvement and satisfaction, parent-child communication, monitoring and conflict management, and parents' and children's family satisfaction (Caprara et al., 2005). Much literature documents the relevance of these dimensions both as indicators and determinants of successful and positive functioning (Capaldi, Chamberlain, & Patterson, 1997; Cumsille & Epstein, 1994; Honess et al., 1997; Noller, 1995; Lavee & Olson, 1991; Scabini, Lanz, & Marta, 1999).

Similar patterns of results for both parents and children attest to the role of efficacy beliefs in contributing to positive family functioning. In particular, efficacy beliefs were positively correlated with open communication and effective monitoring and negatively correlated with aggressive management of conflict. It is likely that these variables influence each other and operate in concert with efficacy beliefs to promote other family variables.

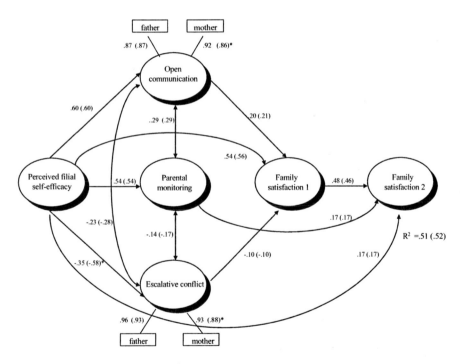

Figure 4.1.   Path analysis of the links of perceived filial self-efficacy and quality of family management to satisfaction with family life. The first path coefficient of the structural links is for the males; the second coefficient in brackets is for the females. Only significant path coefficients ($p < .05$) are included. Coefficients with an asterisk differ significantly across gender.

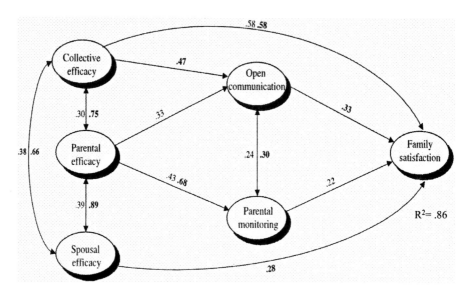

Figure 4.2.   Standardized path coefficients for the contribution of parental family efficacy beliefs and quality of family functioning to level of family satisfaction. The first path coefficient on each of the structural links is for within-level model; the second path coefficient in bold type is for the group-level model. Only path coefficients significant beyond the $p < .05$ level are included

In this regard, the influence of personal and collective family efficacy beliefs on the quality of family functioning and satisfaction has been clarified and further supported by two recent studies. As illustrated in Figure 4.1 , findings of the first study (Caprara et al., 2005) show both concurrently and longitudinally, that adolescents' perceived self-efficacy to manage parental relationships affected their satisfaction with family life, both directly and through its intervening impact on the quality of family management practices. In particular, the stronger the adolescents' self-efficacy, the more likely adolescents were to have open communication with their parents and to be accepting of how their parents monitor their activities outside the home. These young people were also less inclined to experience discord over disagreements. Finally, regardless of whether perceived filial self-efficacy was placed in the conceptual structure as a contributor to the quality of family interactions or as a partial product of family functioning, it consistently predicted satisfaction with family life.

As shown in Figures 4.2 and 4.3, findings of the second study (Bandura et al., 2004) attested instead to the primacy of perceived family collective efficacy, with regard to filial, parental, and marital efficacy

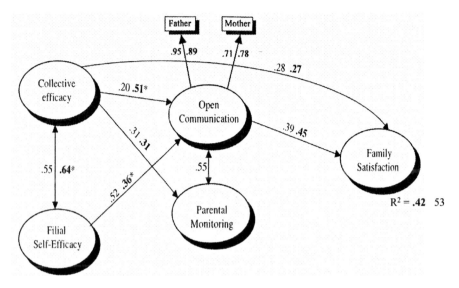

Figure 4.3.   Standardized path coefficients for the contribution of adolescent's family efficacy beliefs and quality of family functioning to level of family satisfaction. The first path coefficient on each of the structural links is for female adolescents; the second path coefficients in bold type is for male adolescents.Only significant path coefficients ($p < .05$) are included. Coefficients with an asterisk differ significantly across gender.

beliefs and to open communication and parental monitoring. In particular, dyadic parent-child, spousal, and filial self-efficacy operated entirely through its mediating links of collective family efficacy. That is, a high sense of collective family efficacy was accompanied by open family communication and enabled monitoring of adolescents' activities outside the home.

Previous studies have shown that the beliefs family members hold about the family's ability to meet its mission are important for its functioning and for the satisfaction of its members. In a third wave of studies, we assessed the extent to which family efficacy beliefs affected not only the quality of relationships inside the family but also the psychosocial correlates of adolescents' lives. Table 4.1 shows the correlations of parents' and children's efficacy beliefs with important variables of adolescents' psychosocial adjustment such as depression, optimism, violent behavior, prosocial behavior, and life satisfaction (Caprara et al., 2001; Regalia et al., 2001).

As hypothesized, the efficacy beliefs children held about being able to deal effectively with their role in the family were highly correlated with psychosocial adjustment—the higher the children's family efficacy beliefs,

**Table 4.1.   Correlation Between Parents' and
Adolescents' Family Perceived Self-Efficacy Scales and
Adolescents' Psychosocial Adjustment**

| | Parents' Perceived Self-Efficacy Scales | | | | | |
| | PPSE | | PMSE | | PCFE | |
Adolescents' Adjustment Variables	Mother-Children (N = 137)	Father-Children (N = 95)	Mother-Children (N = 137)	Father-Children (N = 95)	Mother-Children (N = 137)	Father-Children (N = 95)
Pro-social behavior	.20*	.07	.14	.16	.13	.06
Violent behavior	−.22**	−.20*	−.17*	−.24*	−.18*	−.17
Depression	−.14	−.27**	−.21*	−.33**	−.13	−.32**
Satisfaction with life	.26*	.37**	.22**	.48**	.24**	.41**
Optimism	.15	.16	.17*	.22*	.12	.17

| | Adolescents' Perceived Self-Efficacy Scales | | | |
| | PFSE | | PFCSE | |
	Males (N = 289)	Females (N = 314)	Males (N = 289)	Females (N = 314)
Pro-social behavior	.45**	.43**	.36**	.27**
Violent behavior	−.25**	−.16**	−.21**	−.20**
Depression	−.42**	−.33**	−.42**	−.40**
Satisfaction with life	.36**	.51**	.38**	.50**
Optimism	.43**	.29**	.44**	.34**

*p < .05; **p < .01.
PPSE = Perceived Parental Self-Efficacy Scale; PMSE = Perceived Marital Self-Efficacy Scale
PCFE = Perceived Collective Family Efficacy Scale; PFSE = Perceived Filial Self-Efficacy Scale
PFCSE = Perceived Filial Collective Self-Efficacy Scale

the higher their optimism, life satisfaction, and prosocial behavior, and
the lower their depression and delinquency. As for parents, results concerning efficacy and child adjustment were less impressive and definitive
and differed according to gender. In particular, mothers' family efficacy
was implicated in children's positive and negative social behaviors. In
contrast, fathers' beliefs in their capacity to manage family demands in
relationships with their children and spouses were highly correlated with
their children's depression and life satisfaction, suggesting that these
fathers' beliefs are more likely to affect or enhance children's affective regulation.

In another study, the researchers hypothesized that parents who
believe strongly in their capability to cope with family demands would
enhance their children's efficacy beliefs that, in turn, would affect children's psychosocial adjustment, assessed both concurrently and longitudinally. Findings confirmed the posited relations (see Figure 4.4). Parental
self-efficacy beliefs significantly affected their adolescents' filial self-effi-

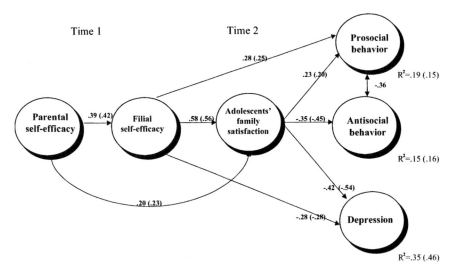

Figure 4.4.   Path analysis of the links of parental family efficacy beliefs and perceived filial self-efficacy to adolescents' satisfaction with family life and depression, pro-social behavior and violent behavior. The first path coefficient on each of the structural links is for mothers-children; the second coefficient in brackets is for fathers-children.

cacy and, through this effect, also had a long-term effect on the family's life evaluation and on adolescents' psychosocial adjustment, indexed by measures of depression and violent and prosocial behavior. Specifically, adolescents' filial self-efficacy had a positive concurrent and longitudinal effect on their psychosocial adjustment, both directly and indirectly, through its influence on family satisfaction. That is, adolescents' confidence in their capability to manage their relationships with their parents played a protective role against depression, a finding that confirms that managing relationships with parents strengthens and improves adolescents' psychological resources.

These findings clearly show the pivotal role of filial efficacy in the system of intergenerational influences within the family. That is, parents' efficacy can affect children's psychosocial outcomes primarily through the intervening effects of filial efficacy. Adolescents are not passive targets of external influences but constructively shape, in a context of interdependence with their parents, a personal developmental trajectory, which can be regarded as an expression of their agentic capabilities to deal effectively with challenges experienced in the family during their transition to adulthood.

CONCLUSION

Promoting one's own self-efficacy is particularly important during adolescence. In fact, this is a period that is marked by many opportunities to prove one's own relational skills and one's own sense of agency in the family, with peers, and in the community at large. Nowadays, adolescents must face multiple choices that can change the course of their careers. Unlike in past years, gender is less constraining with regard to the opportunities that exist in educational and professional domains. Society in general, and significant adults in particular, are less likely to provide adolescents with explicit advice concerning how to deal with life transitions and the steps that young people need to follow to manage them. Adolescents may feel lost as they seem not to have the same degree of certainty that adolescents had in the past concerning their move into adulthood. Yet adolescents are given a great deal of freedom in their affective choices, leisure time, romantic relationships, friendships, and career choices.

An expanded adolescence offers the opportunity and call for continuous refinement of relational skill of both parents and children. Today more than ever, all family members' self-efficacy to successfully undertake the challenges associated with the transition occurring within the families plays a critical role. It becomes crucial for adults to understand how they can exert their protective function in effective ways while at the same time help adolescents decide and act. It becomes critical for adolescents to choose the environments and the situations that best fit their skills and expertise. The beliefs that family members hold and share about the capacity of the family to operate as an effective system is no less important to create the synergies needed to face challenges and changes. Based on the evidence collected, we contend that self-efficacy beliefs depend on the parent-child relationship. It is unlikely that children will develop and maintain strong self-efficacy beliefs if these beliefs are not supported at home.

In environments with fewer rules and norms and greater uncertainty, the family plays a more important role. In such a context, how can parents fulfill their function of monitoring and supporting the children? The rising demand for parent training and parent education programs can provide insights about these new challenges for parents. In fact, parenting programs are one place to learn and develop the skills to help manage the complex challenges of raising children through adolescence (Briesmeister & Schaefer, 1998).

The available literature focuses particularly on the positive outcomes of parenting programs, showing their positive impact on health status, self-esteem, and child development. Such programs actually improve parents' skills, strengthen their authority, improve the relationship between parents and their children, and ameliorate the stress associated with being a parent, a role often marked by high uncertainty (Tucker, Herman, Reid, Keefer, & Vogel, 1988). Program evaluations are often based on the expectations and needs that parents express at the time of enrolling in these programs. Therefore, the question, "which parent education program works best?" should be replaced by the question, "which parent education program works best for which parents and which children?" (Gerris, Van As, Wels, & Janssens, 1998, p. 412).

The proliferation of intervention programs shows a tendency to plan and conduct programs designed for improving parental skills in particular situations at early stages of children's lives, such as in the presence of a child with a chronic disease or a disability, economic hardship, school failures, and problems associated with belonging to a minority group (Gross et al., 2003; Peterson, Tremblay, Ewingman, & Saldana, 2003; Sofronoff & Farbotko, 2002; Warschburger, von Schwering, Buchholz, & Petermann, 2003). Despite their need, there are fewer programs specifically designed for parents of adolescents (Dinkmeyer & McKay, 1990; Patterson & Forgatch, 1987). We believe that more work needs to be done in this direction because we are convinced that it is crucial for those who educate adolescents to be able to fulfill the key role of being flexible guides. As Coleman and Karraker (1998) claim, programs for parents of adolescents should aim to improve parents' sense of efficacy.

The promotion of family self-efficacy beliefs is surely a challenging task that must be engaged at two levels. The first, essentially dyadic, concerns parents' competence with their sons and daughters. At this level, it is necessary to isolate a specific domain for working with parents and to pursue the purpose of learning how to better manage their relationships with their kids, keeping in mind the different roles played by fathers and mothers. It appears critical to structure guided experiences through which parents can master their parental role of controlling, monitoring, and regulating new emotional experiences.

A second level of intervention should be focused on the family as an organized system. At this level, the key is to develop and strengthen forms of collective efficacy. In this context, it is crucial to promote experiences that can strengthen mutual bonding and coaching. Mutual bonding and coaching are typical family resources that can improve the family's collective efficacy for strategies used by the family for coping with unexpected situations and with other challenges and hardships that enter the family's life cycle, particularly those that occur during adolescence. An efficacious family system can profit from past experience and use it for redirecting personal and collective choices. Ultimately the entire family's self-reflective and regulatory processes must be strengthened. To this aim, the body of knowledge we have reviewed could be of great importance in planning interventions in which teachers and parents are involved.

REFERENCES

Ardelt, M., & Eccles, J. S. (2001). Effects of mothers' parental efficacy beliefs and promotive parenting strategies on inner-city youth. *Journal of Family Issues, 22*, 944-972.

Arnett, J. J. (1999). Adolescent storm and stress reconsidered. *American Psychologist, 54*, 317-326.

Arnett, J. J. (2001). Conceptions of the transition to adulthood: Perspectives from adolescence through midlife. *Journal of Adult Development, 8*, 133-143

Bandura, A. (1997). *Self-efficacy: The exercise of control*. New York: Freeman

Bandura, A. (2000). Social cognitive theory: An agentic perspective. *Annual Review of Psychology, 52*, 1-26.

Bandura, A., Barbaranelli, C., Caprara, G. V., & Pastorelli, C. (1996). Mechanisms of moral disengagement in the exercise of moral agency. *Journal of Personality and Social Psychology, 71*, 364-374.

Bandura, A., Barbaranelli, C., Caprara, G. V., & Pastorelli, C. (2001). Self-efficacy beliefs as shapers of children's aspirations and career trajectories. *Child Development, 72*, 187-206.

Bandura, A., Caprara, G. V., Regalia C., Scabini E., & Barbaranelli, C. (2004). *Impact of family efficacy beliefs on quality of family functioning and satisfaction with family life*. Manuscript submitted for publication.

Barnes, G. M., Reifman, A. S., Farrell, M. P., & Dintcheff, B. A. (2000). The effects of parenting on the development of adolescent alcohol misuse: A six-wave latent growth model. *Journal of Marriage and the Family, 62*, 175-186.

Bell, R. Q., & Harper, L. (1977). *Child effects on adults*. New York: Wiley.

Bodenmann, G., Kaiser, A., Hahlweg, K., & Fehm-Wolfsdorf, G. (1998). Communication patterns during marital conflict: A cross-cultural representation. *Personal Relationships, 5*, 343-356.

Brannen, J. (1999). Discourses of adolescence and young people's independence. In M. Woodhead (Ed.), *Making sense of social development* (pp. 214-230). New York: Routledge.

Briesmeister J. M., Schaefer C. E. (1998). *Handbook of Parent Training*. New York: John Wiley & Sons.

Bussey, K., & Bandura, A. (1999). Social cognitive theory of gender development and differentiation. *Psychological Review, 106*, 676-713.

Capaldi, D. M., Chamberlain, P., & Patterson, G. R. (1997). Ineffective discipline and conduct problems in males: Association, late adolescent outcomes, and prevention. *Aggression and Violent Behavior, 2*, 343-353.

Caprara, G. V., & Cervone, D. (2000). *Personality: Determinants, dynamics, and potentials*. New York: Cambridge University Press.

Caprara G. V., Pastorelli, C., Regalia, C., Scabini, E., & Bandura, A. (2005). Impact of adolescents' filial self-efficacy on quality of family functioning and satisfaction. *Journal of Research on Adolescence, 15*, 71-97.

Caprara, G. V., Regalia, C., & Bandura, A. (2002). Longitudinal impact of perceived self-regulatory efficacy on violent conduct. *European Psychologist, 7*, 63-69.

Caprara G. V., Regalia, C., & Scabini, E. (2001). *Autoefficacia familiare* [Family self-efficacy]. In G. V. Caprara (Ed.), *La valutazione dell'autoefficacia* [The self-efficacy assessment] (pp. 63-86). Trento, Italy: Erickson.

Caprara, G. V., Regalia, C., Scabini, E., Barbaranelli, C., Bandura, A. (2004). Assessment of filial, marital, and collective efficacy beliefs. *European Journal of Psychological Assessment, 20*, 247-261.

Caprara, G. V., Scabini, E., Barbaranelli, C., Pastorelli, C., Regalia, C., & Bandura, A. (1998). Impact of adolescents' perceived self-regulatory efficacy on familial communication and antisocial conduct. *European Psychologist, 3*, 125-132.

Caprara, G. V., Scabini, E., Barbaranelli, C., Pastorelli, C., Regalia, C., & Bandura, A. (1999). Autoefficacia percepita emotiva e interpersonale e buon funzionamento sociale [Perceived emotional and interpersonal self-efficacy and good social functioning]. *Giornale Italiano di Psicologia, 26*, 769-789.

Caprara, G. V., Scabini, E., & Sgritta, G. B. (2003). The long transition to adulthood: An Italian view. In F. Pajares & T. Urdan (Eds.), *International perspectives on adolescence* (pp. 71-99). Greenwich, CT: Information Age.

Coleman, P. K., & Karraker, K. H. (1998). Self-efficacy and parenting quality: Findings and future applications. *Developmental Review, 18*, 47-85.

Coleman, P. K., & Karraker, K. H. (2000). Parenting self-efficacy among mothers of school-age children: Conceptualization, measurement, and correlates. *Family Relations: Interdisciplinary Journal of Applied Family Studies, 49*, 13-24.

Cumsille, P. E., & Epstein, N. (1994). Family cohesion, family adaptability, social support, and adolescent depressive symptoms in outpatient clinic families. *Journal of Family Psychology, 8*, 202-214.

Cutrona, C. E., & Troutman, B. R. (1986). Social support, infant temperament, and parenting self-efficacy: A mediational model of postpartum depression. *Child Development, 57*, 1507-1518.

Demo, D., & Acock, A. (1996). Family structure, family process, and adolescent well-being. *Journal of Research on Adolescence, 6*, 457-488.

Dinkmeyer, D., & McKay, G. D. (1990). *Parenting teenagers: Systematic training for effective parenting of teens*. Circle Pines, MN: American Guidance Service.

Eccles, J. S., Midgley, C., Wigfield, A., & Buchanan, C. M. (1993). Development during adolescence: The impact of stage-environment fit on young adolescents' experiences in schools and in families. *American Psychologist, 48*, 90-101.

Elder, G. H., Jr., Eccles, J. S., Ardelt, M., & Lord, S. (1995). Inner-city parents under economic pressure: Perspective on the strategies of parenting. *Journal of Marriage and the Family, 57*, 771-784.

Erel, O., & Burman, B. (1995). Interrelatedness of marital relations and parent-child relations: A meta-analytic review. *Psychological Bulletin, 118*, 108-132.

Fisher, L., & Feldman, S. S. (1998). Familial antecedents of young adult health risk behavior: A longitudinal study. *Journal of Family Psychology, 12*, 66-80.

Forkel, I., & Silbereisen, R. K. (2003). Väterliche selbstwirksamkeit als moderator des zusammenhangs zwischen ökonomischen härten und depressiver gestimmtheit bei jugendlichen. [Paternal self-efficacy as moderator of the link between economic hardship and adolescents' depressed mood]. *Zeitschrift für Entwicklungspsychologie und Pädagogische Psychologie, 35,* 163-170.

Gerris, J. R. M., Van As, N. M. C., Wels, P. M. A., & Janssens, J. M. A. M. (1998). From parent education to family empowerment programs. In L. L'Abate (Ed.), *Family psychopathology: The relational roots of dysfunctional behavior* (pp. 401-426). New York: Guilford Press.

Gross, D., Fogg, L., Webster-Stratton, C., Garvey, C., Julion, W., & Grady, J. (2003). Parent training of toddlers in day care in low-income urban communities. *Journal of Consulting and Clinical Psychology, 71,* 261-278.

Halverson, C. F. J., & Wampler, K. S. (1997). Family influences on personality development. In R. Hogan & J. A. Johnson (Eds.), *Handbook of personality psychology* (pp. 241-267). San Diego, CA: Academic Press.

Hinde, R. A., & Stevenson-Hinde, J. (1988). Interpersonal relationships and child development. *Annual Progress in Child Psychiatry & Child Development, 71,* 5-26.

Honess, T. M., Charman, E. A., Zani, B., Cicognani, E., Xerri, M. L., Jackson, A. E., et al. (1997). Conflict between parents and adolescents: Variation by family constitution. *British Journal of Developmental Psychology, 15,* 367-385.

Kuczynski, L. (2003). *Handbook of dynamics in parent-child relations.* Thousand Oaks, CA: Sage.

Lavee, Y., & Olson, D. H. (1991). Family types and response to stress. *Journal of Marriage and the Family, 53,* 786-798.

Maccoby, E. E. (1988). Social-emotional development and response to stressors. *Seminar on stress and coping in children 1979, Center for Advanced Study in the Behavioral Sciences, Stanford, CA: Stress, coping, and development in children.* Baltimore, MD: Johns Hopkins University Press.

Noller, P. (1995). Parent-adolescent relationships. In M. Fitzpatrick & A. Vangelisti (Eds.), *Explaining family interactions* (pp. 77-111). Thousand Oaks, CA: Sage.

Olson, D. H., & DeFrain, J. (2000). *Marriage and the family: Diversity and strengths* (3rd ed.). Mountain View, CA: Mayfield.

Ozer, E. M. (1995). The impact of childcare responsibility and self-efficacy on the psychological health of working mothers. *Psychology of Women Quarterly, 19,* 315-336.

Parke, R. D. (1988). Families in life-span perspective: A multilevel developmental approach. In E. M. Hetherington, & R. M. Lerner (Eds.), *Child development in life-span perspective* (pp. 159-190). Hillsdale, NJ: Lawrence Erlbaum Associates.

Parke, R. D. (1996). *Fatherhood.* Cambridge, MA: Harvard University Press.

Parke, R. D. (2004). Development in the family. *Annual Review of Psychology, 55,* 365-399.

Parke, R. D., & Buriel, R. (1998), Socialization in the family: Ethnic and ecological perspectives. In W. Damon (Series Ed.) & N. Eisenberg (Vol. Ed.), *Handbook of child psychology,* (5th ed., pp. 463-452). New York: Wiley.

Pastorelli, C., Steca, P., Gerbino, M., & Vecchio, G. (2001). Il ruolo delle convinzioni di efficacia personale e genitoriale rispetto alle condotte delinquenziali e all'uso di sostanze nel corso dell'adolescenza [Personal and parental self-efficacy: Its relations with antisocial behavior and substance use during adolescence]. *Eta evolutiva, 69,* 80-87.

Patterson, G. R., & Forgatch, M. (1987), *Parent and adolescents living together.* Eugene, OR: University Press.

Patterson, G. R., Reid, J. B., & Dishion, T. J. (1992). *Antisocial boys.* Eugene, OR: Castalia.

Peterson L., Tremblay G., Ewingman B., & Saldana L. (2003). Multilevel selected primary prevention of child maltreatment. *Journal of Consulting and Clinical Psychology, 71,* 601-612.

Regalia, C., Barbaranelli, C., Pastorelli, C., & Mazzotti, E. (1999). Convinzioni di efficacia filiale e prevenzione del rischio in adolescenza [Children's self-efficacy beliefs and risk prevention in adolescence]. *Eta evolutiva, 64,* 60-66.

Regalia, C., Pastorelli, C., Barbaranelli, C., & Gerbino, M. (2001). Convinzioni di efficacia personale filiale [Filial self-efficacy beliefs]. *Giornale Italiano di Psicologia, 28,* 575-593.

Scabini, E. (1995). *Psicologia sociale della famiglia* [Social Psychology of the Family]. Torino, Italy: Bollati-Boringhieri.

Scabini, E., & Cigoli, V. (2000). *Il famigliare* [The Family Identity]. Milano: Raffaello Cortina.

Scabini, E., Lanz, M., & Marta, E. (1999). Psychosocial adjustment and family relationships: A typology of Italian families with a late adolescent. *Journal of Youth and Adolescence, 28,* 633-644.

Smetana, J. (1996). Adolescent-parent conflict: Implications for adaptive and maladaptive development. In D. Cicchetti & S. Toth (Eds.), *Adolescence: Opportunities and challenges. Rochester symposium on developmental psychopathology, Vol. 7* (pp. 1-46). Rochester, NY: University of Rochester Press.

Sofronoff, K., & Farbotko, M. (2002). The effectiveness of parent management training to increase self-efficacy in parents of children with Asperger syndrome. *Autism, 6,* 271-286.

Steinberg, L. (2001). We know some things: Parent-adolescent relationships in retrospect and prospect. *Journal of Research on Adolescence, 11,* 1-19.

Steinberg, L., & Morris, A. S. (2000). Adolescent development. *Annual Review of Psychology, 52,* 83-110.

Teti, D. M., & Gelfand, D. M. (1991). Behavioral competence among mothers of infants in the first year: The mediational role of maternal self-efficacy. *Child Development, 62,* 918-929.

Teti, D. M., O'Connell, M. A., & Reiner, C. D. (1996). Parenting sensitivity, parental depression and child health: The mediational role of parental self-efficacy. *Early Development & Parenting, 5,* 237-250.

Tucker, C. M., Herman, K. C., Reid, A. D., Keefer, N. L., & Vogel, D. L. (1998). The Research-Based Model Partnership Education Program: A 4-year outcome study. *Journal of Research and Development in Education, 32,* 32-37.

Walsh, F. (1993). *Normal Family Processes.* New York: Guilford Press.

Warschburger, P., von Schwering, A. D., Buchholz, H. T., & Petermann, F. (2003). An educational program for parents of asthmatic preschool children: Short- and medium-term effects. *Patient Education and Counselling, 51,* 83-91.

Youniss, J., & Smollar, J. (1985). *Adolescent relations with mothers, fathers, and friends.* Chicago: The University of Chicago Press.

CHAPTER 5

TEACHER SELF-EFFICACY AND ITS INFLUENCE ON THE ACHIEVEMENT OF ADOLESCENTS

Anita Woolfolk Hoy and Heather A. Davis

Teachers' sense of efficacy is a judgment about capabilities to influence student engagement and learning, even among those students who may be difficult or unmotivated. Early definitions of teacher self-efficacy were "the extent to which the teacher believes he or she has the capacity to affect student performance" (Berman, McLaughlin, Bass, Pauly, & Zellman, 1977, p. 137) and "teachers' belief or conviction that they can influence how well students learn, even those who may be difficult or unmotivated" (Guskey & Passaro, 1994, p. 4). Tschannen-Moran, Woolfolk Hoy, and Hoy's (1998) definition emphasized the situation-specific nature of self-efficacy: "Teacher efficacy is the teacher's belief in her or his ability to organize and execute the courses of action required to successfully accomplish a specific teaching task in a particular context" (p. 233). A recent review by Labone (2004) encouraged researchers to include tasks beyond the classroom and the context of school reform in the specific tasks and contexts that are the foci of efficacy judgments.

Self-Efficacy Beliefs of Adolescents, 117–137

We begin with a brief explanation of teachers' sense of efficacy, including its conceptual framework and a review of research on teacher self-efficacy and student academic achievement. We also examine emergent work on teachers' sense of efficacy for establishing and maintaining positive relationships with adolescents. We then propose a framework for connecting teachers' sense of efficacy to adolescent learning, considering both immediate and long-term outcomes. In order to bridge past, present, and future, we describe some established relationships and suggest other possible connections to explore. Although we specifically address the role of these teacher judgments in their adolescent students' achievement, we also encourage readers to consider the breadth of potential outcomes, the landscape and coordination of teaching self-efficacy domains, and the underlying mechanisms driving the relationships between teachers' sense of efficacy and adolescent learning and development. We end the chapter with a discussion of two topics: (a) the pre-service teacher as an adolescent learner and (b) questions and caveats for research.

TEACHER SELF-EFFICACY: CONCEPTUALIZATION AND RESEARCH

The model of teacher self-efficacy presented by Tschannen-Moran et al. (1998, see Figure 5.1) suggests that teachers' efficacy judgments are the result of an interaction between (a) the personal appraisal of the relative importance of factors that make accomplishing a specific teaching task easy or difficult (analysis of teaching task in context) and (b) a self-assessment of personal teaching capabilities and limitations specific to the task (analysis of teaching competence). The resultant efficacy judgments influence the goals teachers set for themselves, the effort they invest in reaching these goals, and their persistence when facing difficulties. These decisions and behaviors lead to outcomes that then become the basis for future efficacy judgments.

As shown in Figure 5.1, the major influences on efficacy beliefs about teaching are assumed to be the cognitive interpretation of the four sources of self-efficacy information described by Bandura (1986, 1997)—mastery experience, physiological arousal, vicarious experience, and verbal persuasion. Like all self-efficacy judgments, teacher self-efficacy is context-specific. Teachers can be expected to feel more or less efficacious under different circumstances. A teacher, for example, who feels highly efficacious about instructing her honors literature class may feel less efficacious about teaching freshman composition or vice versa. In a review of the literature examining contextual effects on self-efficacy, Ross (1998) concluded that teacher self-efficacy generally is higher in settings with high-

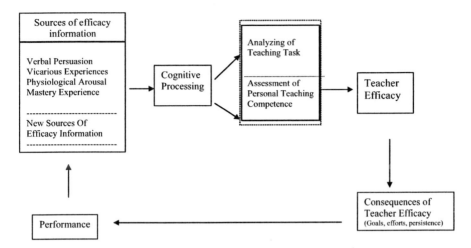

Source: Tschannen-Moran, Woolfolk Hoy, and Hoy (1998, p. 228), Reprinted with permission.

Figure 5.1   The cyclical nature of teacher efficacy.

ability, orderly students, when teachers are working in the area of their expertise, when teacher workloads are moderate, and when the school culture is collaborative. Therefore, in making an efficacy judgment, it is necessary to assess one's strengths and weaknesses *in relation to* the context and requirements of the task at hand. As indicated in the model in Figure 5.1, teachers judge their competence in relation to a specific teaching task, and these judgments result in an efficacy expectation for that task.

One of the things that make teachers' efficacy judgments so powerful is the cyclical nature of the process by which they are formed. As noted in Figure 5.1, the performances and outcomes create a new mastery experience, which provides new information that will be processed to shape future efficacy beliefs. Greater self-efficacy leads to greater effort and persistence, which leads to better performance, which in turn leads to greater self-efficacy. The reverse is also true. Lower self-efficacy leads to less effort and giving up easily, which leads to poor teaching outcomes, which then produce decreased self-efficacy.

Related to conceptualizations of self-efficacy for teaching are concerns with measurement. We will not address these issues here but refer the reader to the chapters addressing general measurement considerations by Bong and by Bandura in this volume and to specific discussions of the assessment of teacher self-efficacy (Henson, 2002; Labone, 2004; Ross, 1998; Tschannen-Moran et al., 1998; Tschannen-Moran & Woolfolk Hoy, 2001).

Teacher Self-Efficacy: Teaching and Learning Outcomes

Research over the past 30 years suggests that a higher sense of efficacy for teaching is related to many positive learning and instructional outcomes. In addition to being related to student achievement (Ashton & Webb, 1986; Muijs & Reynolds, 2001; Ross, 1998), teachers' sense of efficacy has been associated with other student outcomes such as motivation (Midgley, Feldlaufer, & Eccles, 1989) and students' own sense of efficacy (Ross, Hogaboam-Gray, & Hannay, 2001).

In terms of teacher outcomes, teachers' efficacy beliefs appear to affect the effort teachers invest, their level of aspiration, and the goals they set. Teachers with a stronger sense of efficacy tend to exhibit greater levels of planning, organization, direct teaching, and enthusiasm (Allinder, 1994; Muijs & Reynolds, 2001) and spend more time teaching in subject areas where their sense of efficacy is higher, whereas teachers tend to avoid subjects when their self-efficacy is lower (Riggs, 1995). Teachers with higher efficacy judgments tend to be more open to new ideas, more willing to experiment with new methods to better meet the needs of their students (Cousins & Walker, 2000), more likely to use powerful but potentially difficult-to-manage methods such as inquiry and small group work, and less likely to use easy-to-adopt but weaker methods such as lecture (Ashton & Webb, 1986; Chacon, 2005). A greater sense of efficacy is associated with being less critical of students who make errors, working longer with students who are struggling (Ashton & Webb, 1986; Gibson & Dembo, 1984), holding less controlling beliefs about discipline (Chacon, 2005; Woolfolk, Rosoff, & Hoy, 1990), being less inclined to refer a difficult student to special education and more likely to attend to the special needs of exceptional students, and being more likely to work with parents (Podell & Soodak, 1993). In brief, a strong sense of efficacy can support higher motivation, greater effort, persistence, and resilience across the span of a teaching career.

Not all researchers, however, agree that higher levels of self-efficacy are always positive influences. Wheatley (2002) identified a number of benefits for teacher learning that might follow from having doubts about one's own competence. These include the possibility that doubts might foster reflection, motivation to learn, greater responsiveness to diversity, productive collaboration, and change-provoking disequilibrium. We believe a sense of efficacy would be necessary to respond to doubts in these positive ways, but the point is well taken that persistent high efficacy perceptions in the face of poor performance can produce avoidance rather than positive action.

Subject-Specific Research

Much of the subject-specific research on teachers' self-efficacy relates to their instructional goals and strategies. For example, De Laat and Watters (1995) found that the goals of high self-efficacy teachers included students' problem solving and logical thinking skills for real life situations. Rather than depending on curriculum guides, these high self-efficacy teachers used themes to integrate science into other subjects and emphasized hands-on science experiences. Preservice teachers who lack confidence in their abilities to teach science, in contrast, deemphasized or avoided science teaching or taught using transmissive as opposed to inquiry methods (Plourde, 2002; Tosun, 2000). Low self-efficacy for classroom management also can lead beginning teachers to avoid hands-on science activities or to transform inquiry activities into teacher demonstrations (Mulholland & Wallace, 2001).

One source of self-efficacy for teachers is subject matter knowledge (Borko & Putnam, 1995; Muijs & Reynolds, 2001). Beginning teachers who have strong science content knowledge have higher self-efficacy about teaching science (Cantrell, Young, & Moore, 2003). When beginning teachers have taken the minimum required number of science courses and, as a result, they feel that their content knowledge is still lacking, they tend to avoid teaching topics that they do not know well for fear that their students will ask questions that they cannot answer (Rice & Roychoudhury, 2003; Tosun, 2000). Raudenbush, Rowan, and Cheong (1992) noted that teacher self-efficacy mediates the relationship between teacher subject knowledge and action. For example, Chacon (2005) found that Venezuelan teachers with higher self-efficacy for English were more likely to use group work activities, choose challenging tasks, apply humanistic classroom management strategies, and pursue self-directed learning to improve their English proficiency.

We suggest that teachers' sense of efficacy for subject matter understanding and subject teaching may become increasingly important during the middle grades and beyond. This is because academic content grows more complex and difficult. Adolescents in middle school may be working with teachers who are responsible for several subjects; the teachers may not be deeply grounded in each of the subjects they teach, either because they lack specific knowledge for the curriculum taught or experience in teaching that curriculum. Thus teachers' sense of efficacy for knowing and teaching the subject may be increasingly important.

Technology

Today, teachers are expected to prepare their students for the demands of living in this Information Age. With increasing pressure to train and support new and practicing teachers in technology integration, researchers have begun to examine the role of teachers' sense of efficacy for using technology (e.g., Pierson, 2001). Fewer studies have explored the role of teachers' sense of efficacy for teaching with technology (Ropp, 1999) or their self-efficacy for managing their classroom with technology. Davis and Ring (2005) found that "resistance" among a sample of preservice teachers to integrating technology was associated with increased computer anxiety and lower judgments of technology and teaching with technology self-efficacy. These findings persisted in the face of students' participation in a course designed to provide opportunities to observe and reflect on the ways technology can be used to promote learning and cognitive development.

Teacher Self-Efficacy and Relationship With Students

Researchers studying motivation argue that the times of transition to middle school and high school may present challenges for adolescents resulting in changes in their academic motivation and performance (Davis, 2003; Murdock, Anderman, & Hodge, 2000; Roeser, Eccles, & Sameroff, 2000). During early adolescence, this difficulty may derive from the mismatch between the adolescent's needs and the structure of middle and high schools. For example, Eccles et al. (1993) argued that the discontinuity and sharp changes in status that occur as a result of the transition combine to make adjustment to middle school problematic for some students. Middle schools, compared to elementary schools, have been criticized for their bureaucratic structure, impersonal atmosphere, and increased student-teacher ratios.

For teachers, cultural stereotypes of adolescence as a period of increasing detachment from adults (Finders, 1997) combined with greater numbers of students across their classes may make it difficult to know each student. This change in the environment is reflected in middle school students' reports of feeling greater anonymity to their teachers and to other students during their transition to middle school from elementary school (Eccles et al., 1993; Lynch & Cicchetti, 1997; Murdock et al., 2000). Moreover, students' perceptions of a lack of teacher support or conflict in their relationships with teachers during high school may place students at risk of feeling alienated, dropping out, experiencing social and emotional maladjustment, and engaging in deviant behavior (Battin-Pearson et al., 2000; Delpit, 1995; Murdock, 1999). Yet, in spite of pervasive cultural stereotypes that adolescents need distance from adults, research continues to demonstrate adolescents' need to develop relationships with the adults in their school in order to thrive (Murdock, 1999; Resnick et al., 1997, Roeser et al., 2000; Roeser, Midgley, & Urdan, 1996).

In addition to setting goals to meet their own social-emotional needs to belong (Goodenow, 1992), adolescents are beginning to struggle with issues of identity, including who they are and who they want to become. Adolescents' changing conceptions of adults may prompt them to seek mentor relationships with teachers (Hamilton & Darling, 1989). Central to adopting a mentor role would be the ability to help students to envision a "future self" and to guide them in its pursuit (Yowell & Smylie, 1999). Future selves are cognitive representations of what we would like to be or what we fear becoming. Wurf and Markus (1991) argue that the " personalization of motivation" occurs when students explore how to pursue a future or possible self. In their struggle to understand who they are, adolescents may rely more on their relationships with teachers to help them interpret their academic experiences but also explore a possible self within a content area—for example, to see themselves as a future scientist, writer, or teacher.

To be successful, teachers must feel confident in their abilities to read and interpret students' verbal and nonverbal communications; to identify, express, and cope with their own emotions; and to help their students learn to manage and cope with the emotions they experience in the classroom. Teachers' self-efficacy for forming and maintaining positive relationships with students of diverse backgrounds or with those who may seem difficult or unpredictable may also play an important role in determining the kinds of learning environments teachers implement to facilitate adolescents' academic achievement. Because relationships with teachers may prove central to adolescents' development, future research needs to explore the roles that self-efficacy for teaching as well as self-efficacy for developing relationships with students may play in supporting students' achievement. For example, does teachers' sense of efficacy for teaching as well as for relationships predict relational and academic outcomes in the classroom? How does teachers' sense of efficacy relate to behavioral differences in the ways teachers interact with their adolescent students?

A PROPOSED FRAMEWORK: TEACHERS' SENSE OF EFFICACY AND ADOLESCENT LEARNING

The research on teachers' sense of efficacy has identified a number of important relationships between efficacy expectations and teacher/student outcomes. There has been less work on the processes through which efficacy beliefs influence teachers' decisions and actions and how those teacher effects might influence student learning. One exception is Ross's (1998) review suggesting that teachers with higher levels of self-efficacy are more likely to (a) learn and use new approaches and strategies for teaching, (b) use management techniques that enhance student autonomy and diminish student control, (c) provide special assistance to low-achieving students, (d) build students' self-perceptions of their academic skills, (e) set attainable goals, and (f) persist in the face of student failure.

Beginning with Ross's (1998) conclusions, we have developed a framework to link teachers' efficacy beliefs to student outcomes (see Figure 5.2). We outline two types of potential consequences of teachers' efficacy beliefs: *Consequences for Teachers' Beliefs and Behaviors* and *Consequences for Students' Beliefs and Behaviors*. We then differentiate the possible consequences for teachers or students as direct, indirect, or relational. We argue that teachers' behaviors in the classroom, such as their planning and curricular decisions; their attention, monitoring, and verbalizations; and their interactions with students, are partly shaped by their sense of efficacy. In turn, these self-efficacy-influenced teacher behaviors and decisions may have direct, indirect, and relational consequences for students' behaviors, emotions, and decisions. Direct consequences involve instructional decisions and actions; indirect consequences involve communications (verbal and nonverbal) about behavioral and attitudinal expectations, values, motivation, and management. Relational consequences involve the interpersonal and emotional dynamics of the classroom and the relationships among participants. Of course, the distinctions among relational, direct, and indirect are not always clear and sharp, but we believe these categories can be used as heuristics for considering the classroom processes.

Few studies have attempted to model the processes by which self-efficacy beliefs may differentially shape teachers' decisions and actions, which in turn affect students' behaviors and outcomes. For this reason, in Figure 5.2 we have chosen more transparent arrows to suggest that we believe there may be associations among these consequences. In the following sections, we provide a few examples of established, likely, and plausible relationships between teachers' sense of efficacy and adolescent outcomes such as achievement. In doing so, we outline process models that could be investigated in future research.

Direct Teaching Influences and Student Outcomes

Much of the research on the correlates of teachers' sense of efficacy has focused on instruction. We begin with these direct influences of teacher self-efficacy.

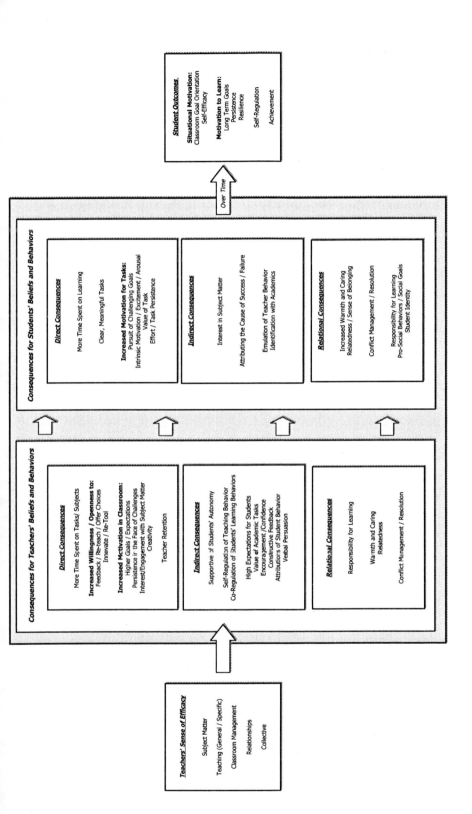

Figure 5.2   Framework to link teachers' efficacy beliefs to student outcomes.

Teachers' Decisions and Actions

Teachers with a higher sense of efficacy are, almost by definition, more motivated to teach. They are more likely to set high but attainable goals for themselves and for their students. Recall that these teachers tend to select strategies that support student learning, including keeping students on task rather than simply covering the curriculum (Ashton & Webb, 1986; Chacon, 2005). They also devote more time to the subject, whereas teachers with lower self-efficacy tend to avoid the subject (Riggs, 1995). Thus, higher self-efficacy teachers in many ways fit the description of those who employ the active teaching or direct instruction associated with greater student learning of basic skills (Brophy & Good, 1986; Rosenshine & Stevens, 1986). In fact, Muijs and Reynolds (2001) found some evidence for a connection between sense of efficacy for teaching mathematics and the use of effective direct instruction practices. If teachers' sense of efficacy for their subject matter knowledge is high, teachers may be confident in answering student questions and providing explanations, which would likely lead to direct teaching, explanation, feedback, and re-teaching in their classes. Higher self-efficacy teachers are more likely to learn new strategies and to persist if initial implementations are less than perfect (Berman et al., 1977; Hani, Czerniak, & Lumpe, 1996).

Student Outcomes

When teachers are active and persist in re-teaching when necessary, academic learning time increases. Almost every study examining time and learning has found a significant relationship between time spent on content and student learning (Berliner, 1988). In fact, the correlations between content studied and student learning are usually larger than are the correlations between specific teacher behaviors and student learning (Rosenshine, 1979). In addition, when teachers set challenging and proximal goals, students are more likely to be motivated to reach the goals because the target is clear. Decades of research on goals attest to the value of setting challenging, attainable goals.

Indirect Teaching Influences and Student Outcomes

By setting higher goals and persisting toward them, teachers with a higher sense of efficacy effectively communicate higher expectations for all their students. In fact, one definition of teacher's self-efficacy is the belief that one can reach even the most difficult students.

Teachers' Indirect Communications and Influences

Researchers have documented the many ways in which teachers' expectations are translated into instructional and interpersonal processes (Woolfolk, 2004). Expectations affect teachers' judgments about the difficulty level or ability group assignment that is appropriate for a particular student. Once teachers assign students to tasks or groups, they usually provide different learning activities. To the extent that teachers choose activities that challenge students and increase achievement, these differences are probably necessary. Activities become inappropriate, however, when students who are ready for more challenging work are not given the opportunity to try it because teachers believe that the students (or the teachers) cannot handle it.

However the class is grouped and whatever the assignments, the quantity and the quality of teacher-student interactions are likely to affect students. Students who are expected to achieve tend to be asked more and harder questions, to be given more chances and a longer time to respond, and to be interrupted less often than do students who are expected to do poorly. Teachers also give these high-expectation students cues and prompts, communicating their belief that the students can answer the question (Allington, 1980; Good & Brophy, 2003; Rosenthal, 1995). Teachers tend to smile at these students more often and to show greater warmth through such nonverbal responses as leaning toward the students and nodding their heads as the students speak (Woolfolk & Brooks, 1985). Higher self-efficacy teachers who hold high expectations for their students are more likely to treat their students in the ways described above. In contrast, if lower self-efficacy teachers hold lower expectations for themselves and for their students, these teachers may ask easier questions, allow less time for answering, give fewer prompts, and express less warmth in their interactions with students.

Higher self-efficacy teachers are more likely to confront management problems and seek solutions rather than being either permissive or controlling (Woolfolk & Hoy, 1990). As part of their teaching, they are more likely to offer students choices and support student autonomy (Midgley, Feldlaufer, & Eccles, 1988), perhaps because they have confidence that they can manage students who are working on different tasks or projects. Having a higher sense of efficacy may cause teachers to make controllable attributions for their own successes and failures and those of their students. Believing in themselves and their students, higher self-efficacy teachers look to controllable factors such as increased effort, improved teaching or learning strategies, better explanations or instructional activities, or improved help and support.

Indirect Student Outcomes

When teachers set higher goals and are persistent and resilient in moving toward them, students may be more willing to adopt the goals. If the goals seem realistic, reasonably difficult, and meaningful (Erez & Zidon, 1984), and if good reasons are given for the value of the goals, goal acceptance is more likely. Intrinsic motivation to learn is also encouraged when students are given choices by their confident teachers and when the students are provided informational rather than controlling communications (Reeve, Bolt, & Cai, 1999; Ryan & Deci, 2000). In addition, students who hear controllable attributions from their teachers and see teachers act in keeping with those attributions may be more likely to make controllable attributions themselves, especially if their teacher is persuasive and confident. Thus, these teachers not only directly teach their students better strategies, they may also model for the students an active, strategic, and effortful approach to overcoming learning problems. These teachers are more self-regulating and provide a model of self-monitoring and regulation for their students.

Relational Influences and Outcomes

Across the fields of educational psychology, researchers are becoming more and more interested in the ways in which the quality of interactions (among students and between students and teachers) shape learning and developmental outcomes.

Teachers' Cognitions and Relationships

Although few studies have examined the effects of teachers' sense of efficacy on their beliefs about relationships and their interactions with students, we believe the next decade will yield increasing interest and findings regarding the social contexts and consequences of teachers' sense of efficacy. One probable connection may exist in the way teachers' sense of efficacy may shape their interactions with students who present challenging, disruptive, or problematic behavior.

Brophy and McCaslin (1992) asked whether teachers perceive different types of "problem behaviors" and "problem students" in their classrooms and whether they have beliefs about the efficacy of different management strategies for different types of problem behaviors. A growing body of research suggests that teachers' beliefs about how to relate to their students as well as their willingness to assume responsibility for developing relationships with students may underlie differences in their beliefs about student behavior (Davis, in press; Delpit, 1995; Stodolsky & Grossman, 2000). For example, Brophy and McCaslin (1992) found that teachers differed in their beliefs about problem students depending on whether they defined their role in the classroom as *instructors* or *socializers*. Socializers assumed responsibility for achieving rapport with students and developing students' social skills whereas instructors were more interested in being an authority figure. Delpit (1995) found that commitment on the part of teachers to establishing and maintaining relationships with diverse students had a transformative effect on students' attitudes and achievement patterns. This was particularly true for negotiating conflict and helping students to regulate negative emotions in the classroom (e.g., frustration, apathy).

Ultimately, we hypothesize that teachers with a strong sense of efficacy for both content and pedagogical knowledge as well as classroom management may be more likely to assume responsibility for working with "problem" students. If teachers' sense of efficacy is not threatened by the challenges and confrontations of their adolescent students, the teachers may feel less need for control and be more inclined to listen to students. If these teachers are confident in their teaching and managerial capabilities, they may be less ego-involved, angered, or insulted by students' misbehaviors and more willing to solve problems rather than punish their students. Further, efficacious teachers may feel freer to appropriately express unpleasant emotions such as frustration or disappointment, to help students to co-regulate their own unpleasant emotions, and to respond with warmth instead of hostility when students express frustration with an activity or question its relevance. In brief, a sense of efficacy may free teachers to care about their students without being overwhelmed by student behaviors they cannot understand or control.

It is also possible that when teachers feel efficacious about their content and pedagogical knowledge, they no longer own sole responsibility for the "successes" and "failures" of a lesson/activity. They create space for reflection on alternative explanations for why things went right or wrong. This shift in the power dynamic, whereby both the teacher and student share the responsibility for bringing about learning, is likely to affect students' sense of belonging to their classrooms. Moreover, teachers with a strong sense of efficacy are likely to present a different type of model of what it means to be a "learner" or "scholar." When failure or struggle in the classroom no longer serves as an indicator of teachers' lack of competence, teachers are free to reflect on and "admit" to their students their own frustration when a lesson does not go as planned and, in doing so, may model how to cope with challenge or failure as well as how to be open to constructive critique. In this way, students may come to understand what it means to be a lifelong learner.

Relational Outcomes

Little research has examined the relationship between teachers' sense of efficacy and relational consequences for students, but there is research on students' perceptions of teachers who care about them. Woolfolk Hoy and Weinstein (in press) document the value that students place on teachers' willingness to "be there" for them, to listen, and to show concern—in short, to *care* (Alder & Moulton, 1998; Cothran, Kulinna, & Garrahy, 2003; Davis, in press; Pomeroy, 1999; Wentzel, 1997, 1998). Cothran and Ennis (2000) interviewed 51 urban high school students about barriers and bridges to engagement. Students reported that they were more willing to engage when they felt that the teacher cared if they learned the subject matter and also cared about their personal lives and welfare. Caring manifested as patience, humor, ability to listen, and expressions of interest in and concern for students was particularly important for students who were experiencing pressures and problems at home (e.g., alcohol-induced fights, physical abuse, verbal conflicts) (Phelan, Yu, & Davidson, 1994).

Katz (1999) found that high expectations for academic achievement combined with caring and support were the essential components of a productive teacher-student relationship, especially for students who have been marginalized:

> High expectations without caring can result in setting goals that are impossible for the student to reach without adult support and assistance. On the other hand, caring without high expectations can turn dangerously into paternalism in which teachers feel sorry for "underprivileged" youth but never challenge them academically. High expectations and caring in tandem, however, can make a powerful difference in students' lives. (p. 814)

Thus, feeling cared for may be particularly important for students representing diverse socioeconomic, cultural, and academic backgrounds. In a 3-year ethnographic study of academic achievement and school orientations among immigrant Mexicans and Mexican Americans, Valenzuela (1999) found that the predominantly non-Latino teaching staff at the school interpreted students' attire and behavior as evidence that they did not care about school, so the teachers "often make no further effort to forge effective reciprocal relationships with this group" (p. 22). At the same time, students saw a caring relationship with teachers as a *precondition* for caring about school; in other words, they needed to be *cared for* before they could *care about* school.

A willingness to listen, easier for a teacher who feels self-efficacious and unthreatened, is related to students' attitudes toward school. Garner (1995), for example, investigated the perceptions of 12 "disruptive" adolescent male students and found that the classroom teacher was the most important factor in students' attitudes toward school. In interviews and through their diaries, the students consistently mentioned the importance of teachers being attentive, respectful, and willing to listen (see Davis, in press). Similarly, Habel, Bloom, Ray, and Bacon (1999) found that students with behavior disorders emphasized the importance of teacher-student relationships characterized by trust and affection, stressing the themes of personal care and academic caring.

A Possible Mechanism for the Influences of Teacher Self-Efficacy on Student Outcomes

Teaching is an ego-involved activity. Teachers must draw on their intellectual and emotional resources if they are to be successful in finding ways to connect with their students and help their students connect with the subject matter. In the classroom, the majority of teachers' successes and failures depend on their ability to cope with the "in-the-moment" problems of managing their classrooms and interacting with their students. For example, new teachers must learn within their first years of their careers how to identify, cope with, and modify their own behavior and instruction based on students' reports of frustration and boredom. Moreover, these strategies need to be flexible over the course of a teaching career to adapt to the needs of a diverse student population. Ultimately, teachers who are focused inward on meeting their own efficacy needs (e.g. finding ways to develop or validate their own sense of instructional, managerial, and relational efficacy) are less likely to allocate their resources towards meeting their students' needs. From this perspective, teachers who have a strong sense of efficacy have more resources to share with their students. Such resources may include more time for planning, more resources for coping with unpleasant emotional experiences in the classroom, and more creativity with regard to designing instruction, management, and discipline techniques that match their students' needs.

IMPLICATIONS FOR STUDYING TEACHERS' SENSE OF EFFICACY

Before concluding, we believe it is important to keep in mind the nature of teacher education, and of the "typical" teacher education student, when considering the development of and the changes in teachers' sense of efficacy over time. In fact, most prospective teachers are themselves adolescent learners and may well be influenced by the sense of efficacy of their own teachers and their teacher educators. Little research has examined this possibility, however. In addition, pre-service teachers as learners bring with them a set of commonsense ideas about teaching and learning such as individual theories of the mind and beliefs about teaching learned during their own "apprenticeship of observation" in over 12 years of being taught (Lortie, 1975). These innate and intuitive ideas of the ways classrooms run are termed "folk pedagogy," which "predispose individuals to think and teach in particular ways, some of which is inconsistent with the concepts and practices characteristic of expert teaching" (Torff, 1999, p. 196). To counter this dysfunctional assimilation, Torff (1999) called for explicit recognition of folk pedagogies during pre-service experiences such as matching folk pedagogy categories to instructional models they experience in the class. Thus, teacher educators have a dual challenge to surface and confront folk pedagogies, support conceptual change in beliefs about teaching, and still build a foundation for authentic efficacy beliefs (for a more extensive discussion of this challenge, see Woolfolk Hoy & Murphy, 2001).

Ultimately, underlying the field of teacher beliefs, including teachers' sense of efficacy, is the assumption that the mental lives of teachers matter both for instructional decision-making and ultimately for affecting student outcomes in the classroom. Initially daunted by the complexity of constructs and the challenges of how to "capture" teachers' beliefs in a meaningful and consistent way, researchers in the field moved away from process-product approaches toward more isolated study of how beliefs are conceptualized (Woolfolk Hoy et al., in press). However, the content of teachers' mental lives, including their self-efficacy expectations, can no longer be studied globally or context free. Many of the newer measures of teacher self-efficacy are context and subject specific. The development of new analysis methods—those that evaluate and compare theoretical models for their fit with empirical data and also explore factors that operate on group/collective levels—calls for renewed exploration using process-product designs to understand the complex processes by which teachers' sense of efficacy shapes their classroom beliefs and behavior and subsequently their students' beliefs, behaviors, and academic outcomes.

The purpose of this paper was threefold: to review literature regarding the nature and conceptualization of teachers' sense of efficacy; to synthesize the findings indicating that teachers' sense of efficacy has important consequences for adolescent learning, motivation, and achievement; and to present a model that can be used, in conjunction with Figure 5.1, as a heuristic for guiding future research. Across these two models we have attempted to identify established, possible, and probable sources of teaching self-efficacy, different domains or dimensions of efficacy judgments, and the proximal and distal outcomes for teachers' and students' beliefs and behaviors. We hope readers will use the models developed to guide theoretically grounded research that begins to explore the processes and mechanisms by which teachers' sense of efficacy influences their behavior, their students' behavior, and, subsequently, their students' abilities to learn in the classroom.

REFERENCES

Alder, N. I., & Moulton, M. R. (1998). Caring relationships: Perspectives from middle school students. *Research in Middle Level Education Quarterly, 21*(3), 15-32.

Allinder, R. M. (1994). The relationship between efficacy and the instructional practices of special education teachers and consultants. *Teacher Education and Special Education, 17*, 86-95.

Allington, R. (1980). Teacher interruption behaviors during primary-grade oral reading. *Journal of Educational Psychology, 71*, 371-377.

Ashton, P. T., & Webb, R. B. (1986). *Making a difference: Teachers' sense of efficacy and student achievement.* New York: Longman.

Bandura, A. (1986). *Social foundations of thought and action: A social cognitive theory.* Englewood Cliffs, NJ: Prentice-Hall.

Bandura, A. (1997). *Self-efficacy: The exercise of control.* New York: W. H. Freeman and Company.

Battin-Pearson, S., Newcomb, M. D., Abbott, R. D., Hill, K. G., Catalano, R. F., & Hawkins, J. D. (2000). Predictors of early high school dropout: A test of five theories. *Journal of Educational Psychology, 92*, 568-582.

Berliner, D. (1988). Simple views of effective teaching and a simple theory of classroom instruction. In D. Berliner & B. Rosenshine (Eds.), *Talks to teachers* (pp. 93–110). New York: Random House.

Berman, P., McLaughlin, M., Bass, G., Pauly, E., & Zellman, G. (1977). *Federal Programs supporting educational change, Vol. VII. Factors affecting implementation and continuation* (Report No. R-1589/7-HEW). Santa Monica, CA: Rand Corporation (ERIC Document Reproduction Service No. 140 432).

Borko, H., & Putnam, R. T. (1995). Expanding a teacher's knowledge base: A cognitive psychological perspective on professional development. In T. R. Guskey & M. Huberman (Eds.), *Professional development in education: New paradigms and practices* (pp. 35-65). New York: Teachers College Press.

Brophy, J. E., & Good, T. (1986). Teacher behavior and student achievement. In M. Wittrock (Ed.), *Handbook of research on teaching* (3rd ed., pp. 328–375). New York: Macmillan.

Brophy, J. E., & McCaslin, M. (1992). Teachers' reports of how they perceive and cope with problem students. *Elementary School Journal, 93*, 3-68.

Cantrell, P., Young, S., & Moore, A. (2003). Factors affecting science teaching efficacy of preservice elementary teachers. *Journal of Science Teacher Education, 14*, 177-192.

Chacon, C. T. (2005). Teachers' perceived efficacy among English as a foreign language teachers in middle schools in Venezuela. *Teaching and Teacher Education, 21,* 257-272.

Cothran, D. J., & Ennis, C. D. (2000). Building bridges to student engagement: Communicating respect and care for students in urban high school. *Journal of Research and Development in Education, 33,* 106-117.

Cothran, D. J., Kulinna, P. H., & Garrahy, D. A. (2003). "This is kind of giving a secret away...": Students' perspectives on effective class management. *Teaching and Teacher Education, 19,* 435-444.

Cousins, J. B., & Walker, C. A. (2000). Predictors of educators' valuing of systemic inquiry in schools. *Canadian Journal of Program Evaluation, Special Issue,* 25-53.

Davis, H. A. (2003). Conceptualizing the role and influence of student-teacher relationships on children's social and cognitive development. *Educational Psychologist, 38,* 207-234.

Davis, H. A. (in press). Exploring the context of relationship quality between middle school students and teachers. *Elementary School Journal.*

Davis, H. A., & Ring, G. (2005). *Integrating technology into the study of teaching and learning: Changes in first-semester pre-service teachers' technology attitudes, motivations, and behaviors.* Manuscript under review.

De Laat, J., & Watters, J. (1995). Science teaching self-efficacy in a primary school: A case study. *Research in Science Education, 25,* 453-464.

Delpit, L. (1995). *Other people's children: Cultural conflict in the classroom.* New York: The New Press.

Eccles, J. S., Midgley, C., Wigfield, A., Bichanan, C. M., Rueman, D., Flanagan, C., et al., (1993). Development during adolescence: The impact of stage-environment fit on young adolescents' experiences in schools and in families. *American Psychologist, 48,* 90-101.

Erez, M., & Zidon, I. (1984). Effects of goal acceptance on the relationship of goal difficulty to performance. *Journal of Applied Psychology, 69,* 69-78.

Ferreira, M. M., & Bosworth, K. (2001). Defining caring teachers: Adolescents' perspective. *Journal of Classroom Interaction, 36*(1), 24-30.

Finders, M. (1997). *Just girls: Hidden literacies and life in junior high.* New York: Teachers College Press.

Garner, P. (1995). Schools by scoundrels: The views of "disruptive" pupils in mainstream schools in England and the United States. In M. Lloyd-Smith & J. D. Davies (Eds.), *On the margins: The educational experience of "problem" pupils* (pp. 17-30). Staffordshire, England: Trentham Books.

Gibson, S., & Dembo, M. (1984). Teacher efficacy: A construct validation. *Journal of Educational Psychology, 76,* 569-582.

Good, T., & Brophy, J. (2003). *Looking in classrooms* (9th ed.). Boston: Allyn & Bacon.

Goodenow, C. (1992). Strengthening the links between educational psychology and the study of social contexts. *Educational Psychologist, 27,* 177-196.

Guskey, T., & Passaro, P. (1994). Teacher efficacy: A study of construct dimensions. *American Educational Research Journal, 31,* 627-643.

Habel, J., Bloom, L. A., Ray, M. S., & Bacon, E. (1999). Consumer reports: What students with behaviour disorders say about school. *Remedial and Special Education, 20,* 93-105.

Hamilton, S. F., & Darling, N. (1989). Mentors in adolescents' lives. In K. Hurrelmann & U. Engle (Eds.), *The social world of adolescents: International perspectives* (pp. 121-139). New York: Walter de Gruyter.

Hani, J., Czerniak, C., & Lumpe, A. (1996). Teacher beliefs and intentions regarding the implementation of science education reform strands. *Journal of Research in Science Teaching, 33,* 971-993.

Henson, R. K. (2002). From adolescent angst to adulthood: Substantive implications and measurement dilemmas in the development of teacher efficacy research. *Educational Psychologist, 37,* 137-150.

Katz, S. R. (1999). Teaching in tensions: Latino immigrant youth, their teachers, and the structures of schooling. *Teachers College Record, 100,* 809-840.

Labone, E. (2004). Teacher efficacy: Maturing the construct through research in alternative paradigms. *Teaching and Teacher Education, 20,* 341-359.

Lortie, D. (1975). *Schoolteachers: A sociological study.* Chicago: University of Chicago Press.

Lynch, M., & Cicchetti, D. (1997). Children's relationships with adults and peers: An examination of elementary and junior high school students. *Journal of School Psychology, 35,* 81-99.

Midgley, C., Feldlaufer, H., & Eccles, J., (1988). The transition to junior high school: Belief of pre- and post-transition teachers. *Journal of Youth and Adolescence, 17,* 543-562.

Midgley, C., Feldlaufer, H., & Eccles, J. S. (1989). Change in teachers' efficacy and student self and task related beliefs in mathematics during the transition to junior high school. *Journal of Educational Psychology, 81,* 247-258.

Muijs, D., & Reynolds, D. (2001). Teachers' beliefs and behaviors: What really matters. *Journal of Classroom Interaction, 37,* 3-15.

Mulholland, J., & Wallace, J. (2001). Teacher induction and elementary science teaching: Enhancing self-efficacy. *Teaching and Teacher Education, 17,* 243-261.

Murdock, T. B. (1999). The social context of risk: Status and motivational predictors of alienation in middle school. *Journal of Educational Psychology, 91,* 62-75.

Murdock, T. B., Anderman, L. H., & Hodge, S. (2000). Middle-grade predictors of students' motivation and behavior in high school. *Journal of Adolescent Research, 15,* 327-351

Phelan, P., Yu, H. C., & Davidson, A. L. (1994). Navigating the psychosocial pressures of adolescence: The voices and experiences of high school students. *American Educational Research Journal, 31,* 415-447.

Pierson, M. E. (2001). Technology integration practice as a function of pedagogical expertise. *Journal of Research on Computing in Education, 33,* 413-430.

Plourde, L. A. (2002). The influence of student teaching on preservice elementary teachers' science self-efficacy and outcome expectancy beliefs. *Journal of Instructional Psychology, 29,* 245-253.

Podell, D. & Soodak, L. (1993). Teacher efficacy and bias in special education referrals. *Journal of Educational Research, 86,* 247-253.

Pomeroy, E. (1999). The teacher-student relationship in secondary school: Insights from excluded students. *British Journal of Sociology of Education, 20,* 465-482.

Raudenbush, S., Rowen, B., & Cheong, Y. (1992). Contextual effects on the self-perceived efficacy of high school teachers. *Sociology of Education, 65,* 150-167.

Reeve, J., Bolt, E., & Cai, Y. (1999). Autonomy-supportive teachers: How they teach and motivate students. *Journal of Educational Psychology, 91,* 537-548.

Resnick, M. D., Bearman, P. S., Blum, R. W., Bauman, K. E., Harris, K. E., Jones, J., et al. (1997). Protecting adolescents from harm: Findings from the national longitudinal study on adolescent health. *Journal of the American Medical Association, 278,* 823-832.

Rice, D. C., & Roychoudhury, A. (2003). Preparing more confident preservice elementary science teachers: One elementary science methods teacher's self-study. *Journal of Science Teacher Education, 14,* 97-126.

Riggs, I. (1995). *The characteristics of high and low efficacy elementary teachers.* Paper presented at the annual meeting of the National Association of Research in Science Teaching, San Francisco, CA.

Roeser, R. W., Eccles, J. S., & Sameroff, A. J. (2000). School as a context of early adolescents' academic social-emotional development: A summary of research findings. *Elementary School Journal, 100,* 443-471.

Roeser, R. W., Midgley, C., & Urdan, T. C. (1996). Perceptions of school psychological environment and early adolescents' psychological and behavioral functioning in school: The mediating role of goals and belonging. *Journal of Educational Psychology, 88,* 408-422.

Ropp, M. M. (1999). Exploring individual characteristics associated with learning to use computers in preservice teacher preparation. *Journal of Computing in Education, 31,* 402-424.

Rosenshine, B. (1979). Content, time, and direct instruction. In P. Peterson & H. Walberg (Eds.), *Research on teaching: Concepts, findings, and implications* (pp. 28-56). Berkeley, CA: McCutchan.

Rosenshine, B., & Stevens, R. (1986). Teaching functions. In M. Wittrock (Ed.), *Handbook of research on teaching* (3rd ed., pp. 376-391). New York: Macmillan.

Rosenthal, R. (1995). Critiquing Pygmalion: A 25-year perspective. *Current Directions in Psychological Science, 4,* 171-172.

Ross, J. A. (1998). The antecedents and consequences of teacher efficacy. In J. Brophy (Ed.), *Advances in research on teaching* (Vol. 7, pp. 49-73). Greenwich, CT: JAI Press.

Ross, J. A., Hogaboam-Gray, A., & Hannay, L. (2001). Effects of teacher efficacy on computer skills and computer cognitions of K-3 students. *Elementary School Journal, 102,* 141-156.

Ryan, R. M., & Deci, E. L. (2000). Intrinsic and extrinsic motivation: Classic definitions and new directions. *Contemporary Educational Psychology, 25,* 54-67.

Stodolsky, S. S., & Grossman, P. L. (2000). Changing students, changing teaching. *Teachers' College Record, 102,* 125-172.

Torff, B. (1999). Tacit knowledge in teaching: Folk pedagogy and teacher education. In R. J. Sternberg & J. A. Horvath (Eds.), *Tacit knowledge in professional practice: Researcher and practitioner perspectives* (pp. 195-214). Mahwah, N J: Erlbaum.

Tosun, T. (2000). The beliefs of preservice elementary teachers toward science and science teaching. *School Science and Mathematics, 100*, 374-379.

Tschannen-Moran, M., & Woolfolk Hoy, A. (2001). Teacher efficacy: Capturing and elusive construct. *Teaching and Teacher Education, 17*, 783-805.

Tschannen-Moran, M., Woolfolk Hoy, A., & Hoy, W. K. (1998). Teacher efficacy: Its meaning and measure. *Review of Educational Research, 68*, 202-248.

Valenzuela, A. (1999). *Subtractive schooling: U.S.-Mexican youth and the politics of caring*. Albany: SUNY Press.

Wentzel, K. R. (1997). Student motivation in middle school: The role of perceived pedagogical caring. *Journal of Educational Psychology, 89*, 411-419.

Wentzel, K. R. (1998). Social relationships and motivation in middle school: The role of parents, teachers, and peers. *Journal of Educational Psychology, 90*, 202-209.

Wheatley, K. F. (2002). The potential benefits of teacher efficacy doubts for educational reform. *Teaching and Teacher Education, 18*, 5-22.

Winfield, L. F. (1986). Teacher beliefs toward academically at risk students in inner urban schools. *The Urban Review, 18*, 253-268.

Woolfolk, A. E. (2004). *Educational psychology* (9th ed.). Boston: Allyn & Bacon.

Woolfolk, A. E., & Brooks, D. (1985). The influence of teachers' nonverbal behaviors on students' perceptions and performance. *Elementary School Journal, 85*, 514-528.

Woolfolk Hoy, A., Davis, H., & Pape, S. (in preparation). Teachers' knowledge, beliefs, and thinking. In P. A. Alexander & P. H. Winne (Eds.), *Handbook of educational psychology* (2nd ed.). Mahwah, NJ: Erlbaum.

Woolfolk, A. E., & Hoy, W. K., (1990). Prospective teachers' sense of efficacy and beliefs about control, *Journal of Educational Psychology, 82*, 81-91.

Woolfolk Hoy, A., & Murphy, P. K. (2001). Teaching educational psychology to the implicit mind. In R. Sternberg & B. Torff (Eds.), *Understanding and teaching the implicit mind* (pp. 145-185). Mahwah, NJ: Erlbaum.

Woolfolk, A. E., Rosoff, B., & Hoy, W. K. (1990). Teachers' sense of efficacy and their beliefs about managing students. *Teaching and Teacher Education, 6*, 137-148.

Woolfolk Hoy, A., & Weinstein, C. S. (in press). Students' and teachers' perspectives about classroom management. In C. Evertson & C. S. Weinstein (Eds.), *Handbook for classroom management: Research, practice, and contemporary issues*. Mahwah, NJ: Erlbaum.

Wurf, E., & Markus, H. (1991). Possible selves and the psychology of personal growth. In D. J. Ozer & J. M. Healy, Jr. (Eds.), *Perspectives in personality, Vol 3: Part A: Self and emotion; Part B: Approaches to understanding lives* (pp. 39-62). Philadelphia: Jessica Kingsley.

Yowell, C. M., & Smylie, M. A. (1999). Self-regulation in democratic communities. The *Elementary School Journal, 99*, 469-490.

CHAPTER 6

SELF-EFFICACY, ADOLESCENTS' RISK-TAKING BEHAVIORS, AND HEALTH

Ralf Schwarzer and Aleksandra Luszczynska

Perceived self-efficacy makes a difference in how people feel, think, and act (Bandura 1997). Thus, it is reasonable that self-efficacy also governs health behaviors. The role that self-beliefs play in the realm of health behaviors, health outcomes, and health care has been the object of many studies, and the construct of self-efficacy has sparked a great deal of valuable research in health psychology. This construct is of particular value when the aim is to predict whether people engage in healthy behaviors or avoid risky ones. We will commence with providing a brief definition of health behaviors and discuss the specificity of health behaviors in adolescence compared to other periods across the life span. We will provide an overview of health behavior theories and will then proceed to review the evidence reported in empirical studies conducted with adolescents.

HEALTH BEHAVIORS ACROSS THE LIFE SPAN

Health behaviors can be defined as actions and habits that are related to health maintenance, restoration, and improvement. Health-compromis-

Self-Efficacy Beliefs of Adolescents, 139–159
Copyright © 2006 by Information Age Publishing
All rights of reproduction in any form reserved.

ing behaviors refer to lack of physical activity, unhealthy diet, substance use, risky sexual behaviors (e.g., unprotected intercourse) or nonadherence to medication or to a therapeutic regimen among individuals with chronic or acute illness. Health-promoting behaviors include dental hygiene, regular physical activity, healthy nutrition, safe sex practices, adherence to medication, and many others.

Various health behaviors such as smoking, alcohol use, and condom use are usually initiated during the developmental periods of adolescence or childhood. Child and adolescent behavior may predict health behaviors and health status in early adulthood. A study of 1000 individuals assessed at regular intervals from age 5 to age 26 revealed that viewing television during childhood and early adolescence predicts body mass index, cardiorespiratory fitness, serum cholesterol, and smoking status at the age of 26 (Hancox, Milne, & Poulton, 2004).

Adolescents differ from adults or seniors in some health behaviors (in particular in physical activity), although for most health behaviors the differences are not very salient (see Pronk et al., 2004). Adolescents meet recommendations regarding physical activity (59%) more frequently than do adults (39%) or seniors (41%). Regarding other health behaviors, there may be no major difference between adolescents and adults or seniors. Approximately 91% of adolescents, 85% of adults, and 93% of seniors meet the recommendations regarding no smoking, and 64% of adolescents, 64% of adults, and 80% of seniors adhere to a healthy diet. Rates of condom use among adolescents and young adults are similar (Siegel, Klein, & Roghmann, 1999). Some health behaviors, such as smoking, may vary to a higher degree within adolescence than across the life span. Among smokers, adolescents in Grade 7 smoke less intensely than do adolescents in Grade 10 (Wills, Resko, Ainette, & Mendoza, 2004). Among 2,387 high school students from Poland, Turkey, and the United States, self-efficacy was found unrelated to age. Across countries, physical activity of adolescents is predicted by age, whereas nutrition is unrelated to age (Luszczynska, Gibbons, Piko, & Tekozel, 2004).

PERCEIVED SELF-EFFICACY IN HEALTH BEHAVIOR CHANGE: BRIEF OVERVIEW OF THEORIES

In this chapter, we examine the role that self-efficacy plays in the process of health behavior change. Self-efficacy instigates the adoption, initiation, and maintenance of health-promoting behaviors. The most prominent theories of health behavior change—such as the Theory of Planned Behavior (TPB), Social Cognitive Theory (SCT), the Transtheoretical

Model (TTM), and the Health Action Process Approach (HAPA)—include a variety of cognitions that either directly or indirectly influence health behaviors.

According to the *Theory of Planned Behavior* (Ajzen, 1991), intention is the most proximal predictor of behavior. Cognitions that affect a specific intention are (a) *attitude toward the behavior* (evaluation of performing the behavior), (b) *subjective norm* (the extent to which a person believes that significant others would want the individual to perform a behavior), and (c) *perceived behavioral control* (perception about being able to perform a specific behavior). Self-efficacy and behavioral control are seen as nearly synonymous constructs.

According to social cognitive theory (Bandura, 1997), personal sense of control facilitates a change of health behavior. Self-efficacy pertains to a sense of control over one's environment and behavior. Self-efficacy beliefs are cognitions that determine whether health behavior change will be initiated, how much effort will be expended, and how long it will be sustained in the face of obstacles and failures (Schwarzer, 2001). Self-efficacy influences the effort one puts forth to change risk behavior and the persistence to continue striving despite barriers and setbacks that may undermine motivation. Self-efficacy is directly related to health behavior, but it also affects health behaviors indirectly through its impact on goals. Self-efficacy influences the challenges that people take on as well as how high they set their goals (e.g., "I intend to reduce my smoking" or "I intend to quit smoking altogether"). Individuals with strong self-efficacy select more challenging and ambitious goals (DeVellis & DeVellis, 2000). They focus on opportunities, not on obstacles (e.g., "At my university there is a smoking ban, anyway," instead of "There are still a lot of ashtrays at my university.").

The Transtheoretical Model (Prochaska, DiClemente, & Norcross, 1992) proposes five *stages of change*. The first one is the pre-contemplation stage, in which individuals consider changing a specific health behavior, but they have not yet decided to make any changes. In the preparation stage, they prepare to change the behavior. In the action stage, a new goal behavior is initiated. When the action is performed for a longer time period, the maintenance stage is reached (Prochaska et al., 1992). A sixth stage is sometimes mentioned, the termination stage, in which individuals no longer experience any temptation to revert to their old habits. According to the TTM, self-efficacy and perceived positive ("pros") and negative ("cons") outcomes are seen as the main social-cognitive variables that change across the stages. Self-efficacy is typically low in early stages and increases when individuals move on to the later stages.

Health Action Process Approach (Schwarzer, 2001) applies to all health behaviors, paying particular attention to post-intentional mechanisms. HAPA theorists argue for a distinction between (a) pre-intentional motivation processes that lead to a behavioral intention and (b) post-intentional volition processes that lead to actual health behavior. Within both phases, different patterns of social-cognitive predictors may emerge.

In the initial *motivation phase*, a person develops an intention to act. In this phase, risk perception ("I have a high risk of suffering from diabetes because of my body weight") is merely seen as a distal antecedent within the motivation phase. Risk perception in itself is not enough to entice a person to form an intention. Rather, it sets the stage for a contemplation process and further elaboration about consequences and competencies. Similarly, outcome expectancies ("If I eat healthful foods, I will reduce my weight") are chiefly seen as being important in the motivation phase, when a person balances the pros and cons of the consequences of a certain behavior. Further, one needs to believe in one's capability to perform a desired action ("I am capable of initiating a healthier diet in spite of temptations"), otherwise one will fail to initiate that action. Outcome expectancies operate in concert with perceived self-efficacy, both of which contribute substantially to the formation of an intention.

In the subsequent *adherence phase*, after a person has developed an inclination toward adopting a particular health behavior, the "good intention" has to be transformed into detailed instructions on how to perform the desired action. These plans, which specify the *when, where,* and *how* of a desired action, carry the structure of "When situation S arises, I will perform response R." Thus, a global intention can be specified by a set of subordinate intentions and action plans that contain algorithms of action sequences. The adherence phase (also called the volition phase) is strongly affected by self-efficacy. The number and quality of action plans depend on one's perceived competence and experience. Self-efficacy influences the cognitive construction of specific action plans, such as visualizing scenarios that may guide goal attainment. The adherence phase includes the processes of taking initiative, maintaining behavior change, and managing relapse. Self-efficacy beliefs may be specific to these processes (see Luszczynska & Schwarzer, 2003; Marlatt, Baer, & Quigley, 1995).

As seen in the examples above, most prominent health behavior theories include self-efficacy (or similar constructs). Self-efficacy is a proximal and direct predictor of intention and of behavior. Its effects on behavior can also be mediated by other cognitions, such as intentions. Across stages of change, an increase of self-efficacy is expected.

SELF-EFFICACY, RISK REDUCTION, HEALTH PROMOTION, HEALTH AND DISEASE MANAGEMENT: SUMMARY OF RESEARCH

Sexual Risk Behaviors

Adolescents form a particularly vulnerable group for human immuno-deficiency virus (HIV) infection, given that approximately 20% of HIV-positive adults contract the virus during adolescence (Hein, 1989). Among sexually active adolescents, those who expressed confidence in their ability to put on a condom and in being able to refuse intercourse with a sexual partner were more likely to use condoms consistently. In addition, holding favorable outcome expectancies associated with condom use predicted protective behaviors (Dilorio et al., 2001).

Interventions that aim at reducing risky sexual behaviors usually affect self-efficacy beliefs. Compared to people in control groups, higher levels of self-efficacy regarding safe sexual behaviors are observed in intervention groups at the 10-month follow-up (Siegel, Aten, & Enaharo, 2001). In addition, stronger effects of intervention are found among youths who were not sexually active prior to the intervention. A short intervention (2 hours) addressing knowledge and self-efficacy in condom use negotiation skills affects knowledge, planning, beliefs about one's ability to negotiate condom use, and intention to use condoms (Dunn, Ross, Caines, & Howorth, 1998). Additionally, if the intervention is led by peer educators (compared to health care professionals), the effects are even stronger: in one study, 87% of the participants were confident that they could use condoms properly (compared to 67% and 57% in interventions led by health care professionals and controls, respectively).

Some adolescents are particularly at risk for sexually transmitted diseases (STD). Gay, lesbian, and bisexual youths are at high risk for HIV infection primarily because of their more frequent unprotected sexual behaviors. Rosario, Mahler, Hunter, and Gwadz (1999) reported that, for gay and bisexual boys, intentions were the strongest predictors of unprotected anal sex and unprotected oral sex. Self-efficacy emerged as the only predictor of the intention itself. Besides intention, variables such as attitudes, social norms, and skills were also directly or indirectly related to behavior, but the associations were weaker. A similar pattern was found in a sample of lesbian and bisexual girls, with intentions as the strongest predictor of unprotected oral sex and unprotected vaginal-digital sex, and self-efficacy as the strongest predictor of intentions. Employing a natural experimental paradigm, Brown and Baranowski (1996) showed that self-efficacy may be more easily enhanced in low-risk groups (i.e., never having had sex or always using condoms, absence of intravenous drug use) than in high-risk groups.

HIV prevention projects should be directed to adolescents who are HIV infected. Such interventions should aim to reduce risky sexual behaviors, increase self-efficacy, and kindle a transition to more advanced stages of behavior change. Butler et al. (2003) designed an intervention for HIV-positive adolescents and young adults with hemophilia. Patients tuned their social skills and participated in self-efficacy exercises during 1 year. Increased self-efficacy but unchanged positive or negative outcome expectations or peer norms were found at posttest. Cognitions or knowledge about risk behaviors did not change, but the increase of self-efficacy was sufficient to increase safer sex rates (consistent condom use, outercourse, or abstinence) and to observe progress in stages of health behavior change. Regarding safe sex, 79% of the participants were in the action or maintenance stages at posttest, compared with 62% at pretest.

In preventing STD, self-efficacy beliefs could refer to the ability to communicate about condom use and HIV/AIDS. This kind of self-efficacy distinguishes between sexually active adolescents who are at high risk from those who are at low risk for STD. According to Holschneider and Alexander (2003), youths who consistently use condoms and report having fewer sexual partners have high optimistic beliefs about their ability to negotiate condom use. Such results, often obtained in cross-sectional studies, might be interpreted in two ways: (a) self-efficacy is enhanced as a result of past mastery experiences (when an individual has successfully negotiated condom use), or (b) high self-efficacy led to successful performance (e.g., negotiation of condom use). Further support for SCT has been provided by experimental studies designed to increase adolescents' confidence in refusing unprotected sex, using condoms, and communicating about safe-sex practices. For example, Coyle et al. (1999) found that changes in condom use self-efficacy were observed 7 months after the intervention. Sexually active high-school students reported more frequent use of condoms than did peers in a control group. They also tended to report a smaller number of partners with whom they had unprotected sex.

It is possible that more general social self-efficacy, such as the perceived ability to engage in successful social interactions, might reduce risk behaviors among adolescents. For African American adolescent boys, refusal and condom-use self-efficacy are significant predictors of condom use, whereas social self-efficacy is not (Colon, Wiatrek, & Ewans, 2000). Similarly, condom-use self-efficacy is a significant predictor of the intention to use condoms, whereas social self-efficacy is not. When behavior-specific beliefs (e.g., ability to refuse having sexual intercourse if one's partner does not agree to use condoms) are entered into a regression equation, more general beliefs (e.g., ability to act on one's intentions in various problematic peer contexts) no longer predict behavior.

In addition to frequency of performing a healthy behavior, it is necessary to measure the behavior as adequately as possible. For example, prevalence of laboratory-diagnosed STDs may be employed as a measure of unsafe sexual behavior. A study conducted with sexually active African American girls revealed that self-efficacy for correct use of condoms were unrelated to skills, measured by demonstrating condom application skills on a penile model (Crosby et al., 2001). Skills of proper condom use determine whether condom use can prevent an infection. Condom use skills are considered a direct and proximal predictor of safe sex practices (Kalichman et al., 2002). However, condom application skills are unrelated to the sexual risk behavior of adolescent girls, self-reported STD symptoms, or laboratory-diagnosed STDs (Crosby et al., 2001). Other studies have confirmed that condom use skills and knowledge may not be good predictors of safe sex practices among adolescents. Kalichman et al. (2002) found that self-efficacy had a direct, unmediated effect on the frequency of unprotected sex whereas condom application skills did not. The relationship between self-efficacy and condom use was stronger than were the relationships between condom use and either gender, age, procondom norms, or risky sexual practices within a 3-month period. It is likely that self-efficacy is the most proximal predictor of safe sex practices.

Christ, Raszka, and Dillon (1998) reported that self-efficacy to apply condoms correctly were unrelated to the intention of using condoms. A closer look at the data collected among sexually active girls suggests, however, that the lack of relationship may have resulted from a ceiling effect: 91% of the girls were sure that they were able to use condoms properly, 97% declared optimistic self-beliefs regarding their ability to convince a partner to use condoms, and 94% were sure that they were able to discuss condom use with a new partner. However, only 22% reported regular condom use, and 38% reported that they used condoms usually. Condom use may be predicted by self-efficacy and by expected outcomes of condom use (e.g., reduction of pleasant sensations during sexual intercourse). Girls with high self-efficacy and low negative outcome expectations regarding condom use are most likely to use condoms regularly.

Some studies report very high levels of condom use self-efficacy (Christ et al., 1998). This may be due to measurement problems. Self-efficacy is sometimes assessed in terms of being able to perform a task (e.g., "I am able to buy condoms"). Such an assessment may result in high rates of positive responses. Measures of self-efficacy should include specific barriers (e.g., "I am able to buy condoms even if my friends would laugh at me while I am doing this").

Contraceptive Behavior

Teenage girls with a high rate of intercourse have been found to use contraceptives more effectively if they believed they could exercise control over their sexual activities (Wang, Wang, & Hsu, 2003). Several variables may moderate the effects of self-efficacy on contraceptive behavior. Data from the National Longitudinal Study of Adolescent Health showed that being female, being older, and living with stepparents resulted in high self-efficacy for contraceptive use. Conversely, adolescents whose mothers had less education (high school dropouts) reported low self-efficacy for contraception use (Longmore, Manning, Giordano, & Rudolph, 2003). Contraceptive self-efficacy also predicts girls' use of contraceptives.

Addictive Behaviors

Self-efficacy to resist smoking temptations is related to the current smoking status of adolescents, together with intention to smoke, attitude toward smoking, impediments to smoking, and social norms (Hanson, Downing, Coyle, & Pederson, 2004). Social norms and self-efficacy together may predict whether adolescents ever smoked and whether they had smoked during the 30 days prior to the measurement. The more strongly they believed that they were able to refuse offered cigarettes, the less likely they were to have ever smoked. Students who perceived their peers as smokers were more likely to have smoked themselves (Zapata et al., 2004). The same associations were found for smoking during the 30 days prior to the time of measurement. Adolescents' self-efficacy for refusing to smoke or drink predicted cigarette, alcohol, and marijuana use measured 12 months later. The direct effect of self-efficacy was similar to the direct effect of past behavior (measured 18 months earlier) on smoking. Self-efficacy emerged as a mediator between social influence variables (such as perceived norms), substance offer, and past behavior on the one hand and smoking on the other (Li, Pentz, & Chou, 2002).

Some adolescents who are already involved in addictive behaviors try to overcome them. When asked to provide reasons for quitting smoking, young people spontaneously list athletic performance, health, and costs, as well as their self-efficacy (Aung, Hickman, & Moolchan, 2003). Although there are gender differences in the reasons that adolescents give for not smoking—such as health and athletic performance—self-efficacy leads to intention formation in both sexes. Recognizing the concerns that young people have is important for designing cessation interventions for young smokers.

Stage models such as the TTM offer useful heuristics for developing smoking cessation programs for adolescents. Such programs should take into account that stage distribution is different for adolescent smokers than for adults. Compared to adults, more adolescent smokers are in an early stage of health behavior change, that is, pre-contemplation. Smoking cessation programs should aim at moving adolescent smokers to later stages, that is, to the contemplation (of pros and cons of smoking), preparation, or action (quitting smoking) stage. Transition to more advanced stages is associated with increased self-efficacy (Coleman-Wallace, Lee, Montgomery, Blix, & Wang, 1999). The question remains, however, what is crucial for the health behavior change process? Do changes in self-efficacy facilitate behavior change and promote stage transition, or do behavior changes themselves (e.g., attempts to quit smoking) have side-effects, namely an increase of self-efficacy?

Self-efficacy may be indirectly related to changing a behavior, performing advocacy against tobacco use, via its effect on knowledge about anti-smoking campaigns. Awareness of anti-smoking policies in schools and in the mass media, as well as support for an anti-tobacco policy, is higher among self-efficacious adolescents. These adolescents, who believe that they can refuse a cigarette, know more about local anti-tobacco campaigns and policies restricting youth access to tobacco and smoking bans in schools, bars, and workplaces. In addition to higher awareness, self-efficacious adolescents have more favorable attitudes toward these campaigns (Unger et al., 1999). Knowledge about anti-tobacco campaigns and policies predict behavior, namely advocacy against tobacco use.

Results of longitudinal studies on adolescents' alcohol consumption have also shown that not all interventions designed to increase self-efficacy and to change addictive behaviors lead to expected changes in target health behaviors or cognitions. In one study, sense of community, self-efficacy, outcome expectancy, incentive value, policy control, and leadership competence were part of a program designed for teens from low-income neighborhoods. No reduction of alcohol consumption or use of tobacco and other psychoactive substances was observed after the program was completed. Post-treatment measurements, however, showed growth in the social-cognitive constructs (Winkleby, Feighery, Altman, Kole, & Tencati, 2001). Perry et al. (1996) reported that some changes in behavior were observed at the 2-year follow-up (lower alcohol consumption in an intervention group compared to controls). However, no differences in self-efficacy were found, both among baseline users and nonusers.

Health-Promoting Behaviors: Physical Exercise and Nutrition

Most adolescents do not meet moderate to vigorous physical activity criteria (Bungum, Pate, Dowda, & Vincent, 1999). Studies employing a motion detector to measure physical activity in preadolescents and adolescents showed that they spent 12.6 minutes daily ($SD = 12.2$) on vigorous physical activity (Strauss, Rodzilsky, Burack, & Colin, 2001). In addition to determinants of physical activity such as demographics, biological factors, physical environment factors, and physical activity characteristics, psychological determinants (such as self-efficacy, intention, and perceived barriers) play a crucial role in the adoption of an active lifestyle (Sallis & Owen, 1999). Although self-efficacy is expected to operate independent of ethnic and cultural background, optimistic self-beliefs are associated with moderate physical activity among White girls, but not among African American girls (Bungum et al., 1999).

Self-efficacy is related to current physical activity and is one of the strongest predictors of future activity among adolescents (Nahas, Goldfine, & Collins, 2003). Studies using objective measures of physical activity, such as a motion detector to monitor physical activity over a specified time period, have shown that self-efficacy is related to high level of physical activity of 10- to 16-year-old adolescents (Strauss et al., 2001). Moreover, across a set of psychosocial and environmental variables, perceived confidence in the ability to be active was the only variable that differentiated between active and low-active African American adolescents (Trost, Pate, Ward, Saunders, & Riner, 1999). For boys, involvement in sport organizations was the other predictor of activity levels. Girls who perceived more positive outcomes were also more active.

Some interventions that aim to increase self-efficacy and healthy nutrition employ computer games to facilitate mastery experience. In one such activity based on SCT, the educational activities in a game were aimed at increasing preference for healthy foods (Baranowski et al., 2003). Using multiple exposures, this approach increased mastery in asking for healthy food at home and when eating out. It also enhanced the skills in preparing healthy foods by means of virtual recipes and virtual food preparation. Compared to persons in control groups, preadolescents participating in such an intervention increased their consumption of fruits and vegetables (Baranowski et al., 2003).

Self-efficacy may mediate between other cognitions and adolescents' physical activity. Assessing self-efficacy in conjunction with constructs from the TPB, Motl et al. (2002) searched for predictors of moderate and vigorous physical activity among Black and White adolescent girls. Only self-efficacy predicted moderate physical activity. Self-efficacy and behavioral control predicted vigorous activity. Intentions, attitudes, and subjective norms were correlated and were related to self-efficacy, but they were only indirectly related to physical activity, mediated by self-efficacy. Self-efficacy may also mediate the relationship between physical activity and constructs such as parental support for the child's physical activity (Trost et al., 2003). Some studies provide evidence that self-efficacy is a stronger correlate of adolescents' physical activity than are cognitions such as perceived benefits, perceived barriers, and social norms (Wu, Pender, & Noureddine, 2003).

Interventions aimed at changing self-efficacy and other social-cognitive variables are effective in changing physical activity and nutrition. In a sample of over 6,000 children and adolescents, self-efficacy and intentions determined healthy food choices, and self-efficacy and perceived social support predicted physical activity three years later (Edmundson et al., 1996). Treatment based on SCT combined with an intervention aimed at increasing motivation predicts self-efficacy levels and fruit and vegetable intake among adolescents (Wilson et al., 2002).

Healthy Lifestyle and Perception of Health

Self-efficacy predicts intentions to engage in a healthy lifestyle. In one sample of adolescents, consistent effects of self-efficacy on intentions were found across behaviors such as nicotine abstinence, fat consumption, and physical exercise (Umeh, 2003). These effects were also significant after controlling for past behavior. Additionally, other cognitions such as perceived severity of disease, perceived vulnerability, or benefits did not produce a consistent effect on intentions to adopt behaviors promoting cardiovascular health.

Perceptions of good health are related moderately to general self-efficacy and weakly to risk-taking behaviors (Honig, 2002). General self-efficacy predicts an index of psychosomatic distress that includes headache, stomachache, backache, dizziness, irritability, and insomnia, especially if teenagers perceived low support from their teachers (Natvig, Albrektsen, Anderssen, & Qvarnstrøm, 1999). Relations between specific symptoms of psychosomatic distress and school-related self-efficacy are also found, particularly in girls. Girls who report increased backaches and an increase in school problems also report low school-related self-efficacy. But not all relations are in line with expectations. In some cases, high school-related self-efficacy is associated with higher levels of complaints (e.g., headaches in girls). However, this may be explained by a mismatch between the self-efficacy and outcome measures. School-related self-efficacy is associated with school achievement rather than with self-reported wellness. Perhaps self-efficacious girls are highly motivated to achieve good grades, and, if their health-related self-efficacy is low, they will not engage in health-enhancing behaviors (e.g., physical activity).

Disease Management

When faced with a chronic disease, individuals should take action (such as taking medication, engaging in daily physical activity) to reduce the effects of the disease on their well-being. Self-efficacy predicts adherence to medication. In one study of adolescents with asthma, social norms, attitudes, and self-efficacy explained 21% of the variance in adherence to medication after a one-year follow-up (Es et al., 2002). In another study of adolescents with tuberculosis, self-efficacy predicted adherence to recommended treatment (Moriski et al., 2001). Youth infected with tuberculosis who participated in a self-efficacy-enhancing intervention acquired higher self-efficacy for medication taking, and self-efficacy for medication-taking was related to the completion of medication.

Self-efficacy predicts adherence to a recommended lifestyle by adolescents with chronic diseases as well as whether youths with trivial, mild, or moderate congenital cardiac malformations will adhere to recommended physical activity (Bar-Mor, Bar-Tal, Krulik, & Zeevi, 2000). In adolescents with chronic arthritis knowledge about the disease, self-efficacy (referring to physical activity and pain management) and social support are among the predictors of disease management (Andre, Hedengren, Hagelberg, & Stenstrom, 1999).

Interventions designed to enhance the self-efficacy of adolescents with type I diabetes mellitus to improve their adherence to a recommended lifestyle are successful in preventing weight gain in girls and improving their metabolic control and overall psychosocial well-being (Grey, Boland, Davidson, Li, & Tamborlane, 2000). Grey et al. (2004) tried to replicate these findings in a group of obese minority adolescents. Compared to control group participants (who took part in an education program on nutrition and physical activity), participants in the intervention group (who additionally received a self-efficacy treatment) demonstrated improved food choices one year later.

Behavior-specific self-efficacy and generalized self-efficacy improve adherence to complex medical recommendations in diabetic patients. Diabetes-related self-efficacy focusing on diet, physical activity, glucose control, and insulin injections is moderately related to general self-efficacy (Griva, Myers, & Newman, 2000). In a sample of diabetic adolescents and young adults, self-reported adherence to diet was correlated with general self-efficacy and with diabetic self-efficacy. However, when an objective measure of adherence to a diabetes regimen was used (levels of glycosylated hemoglobin), it correlated better with diabetes-specific self-efficacy than with general self-efficacy. When age, diabetes duration, and self-reported adherence were controlled, diabetes-related self-efficacy continued to prove a significant predictor of glycosylated hemoglobin levels, whereas general self-efficacy did not.

Self-efficacy may also mediate the influence of parental behaviors on adolescents' disease management. For example, self-efficacy for blood glucose monitoring mediates the influence of parents' support regarding diabetes control on adolescents' adherence to blood glucose monitoring (Ott, Greening, Palardy, Holderby, & DeBell, 2000). Self-efficacious adolescents report higher adherence to the recommendations for diabetic diet, physical activity, insulin injections, and blood glucose monitoring. Among adolescents with trivial, mild, or moderate congenital cardiac malformations, self-efficacy is not only directly related to physical activity but also mediates the attitudes of their parents and the recommendations of their cardiologists (Bar-Mor et al., 2000).

DEVELOPMENTS: GENERAL, BEHAVIOR-SPECIFIC, AND PHASE-SPECIFIC SELF-EFFICACY

Bandura (1997) suggested that self-efficacy assessments should be particularized judgments that carefully correspond to the outcome with which they will be compared. Some researchers have proposed that optimistic self-beliefs may be more generally conceptualized or that they should be tailored to particular stages of behavior change. General optimistic beliefs refer to a global confidence in one's coping ability across a wide range of demanding or novel situations (Schwarzer & Jerusalem, 1995; Sherer et al., 1982). General self-efficacy assesses a broad and stable sense of personal competence to deal effectively with a variety of stressful situations. This approach is not in opposition to Bandura's (1997) suggestion that self-efficacy should be conceptualized in a situation-specific manner. Rather, general self-efficacy can be used to explain a complex set of adherence behaviors (e.g., in diabetes) or the perception of health or various symptoms.

General self-efficacy may be useful in predicting multiple health behaviors (rather than a single behavior). In a study by Luszczynska et al. (2004), general self-efficacy was related to more frequent physical activity in adolescents in Hungary, Poland, Turkey, and the United States. Coefficients were low, ranging from .17 to .18 (n = 539 to 662), and relations were similar across countries. Similar patterns were found for a healthy diet: Adolescents watched their diet more frequently if they had high general self-efficacy. Again, coefficients were low (.09 to .10) and similar across countries. Although these relationships are weak, interventions designed to increase general self-efficacy may influence a wide range of health behaviors such as risk-taking, improvement of life skills, and health perception. Experimental studies are needed to test the benefits of increasing general self-efficacy versus behavior-specific self-efficacy (e.g., fiber intake self-efficacy).

Researchers have also argued that optimistic self-beliefs should be tailored to particular stages of the behavior change process. Endorsing a process approach to behavior change, Marlatt et al. (1995) proposed five categories of self-efficacy. They differentiated the kinds of self-efficacy crucial for primary and secondary prevention, namely resistance self-efficacy and harm-reduction self-efficacy. Action self-efficacy, coping self-efficacy, and recovery self-efficacy were advocated as making a difference in treatment adherence and relapse prevention.

Resistance self-efficacy refers to confidence in one's ability to avoid substance use. This includes resisting peer pressure to smoke, drink, or take drugs. It has repeatedly been found that the combination of peer pressure and low resistance self-efficacy predicts the onset of smoking and substance use in adolescents (Conrad, Flay, & Hill, 1992). Ellickson and Hays (1991) studied the determinants of future substance use of students in Grades 8 and 9. Social influence or exposure to drug users combined with low self-efficacy for drug resistance predicted experimentation with drugs nine months later. Resistance self-efficacy was not predictive for students already involved with drugs. In a study of smoking onset among high school students, resistance self-efficacy moderated the effect of peer pressure (Stacy, Sussman, Dent, Burton, & Flay, 1992). Many adolescents succumb to pro-smoking influences, but those high in resistance self-efficacy are less vulnerable. Interventions can increase smoking-resistance self-efficacy, and these increases lower smoking in students who participate in the interventions (De Vries et al., 2003). Interventions may vary across countries. De Vries et al. found that an intervention aimed at social influence processes and self-efficacy had short-term effects on smoking rates among Finnish and Spanish adolescents but not among youths from the UK and Denmark.

Harm-reduction self-efficacy refers to confidence to reduce known risks after becoming involved with alcohol, tobacco, or illegal drugs. Adolescents recognize that if they become involved in risky behaviors such as smoking, they risk a loss of autonomy (Johnson, Kalaw, Lovato, Baillie, & Chambers, 2004). They attempt to reduce the harm of losing this autonomy by rationing cigarettes or limiting situations for smoking. Once a risk behavior has commenced, the notion of resistance loses its significance, and it becomes more important to control further damage and strengthen the belief that one is capable of minimizing the risk of losing autonomy.

This is particularly useful because many young people experiment with cigarettes and alcohol during puberty, when adolescents face developmental tasks, including self-regulation in tempting situations. Substance use is thus regarded as normative rather than deviant, and it may reflect a healthy exploratory behavior and constructive learning process (Newcomb & Bentler, 1988). The conflict is between solving normative developmental tasks and initiating a risk behavior that may become a daily habit. Adolescents must acquire not only the competence and skills but also the optimistic belief in control of the impending risk.

Resistance self-efficacy and harm-reduction self-efficacy are related to prevention. The process requires self-regulatory skills that enable an individual to deal with barriers specific for initiation, maintenance, and recovery. The distinction proposed by Marlatt et al. (1995) was further developed to specify self-efficacy beliefs typical for a particular stage of health behavior change process (Luszczynska & Schwarzer, 2003; Schwarzer & Renner, 2000). This development refers to stages included in the HAPA (Schwarzer, 2001).

People initiate behavior change when a critical situation arises. For this, they need to believe firmly that they are capable of performing a particular action. *Pre-action self-efficacy* is an optimistic belief through which one develops an intention to change. People high in pre-action self-efficacy imagine success, anticipate potential outcomes of diverse strategies, and are more likely to initiate a new behavior. Pre-action self-efficacy refers to the first phase of a process in which one does not yet act but develops a motivation to do so. Later, a health-related behavior is maintained. *Maintenance self-efficacy* refers to optimistic beliefs about one's capability to deal with barriers that arise during the maintenance period. A new health behavior may turn out to be much more difficult to adhere to than expected, but a self-efficacious person responds confidently with better strategies, more effort, and prolonged persistence to overcome such hurdles. This kind of self-efficacy refers to mobilizing resources to continue with the successful adoption. *Recovery self-efficacy* refers to beliefs in one's ability to get back on track after being derailed and trusting in one's competence to regain control after a setback or failure.

Some studies show that pre-action, maintenance, and recovery self-efficacy act in a phase-specific way. Pre-action self-efficacy predicts intentions and planning, but it does not predict behavior. In a sample of 500 adolescents, pre-action self-efficacy was related to the intention to use a seat belt while driving (Luszczynska, 2004). Optimistic self-beliefs about one's ability to initiate the action were better related to developing plans (measured 6 months later) than was intention. Maintenance self-efficacy predicted precaution behavior, namely seat belt use (measured one month later), and this relation was stronger than the relation between planning and behavior. Additionally, maintenance self-efficacy had an indirect effect on behavior mediated by planning. In a study of youths who smoked and who had experienced a relapse after attempting to quit, recovery self-efficacy predicted the seriousness of the lapse or relapse. Individuals with higher recovery self-efficacy (that is, beliefs about one's ability to resume the action) smoked fewer cigarettes during a relapse episode (Luszczynska, 2004).

Small long-term effects of some self-efficacy interventions (Barnett, O'Loughlin, & Paradis, 2002; Bungum et al., 1999; Grey et al., 2004; Perry et al., 1996; Winkleby et al., 2001) may be due to a mismatch between the wording of the self-efficacy measures or to the self-efficacy beliefs targeted during intervention and the stage within the behavior change process. High self-beliefs about the ability to use condoms properly, which are crucial in the maintenance phase, do not influence the intention to use condoms in the first place (see Christ et al., 1998).

A larger proportion of adolescents than of adults may be in early motivational stages of the health behavior change process rather than later volitional stages. This may be the case for such behaviors as smoking, risky driving, or drug use. Adolescents are also less likely to alter their smoking behavior (Coleman-Wallace et al, 1999). For individuals in the early motivation phase, an intervention should target pre-action self-efficacy, that is, optimistic self-beliefs about their ability to deal with barriers specific to this phase (e.g., how to develop plans and imagine success scenarios about initiating a healthy behavior). Interventions that enhance beliefs about the ability to maintain nicotine abstinence may have only a minor effect if adolescents are still in the initial motivation phase and do not intend to give up smoking at all.

If individuals are in a more advanced stage in the health behavior change process and have already engaged it, interventions should aim at maintenance self-efficacy (similar to "coping self-efficacy"; see Marlatt et al., 1995). For example, if adolescents try to adhere to a healthy diet, an intervention should address their ability to deal with specific barriers that arise during the maintenance phase, such as high-risk situations that impose temptations and may be a trap for relapse. Self-efficacy that refers to the maintenance of physical activity, however, is a poor predictor of the intensity of relapse to a sedentary lifestyle (Barnett et al., 2002). Adolescents who relapse to their old habits (e.g., not using condoms) should be treated in a manner that enhances their beliefs about their ability to regain control after a setback. It may not be sufficient for an intervention to raise optimistic beliefs about being able to maintain condom use. Instead, improved beliefs about the ability to renegotiate condom use may get adolescents who experienced a relapse back on track (recovery self-efficacy).

Future interventions for changing health behaviors and health perceptions should distinguish between three research perspectives. The one employed most often focuses on enhancing behavior-specific self-efficacy but does not take into account the stages within the health behavior change process. The second perspective may focus on general self-efficacy beliefs under the assumption that interventions aimed at more general beliefs will affect a wider range of behaviors and life skills. These, in turn, will generalize to other behaviors. The focus of the third approach could be on the distinct mindsets of those currently in the motivation, volition, or relapse stages. Here, the object would be to enhance the optimistic beliefs that are exclusive to a particular stage. Such a process strategy, as part of a more comprehensive health behavior theory, may increase the likelihood that adolescents will reduce their risk-taking and adhere to a healthier lifestyle.

REFERENCES

Ajzen, I. (1991). The theory of planned behavior. *Organizational Behavior and Human Decision Processes, 50*, 179-211.

Andre, M., Hedengren, E., Hagelberg, S., & Stenstrom, C. H. (1999). Perceived ability to manage juvenile chronic arthritis among adolescents and parents: Development of a questionnaire to assess medical issues, exercise, pain, and social support. *Arthritis Care and Research, 12*, 229-237.

Aung, A. T., Hickman, N. J. 3rd, & Moolchan, E. T. (2003). Health and performance related reasons for wanting to quit: Gender differences among teen smokers. *Substance Use & Misuse, 38*, 1095-1107.

Bandura, A. (1997). *Self-efficacy: The exercise of control.* New York: Freeman.

Baranowski, T., Baranowski, J., Cullen, K. W., Marsh, T., Islam, N., Zakerei, I., et al. (2003). Squire's Quest: Dietary outcome evaluation of a multimedia game. *American Journal of Preventive Medicine, 24*, 52-61.

Bar-Mor, G., Bar-Tal, Y., Krulik, T., & Zeevi, B. (2000). Self-efficacy and physical activity in adolescents with trivial, mild or moderate congenital cardiac malformations. *Cardiology in the Young, 10*, 561-566.

Barnett, T. A., O'Loughlin, J., & Paradis, G. (2002). One- and two-year predictors of decline in physical activity among inner-city schoolchildren. *American Journal of Preventive Medicine, 23*, 121-128.

Brown, B. R., Jr., & Baranowski, M. D. (1996). Searching for the Magic Johnson effect: AIDS, adolescents, and celebrity disclosure. *Adolescence, 31*, 253-264.

Bungum, T., Pate, R., Dowda, M., & Vincent, M. (1999). Correlates of physical activity among African-American and Caucasian female adolescents. *American Journal of Health Behavior, 23*, 25-31.

Butler, R. B., Schultz, J. R., Forsberg, A. D., Brown, L. K., Parsons, J. T., King, G., et al. (2003). Promoting safer sex among HIV-positive youth with hemophilia: Theory, intervention, and outcome. *Haemophilia, 9*, 214-222.

Christ, M. J., Raszka, W. V., Jr., & Dillon, C. A. (1998). Prioritizing education about condom use among sexually active adolescent females. *Adolescence, 132,* 735-744.

Coleman-Wallace, D., Lee, J. W., Montgomery, S., Blix, G., & Wang, D. T. (1999). Evaluation of developmentally appropriate programs for adolescent tobacco cessation. *Journal of School Health, 69,* 314-319.

Colon, R. M., Wiatrek, D. E., & Ewans, R. I. (2000). The relationship between psychosocial factors and condom use among African-American adolescents. *Adolescence, 35,* 559-569.

Conrad, K. M., Flay, B. R., & Hill, D. (1992) Why children start smoking cigarettes: Predictors of onset. *British Journal of Addiction, 87,* 1711-1724.

Coyle, K., Basen-Engquist, K., Kirby, D., Parcel, G., Banspach, S., Harrist, R., et al. (1999). Short-term impact of Safer Choices: A multicomponent, school-based HIV, other STD, and pregnancy prevention program. *Journal of School Health, 69,* 181-188.

Crosby, R., DiClemente, R. J., Wingood, G. M., Sionean, C., Cobb, B. K., Harrington, K., et al. (2001). Correct condom application among African-American adolescent females: The relationship to perceived self-efficacy and the association to confirmed STDs. *Journal of Adolescent Health, 29,* 194-199.

De Vries, H., Mudde, A., Kremers, S., Wetzels, J., Uiters, E., Ariza, C., et al. (2003). The European Smoking Prevention Framework Approach (ESFA): Short-term effects. *Health Education Research, 18,* 649-677.

DeVellis, B. M., & DeVellis, R. F. (2000). Self-efficacy and health. In A. Baum, T. A. Revenson, & J. E. Singer (Eds.), *Handbook of health psychology* (pp. 235-247). Mahwah, NJ: Erlbaum.

Dilorio, C., Dudley, W. N., Kelly, M., Soet, J. E., Mbwara, J., & Sharpe Potter, J. (2001). Social cognitive correlates of sexual experience and condom use among 13- through 15-year-old adolescents. *Journal of Adolescent Health, 29,* 208-216.

Dunn, L., Ross, B., Caines, T., & Howorth, P. (1998). A school-based HIV/AIDS prevention education program: Outcomes of peer-led versus community health nurse-led interventions. *Canadian Journal of Human Sexuality, 7,* 339-345.

Dwyer, J. J., Allison, K. R., & Makin, S. (1998). Internal structure of a measure of self-efficacy in physical activity among high-school students. *Social Science and Medicine, 46,* 1175-1182.

Edmundson, E., Parcel, G. S., Feldman, H. A., Elder, J., Perry, C. L., Johnson, C. C., et al. (1996). The effects of the child and adolescent trial for cardiovascular health upon psychosocial determinants of diet and physical activity behavior. *Preventive Medicine, 25,* 442-454.

Ellickson, P. L., & Hays, R. D. (1991). Beliefs about resistance self-efficacy and drug prevalence: Do they really affect drug use? *International Journal of the Addictions, 25,* 1353-1378.

Es, S. M., Kaptein, A. A., Bezemer, P. D., Nagelkerke, A. F., Colland, V. T., & Bouter, L. M. (2002). Predicting adherence to prophylactic medication in adolescents with asthma: An application of ASE-model. *Patient Education and Counseling, 47,* 165-171.

Grey, M., Berry, D., Davidson, M., Galasso, P., Gustafson, E., & Melkus, G. (2004). Preliminary testing of a program to prevent type 2 diabetes among high-risk youth. *Journal of School Health*, *74*, 10-15.

Grey, M., Boland, E. A., Davidson, M., Li, J., & Tamborlane, W. V. (2000). Coping skills training for youth with diabetes mellitus has long-lasting effects on metabolic control and quality of life. *Journal of Pediatrics*, *137*, 107-113.

Griva, K., Myers, L. B., & Newman, S. (2000). Illness perceptions and self-efficacy beliefs in adolescents and young adults with insulin dependent diabetes mellitus. *Psychology and Health*, *15*, 733-750.

Hancox, R. J., Milne, B. J., & Poulton, R. (2004). Association between child and adolescent television viewing and adult health: A longitudinal birth cohort study. *Lancet*, *364*, 257-262.

Hanson, C., Downing, R. A., Coyle, K. K., & Pederson L. L. (2004). Theory-based determinants of youth smoking: A multiple influence approach. *Journal of Applied Social Psychology*, *34*, 59-84.

Hein, K. (1989). AIDS in adolescence: Exploring the challenge. *Journal of Adolescent Health Care*, *10*, 10-35.

Holschneider, S. O., & Alexander, C. S. (2003). Social and psychological influences on HIV preventive behaviors of youth in Haiti. *Journal of Adolescent Health*, *33*, 31-40.

Honig, J. (2002). Perceived health status in urban minority young adolescents. *The American Journal of Maternal Child Nursing*, *27*, 233-237.

Johnson, J. L., Kalaw, C., Lovato, C. Y., Baillie, L., & Chambers, N. A. (2004). Crossing the line: Adolescents' experiences of controlling their tobacco use. *Qualitative Health Research*, *14*, 1276-1291.

Kalichman, S., Stein, J. A., Malow, R., Averhart, C., Devieux, J., Jennings, T., et al. (2002). Predicting protected sexual behavior using Information-Motivation-Behaviour skills model among adolescent substance abusers in court-ordered treatment. *Psychology, Health, and Medicine*, *7*, 327-338.

Li, C., Pentz, M. A., & Chou, C.-P. (2002). Parental substance use as a modifier of adolescent substance use risk. *Addiction*, *97*, 1537-1550.

Longmore, M. A., Manning, W. D., Giordano, P. C., & Rudolph, J. L. (2003). Contraceptive self-efficacy: Does it influence adolescents' contraceptive use. *Journal of Health and Social Behavior*, *44*, 45-60.

Luszczynska, A. (2004). *Effects of phase-specific self-efficacy on initiation and maintenance of health behavior, and intensity of relapse*. Manuscript submitted for publication.

Luszczynska, A., Gibbons, F. X., Piko, B., & Tekozel, M. (2004). Self-regulatory cognitions, social comparison, and perceived peers' behaviors as predictors of nutrition and physical activity: A comparison among adolescents in Hungary, Poland, Turkey, and USA. *Psychology and Health*, *19*, 577-593.

Luszczynska, A., & Schwarzer, R. (2003). Planning and self-efficacy in the adoption and maintenance of breast self-examination: A longitudinal study on self-regulatory cognitions. *Psychology and Health*, *18*, 93-108.

Marlatt, G. A., Baer, J. S., & Quigley, L. A. (1995). Self-efficacy and addictive behavior. In A. Bandura (Ed.), *Self-efficacy in changing societies* (pp. 289-315). New York: Cambridge University Press.

Morisky, D. E., Malotte, C. K., Ebin, V., Davidson, P., Cabrera, D., Trout, P. T., et al. (2001). Behavioral interventions for the control of tuberculosis among adolescents. *Public Health Reports, 116*, 568-574.

Motl, R. W., Dishman, R. K., Saunders, R. P., Dowda, M., Felton, G., Ward, D. S., et al. (2002). Examining social-cognitive determinants of intention and physical activity among black and white adolescent girls using structural equation modeling. *Health Psychology, 21*, 459-467.

Nahas, M. V., Goldfine, B., & Collins, M. A. (2003). Determinants of physical activity and young adults: The basis for high school and college physical education to promote active lifestyles. *Physical Educator, 60*, 42-56.

Natvig, G. K., Albrektsen, G., Anderssen, N., & Qvarnstrøm, U. (1999). School-related stress and psychosomatic symptoms among school adolescents. *Journal of School Health, 69*, 362-368.

Newcomb, M. D., & Bentler, P. M. (1988). *Consequence of adolescent drug use: Impact on the lives of young adults.* Beverly Hills, CA: Sage.

Ott, J., Greening, L., Palardy, N., Holderby, A., & DeBell, W. K. (2000). Self-efficacy as a mediator variable for adolescents' adherence to treatment for insulin-dependent diabetes mellitus. *Children's Health Care, 29*, 47-63.

Perry, C. L., Williams, C. L., Veblen-Mortenson, S., Toomey, T. L., Komro, K. A., Anstine, P. S., et al. (1996). Project Northland: Outcomes of a community-wide alcohol use prevention program during early adolescence. *American Journal of Public Health, 86*, 956-965.

Prochaska, J. O., DiClemente, C. C., & Norcross, J. C. (1992). In search of how people change: Applications to addictive behaviors. *American Psychologist, 47*, 1102-1114.

Pronk, N. P., Anderson, L. H., Crain, A. L., Martinson, B. C., O'Connor, P. J., Sherwood, N. E., et al. (2004). Meeting recommendations for multiple healthy lifestyle factors: Prevalence, clustering, and predictors among adolescent, adult and senior health plan members. *American Journal of Preventive Medicine, 27*, 25-33.

Rosario, M., Mahler, K., Hunter, J., & Gwadz, M. (1999). Understanding the unprotected sexual behaviors of gay, lesbian, and bisexual youths: An empirical test of the Cognitive-Environmental Model. *Health Psychology, 18*, 272-280.

Sallis, J. F., & Owen, N. (1999). *Physical activity and behavioral medicine.* Thousand Oaks, CA: Sage.

Schwarzer, R. (2001). Social-cognitive factors in changing health-related behavior. *Current Directions in Psychological Science, 10*, 47-51.

Schwarzer, R., & Jerusalem, M. (1995). Generalized Self-Efficacy scale. In J. Weinman, S. Wright, & M. Johnston (Eds.), *Measures in health psychology: A user's portfolio. Causal and control beliefs* (pp. 35-37). Windsor, England: NFER-NELSON.

Schwarzer, R., & Renner, B. (2000). Social-cognitive predictors of health behavior: Action self-efficacy and coping self-efficacy. *Health Psychology, 19*, 487-495.

Sherer, M., Maddux, J. E., Mercandante, B., Prentice-Dunn, S., Jacobs, B., & Rogers, R. W. (1982). The Self-Efficacy Scale: Construction and validation. *Psychological Reports, 51*, 663-671.

Siegel, D. M., Aten, M. J., & Enaharo, M. (2001). Long-term effects of a middle school- and high school-based human immunodeficiency virus sexual risk prevention intervention. *Archives of Pediatrics and Adolescent Medicine*, *155*, 1117-1126.

Siegel, D. M., Klein, D. I., & Roghmann, K. J. (1999). Sexual behavior, contraception, and risk among college students. *Journal of Adolescent Health*, *25*, 336-343.

Stacy, A. W., Sussman, S., Dent, C. W., Burton, D., & Flay, B. R. (1992). Moderators of peer social influence in adolescent smoking. *Personality and Social Psychology Bulletin*, *18*, 163-172.

Strauss, R. S., Rodzilsky, D., Burack, G., & Colin, M. (2001). Psychosocial correlates of physical activity in healthy children. *Archives of Paediatrics and Adolescent Medicine*, *155*, 897-902.

Trost, S. G., Pate, R. R., Ward, D. S., Saunders, R., & Riner, W. (1999). Determinants of physical activity in active and low-active, sixth-grade African American youth. *Journal of School Health*, *69*, 29-34.

Trost, S. G., Sallis, J. F., Pate, R. R., Freedson, P. S., Taylor, W. C., & Dowda, M. (2003). Evaluating a model of parental influence on youth physical activity. *American Journal of Preventive Medicine*, *25*, 277-282.

Umeh, K. (2003). Social cognitions and past behavior as predictors of behavioral intentions related to cardiovascular health. *Journal of Applied Social Psychology*, *33*, 1417-1436.

Unger, J. B., Rohrbach, L. A., Howard, K. A., Boley Cruz, T., Anderson Johnson, C., & Chen, X. (1999). Attitudes toward anti-tobacco policy among California youth: Associations with smoking status, psychosocial variables, and advocacy actions. *Health Education Research*, *14*, 751-763.

Wang, R.-H., Wang, H.-H., & Hsu, M.-T. (2003). Factors associated with adolescent pregnancy: A sample of Taiwanese female adolescents. *Public Health Nursing*, *20*, 33-41.

Wills, T. A., Resko, J. A., Ainette, M. G., & Mendoza, D. (2004). Smoking onset in adolescence: A person-centered analysis with time-varying predictors. *Health Psychology*, *23*, 158-167.

Wilson, D. K., Friend, R., Teasley, N., Green, S., Reaves, I. L., & Sica, D.A. (2002). Motivational versus social cognitive interventions for promoting fruit and vegetable intake and physical activity in African American adolescents. *Annals of Behavioral Medicine*, *24*, 310-319.

Winkleby, M. A., Feighery, E. C., Altman, D. A., Kole, S., & Tencati, E. (2001). Engaging ethnically diverse teens in a substance use prevention advocacy program. *American Journal of Health Promotion*, *15*, 433-436.

Wu, S. Y., Pender, N., & Noureddine, S. (2003). Gender differences in the psychosocial cognitive correlates of physical activity among Taiwanese adolescents: A structural equation modeling approach. *International Journal of Behavioral Medicine*, *10*, 93-105.

Zapata, L. B., Forthofer, M. S., Eaton, D. K., McCormack Brown, K., Bryant, C. A., Reynolds, S. T., et al. (2004). Cigarette use in 6th through 10th grade: The Sarasota county demonstration project. *American Journal of Health Behavior*, *28*, 151-165.

CHAPTER 7

SELF-EFFICACY AND ADOLESCENTS IN SPORT AND PHYSICAL ACTIVITY

Deborah L. Feltz and T. Michelle Magyar

Physical activity and participation in sport expose young people to situations that create optimal challenges, moments of uncertainty, or even great frustration and disappointment. What distinguishes sport and physical activity from other achievement domains is that the learning and performance of a skill is physical, and, thus, performance markers are observable to others. In addition, in competitive sport, performance markers are also often normative. For example, how well one performs in a tennis match is understood in relation to the opponent's performance. With physical ability and the consequences of competition readily on display, the likelihood of adolescents continuing their involvement and enjoyment highly depends on how they navigate the highs and lows of these sport and physical activity experiences.

One belief central to navigating positive and negative experiences in sport and physical activity is *self-efficacy*, which is the belief in one's capabilities to learn or perform motor skills and/or sport tasks to obtain a certain outcome. In this chapter, we review the literature that examines self-efficacy in youth sport and physical activity, and we provide recommenda-

Self-Efficacy Beliefs of Adolescentss, 161–179

tions for future research. We define youth sport as adult organized sports programs for children and youth, typically between the ages of 7 and 18 years, which have designated coaches, organized practices, and scheduled competitions (Gould, 1982). Physical activity is typically a more inclusive term and includes any bodily movement that is produced by the contracting of skeletal muscle and that substantially increases energy expenditure (Bouchard, Shepard, Stephens, Sutton, & McPerson, 1990). This can include exercise, dance, or physical leisure-time activities.

SELF-EFFICACY RESEARCH CONDUCTED WITH YOUTH AND ADOLESCENTS IN SPORT AND PHYSICAL ACTIVITY

Self-efficacy beliefs are an important aspect of motivation in youth sport and physical activity because they influence task choice, effort, persistence, and resilience (Bandura, 1990; Feltz, 1994; Schunk, 1995). When compared to participants who doubt their motor skill and sport capabilities, those who feel efficacious about learning and/or performing a motor skill are more likely to attempt that skill, exert more effort, persist longer when faced with difficulties, and achieve higher levels of performance (Chase, 2001; Feltz & Lirgg, 2001; George, 1994). Given the recent trend of inactivity in adolescents, the ability to develop and sustain motivation in sport and physical activity is of critical importance to keep adolescents engaged and on the pathway to adopting physically healthy lifestyles.

Self-Efficacy as a Predictor of Performance

A number of researchers have reported that self-efficacy predicts athletic performance, assessed either as single competition performance scores or average performance scores across multiple trials (Martin & Gill, 1995; Treasure, Monson, & Lox, 1996; Weiss, Wiese, & Klint, 1989). We should note that, in competitive contexts, self-efficacy is often based on normative criteria and does not have to be based solely on a mastery-oriented criterion of performance. As Bandura (1997) observed, "It is difficult to perform well while wrestling with self-doubts about one's comparative ability. This is most evident when players have the necessary skills but lack the perceived efficacy to beat higher ranking opponents" (p. 385). Feltz and Chase (1998) have labeled this "competitive" or "comparative" self-efficacy. The research conducted in this context has included a range of competitive activities such as gymnastics, distance running, and wrestling. This research has demonstrated that, as athletes become more confident in their ability to perform successfully and best their opponents, their subsequent performance is also enhanced. More importantly, self-efficacy differs from other psychological constructs proposed to significantly influence athletic performance (e.g., anxiety) and has emerged as the strongest predictor of performance.

When other variables better predict athletic performance than self-efficacy, this is largely due to methodological and/or measurement errors (Feltz & Chase, 1998). For example, research on female youth gymnasts revealed that past performances in training were stronger predictors of competitive gymnastic performance than were the gymnasts' self-efficacy (Lee, 1986). The youth and inexperience of the participants, as well as the two weeks allotted between self-efficacy assessment and actual performance may have worked to minimize the effects of self-efficacy (Feltz & Lirgg, 2001). Kane, Marks, Zaccaro, and Blair (1996) found that the self-efficacy of high school wrestlers did not directly influence overall tournament performance. This was likely due to the poor correspondence between the self-efficacy and tournament performance measures used. Athletes were asked to report their confidence specific to wrestling moves (e.g., performing and/or defending takedowns) to determine if these beliefs predicted their camp performance (number of matches won divided by total number of matches). Methodological and measurement limitations in these studies likely contributed to self-efficacy failing to emerge as the strongest predictor of performance.

Few research studies have investigated whether self-efficacy predicts initiation of or adherence to physical activity in adolescents. Most research in this area has been conducted in asymptomatic and diseased adult populations (e.g., McAuley, Pena, & Jerome, 2001). Consistent with the sport performance literature, research on adult populations has demonstrated that efficacy beliefs are strong predictors of exercise participation, especially in the initial stages of exercise adoption (McAuley, 1992) and for long-term maintenance of physical activity (McAuley, Lox, & Duncan, 1993).

Of the studies that have been conducted on adolescents, efficacy beliefs have been shown to significantly predict the adoption of, adherence to, and performance of exercise-related activities (Bungum, Pate, Dowda, & Vincent, 1999; Dwyer, Allison, & Makin, 1998; Reynolds et al., 1990). Allison, Dwyer, and Makin (1999) examined the relationship between self-efficacy and physical education, school-based sports, and community/club-based recreation or sports among high school students. They reported that self-efficacy based on overcoming external barriers (e.g., confidence to participate in vigorous physical activity if there was lack of support from family) predicted vigorous physical activity in sports and recreation settings over a number of other competing demands on time, such as homework, part-time work, and TV watching.

Bungum et al. (1999) found that self-efficacy and school sport participation predicted physical activity among African American and Caucasian female adolescents. As the authors noted, the competitive aspects of sport limits the potential to increase physical activity for large numbers of adolescents. Recreational sports such as inline skating, tennis, bicycling, or intramural sports that are more participation oriented may provide better opportunities for a greater number of adolescents to be active while building their sense of mastery and enjoyment.

Antecedents of Self-Efficacy Beliefs in Sport and Physical Activity

Sport and exercise psychology researchers contend that understanding the sources of self-efficacy is essential to understanding how individuals develop and sustain their efficacy beliefs over time and in different competitive situations (Feltz, 1994; Vealey, 2001). Bandura (1997) proposed that people obtain information about their self-efficacy for sport and physical activity primarily from their performance accomplishments, followed by their vicarious experiences, the persuasions they receive from others, and their physiological states. Maddux (1995) suggested that participants also receive self-efficacy information from their imaginal states (e.g., the use of mental imagery and picturing the performance of a skill).

Perceptions of successful mastery enhance self-efficacy in sport, whereas repetitive failure lowers it (Chase, 1998; Kane et al., 1996; Lee, 1986; Magyar & Feltz, 2003). By examining the influence of prior mastery experiences on self-efficacy across multiple performance trials, sport researchers have tracked the recursive pattern of the mastery/self-efficacy relationship (Feltz, 1982; George, 1994). Watkins et al. (1994) examined the relationship between self-efficacy and baseball hitting across four trials and reported that past performance was a better predictor of hitting than was self-efficacy. Feltz and Lirgg (2001) explained that previous hitting likely emerged as the stronger predictor of subsequent hitting because athletes were performing in invariant conditions (e.g., hitting controlled pitches from a machine). In unrealistic performance conditions, the predictive utility of past performance is inflated and supersedes the influence of self-efficacy (Bandura, 1997).

George (1994) tracked the relationship between self-efficacy and baseball hitting across nine competitive summer league games and found that self-efficacy was a stronger predictor than was past performance. Instead of hitting against a machine, the players hit against a live pitcher in each game and different pitchers across games. Given the uncertainty of live competition, athletic performance can be difficult to predict. For example, a baseball hitter may report high self-efficacy before hitting, but this self-efficacy may be nonsignificant due to factors beyond one's control (e.g., bad weather, an umpire's decision, or injury) that negatively affect performance and have little to do with self-efficacy.

The strength of past performance accomplishments as predictors of self-efficacy also depends on athletes' perceptions of task difficulty. By modifying basketball equipment, Chase, Ewing, Lirgg, and George (1994) minimized task difficulty in basketball shooting. Children made more baskets and had higher self-efficacy on an 8-foot high basket than on a 10-foot high one. This suggests that minimizing task difficulty and facilitating mastery experiences through equipment modification that is developmentally appropriate may foster performance, which in turn enhances beliefs about one's capabilities.

Despite minimizing task difficulty, Chase et al. (1994) revealed a discrepancy between athletes' self-efficacy and performance. Pre-performance self-efficacy had a lower correlation with shooting than did shooting with post-performance self-efficacy. Self-efficacy assessed just prior to performing was not a strong predictor of performance, but efficacy beliefs were raised as a consequence of participation. The authors tracked this relationship across four trials and noted that efficacy beliefs remained high despite performance being relatively low. Schunk (1995) argued that it is not uncommon for children to report high self-efficacy that is disproportional to performance outcome even when feedback indicates low performance. He proposed that discrepancies between self-efficacy and performance may be attributed to many things, including ambiguous task factors and insufficient knowledge about task requirements and performance capability. Chase et al. observed that it was possible that the children's inaccuracy stemmed from the use of additional sources to judge personal capability, such as focusing on the qualitative form of technique than on the outcome score and relying on other performance indicators (e.g., peer comparison or adult feedback).

Sport and physical activity researchers have also examined the influence of vicarious sources of information on the self-efficacy of youth performers. Individuals may observe significant others, older athletes, or peers modeling performances and may use this information to make judgments and evaluate the consequences of their own performance (Chase, 1998; Feltz, 1994; Magyar & Feltz, 2003). For example, novice performers may observe expert performers to learn how to execute a certain skill, whereas elite performers may rely on vicarious information to obtain specific details that can be used to improve technique and/or master a particularly difficult skill (Feltz, 1994; Schunk, 1995).

Weiss, McCullagh, Smith, and Berlant (1998) investigated the extent to which visual demonstrations help children overcome the fearful motor task of learning how to swim. Children were randomly assigned to one of three conditions: no model, peer-mastery model, and peer-coping model. The peer-mastery model demonstrated confidence and successful completion of the swimming skills, whereas the peer-coping model initially demonstrated low confidence and failure but gradually progressed to enhanced confidence and successful completion of the swimming task. Participants from both model groups demonstrated stronger swimming skills and reported higher self-efficacy than did the control group, with the coping-model group reporting higher self-efficacy than did the mastery-model group.

Information from verbal feedback, expectations of others, and self-talk represent persuasive sources of self-efficacy. Aside from assessing their own performance experiences, young athletes rely on verbal praise, encouragement, and support from significant others such as parents and coaches to build their confidence in sport (Chase, 1998; Magyar & Feltz, 2003). Coaches have ranked verbal persuasion as one of the most effective techniques for increasing the efficacy beliefs of young athletes (Weinberg & Jackson, 1990). Chase (1998) also noted that younger athletes may enhance their beliefs in their ability through self-talk.

Vargas-Tonsing (2004) found that youth soccer coaches' pre-game speeches significantly increased self-efficacy about the impending game in athletes who perceived the speech as informational and strategic. The perceived emotional content of the speeches was not related to post-speech perceptions of efficacy. Thus, a coach's persuasive attempts to heighten a team's ability have a more potent effect on players' self-efficacy than do attempts to heighten a team's emotional arousal.

Coaches' expectations of their athletes and corresponding feedback also convey subtle efficacy messages. Horn (1985) found that middle school coaches gave low-expectancy athletes more praise for mediocre performances and ignored their mistakes more. They gave their high-expectancy athletes more criticism and corrective instruction in response to skill errors. Low-expectancy athletes interpreted their coach's feedback as conveying a message of low ability, whereas high-expectancy athletes interpreted it as conveying higher expectations.

Self-efficacy information also emanates from a performer's physiological state. Bandura (1997) joined physiological and affective/emotional states because they both have a physiological basis, but Feltz, Short, and Sullivan (2005) separated them because they relate to different aspects of performance in sport. Physiological information in sport includes one's fitness level, fatigue, and pain. This has been shown to be a more important source of efficacy information in sport and physical activity tasks than in nonphysical tasks (Chase, Feltz, & Lirgg, 2003). Young athletes with less training may dwell more on their physical discomforts and interpret these signals as indicative of lower capability rather than as part of physical performance, especially in strength and endurance activities.

In addition to physiological status, autonomic arousal associated with fear and self-doubt or with being psyched-up and ready for performance may also influence motor skill activities (Bandura, 1997; Feltz & Lirgg, 2001; Maddux, 1995). For example, Treasure, Monson, and Lox (1996) found significant negative relationships between self-efficacy and both state anxiety and negative affect. Positive affect positively correlated with self-efficacy. Thus, anxious and pessimistic athletes were not as confident in their abilities to compete successfully. What is also interesting about these findings was that positive affect made a small but significant contribution to competitive wrestling performance, whereas anxiety did not. Furthermore, Chase (1998) found that children rely on positive affect or "liking" the sport or physical activity as a meaningful source of confidence.

Performers also appraise their capabilities through their imaginal experiences. Positive imagery is a common psychological technique used by athletes to prepare for competition and to enhance efficacy beliefs. Garza and Feltz (1998) examined the effects of imaginal experiences by comparing two mental practice techniques to enhance self-efficacy, competition confidence, and performance ratings of competitive figure skaters. Junior figure skaters were randomly assigned to one of two 4-week mental practice interventions (drawing one's freestyle routine on paper or walking through one's routine on the floor) or a stretching control group. On completion of the intervention training, the skaters competed in their club's annual competition. Both mental practice groups demonstrated significant improvement in performance ratings and competition confidence compared to the stretching control group. Self-efficacy judgments improved in all groups, but the walk-through intervention group yielded greater improvements in spin self-efficacy compared to the other two groups.

MODERATORS OF THE SELF-EFFICACY AND PERFORMANCE RELATIONSHIP

Researchers have considered the influence of individual difference variables such as gender as a critical factor in self-efficacy in sport and physical activity. Researchers who investigated gender differences in children's self-efficacy/confidence about performing motor skills offer inconsistent results (Corbin, Landers, Feltz, & Senior, 1983; Lewko & Ewing, 1980). Lirgg (1991) attributed gender differences to the type of task. She explained that studies incorporating masculine motor tasks may have increased the chances of boys reporting higher confidence. She also noted that boys and girls in elementary school had similar confidence in motor tasks. By high school, however, boys reported higher confidence for most motor tasks.

Self-Efficacy Beliefs as a Predictor of Achievement-Related Beliefs

With the growing concern about childhood obesity and the declining levels of physical activity during adolescence, there is a developing interest in the motivational implications of youth sport and physical activity. Although the literature is not fully developed, researchers are beginning to identify factors that will enhance motivation and adherence to a physically active lifestyle. Given the evidence for the effectiveness of self-efficacy as an influential psychological mechanism in adults, researchers have naturally turned their attention to self-efficacy in predicting other achievement-related beliefs, such as the attributions that adolescents make following failure and the motivational intentions to exercise that they possess (Chase, 2001; Feltz, 1994; Hagger, Chatzisarantis, & Biddle, 2001; Umeh, 2003).

Chase (2001) examined how individual differences in self-efficacy, age, and gender influence motivational intentions, future self-efficacy, and attributions following perceptions of failure. Specifically, children with higher self-efficacy chose to participate at a higher rate, reported higher future self-efficacy, and attributed failure to lack of effort rather than to ability when compared to children with lower self-efficacy. There were no gender differences in attributions, efficacy beliefs, or motivational intentions in response to the failure scenario.

Self-efficacy beliefs also function as a significant determinant of intentions to engage in physical activity, even after controlling for past behavior (Umeh, 2003). For example, Hagger et al. (2001) found that adolescents' self-efficacy to overcome barriers to physical activity (e.g., "going out with friends") was the strongest predictor of intentions to be physically active. Thus, it may be that when young people feel confident in their ability to participate in a given activity in the face of barriers, they are more likely to engage in that activity.

CURRENT TRENDS IN YOUTH SPORT AND PHYSICAL ACTIVITY RESEARCH

In her initial reviews of the sport and exercise self-efficacy literature, Feltz (1988, 1994) identified areas for additional research. She recommended that future researchers consider (a) the emotional aspects of performance and resiliency of efficacy beliefs, (b) the appraisal process of multidimensional self-efficacy over time and in different situations, and (c) the comprehensive examination of collective efficacy in teams. This section outlines current efforts to address these calls for research.

Specific to the emotional aspects of sport performance and the resiliency of efficacy beliefs, the role of self-efficacy in overcoming the fear of (re)injury in youth sport has been examined (Chase, Magyar, & Drake, in press). A qualitative examination of female gymnasts revealed that, for this particular sample, athletes were most fearful of injuries because of the difficulty in returning to full participation and being unable to participate in practices and competitions (e.g., time away results in loss of conditioning/technique). The gymnasts discussed the importance of performance experiences—in particular, graded mastery that is facilitated by the coach—in addition to communication with significant others, such as parents and teammates, as the two primary sources of self-efficacy information important to overcoming the fear of being (re)injured. Other sources of self-efficacy that diminish fears of (re)injury were self-awareness (feeling mentally and physically strong), physical and mental preparation (the use of mental imagery), and social comparison (observing peer models). Current findings illustrate how the sources of self-efficacy can function as a resilient cognitive buffer in fearful situations and assist the athlete in eventually overcoming injury-related fears altogether.

Other researchers (Chase, Vealey, & Magyar, 2004; Magyar, Chase, Vealey, & Gano-Overway, 2004; Vealey, Chase, & Magyar, 2004) have addressed Feltz's (1994) call for research by providing a mixed-method approach to the study of how athletes process multidimensional efficacy information over time and in different situations. Developmental differences in processing sources of sport confidence have been tracked in youth, high school, and college female softball players over the course of a competitive softball season. The athletes completed the Sources of Sport Confidence Questionnaire (SSCQ; Vealey, Hayashi, Garner-Holman, & Giacobbi, 1998) at the beginning, middle, and end of the season (Chase et al., 2004). The SSCQ measures sources of self-efficacy that reflect achievement (mastery and demonstration of ability), self-regulation (physical/mental preparation and physical self-presentation), and social climate (social support, vicarious experience, coach's leadership, environmental comfort, and situational favorableness).

Mastery emerged as the most consistent predictor of overall sport confidence across the season for youth athletes. For high school athletes, mental/physical preparation emerged as the strongest predictor of confidence; vicarious experience also predicted confidence at the end of the season. Mastery and vicarious experience predicted the confidence of college athletes at the beginning of the season, mental/physical preparation predicted confidence at the middle, and preparation and demonstration of ability predicted confidence at the end.

Following the quantitative phase of the study, the researchers used qualitative interviews to provide a more in-depth account of the weighting process. There were important consistencies across the mixed methods (Magyar, Chase, et al., 2004). The athletes provided a retrospective account of the reasons why they felt confident in softball, and how (and why) they changed, combined, and weighed their sources of confidence over the course of the season. Youth athletes targeted practice effort and peer approval, high school athletes emphasized practice performance and social support, and college athletes focused on mental skills training and preparation, performance experience, and support from others as critical sources of confidence. All participants mentioned the significance of "social" sources of information as meaningful and more salient to confidence later in the season.

This line of research revealed cross-sectional differences that reflect important and consistent developmental differences (Horn, 2004). Age-related changes from late childhood to adolescence reflect changes in cognitive abilities in addition to changes in the social environment. Athletes in late childhood begin to learn how to differentiate and integrate the various sources of information. Peer comparison and evaluative feedback from peers and coaches increases in importance as the child approaches adolescence, whereas feedback from parents declines in importance. By adolescence, however, athletes can fully differentiate task difficulty, effort, and ability and through this differentiation, rely on a greater number of sources than they could during late childhood. These athletes begin to use more sophisticated cognitive and internal information that is more psychologically based. Horn (2004) also described how peer comparisons become more advanced through the distinction of "near" peers such as teammates, versus "extended" peers or opponents. There is also greater differentiation in using peers as a source of information. Peers can provide evaluative information for personal mastery or comparison information to gauge their personal ability. As athletes' cognitive abilities mature, they differentiate sources of information and integrate sources, weighting and combining multiple sources simultaneously. Parallel to this cognitive maturation, athletes become more motorically advanced through growth and experience. With an increase in physical skill, athletes broaden their repertoire or awareness of the various sources of information available to them.

Bandura (1997) noted that mastery experiences increase self-efficacy, but he also acknowledged that there are individual differences in definitions of successful mastery. Because of these differences, he considered conceptions of ability and perceptions of controllability to be meaningful determinants of efficacy judgments. Developmental researchers in the cognitive and physical domains, however, note that children under age 12 may not be able to differentiate between effort, ability, and luck (Fry, 2000; Fry & Duda, 1997). Therefore, changes in appraisal and accuracy of efficacy beliefs may parallel changes in conceptions of ability and in the development of children's capacity to differentiate between ability and effort as they grow older. As a consequence of this change, there are individual differences in the use of subjective versus normative criteria to define ability and success (Ames, 1992; Bandura, 1997; Horn, 2004; Nicholls, 1992). Youth sport researchers support this contention, as athletes of all ages cite past performance accomplishments as an important source of self-efficacy information. How they define successful performance accomplishments, however, varies by age (Chase, 1998; Chase et al., 2004; Magyar, Chase, et al., 2004).

Contemporary sport self-efficacy researchers integrate the social cognitive theories of achievement goals (Ames, 1992; Nicholls, 1984) and self-efficacy/confidence in sport (Bandura, 1997; Vealey, 2001) to understand how individual differences in achievement goals, or definitions of success and ability, may influence the cognitive appraisal of self-efficacy/confidence information. Previous sport studies demonstrated a relationship between athletes' competitive orientations (e.g., desire to win/perform better than others or to perform well relative to one's own standard) and efficacy expectations (e.g., Martin & Gill, 1995), but these studies did not adopt the developmental framework of achievement goal theory.

According to achievement goal theory, there are two major goal perspectives: self-referenced task (also known as learning or mastery) and norm-referenced ego (also known as ability or performance). Task goals represent a focus on learning, trying hard, improving, and mastering the task in developing ability. Such goals can yield adaptive achievement patterns such as choosing a task that is challenging, exerting maximal effort, and persisting when faced with difficulty. In contrast, ego goals reflect the desire to demonstrate one's superior ability via social comparison, and, when combined with perceptions of low ability, there is a potential for maladaptive behaviors such as choosing tasks that are too easy or too hard, not trying as hard as possible, and dropping out.

Achievement goal theory provides the framework from which to study variations in goal perspectives at the individual level, through personal goal orientations, and at the situational level, through perceptions of the motivational climate. Personal goal orientations represent the way an athlete evaluates personal ability and success in athletic performance. Motivational climate, on the other hand, reflects the athlete's perceptions of the goal structure, or the messages in the environment that are created by members of the team that make certain goals salient. For example, a coach may create a climate that is task-involving (i.e., "On this team, the coach makes sure everyone has a role on the team") or ego-involving (i.e., "On this team, only the best athletes get noticed by the coach").

By merging the achievement goal and self-efficacy/confidence conceptual viewpoints, sport researchers can simultaneously examine the independent effects of task and ego goal perspectives and how they differentially influence self-efficacy appraisal in athletes and teams. Therefore, both at the individual level of the athlete and at the group level of the team, task goal perspectives should align with self-referenced mastery sources of self-efficacy, whereas ego goal perspectives should link to norm-referenced sources.

Magyar and Feltz (2003) examined the relationship between goal orientations, perceptions of the motivational climate, and sources of sport confidence in competitive adolescent female volleyball players. Task orientation was positively related to adaptive sources (mastery, mental/physical preparation, and vicarious experience) and to coach's leadership and social support sources of confidence. In contrast, ego orientation positively correlated with more maladaptive sources (demonstration of ability, physical self-presentation, and situational favorableness). Perceptions of a task-involving climate positively correlated with mastery, coach's leadership, and social support sources, whereas perceptions of an ego-involving climate negatively related to the coach's leadership sources of sport confidence. These findings demonstrate how individual differences in the emphasis of sport confidence sources relate to how one defines and perceives success and mastery in a sport setting.

Another notable contribution of this research is that motivational climate mediated the relationship between goal orientations and appraisal of sport confidence sources (Magyar & Feltz, 2003). In particular, perceptions of the motivational climate mediated the influence on the coach's leadership and social support sources. The more task-oriented athletes perceived a task-involved climate, which influenced their selection of coach's leadership as a source of confidence; ego-oriented athletes perceived an ego-involved climate, which negatively influenced their consideration of this source. Perceptions of a task-involving climate also partially mediated the influence of task orientation on the social support source. These findings suggest that selecting and weighting "social" sources of sport confidence is not just a function of goal orientation but is also indirectly influenced by the motivational climate of the sport setting.

Feltz (1994) also recommended that researchers adopt a comprehensive approach to the study of the cognitive appraisal of potential self-efficacy determinants that occur at both the personal self-efficacy level and at the collective efficacy level. The simultaneous consideration of both individual- and group-level efficacy beliefs requires the application of multilevel modeling to account for data that are hierarchically nested (e.g., athletes grouped within teams).

To date, there is only one published research study that examines collective efficacy in youth and adolescent sport. Magyar, Feltz, and Simpson (2004) integrated achievement goal theory with self-efficacy to examine individual and group (boat) level determinants of collective efficacy in rowing. Just before their regional championship regatta, adolescent competitive rowers' goal orientations, perceptions of the motivational climate, task self-efficacy, and collective efficacy beliefs were assessed. Results demonstrated that self-efficacy in individual rowing ability positively predicted individual perceptions of collective efficacy. However, when individual perceptions of collective efficacy were averaged by boat, perceptions of a task-involving motivational climate emerged as a significant positive predictor of collective efficacy. Although task orientation demonstrated a positive relationship with individual perceptions of collective efficacy, this relationship was not significant when task self-efficacy was also considered. Therefore, individual perceptions of capability significantly influence individual perceptions of group ability, but it is the coaches who create a task-involving climate that underpins the performance emphasis inherent to sport that stand a better chance of maximizing the motivation of athletes at the group level.

FUTURE DIRECTIONS FOR RESEARCH

Research on efficacy beliefs in youth sport and physical activity is still in the early stages of development, but much progress has been made. Current contributions illustrate the complexities and developmental nature of self-efficacy sources salient to youth performers in a variety of achievement settings. Furthermore, sport and exercise researchers have set the agenda for future self-efficacy researchers to continue to augment the current body of knowledge in important and meaningful ways. In the following section, we delineate future research directions.

One primary direction for future research would be to focus on Vealey's (2001) social cognitive model of sport confidence. Findings would establish the external validity of the Sport Confidence Model and determine if current findings on sport confidence generalize across gender, sport type, and level of athlete. Additional research on the multidimensional nature of self-efficacy/confidence sources of information in the youth physical activity setting will provide a fruitful extension of the current self-efficacy literature.

One conceivable way to examine the appraisal of self-efficacy information is through the integration of achievement goal and self-efficacy theories. This integrative approach should help clarify how adolescents appraise efficacy-related information with regard to their exercise ability. Previous research has identified a promising link between achievement goal constructs and physically active lifestyles. Specifically, task goal orientation and mastery motivational climate have been found positively correlated with moderate to vigorous physical activity (Dempsey, Kimiecik, & Horn, 1993) and self-reported intentions to exercise (Biddle & Goudas, 1996) in adolescents. Furthermore, links between achievement goals and exercise self-efficacy of young adults suggest that high task orientation is related to greater task and coping self-efficacy beliefs in the exercise setting (Cumming & Hall, 2004). Additional research to determine whether similar motivational patterns emerge during adolescence will advance the understanding of how to structure the physical activity setting to best maximize motivation.

Additional research is needed on the resilience of self-efficacy beliefs and self-efficacy restoration that coincides with developmental transitions observed during adolescence. Bandura (1990) suggested that young performers must have a resilient sense of self-efficacy to sustain persistent effort in the face of failure, pain, fatigue, competitive pressure, or injury. Experiences with performance slumps and temporary injuries represent important developmental periods of growth that youth and adolescents must encounter in sport and physical activity. During these difficult times, self-efficacious individuals will not ruminate or allow distracting thoughts to interfere with their ever-persistent sense of knowing that they are capable no matter what the circumstances. More research on resilient self-efficacy is essential for sport and exercise practitioners to understand how adolescents can be tenacious and efficacious through adversity. Furthermore, when children suffer a complete loss of confidence, self-efficacy restoration is critical. Researchers have demonstrated that, when dealing with athletic injury, coaches, athletic trainers, and significant others play a vital role in intercollegiate athletes' self-efficacy restoration and their ability to return to full participation (Magyar & Duda, 2000). Future researchers should consider if the same findings apply to the youth sport and physical activity contexts.

A related developmental issue in need of attention is the testing of self-efficacy for learning (Schunk, 1995). With the exception of the few studies that investigate the self-regulated learning of motor skills (Kitsantas & Zimmerman, 1998; Kitsantas, Zimmerman, & Cleary, 2000; Schunk, 1995), most of the research on self-efficacy in youth sport focuses on performance, with little emphasis on learning. To capture the transitions from novice to expert, self-efficacy for learning sport and motor skills should be considered, particularly in training and competitive environments. Researchers should also examine the sources of self-efficacy that coincide with the different stages of learning to better understand the interaction between learning and self-efficacy in sport and physical activity (Feltz, 1994).

Research on the sources of collective efficacy and on the appraisal of these sources at the group level over time has been examined in adult sport (Feltz & Lirgg, 2001) and exercise (McAuley et al., 2001) settings. The influence of coaches and exercise instructors on collective achievement and attributes has also been investigated with adult samples (Magyar, 2002). Much of the sport and physical activity settings afford adolescents with the opportunities to interact and rely on each other to perform. However, researchers have not examined how collective efficacy perceptions may differ developmentally.

A final direction for future research pertains to the use of interventions to enhance efficacy beliefs in athletes and teams. Although there is research that introduces interventions as a way to enhance self-efficacy and performance in sport and physical activity (Garza & Feltz, 1998; Kitsantas et al., 2000; Kitsantas & Zimmerman, 1998; Weiss et al., 1998), additional research on nonperformance consequences of youth sport warrants investigation. A review of effective classroom practices reveals that a long-term and consistent emphasis on creating a caring environment fosters motivation as well as important social and emotional outcomes in youth and adolescents (Elias, 2003). Specific to efficacy beliefs, Bandura, Caprara, Barbaranelli, Gerbino, and Pastorelli (2003) examined the roles of empathic and affective self-regulatory self-efficacy during the transitional phase of adolescence and found that emotionally self-efficacious adolescents are more confident in negotiating important developmental issues and behaviors (e.g., depression and delinquency). Parallel to this developmental focus, sport and exercise researchers should consider broadening the scope of study to include the social and emotional implications of physical movement during adolescence. For example, researchers could create interventions that educate sport and physical activity leaders on how to establish a more caring climate and examine the influence of this caring climate on important social and emotional outcomes, such as empathic and affective self-regulatory efficacy beliefs (Newton et al., 2004). Ultimately, this research will encourage leaders to adopt innovative instructional methods designed to benefit adolescents through participation in sport and physical activity.

REFERENCES

Allison, K. R., Dwyer, J. M. J., & Makin, S. (1999). Self-efficacy and participation in vigorous physical activity by high school students. *Health Education & Behavior, 26*, 12-24.

Ames, C. (1992). Achievement goals, motivational climate, and motivational processes. In G. C. Roberts (Ed.), *Motivation in sport and exercise* (pp. 161-176). Champaign, IL: Human Kinetics.

Bandura, A. (1990). Perceived self-efficacy in the exercise of personal agency. *Journal of Applied Sport Psychology, 2*, 128-163.

Bandura, A. (1997). *Self-efficacy: The exercise of control.* New York: Freeman.

Bandura, A., Caprara, G. V., Barbarelli, C., Gerbino, M., & Pastorelli, C. (2003). Role of affective self-regulatory efficacy in diverse spheres of psychosocial functioning. *Child Development, 74*, 769-782.

Biddle, S., & Goudas, M. (1996). Analysis of children's physical activity and its association with adult encouragement and social cognitive variables. *Journal of School Health, 66*, 75-78.

Bouchard, C., Shepard, R. J., Stephens, T., Sutton, J. R., & McPerson, B. D. (Eds.). (1990). *Exercise, fitness, and health.* Champaign, IL: Human Kinetics.

Bungum, T., Pate, R., Dowda, M., & Vincent, M. (1999). Correlates of physical activity among African-American and Caucasian female adolescents. *American Journal of Health Behavior, 23*, 25-31.

Chase, M. A. (1998). Sources of self-efficacy in physical education and sport. *Journal of Teaching Physical Education, 18*, 76-89.

Chase, M. A. (2001). Children's self-efficacy, motivational intentions, and attributions in physical education and sport. *Research Quarterly for Exercise and Sport, 72*, 47-54.

Chase, M. A., Ewing, M. E., Lirgg, C. D., & George, T. R. (1994). The effects of equipment modification on children's self-efficacy and basketball shooting performance. *Research Quarterly for Exercise and Sport, 65*, 159-168.

Chase, M. A., Feltz, D. L., & Lirgg, C. D. (2003). Sources of collective and individual efficacy of collegiate athletes. *International Journal of Exercise and Sport Psychology, 1*, 180-191.

Chase, M. A., Magyar, T. M., & Drake, B. M. (in press). Fear of injury in gymnastics: Self-efficacy and psychological strategies to keep on tumbling. *Journal of Sport Sciences.*

Chase, M. A., Vealey, R. S., & Magyar, T. M. (2004). *Sources of confidence in female athletes: Age-related and seasonal influences.* Paper presented at the Association for the Advancement of Applied Sport Psychology, Minneapolis, MN.

Corbin, C. B., Landers, D. M., Feltz, D. L., & Senior, K. (1983). Sex differences in performance estimates: Female lack of confidence vs. male boastfulness. *Research Quarterly for Exercise and Sport, 54*, 407-410.

Cumming, J., & Hall, C. (2004). The relationship between goal orientation and self-efficacy for exercise. *Journal of Applied Social Psychology, 34*, 747-763.

Dempsey, J. M., Kimiecik, J. C., & Horn, T. S. (1993). Parental influence on children's moderate to vigorous physical activity participation: An expectancy value approach. *Pediatric Exercise Science, 5*, 151-167.

Dwyer, J. M. J., Allison, K. R., & Makin, S. (1998). Internal structure of a measure of self-efficacy in physical activity among high school students. *Social Science and Medicine, 46*, 1175-1182.

Elias, M. J. (2003). *Academic and social-emotional learning.* Brussels, Belgium: International Academy of Education.

Feltz, D. L. (1982). A path analysis of the causal elements in Bandura's theory of self-efficacy and an anxiety-based model of avoidance behavior. *Journal of Personality and Social Psychology, 42*, 764-781.

Feltz, D. L. (1988). Self-confidence and sports performance. In K. B. Pandolf (Ed.), *Exercise and sport sciences reviews* (pp. 423-457). New York, NY: Macmillan.

Feltz, D. L. (1994). Self-confidence and performance. In D. Druckman & R. A. Bjork (Eds.), *Learning, remembering, believing* (pp. 173-206). Washington, DC: National Academy of Sciences.

Feltz, D. L., & Chase, M. A. (1998). The measurement of self-efficacy and confidence in sport. In J. L. Duda (Ed.), *Advances in sport and exercise psychology measurement* (pp. 63-78). Morgantown, WV: Fitness Information Technology.

Feltz, D. F., & Lirgg, C. D. (2001). Self-efficacy beliefs of athletes, teams, and coaches. In R. N. Singer, H. A. Hausenblas, & C. M. Janelle (Ed.), *Handbook of sport psychology* (pp. 340-361). New York: John Wiley & Sons, Inc.

Feltz, D. L., Short, S. A., & Sullivan, P. J. (2005). *Self-efficacy theory and applications in sport*. Book in preparation.

Fry, M. D. (2000). A developmental analysis of children's and adolescents' understanding of luck and ability in the physical domain. *Journal of Sport and Exercise Psychology, 22*, 145-166.

Fry, M. D., & Duda, J. L. (1997). A developmental examination of children's understanding of effort and ability in the physical and academic domains. *Research Quarterly for Exercise and Sport, 68*, 331-344.

Garza, D. L., & Feltz, D. L. (1998). Effects of selected mental practice on performance, self-efficacy, and competition confidence of figure skaters. *The Sport Psychologist, 12*, 1-15.

George, T. R. (1994). Self-confidence and baseball performance: A causal examination of self-efficacy theory. *Journal of Sport and Exercise Psychology, 16*, 381-399.

Gould, D. (1982). Sport psychology in the 1980s: Status, direction, and challenge in youth sports research. *Journal of Sport Psychology, 4*, 203-218.

Hagger, M. S., Chatzisarantis, N., & Biddle, S. J. H. (2001). The influence of self-efficacy and past behaviour on the physical activity intentions of young people. *Journal of Sport Sciences, 19*, 711-725.

Horn, T. S. (1985). Coaches' feedback and changes in children's perceptions of their physical competence. *Journal of Educational Psychology, 77*, 174-186.

Horn, T. S. (2004). Developmental perspectives on self-perceptions in children and adolescents. In M. R. Weiss (Ed.), *Developmental sport and exercise psychology: A lifespan perspective* (pp. 101-143). Morgantown, WV: Fitness Information Technology Inc.

Kane, T. D., Marks, M. A., Zaccaro, S. J., & Blair, V. (1996). Self-efficacy, personal goals, and wrestlers' self-regulation. *Journal of Sport and Exercise Psychology, 18*, 36-48.

Kitsantas, A., & Zimmerman, B. J. (1998). Self-regulation of motoric learning: A strategic cycle view. *Journal of Applied Sport Psychology, 10*, 220-239.

Kitsantas, A., Zimmerman, B. J., & Cleary, T. (2000). The role of observation and emulation in the development of athletic self-regulation. *Journal of Educational Psychology, 92*, 811-817.

Lee, C. (1986). Efficacy expectations, training performance, and competitive performance in women's artistic gymnastics. *Behaviour Change, 3*, 100-104.

Lewko, J. H., & Ewing, M. E. (1980). Sex differences and parental influences in the sport involvement of children. *Journal of Sport Psychology, 2*, 62-68.

Lirgg, C. D. (1991). Gender differences in self-confidence in physical activity: A meta-analysis of recent studies. *Journal of Sport and Exercise Psychology, 8*, 294-310.

Maddux, J. E. (1995). Self-efficacy theory: An introduction. In J. E. Maddux (Ed.), *Self-efficacy adaptation, and adjustment: Theory, research, and application* (pp. 3-33). New York: Plenum Press.

Magyar, T. M. (2002). *A social-cognitive perspective of motivational and self-regulatory mechanisms of leadership in female collegiate rowers.* Unpublished doctoral dissertation. Michigan State University, East Lansing.

Magyar, T. M., Chase, M. A., & Vealey, R. S., & Gano-Overway, L. A. (2004). *Age-related sources of confidence and psychological strategies used by female athletes: A structured interview approach.* Paper presented at the Association for the Advancement of Applied Sport Psychology, Minneapolis, MN.

Magyar, T. M., & Duda, J. L. (2000). Confidence restoration following athletic injury. *The Sport Psychologist, 14*, 372-390.

Magyar, T. M., & Feltz, D. L. (2003). The influence of dispositional and situational tendencies on adolescent girls' sport confidence sources. *Psychological of Sport and Exercise, 4*, 175-190.

Magyar, T. M., & Feltz, D. L., & Simpson, I. . (2004). Individual and crew level determinants of collective efficacy in rowing. *Journal of Sport and Exercise Psychology, 26*, 136-153.

Martin, J. J., & Gill, D. L. (1995). The relationship of competitive orientations and self-efficacy to goal importance, thoughts, and performance in high school distance runners. *Journal of Applied Sport Psychology, 7*, 50-62.

McAuley, E. (1992). The role of efficacy cognitions in the prediction of exercise behavior in middle-aged adults. *Journal of Behavioral Medicine, 15*, 65-88.

McAuley, E., Lox, D. L., & Duncan, T. (1993). Long-term maintenance of exercise, self-efficacy, and physiological change in older adults. *Journal of Gerontology, 48*, P218-P223.

McAuley, E., Pena, M. M., & Jerome, G. J. (2001). Self-efficacy as a determinant and an outcome of exercise. In G. C. Roberts (Ed.), *Advances in sport and exercise* (pp. 235-261). Champaign, IL: Human Kinetics.

Newton, M., Fry, M., Kim,M. Gano-Overway, L., Magyar, M., Watson, D., et al., (2004). *Caring about the motivation of youth involved in physical activity.* Paper presented at the Association for the Advancement of Applied Sport Psychology, Minneapolis, MN.

Nicholls, J. G. (1984). Achievement motivation: Conceptions of ability, subjective experience, task choice, and performance. *Psychological Review, 91*, 328-346.

Nicholls, J. G. (1992). The general and the specific in the development and expression of achievement motivation. In G. . Roberts (Ed.), *Motivation in sport and exercise* (pp. 31-57). Champaign, IL: Human Kinetics.

Reynolds, K. D., Killen, J. D., Bryson, S. W., Maron, D. J., Taylor, C. B., Maccoby, N., et al. (1990). Psychosocial predictors of physical activity in adolescents. *Preventative Medicine, 19*, 541-551.

Schunk, D. H. (1995). Self-efficacy, motivation, and performance. *Journal of Applied Sport Psychology, 7*, 112-137.

Treasure, D. C., Monson, J., & Lox, C. L. (1996). Relationship between self-efficacy, wrestling performance, and affect prior to competition. *The Sport Psychologist, 10*, 73-83.

Umeh, K. (2003). Social cognitions and past behavior as predictors of behavioral intentions related to cardiovascular health. *Journal of Applied Social Psychology, 33*, 1417-1436.

Vargas-Tonsing, T. (2004). *An examination of pre-game speeches and their effectiveness in increasing athletes' levels of self-efficacy and emotion.* Unpublished doctoral dissertation, Michigan State University, East Lansing.

Vealey, R. S. (2001). Understanding and enhancing self-confidence in athletes. In R. N. Singer, H. A. Hausenblas, & C. M. Janelle (Eds.), *Handbook of sport psychology* (pp. 550-565). New York: Wiley.

Vealey, R. S., Chase, M. A., & Magyar, T. M. (2004). *Relationships between sources and levels of confidence across a competitive season: Are some sources better than others?* Paper presented at the Association for the Advancement of Applied Sport Psychology, Minneapolis, MN.

Vealey, R.S., Hayashi, S., Garner-Holman, M., & Giacobbi, P. (1998). Sources of sport-confidence: Conceptualization and instrument development. *Journal of Sport and Exercise Psychology, 20*, 54-80.

Watkins, B., Garcia, A. W., & Turek, E. (1994). The relation between self-efficacy and sport performance: Evidence from a sample of youth baseball players. *Journal of Applied Sport Psychology, 6*, 21-31.

Weinberg, R., & Jackson, A. (1990). Building self-efficacy in tennis players: A coach's perspective. *Journal of Applied Sport Psychology, 2*, 164-174.

Weiss, M. R., McCullagh, P. Smith, A. L., & Berlant, A. R. (1998). Observational learning and the fearful child: Influence of peer models on swimming skill performance and psychological responses. *Research Quarterly for Exercise and Sport, 69*, 380-394.

Weiss, M. R., Wiese, D. M., & Klint, K. A. (1989). Head over heels with success: The relationship between self-efficacy and performance in competitive youth gymnastics. *Journal of Sport and Exercise Psychology, 11*, 444-451.

CHAPTER 8

TOO MUCH CONFIDENCE?

The Self-Efficacy of Adolescents
with Learning Disabilities

Robert M. Klassen

Le trop de confiance attire le danger.
(Overconfidence can be dangerous.)

—Pierre Corneille, 1637

How do self-efficacy beliefs operate in adolescents who have learning disabilities (LDs)? For most people, optimistic efficacy beliefs enhance and maintain motivation and result in comparatively strong performance. But there is evidence that students with specific learning difficulties are sometimes *over*confident about their academic skills and consequently fail to adequately prepare to carry out academic tasks. The optimistic efficacy beliefs of adolescents with LDs might signal faulty self-knowledge and an inadequate awareness of the task at hand, with the result that performance suffers and motivation eventually wavers.

This chapter is divided into five sections. First, I define the central concepts of the chapter: *LD* and *self-efficacy.* Second, I address the motivational and metacognitive problems of students with LDs and examine

Self-Efficacy Beliefs of Adolescents, 181–200
Copyright © 2006 by Information Age Publishing

possible causes and consequences of problems related to the calibration of self-efficacy and performance. Third, I review findings of studies that examine the self-efficacy of LD students in a variety of academic contexts. In the fourth section, I present initial results of a study investigating literacy-related (reading, spelling, and writing) self-efficacy and predictions of early adolescents with and without LDs. I conclude by making recommendations to improve the self-efficacy calibration and academic functioning of adolescents with LDs.

LEARNING DISABILITIES IN ADOLESCENCE

Adolescents with LDs undergo the same physiological, educational, and social transitions experienced by their non-disabled peers but with the added overlay of powerful learning challenges in specific domains. The term LD refers to any of a number of intrinsic disorders that interfere with the acquiring, organizing, retaining, or understanding of information and that are caused by impairments to psychological processes such as phonological processing, executive functions (i.e., planning, monitoring, and metacognition), or memory (Learning Disabilities Association of Canada, 2002). Learning disabilities range in severity and interfere with academic skills, including oral language, reading, writing, and mathematics. The incidence of LD varies depending on definition, but it is generally accepted that an estimated 3% to 6% of all students are affected with some form of LD (Kibby & Hynd, 2001), with literacy areas most commonly affected. In school, LD students have considerable academic difficulties and display a pattern of unexpected underachievement, rather than global low achievement.

In light of the academic difficulties experienced by LD students, it is not surprising that previous research has found that children and adolescents with LD display low academic self-concept, a tendency toward learned helplessness, and low expectations of future academic success (e.g., Ayres, Cooley, & Dunn, 1990; Chapman, 1988). The lower self-concept of LD students may be limited to the school context. Gans, Kenny, and Ghany (2003) found that early adolescents with LD scored lower than did students who were not learning disabled (NLD) on intellectual and school status self-concept but not on more generalized self-concept perceptions. Relatively lower self-concept beliefs do not necessarily mean *low* self-concept beliefs. Meltzer, Roditi, Houser, and Perlman (1998) reported that LD students expressed lower academic self-concepts than did students without LD, but they were within the "average" to "above-average" ratings. These comparatively lower self-beliefs are thought to reflect the academic difficulties inherent in an LD profile and to reciprocally contribute to continuing failure in which poor academic performance reinforces already negative feelings about school (Chapman, 1988).

SELF-EFFICACY AND CALIBRATION

Self-efficacy beliefs—the context-specific judgments of the capability to successfully complete a task—differ from self-concept beliefs. Whereas self-concept is comparative (e.g., "Compared to others, I'm good at math") and consists of both cognitions and related feelings, self-efficacy is more task-specific, less based on one's feelings about a task, and is established through criterion reference (e.g., "I'm confident that I can solve most of these math problems") rather than through comparison with others (Bong & Skaalvik, 2003). Self-efficacy perceptions influence choice of activity, task perseverance, level of effort expended, and degree of success achieved. Inaccurate estimates of self-efficacy may develop from faulty task analysis or from a lack of self-knowledge (Bandura & Schunk, 1981), two problems shown to be prevalent in students with LDs (Butler, 1999; Meltzer et al., 1998; Swanson, 1989). The issue of calibration—that is, the congruence of self-efficacy beliefs with subsequent performance—has been described by self-efficacy researchers (e.g., Bandura, 1997), who maintain that optimistic self-efficacy is instrumental to the successful completion of challenging tasks.

Optimistic estimates of one's competence are hypothesized to increase effort and persistence and to promote accomplishment in challenging circumstances (Bandura, 1997), but is there a point at which optimism is maladaptive? As queried by Pajares (1996, p. 565), "How much confidence is too much confidence?" In an academic setting, optimistic competence beliefs are necessary for attempting novel tasks or for learning new material, and there is evidence that most normally-achieving students are moderately overconfident when asked to rate their academic abilities (e.g., Pajares & Kranzler, 1995; Pajares & Miller, 1994). Although modest overconfidence is posited to promote achievement, significant incongruence between efficacy beliefs and subsequent performance may not be so benign—naïve optimism or "gross miscalculation (between efficacy judgments and performance) can create problems" (Bandura, 1989, p. 1177). The optimistic efficacy beliefs held by some students with learning problems may not provide the same academic boost that they do for their more able peers. Rather, optimistic beliefs may lead to poor preparation, ineffective self-advocacy, and a lack of awareness of one's strengths and weaknesses. Assessments of self-efficacy can be viewed as a function of metacognitive knowledge and are derived from task analysis and self-understanding.

MOTIVATION, METACOGNITION,
AND LEARNING DISABILITIES

Motivational beliefs such as self-efficacy influence task approaches and affect the development of metacognitive skills. Well-developed skills in metacognition—awareness of one's cognitive processes, cognitive strengths and weaknesses, and self-regulation (Flavell, 1976)—are necessary for successful academic functioning. But LD students have been shown to experience difficulties analyzing task requirements, selecting and implementing strategies, and monitoring and adjusting performance (Butler, 1998). Learning disabled students display lower levels of metacognitive awareness of reading strategies in comparison to NLD students (Pintrich, Anderman, & Klobucar, 1994). In writing tasks, LD students have been found to focus on lower-order processes, like spelling or grammar, while ignoring higher-order demands such as writing to an audience or organizing ideas (Wong, Butler, Ficzere, & Kuperis, 1996). In mathematics, the persistent skills deficits of LD students adversely affect their ability to decipher the demands of higher-level mathematics problems (Jones, Wilson, & Bhojwani, 1997). When compared with their normally-achieving peers, learning disabled students are in general less metacognitively aware and tend to focus on the concrete demands of tasks rather than on the more obscure evaluative and self-awareness skills demanded by metacognitive processes (Butler, 1998).

An understanding of task demands—what Borkowski (1992) calls the "sizing up" of a task—is essential for successful academic performance. LD students may misanalyze tasks because of misconceptions held about the nature of the task, or because of a lack of awareness that analyzing tasks is an important step in learning (Butler, 1996). The level of effort and persistence expended by a learner is at least partly the result of awareness of task demands and personal capabilities (Butler & Winne, 1995). Learning disabled students struggle with various aspects of metacognition (Butler, 1998), one component of which is the assessment or evaluation of the nature of the task encountered. The formation of self-efficacy beliefs is a metacognitive activity, demanding a conscious awareness of self and task. Since LD students have been shown to experience difficulty with metacognition, it should come as no surprise that considerable literature has found that students with LDs miscalibrate their efficacy beliefs. In the following section, I review some of the literature exploring the efficacy beliefs of LD students and pay particular attention to issues of calibration.

REVIEW OF PREVIOUS STUDIES

In a search of relevant education and psychology databases, I found 28 journal articles, published between 1977 and 2003, that explored the self-efficacy beliefs of students with LDs. Because research on reading disabilities dominates the LD field (Shaywitz, Fletcher, Holahan, & Shaywitz, 1992), it may have been predicted that the reading domain would figure prominently in these self-efficacy studies. This was not the case. Of the 28 studies that explored the self-efficacy of LD students, 8 investigated writing skills, 10 explored general academic or "mixed" functioning, 5 examined mathematics, 4 explored self-efficacy for social or vocational functioning, and only 1 explored reading. Most (22) of the studies explored the efficacy beliefs of students in K-12 settings, of which 11 were set in elementary schools, 7 in high schools, and 4 included students spanning both elementary and high school. The remaining 6 studied focused on college students.

LD Students Compared to Students Without LD

Most of the studies (17 of 28) were designed to examine the effectiveness of a particular academic intervention and were not directly concerned with self-efficacy differences between LD and NLD groups. In general, authors of these studies reported that increases in performance were mirrored by increases in self-efficacy. The brief review presented here will examine a few of the trends found in the literature. For a more extensive review of these studies, see Klassen (2002). Of the studies not investigating a specific academic intervention (11 of 28), most explored differences in self-efficacy between LD and normally-achieving students. For example, Baum and Owen (1988) found that the self-efficacy of high-ability LD students was lower than was that of either the LD/Average or NLD/High-Ability students. In answer to their research question "Why do bright, learning disabled students have such a poor sense of self-efficacy when they possess greater intellectual and creative potential?" (p. 325), the authors suggested that bright LD students do not view their classroom accomplishments as meaningful or as meeting their own elevated internal standards. Gresham, Evans, and Elliott (1988) reported that the mainstreamed mildly handicapped students (including LD students) displayed lower levels of academic and social self-efficacy than did the non-handicapped and gifted students. Hampton (1998) investigated the sources of self-efficacy of LD students and found that adolescents with LD rated each of the four sources of academic self-efficacy—past performance, vicarious learning, social persuasion, and physical arousal—lower than did the NLD control group.

Gender was analyzed in only 7 of the studies. In some cases, the low proportion of girls in the sample of LD students made it difficult to conduct statistical analyses. Gresham et al. (1988) and Hampton and Mason (2003) found no significant gender effects. In a study investigating the social and academic self-efficacy of LD university students, Saracoglu, Mindan, and Wilchesky (1989) found that female students reported lower self-esteem than did male students, but not significantly lower self-efficacy beliefs. Schunk (1985) included gender as a variable in a study on goal setting in arithmetic and found no significant gender differences. Likewise, Schunk and Cox (1986) found no significant effects for gender in their study of strategy training and attributional feedback.

Calibration

In eight of the studies, the authors address the LD students' miscalibration of efficacy beliefs with performance. In each case, the authors determined whether or not the self-beliefs measured were underestimates, accurate, optimistic, or serious overestimates. It is not always easy to label self-efficacy beliefs as "accurate" or as "overestimated." For example, a mean self-efficacy rating of 65 on a 10- to 100-point self-efficacy scale might be difficult to interpret in terms of accuracy of perceived efficacy for writing essays. In a few of the studies (e.g., Alvarez & Adelman, 1986; Schunk, 1985; Schunk & Cox, 1986), the domain investigated—arithmetic—and the methodology used made the assessment of the accuracy of the judgments clear. In studies involving arithmetic, it is possible to briefly display the actual task to the student for purposes of self-efficacy assessment and then follow up with the same task as a performance measure. This approach cannot be easily used in other academic domains, such as reading or writing, where the researcher must take a more "qualitative" approach to calibration issues. Of the eight studies in which overestimates of efficacy beliefs are discussed, five investigated the domain of writing, one explored self-efficacy for reading, one examined arithmetic, and one looked at a mix of these academic areas.

Alvarez and Adelman (1986) observed that students with "psycho-educational problems" (including LD and dyslexia) typically miscalibrated on academic tasks that were viewed as potentially within their capability but were accurate in judging their competence when the task items were seen as either obviously easy or obviously difficult. This phenomenon of overconfidence for realistically challenging tasks was attributed to a "self-protective" function in which students erected a "facade of competence" to hide their academic difficulties. Graham and Harris (1989a), investigating self-instructional strategy training for LD students with writing deficiencies, found that "LD students consistently overestimated their composition abilities" (p. 360). They postulated that the unrealistic pre-task expectancies of the students in their study might be due to "comprehension deficiencies, use of a self-protective coping strategy, or a developmental delay in the ability to match task demands to ability level" (p. 360).

In their case study of three LD students exposed to strategy training, Graham and Harris (1989b) found the students consistently overestimated their writing skills. Graham, MacArthur, Schwartz, and Page-Voth (1992) found that LD students overestimated self-efficacy for writing on the pre-test but displayed more realistic confidence beliefs after goal setting instruction. The authors had predicted that the students' efficacy beliefs would become more realistic because "the process of goal setting has been shown to facilitate self-evaluation" (p. 332). In other words, the students' self-knowledge was enhanced by the intervention, resulting in more accurate self-appraisals. Again in the domain of writing, Graham, Schwartz, and MacArthur (1993) and Sawyer, Graham, and Harris (1992) found that LD students expressed relatively high confidence for composition tasks despite poor performance on pre-test writing measures. Graham et al. (1993) concluded with a call for further investigation into why LD students tend to miscalibrate and overestimate their writing abilities. It should be noted that *overestimation* of efficacy beliefs can be defined either as average task performance coupled with overly-optimistic self-efficacy ratings or as average self-efficacy ratings coupled with low task performance. In Graham et al. (1993), the self-efficacy ratings of the two groups were not significantly different, but the level of performance was much lower for the LD students.

In the only study reviewed that specifically examined perceived efficacy for reading tasks, Pintrich et al. (1994) found that LD students displayed levels of reading confidence that were the equal to those of the more capable readers without LDs. The LD students averaged a rating of 5.37 on a 7-point scale, whereas the NLD students displayed a mean of 5.71 on this same scale—a nonsignificant difference. In light of the LD students' documented disability in reading, the authors commented that these students felt "rather efficacious" at reading; that is, the LD students expressed equal confidence for reading, even though their skill level was considerably lower. The authors also found that the LD group displayed significantly lower metacognitive skills but a "somewhat positive" attributional style. Although these findings of the overconfidence and weak metacognitive skills of LD students in the area of reading are valuable, the sample of fifth-grade LD students was small ($n = 19$) and the results may not be reflective of students in other age groups.

Summary of Reviewed Studies

What can be concluded from this brief review of the literature examining the self-efficacy beliefs of students with LDs? Results from several of the studies suggest that students with LDs frequently overestimate their capabilities to perform certain tasks. This finding may not generalize to all subject matters and to all age levels, but in some circumstances—particularly in writing—students with LDs appear to be unrealistically optimistic about their capabilities. There are a number of possible factors underpinning the finding of optimistic efficacy beliefs in LD students. Estimations of self-efficacy can be construed as a form of metacognition, and students with LDs have been found to display significant metacognitive deficiencies (see Butler, 1999; Wong, 1985, 1986). Pintrich et al. (1994) reported that LD students possess significantly lower metacognitive skills than do NLD students. Bandura and Schunk (1981) proposed that discrepancies between perceived efficacy and performance may be the result of task misunderstanding and deficiencies in self-evaluation. Writing is a complex task, and self-assessment or reflection about challenging tasks like writing is a difficult process for many children with LD. Wong, Wong, and Blenkinsop (1989) found that LD students focus on lower-order writing processes whereas normally-achieving students focus on higher-order processes. Although findings about the writing self-efficacy of LD students point to a tendency to miscalibrate, few studies have included adolescents as participants, and the academic domains explored have been limited.

Several gaps were noted in this review of research. First, although several studies addressed the issue of calibration in an indirect fashion (e.g., using a 0-100 self-efficacy scale and a different scale for the performance task), more direct measurement of calibration would shed light on the nature of the incongruence between self-efficacy and subsequent performance. Second, only one study addressed the reading efficacy beliefs of LD students despite the high proportion of LD students who have reading problems (Shaywitz et al., 1992). Third, none of the studies examined spelling, a domain that influences writing success (Graham, Harris, & Chorzempa, 2002). Finally, few of the studies have focused on the efficacy beliefs of early adolescents, although domain-specific attitudes and motivation have been shown to drop significantly during these ages (Anderman & Maehr, 1994).

AN EMPIRICAL STUDY OF
THE SELF-EFFICACY BELIEFS OF ADOLESCENTS

Previous studies have investigated various aspects of the self-beliefs of adolescents with LDs, but few have investigated self-efficacy with a particular eye to the calibration of self-efficacy with performance, and fewer still have explored the reading and spelling beliefs of early adolescents with LD. In this section, I present initial results from a recent research project that addresses these research gaps with a focus on the reading, spelling, and writing efficacy beliefs of early adolescents with and without LDs. In addition to measuring self-efficacy using well-validated self-efficacy measures used in other self-efficacy studies (as proposed by Bandura, this volume), adolescents' *direct* predictions of their performance were also assessed so that predictions and performance can be compared.

Students' predictions of their performance can be seen as an indication of their self-efficacy to complete a task or as an indicator of their metacognitive self-appraisal, i.e., judgments about personal cognitive abilities (Paris & Winograd, 1990). In addition, to explore whether students became more aware of task demands and personal functioning after completing each task, participants also gave *self-evaluations—post hoc* analyses of their performance on completion of each task—and were asked to compare their own performance with that of other students in their grade. Finally, to provide further insights regarding the metacognitive beliefs of these early adolescents, participants also rated their self-efficacy for self-regulated learning.

Based on previous research, I hypothesized that LD students would display lower levels of self-efficacy and performance but that their predictions of performance would be more optimistic than would those of the NLD students. In addition, I predicted that all students would become more aware of task demands and of their own skills (i.e., more accurate in the calibration of self-efficacy and performance) *after* completing each of the academic tasks. Finally, I predicted that LD students would display lower levels of self-efficacy for self-regulation and would rate themselves lower in comparison to other students in their grade.

Participants were 133 (68 LD and 65 NLD) students in Grades 8 and 9 selected from two public and one independent Grade 8-12 high schools in an urban metropolitan area in Western Canada. Students in these schools were predominantly of European or East Asian backgrounds and middle class. All students with LDs in this study had been assessed by a qualified professional (certified school psychologist or registered clinical psychologist) and had met provincial LD criteria that stipulate a significant (two standard deviation) discrepancy between IQ and an achievement area, usually reading or writing. Students in the normally-achieving

NLD group were selected from social studies classes and were assumed to possess average IQ scores. Teachers were asked to identify students who received learning support or support for English as a Second Language (ESL), and these students were excluded from the analyses. All three schools were situated in similar middle class areas.

Background information collected included father's highest level of education, country of birth, language(s) spoken at home, and previous and predicted English marks. Students responded to a self-report questionnaire that included performance measures of reading (50 true-false questions with a 2-minute time limit), spelling (20 words selected from various published spelling tests), and writing (20 items asking the student to write a short, complete sentence using three given words to make a meaningful sentence within a 4-minute time limit, e.g., "food, puts, oven"). For each performance task, students were given a written example, and the directions were read aloud by the researcher.

Self-efficacy was assessed in two ways. First, using procedures outlined by Bandura (see the Guide in this volume), students were given examples of each task and then asked to "rate your degree of confidence (from 0 "Cannot do at all" to 10 "Certain can do") of getting 30% to 100% correct for this (writing) test by circling a number to the right of each of the percentages." Scores for the eight levels of confidence (30% to 100% with increments of 10%) were summed for a total self-efficacy score. Next, to facilitate direct comparison of self-efficacy with performance, self-efficacy was assessed as students' predictions of their performance (e.g., "*Prediction:* I believe that I can correctly write _____ (out of 20) sentences in 4 minutes."). Predictions are a form of self-efficacy: they are "task-specific performance expectations" (Zimmerman, 2000) that reflect one's beliefs about one's capabilities to complete a task. In addition, students were asked to estimate their performance *after* each task ("self-evaluations") and were also asked to answer how well they thought they compared with others in their grade. Finally, a scale was included to assess perceived capabilities to use a variety of self-regulated learning strategies (e.g., "How well can you concentrate on school subjects?") (Zimmerman, Bandura, & Martinez-Pons, 1992).

The measures were pilot tested on one Grade 8 social studies class in one of the target schools. A few of the performance items were changed as a result of the pilot test and the data were not used in the subsequent analyses.

Results

There were significant differences between the LD and NLD groups on all variables, with the exception of reading prediction. Learning disabled

students scored lower on literacy (reading, spelling, and writing) self-efficacy, self-evaluation, comparison with others, and performance in all
three domains. For example, in the area of reading, LD students displayed a mean self-efficacy rating of 56.2, compared to 65.7 for the NLD
students. The predictions of the LD group were also lower than were
those of the NLD group in spelling and writing, but not in reading. Table
1 provides ratings for self-efficacy, predictions and self-evaluations, comparison with others, and performance scores for all three domains by
group. These results were not unexpected. The LD students experienced
more difficulty with the academic tasks and were less efficacious than were
the NLD students. A closer look at the results provides information about
the accuracy of these students' predictions.

Recall that prediction scores can be viewed as a type of self-efficacy
assessment that can be compared with subsequent performance. The prediction and self-efficacy scores were highly correlated in each domain,
and both of these forms of self-efficacy correlated with subsequent perfor-

Table 8.1. Means and Standard Deviations for Reading, Spelling, and Writing Predictions, Performance, Self-Evaluations, Self-Efficacy, and Comparisons

	LD students (N = 68)		NLD students (N = 65)		
	M	SD	M	SD	η^2
Reading prediction	35.87	9.06	37.80	7.99	.01
Reading score[**]	32.59	9.25	44.60	5.19	.39
Reading self-evaluation[**]	33.00	9.33	41.97	6.20	.24
Reading self-efficacy[**]	56.24	16.73	65.72	11.49	.10
Reading compared to others[*]	6.21	1.99	7.01	1.40	.05
Spelling prediction[**]	11.37	5.24	15.15	3.35	.16
Spelling score[**]	7.46	4.66	14.58	3.57	.43
Spelling self-evaluation[**]	10.25	5.20	15.40	3.48	.25
Spelling Self-Efficacy[**]	44.79	21.70	64.88	13.12	.24
Spelling compared to others[**]	4.43	2.56	6.65	1.98	.19
Writing prediction[**]	12.39	4.69	14.94	3.16	.09
Writing score[**]	10.40	3.40	15.82	3.34	.40
Writing self-evaluation[**]	10.88	3.83	15.17	3.59	.25
Writing self-efficacy[**]	52.35	17.64	65.38	11.89	.16
Writing compared to others[**]	4.82	2.15	6.46	1.81	.15

*$p < .05$, **$p < .01$

mance. The LD students overestimated their performance in reading, spelling, and writing, whereas the NLD adolescents did not overestimate any of the performance outcomes. In the area of reading, however, NLD students *underestimated* their performance. In other words, NLD students were generally accurate in their predictions, except for reading, where they scored better than they thought they would. In comparison, LD students were overly optimistic for each task. As an example, in the area of spelling, LD students predicted a mean score of 11.4 out of 20 and scored 7.5. The NLD students predicted a score of 15.1 out of 20 and actually scored 14.6—a nonsignificant difference. This pattern of overestimation can be seen in Figures 8.1 through 8.3, which provide the predicted, actual, and self-evaluation scores across the three domains.

In terms of *post hoc* assessments of performance (self-evaluations), LD students persisted with overestimation of their performance in the area of spelling but accurately adjusted their self-ratings in reading and writing. The NLD students were accurate (i.e., their performance scores and self-evaluations were not significantly different) with all three of their self-evaluation assessments. When asked to compare their performance with that of other students in their grade, LD students ranked their reading performance surprisingly highly (at 6.2 on a 0-10 scale, or slightly better than their peers, with 5 indicating "about the same" [as others]). The LD students rated their spelling and writing performance slightly below that

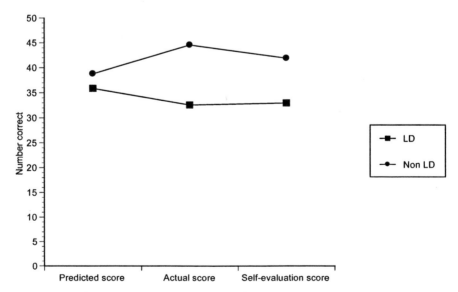

Figure 8.1.   Mean Levels of Predicted, Actual, and Self-Evaluation Reading Scores as a Function of LD Status.

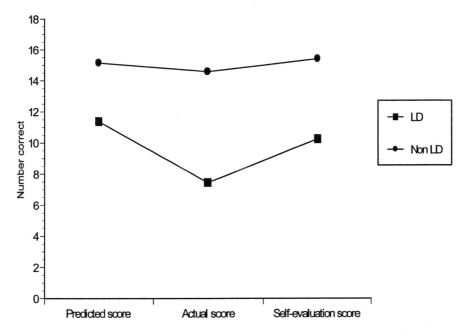

Figure 8.2.   Mean Levels of Predicted, Actual, and Self-Evaluation Spelling Scores as a Function of LD Status.

of their peers, at 4.4 and 4.8, respectively. The NLD students rated their performance as 7.0 in reading, 6.7 in spelling, and 6.5 in writing, which was better than the rated performance of their same-grade peers.

Students with LDs rated their self-efficacy for self-regulated learning lower than did students without LD. A look at the individual items of this scale showed significant differences and largest effect sizes for how well can you (a) finish homework assignments by deadline, (b) concentrate on school subjects, (c) plan your schoolwork, and (d) motivate yourself to do schoolwork.

Finally, to investigate whether low performers overestimate their performance regardless of disability status, the LD and NLD students were divided into four equal-sized skill-level groups to explore calibration according to performance levels. In each of the three academic domains, the lowest performers were the most optimistically miscalibrated. For example, in spelling (with both groups combined), the lowest performing group predicted they would score 8.6 out of 20 and actually scored 3.4. The highest-performing group estimated they would score 16.3 and actually scored 17.4. Both middle-performing groups overestimated their

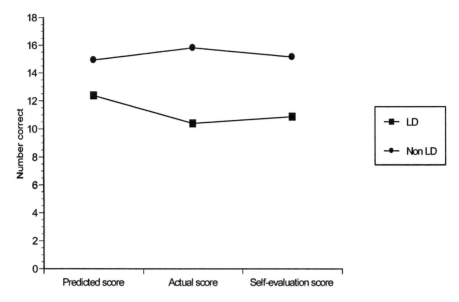

Figure 8.3.   Mean Levels of Predicted, Actual, and Self-Evaluation Writing Scores as a Function of LD Status.

performance, although not to the same extent as did the lowest performing group.

Discussion

In the literature earlier reviewed, findings reveal that LD students appear to overestimate their competence for writing tasks. The purpose of the study presented above was to examine early adolescents' calibration of efficacy beliefs and literacy-related academic performance. I found that normally-achieving adolescents were generally accurate or slightly optimistic when estimating their performance, although they significantly underestimated their reading scores. In contrast, the students with LDs significantly overestimated their performance in all three domains. It may be that LD students are *too* self-efficacious in reading, spelling, and writing tasks and, at least in the area of spelling, continue to hold these mistaken beliefs even after completing a task. In reading, LD students rated their skills as better than average in spite of their comparatively poor performance. In spelling and writing, LD students were more modest when comparing themselves with their peers. Although modest overconfidence is posited to promote achievement (Bandura, 1997),

significant incongruence between efficacy beliefs and subsequent performance may not be so benign. The "gross miscalculations" warned against
by Bandura (1989) appear to be linked with poor performance and reflect
a continued lack of awareness of self-capabilities and task demands. In
this study, students with LDs (and the lowest-achieving students across
disability categories) "grossly miscalculated" their ability to complete literacy tasks—their optimistic beliefs did not lead to superior performance.

Why do LD students who experience negative feedback about their
performance (e.g., failed tests or poor grades) in their domains of greatest weakness persist in overestimating their skills to complete a particular
task? Kruger and Dunning (1999) argued that the skills required to succeed in a domain are the same skills required to evaluate competence in
that domain. They suggest that people who lack skill and understanding
in a domain suffer from a "dual burden": they are unskilled but also
unaware. They lack the metacognitive ability to recognize their own lack
of skill. To paraphrase Miyake and Norman (1978), to solve a problem,
one must know enough to know what is not known. From this point of
view, the overconfidence of students with LDs might be expected. These
students may lack skill in the area of writing, for example, but they also
lack the awareness skills to recognize their lack of potential success in this
particular task. Perhaps, as suggested by Stone and May (2002), LD students may hold strongly negative views of their self-concept in a domain,
but, due to poor metacognitive awareness and a need for self-protection,
they continue to overestimate their academic skills and performance in
that domain.

Some LD students may misanalyze tasks because of misconceptions
held about the nature of the task or because of a lack of awareness that
analyzing tasks is an important step in learning (Butler, 1996). Results
from the self-efficacy for self-regulated learning measure showed that LD
students struggled with concentration, planning, and motivation, and
they tended not to complete homework on time. The level of effort and
persistence expended by a learner is at least partly the result of awareness
of task demands and personal capabilities (Butler & Winne, 1995) as well
as self-efficacy. Students with LDs have been shown to struggle with various aspects of metacognition. The present study provides evidence that
LD students have considerable difficulty with task analysis and with
understanding their strengths and weaknesses.

Social cognitive theory holds that optimistic self-efficacy beliefs foster
increased perseverance and effort. As demonstrated by previous findings
and results of the study presented, for students with learning problems,
positive efficacy beliefs—especially in the face of specific academic weaknesses—may not operate as they do for normally-achieving students.
Bandura (1997) warned that "deficient information leads to poor aca-

demic preparation" (p. 65). If self-evaluation can be seen as a reflection of self-knowledge or as a form of metacognition, then serious misjudgments about one's competence can potentially be academically harmful. Butler (1998) stressed the importance for LD students to construct accurate metacognitive understandings and to mindfully reflect about learning processes. To a certain extent, cognitive strategy use depends on accurate self-awareness or self-knowledge. Deficient self-knowledge may result in appropriate strategies not used, faulty task understanding, and difficulties with self-regulating and monitoring of one's progress. In some situations, the overly-optimistic self-efficacy reported by LD students may, in fact, result in inferior academic functioning.

CONCLUSION

The implications for educational practice are clear. Adolescents with LDs are sometimes "unskilled and unaware of it" (Kruger & Dunning, 1999). With some academic tasks, adolescents with LD appear to not only lack the cognitive skills to complete certain tasks but also the "reflective awareness about knowledge" (Butler, 1998, p. 282) that defines metacognition. Because of overconfidence, adolescents with LD may study less than do their NLD peers and may spend less time completing reading and writing tasks. The student who needs to work the hardest ends up working the least! In the classroom, teachers need to be aware that, for some students, high levels of optimism may signal difficulties with task-analysis and self-awareness or may serve a self-protective role. Pajares (1996) suggested that teachers should focus on improving their students' calibration skills through improved task understanding without lowering students' efficacy beliefs. Improving students' metacognitive skills, specifically the awareness of task demands and personal strengths and weaknesses, should bring about greater congruence between efficacy beliefs and performance.

For teachers, it is one thing to work at boosting the beliefs of students who are pessimistic about their self-efficacy (Pajares & Johnson, 1996), but dealing with excessive overconfidence in certain domains may not be so easily managed. The findings I have presented suggest that some LD students overestimate their ability to complete literacy-related tasks. For these students, optimistic efficacy beliefs may not increase effort and persistence, but rather may mask strategy and skill deficits. If these miscalibrated beliefs are based on inadequate self-awareness (Butler, 1999) or deficient information (Bandura, 1997), then students' approaches to some tasks may prove inadequate. Approaches that foster the self-awareness and self-regulative functions associated with metacognition (e.g.,

Butler, 1998; Meltzer et al., 1998) may improve the accuracy of students' calibration and subsequent performance.

Little is known about *why* students with LDs overestimate their academic capabilities. Previous researchers have hypothesized either a self-protective function (Alvarez & Adelman, 1986) or faulty task and self-understanding (Borkowski, 1992). Carefully designed qualitative studies that examine LD students' voices in school settings will help provide an *emic*, or insider's perspective, about the academic motivation of these students. The next research step should involve exactly this insider's perspective—a qualitative study investigating the efficacy beliefs of adolescents with LD, with a focus on the students' self-beliefs and reasons behind their miscalibration. Listening to LD students should lead to a clearer understanding of why some persistently engage in miscalibration. Because one goal of motivation research is to improve students' academic performance, researchers should examine whether improving LD students' task analysis improves self-efficacy calibration and subsequent performance.

REFERENCES

Alvarez, A., & Adelman, H. S. (1986). Overstatements of self-evaluations by students with psychoeducational problems. *Journal of Learning Disabilities, 19*, 567-571.

Anderman, E. M., & Maehr, M. L. (1994). Motivation and schooling in the middle grades. *Review of Educational Research, 64*, 287-309.

Ayres, R., Cooley, E., & Dunn, C. (1990). Self-concept, attribution, and persistence in learning-disabled students. *Journal of School Psychology, 28*, 153-163.

Bandura, A. (1989). Human agency in social cognitive theory. *American Psychologist, 44*, 1175-1184.

Bandura, A. (1997). *Self-efficacy: The exercise of control*. New York: W.H. Freeman and Company.

Bandura, A., & Schunk, D. H. (1981). Cultivating competence, self-efficacy, and intrinsic interest through proximal self-motivation. *Journal of Personality and Social Psychology, 41*, 586-598.

Baum, S., & Owen, S. V. (1988). High ability/learning disabled students: How are they different? *Gifted Child Quarterly, 32*, 321-326.

Bong, M., & Skaalvik, E. M. (2003). Academic self-concept and self-efficacy: How different are they really? *Educational Psychology Review, 15*, 1-40.

Borkowski, J. G. (1992). Metacognitive theory: A framework for teaching literacy, writing, and math skills. *Journal of Learning Disabilities, 25*, 253-257.

Butler, D. L. (1996). Promoting strategic content learning by adolescents with learning disabilities. *Exceptionality Education Canada, 6*, 131-157.

Butler, D. L. (1998). Metacognition and learning disabilities. In B. Y. L. Wong (Ed.) *Learning about learning disabilitie* (2nd ed., pp. 277-307). New York: Academic Press.

Butler, D. L. (1999, April). *Identifying and remediating students' inefficient approaches to tasks.* Paper presented at the annual meeting of the American Educational Research Association, Montreal, Canada.

Butler, D. L. & Winne, P. H. (1995). Feedback and self-regulated learning: A theoretical synthesis. *Review of Educational Research, 65,* 245-281.

Chapman, J. W. (1988). Cognitive-motivational characteristics and academic achievement of learning disabled children: A longitudinal study. *Journal of Educational Psychology, 80,* 357-365.

Flavell, J. H. (1976). Metacognitive aspects of problem solving. In L. B. Resnick (Ed.), *The nature of intelligence* (pp. 231-235). Hillsdale, NJ: Erlbaum.

Gans, A. M., Kenny, M. C., & Ghany, D. L. (2003). Comparing the self-concept of students with and without learning disabilities. *Journal of Learning Disabilities, 36,* 287-295.

Graham, S., & Harris, K. R. (1989a). Components analysis of cognitive strategy instruction: Effects on learning disabled students' compositions and self-efficacy. *Journal of Educational Psychology, 81,* 353-361.

Graham, S., & Harris, K. R. (1989b). Improving learning disabled students' skills at composing essays: Self-instructional strategy training. *Exceptional Children, 56,* 201-214.

Graham, S., Harris, K. R., & Chorzempa, B. F. (2002). Contribution of spelling instruction to the spelling, writing, and reading of poor spellers. *Journal of Educational Psychology, 94,* 669-686.

Graham, S., Macarthur, C., Schwartz, S., & Page-Voth, V. (1992). Improving the compositions of students with learning disabilities using a strategy involving product and process goal setting. *Exceptional Children, 58,* 322-334.

Graham, S., Schwartz, S., & MacArthur, C. (1993). Learning disabled and normally achieving students' knowledge of writing and the composing process, attitude toward writing, and self-efficacy for students with and without learning disabilities. *Journal of Learning Disabilities, 26,* 237-249.

Gresham, F. M., Evans, S., & Elliott, S. N. (1988). Self-efficacy differences among mildly handicapped, gifted, and nonhandicapped students. *The Journal of Special Education, 22,* 231-241.

Hampton, N. Z. (1998). Sources of academic self-efficacy scale: An assessment tool for rehabilitation counselors. *Rehabilitation Counseling Bulletin, 41,* 260-277.

Hampton, N. Z., & Mason, E. (2003). Learning disabilities, gender, sources of efficacy, self-efficacy beliefs, and academic achievement in high school students. *Journal of School Psychology, 41,* 101-112.

Jones, E. D., Wilson, R., & Bhojwani, S. (1997). Mathematics instruction for secondary students with learning disabilities. *Journal of Learning Disabilities, 30,* 151-163.

Kibby, M. Y., & Hynd, G. W. (2001). Neurobiological basis of learning disabilities. In D. P. Hallahan & B. K. Keogh (Eds.), *Research and global perspectives in learning disabilities: Essays in honor of William M. Cruickshank* (pp. 25-42). Mahwah, NJ: Erlbaum.

Klassen, R. (2002). A question of calibration: A review of the self-efficacy beliefs of students with learning disabilities. *Learning Disability Quarterly, 25,* 88-103.

Kruger, J., & Dunning, D. (1999). Unskilled and unaware of it: How difficulties in recognizing one's own incompetence lead to inflated self-assessments. *Journal of Personality and Social Psychology, 77,* 1121-1134.

Learning Disabilities Association of Canada. (2002). *Official definition of learning disabilities.* Retrieved August 12, 2004, from http://www.ldac-taac.ca/english/defined/definew.htm

Meltzer, L., Roditi, B., Houser, R. F., Jr., & Perlman, M. (1998). Perceptions of academic strategies and competence in students with learning disabilities. *Journal of Learning Disabilities, 31,* 437-451.

Miyake, N., & Norman, D. (1978). To ask a question, one must know enough to know what is not known. *Journal of Verbal Learning and Verbal Behavior, 18,* 357-364.

Pajares, F. (1996). Self-efficacy beliefs in academic settings. *Review of Educational Research, 66,* 543-578.

Pajares, F., & Johnson, M. J. (1996). Self-efficacy beliefs in the writing of high school students: A path analysis. *Psychology in the Schools, 33,* 163-175.

Pajares, F., & Kranzler, J. (1995, April). *Competence and confidence in mathematics: The role of self-efficacy, self-concept, anxiety, and ability.* Paper presented at the meeting of the American Educational Research Association, San Francisco.

Pajares, F., & Miller, M. D. (1994). The role of self-efficacy and self-concept beliefs in mathematical problem-solving: A path analysis. *Journal of Educational Psychology, 86,* 193-203.

Paris, S. G., & Winograd, P. (1990). How metacognition can promote academic learning and instruction. In B. F. Jones & L. Idol (Eds.), *Dimensions of thinking and cognitive instruction* (pp. 15-51). Hillsdale, NJ: Erlbaum.

Pintrich, P. R., Anderman, E. M., & Klobucar, C. (1994). Intraindividual differences in motivation and cognition in students with and without learning disabilities. *Journal of Learning Disabilities, 27,* 360-370.

Saracoglu, B., Minden, H., & Wilchesky, M. (1989). The adjustment of students with learning disabilities to university and its relationship to self-esteem and self-efficacy. *Journal of Learning Disabilities, 22,* 590-592.

Sawyer, R. J., Graham, S., & Harris, K. R. (1992). Direct teaching, strategy instruction, and strategy instruction with explicit self-regulation: Effects on the composition skills and self-efficacy of students with learning disabilities. *Journal of Educational Psychology, 84,* 340-352.

Schunk, D. H. (1985). Participation in goal setting: Effects on self-efficacy skills and skills of learning disabled children. *Journal of Special Education, 19,* 307-317.

Schunk, D. H., & Cox, P. D. (1986). Strategy training and attributional feedback with learning disabled students. *Journal of Educational Psychology, 78,* 201-209.

Shaywitz, B. A., Fletcher, J. M., Holahan, J. M., & Shaywitz, S. E. (1992). Discrepancy compared to low achievement definitions of reading disability: Results from the Connecticut Longitudinal Study. *Journal of Learning Disabilities, 25,* 639-648.

Stone, C. A., & May, A. L. (2002). The accuracy of academic self-evaluations in adolescents with learning disabilities. *Journal of Learning Disabilities, 35*, 370-383.

Swanson, H.L. (1989). Strategy instruction: Overview of principles and procedures for effective use. *Learning Disability Quarterly, 12*, 3-15.

Wong, B. Y. L. (1985). Metacognition and learning disabilities. In T. G. Waller, D. Forrest-Pressley, & E. MacKinnon (Eds.), *Metacognition, cognition, and human performance* (pp. 137-180). New York: Academic Press.

Wong, B. Y. L. (1986). Metacognition and special education: A review of a view. *Journal of Special Education, 20*, 9-29.

Wong, B. Y. L., Butler, D. L., Ficzere, S. A., & Kuperis, S. (1996). Teaching low achievers and students with learning disabilities to plan, write, and revise opinion essays. *Journal of Learning Disabilities, 29*, 197-212.

Wong, B. Y. L., Wong, R., & Blenkinsop, J. (1988). Cognitive and metacognitive aspects of learning disabled adolescents' composing problems. *Learning Disability Quarterly, 12*, 300-322.

Zimmerman, B. J. (2000). Self-efficacy: An essential motive to learn. *Contemporary Educational Psychology, 25*, 82-91.

Zimmerman, B. J., Bandura, A., & Martinez-Pons, M. (1992). Self-motivation for academic attainment: The role of self-efficacy beliefs and personal goal-setting. *American Educational Research Journal, 29*, 663-676.

CHAPTER 9

PREPARING ADOLESCENTS TO MAKE CAREER DECISIONS

A Social Cognitive Perspective

Steven D. Brown and Robert W. Lent

Deciding on a career direction can be a challenging task for even the most prepared adolescent in contemporary society. For those less well off economically and less accomplished academically, this task may seem overwhelming. Some may feel as if they have no choice at all. The modern world offers individuals a range of occupational possibilities that is vastly larger than what was available a century ago. On top of this, a large majority of occupations available in the world today (especially the fastest growing ones in the service and technology industries) require skills that were unheard of a century ago and levels of education (e.g., college) that the ancestors of today's adolescents rarely attained (U.S. Census Bureau, 2002; U.S. Department of Labor, 2002). Indeed, in today's world educational attainment seems to be critical for making the idea of a career imaginable to many adolescents (Arbona, 2005).

There are, in fact, compelling, large sample longitudinal data suggesting that early (pre-high school) educational attainment is strongly linked to the types of occupations to which children and adolescents aspire, to

Self-Efficacy Beliefs of Adolescents, 201–223
Copyright © 2006 by Information Age Publishing
All rights of reproduction in any form reserved.

the types of post-high school choices they make, and to their subsequent ability to achieve success and sustain involvement in chosen occupational paths (Arbona, 2005; Rojewski, 2005). For example, a series of recent longitudinal studies, using data drawn from some 25,000 children and adolescents in the National Education Longitudinal Study (NELS: 88; U.S. Department of Education, 2002) database, has found that the occupational aspirations that students reported in Grade 8 were remarkably stable and served as the strongest predictors of aspirations at Grade 12 (Rojewski & Kim, 2003; Rojewski & Yang, 1997). Perhaps more importantly, the single strongest predictor of occupational aspirations at Grade 8 was students' levels of pre-high school academic performance. Those who performed better academically up through Grade 8 had higher adult occupational aspirations than did those whose academic performance was more marginal. Academic performance was indeed a better predictor of occupational aspirations than were such other factors as gender, socioeconomic status, race/ethnicity, locus of control, and self-esteem.

Perhaps these results are not terribly surprising. One might expect children who do better in school to have more optimistic expectations about the level of jobs they will attain when they graduate from high school. It is important to note, however, that levels of high school academic performance were shown to be quite consistent with earlier levels of academic performance, and even where adolescents experienced increased success in high school, this improvement did not necessarily offset the aspiration-lowering effects of their earlier performance. In short, these data suggest that, by the time adolescents make the transition from middle school to high school, many may already be locked-in (based on their elementary and middle school academic performance) to a particular way of occupational life in adulthood (Rojewski & Kim, 2003).

Although there are a variety of explanations for these findings, including the natural weeding-out influence of intelligence and cognitive abilities, it is clear that intellectual ability is not the whole story. Rather, as teachers invariably discover in their interactions with students, adolescents at the same level of measured cognitive ability can achieve quite varying levels of academic performance. Some very cognitively-able children do not do well in school, and some children with lesser cognitive abilities do much better than would be expected from their standardized aptitude scores. However, given the apparent influence of early educational performance on future career aspirations and choices (and on the lifestyles that result from such choices), it is important for parents, teachers, and other educational personnel to try to ensure that the children in their charge perform as well as they can academically and to help them aim as high occupationally as their talents and motivation can take them.

Fortunately, this volume contains chapters that can aid in these efforts—chapters that demonstrate the power of self-efficacy and other variables derived from Bandura's (1986, 1993, 1997) social cognitive theory in promoting academic achievement and empowerment. In particular, our colleagues highlight motivational variables and processes that enable students to organize and make the most of their academic efforts. The insights provided by these chapters may provide valuable tools for promoting the academic success of elementary and middle school students as well as for undoing the debilitating effects of earlier academic troubles on high school students' occupational aspirations. Indeed, such academic success, and the dreams nurtured by it, may be intimately related to students' later occupational options.

Our chapter, therefore, begins by recognizing the essential connection between academic and career development. Our primary emphasis will be on how adolescents might be helped to transform their aspirations into eventual occupational choices—ideally, choices to which they can commit, that make full use of their talents, and that will lead to a satisfying lifestyle in adulthood. In particular, we will present a synopsis of a social cognitive theory of academic and occupational interest, choice, and performance that we, along with our colleague Gail Hackett, introduced into the psychological literature about a decade ago (Lent, Brown, & Hackett, 1994). We will also summarize the research that has been generated by the theory and end with a series of suggestions for how various aspects of the theory might be used to promote career choice-making among adolescents.

Because our theoretical framework involves educational as well as occupational choice and performance, some of our discussion may overlap with other chapters, but we will try to keep the overlap to a minimum by focusing on the implications of the theory for career choice-making. Our hope is that this chapter will be useful to parents, teachers, and counselors who want to help adolescents to think about, and prepare for, their occupational futures.

SOCIAL COGNITIVE CAREER THEORY

Theoretical Overview

Social Cognitive Career Theory (SCCT; Lent et al., 1994) is aimed at explaining the processes through which (a) academic and career interests develop, (b) educational and career choice are made, and (c) academic and career success is obtained. The framework was designed to integrate a variety of constructs (e.g., interests, abilities, goals, contextual influences) that appear in a number of different career theories and have been found to be important to the career development process. However, as its name implies, SCCT is centrally linked to Bandura's (1986) larger framework, adapting social cognitive theory as a conceptual scaffold to explain key educational and career development processes. In particular, three intricately-linked social cognitive variables—self-efficacy beliefs, outcome expectations, and goals—serve as the basic "building blocks" of SCCT.

Self-efficacy, as the reader is by now well informed, refers to context-specific, personal beliefs about an individual's capabilities to perform particular behaviors or courses of action (Bandura, 1986, 1997). Self-efficacy beliefs are not static estimates of global confidence or self-esteem, but rather are dynamic (i.e., changeable) and intimately tied to specific performance domains. For example, in career decision-making contexts, people vary in their self-efficacy regarding the behaviors required in different occupational domains. One adolescent might feel very confident in being able to accomplish tasks for successful entry into, and performance in, scientific fields, but feel much less self-efficacious about his or her abilities in more enterprising fields (e.g., politics or sales). Another adolescent may hold opposite efficacy beliefs (confidence in enterprising fields, but not in scientific fields). Even though both young persons differ in their occupational self-efficacy beliefs, it is possible for them to hold equal views of their self-worth or self-esteem; such broad feelings about the self are conceptually distinct from more domain- and situation-specific self-efficacy beliefs that focus on what one can do rather than how fundamentally worthy one is.

As dynamic and context-specific personal competency estimates, self-efficacy beliefs are assumed to develop from four major sources and how information provided by these sources is interpreted: personal accomplishments, vicarious experiences, social persuasion, and physiological and affective states. Personal accomplishments (successes and failures with specific tasks) are posited to offer a particularly compelling source of efficacy information, but the nature of the models and reinforcing messages to which one is exposed, and the types of physiological states one experiences while engaged in particular tasks (e.g., low levels of anxiety), can all have important effects on developing self-efficacy beliefs in different performance domains. These same information sources may be used as the basis for developmental and remedial interventions aimed at promoting academic and occupational self-efficacy beliefs (and the performance and choice outcomes they enable).

Outcome expectations refer to beliefs about the consequences or outcomes of performing particular behaviors (e.g., what will happen if I do this?). Although outcome expectations may not be as central to this book as are self-efficacy beliefs, the choices that people make about the activities in which they will engage, and their effort and persistence at these activities, entail consideration of outcome as well as self-efficacy beliefs. It is hard, for example, to imagine that an adolescent will choose to engage in an activity if he or she sees the likely outcomes of activity engagement to be negative, regardless of how competent the person might feel about his or her abilities to perform the task. Similarly, it is unlikely that an adolescent will choose to engage and persist in an activity in which he or she feels incompetent (e.g., taking advanced, elective math and science courses in high school), regardless of the positive occupational outcomes to which it might lead. Thus, according to SCCT and the larger social cognitive theory from which it was derived, persons' engagement in activities, the effort and persistence they put into these activities, and their ultimate success are partly and jointly determined by their self-efficacy beliefs and outcome expectations.

Personal goals may be defined as one's intentions to engage in a particular activity (e.g., to pursue a given academic major) or to attain a certain level of performance (e.g., to receive an A in a particular course) (Bandura, 1986). In SCCT, these two types of goals are referred to as choice goals and performance goals, respectively. By setting goals, people help to organize and guide their own behavior and to sustain it in the absence of more immediate positive feedback and in spite of inevitable setbacks. Social cognitive theory posits that goals are centrally linked to both self-efficacy and outcome expectations: adolescents will tend to set goals that are consistent with their views of their personal capabilities and of the outcomes they expect to attain from taking a particular course of action. Success or failure in reaching personal goals, in turn, becomes important information that helps to alter (e.g., strengthen or weaken) or confirm self-efficacy beliefs and outcome expectations.

SCCT's Interest Model

SCCT encompasses three interlocking, segmental models of educational and vocational interest development, choice-making, and performance attainment. The interest model, displayed in Figure 9.1, depicts interests in career-relevant activities as the outgrowth of self-efficacy and outcome expectations. Over the course of childhood and adolescence, people are exposed, directly and vicariously, to a variety of occupationally-relevant activities in school, at home, and in their communities. They are also differentially reinforced for continuing their engagement and for developing their skills in different activity domains. The types and variety of activities to which children and adolescents are exposed is partly a function of the context and culture in which they grow up. Girls, for example, are typically more exposed to and reinforced for engaging in

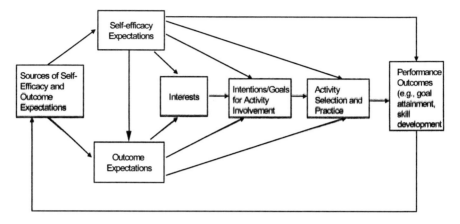

Source: Lent, Brown, and Hackett (1993), Reprinted with permission.

Figure 9.1.   Model of how basic career interests develop over time.

different types of activities than are boys, and wealthy children have access to a greater range of activity options than do children from less affluent homes.

Through continued activity exposure, practice, and feedback, children and adolescents refine their skills, develop personal performance standards, form a sense of their efficacy in particular tasks, and acquire certain expectations about the outcomes of activity engagement. They are most likely to develop interest in activities at which they both feel efficacious and from which they expect positive outcomes. As adolescents develop interest in an activity, they are likely to develop goals for sustaining or increasing their involvement in it. Further activity involvement leads to subsequent mastery or failure experiences which, in turn, help to revise self-efficacy, outcome expectations, and, ultimately, interests within an ongoing feedback loop.

Although we believe this process occurs repeatedly over the life span, interest development may be most fluid up until late adolescence, the point at which general interests (e.g., in art, science, social, or mechanical activities) tend to become fairly stable (Hansen, 2005). We believe that this stability is partly due to the relatively crystallized self-efficacy and outcome expectations that adolescents and adults hold regarding their performance in diverse activity domains. At the same time, data on the stability of interests suggests that, although stability is the rule, interest change does occur for some people during their post-adolescent years. SCCT posits that when such changes do occur, they can be explained by changes in self-efficacy beliefs and/or outcome expectations—more precisely, by exposure to potent new learning experiences (e.g., parenting, technological advances, job training or restructuring) that enable people to alter their sense of efficacy and outcome expectations in new occupational and avocational directions.

In sum, people, by mid- to late-adolescence, are likely to form enduring interest in an activity when they view themselves as competent at performing it *and* when they expect the activity to produce valued outcomes. Conversely, interests are unlikely to develop in activities for which people doubt their competence and expect negative, or neutral, outcomes (Betz, 1989). Further, SCCT posits that for interests to blossom in areas for which people have talent, their environments must expose them to the types of direct, vicarious, and persuasive experiences that can give rise to robust efficacy beliefs and positive outcome expectations. Interests are impeded from growing when individuals do not have the opportunity to form strong self-efficacy and positive outcome beliefs, regardless of their level of objective talent. Indeed, findings suggest that perceived capabilities and outcome expectations form key intervening links between objective abilities and interests (Lent et al., 1994).

Among other things, these interest hypotheses may help explain gender, race/ethnicity, and socioeconomic status differences in occupational distributions. For example, Hackett and Betz (1981) have considered ways in which gender, particularly gender role socialization, can influence the context in which self-efficacy beliefs are acquired and interests formed. According to their analyses, which are consistent with the predictions of SCCT, girls are more likely to be exposed to, and encouraged to engage in, female-typed activities such as artwork, social, and domestic tasks, whereas boys tend to be rewarded more for engaging in male-typed pursuits such as science and athletics. As a consequence of differential exposure, experiences, and reinforcement, boys and girls are likely to develop skills, self-efficacy beliefs, positive outcome expectations, and interests in tasks that are defined by their culture as gender-appropriate. Although behavior genetics research suggests that gender-typed values (e.g., altruistic versus theoretical) explain some of the variance in the distribution of men and women in different occupations (Achter & Lubinski, 2005), we maintain that gender and culture-based socialization experiences, which give rise to differential patterns of efficacy beliefs and outcome expectations, add unique variance to understanding the unequal distribution of men and women in different occupations. One implication of this analysis is that many young women and men likely under-utilize their talents and prematurely foreclose viable occupational options because of unsupportive social learning conditions.

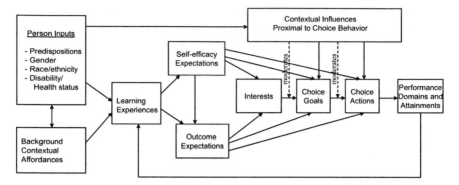

Source: Lent, Brown, and Hackett (1993), Reprinted with permission.

Figure 9.2.   Model of person, contextual, and experiential factors affecting career-related choice behavior. Note. Direct relations between variables are indicated with solid lines; moderator effects (where a given variable strengthens or weakens the relations between two other variables) are shown with dashed lines.

SCCT's Choice Model

Our basic model of the career choice process is embedded within Figure 9.2. This figure also incorporates the basic causal sequence depicted in Figure 1, only now the activity goal and practice variables have been transformed into career-related goals and the actions required to implement them. As outlined in the interest model, self-efficacy and outcome beliefs are seen as jointly and additively promoting occupational interests. Interests, in turn, foster corresponding choice goals (e.g., intentions to pursue a particular occupational path). One's choice goals, in turn, motivate goal-consistent actions (e.g., efforts to gain entry into a particular academic major, training program, or job).

The balance of positive and negative experiences accrued via activity engagement serve to strengthen or weaken earlier self-efficacy and outcome expectations. For example, poor performance in a training program is likely to prompt revision of self-efficacy (e.g., I may not be as good at this as I thought I was) and outcome expectations (e.g., I may have trouble getting a job if I do this poorly in training), leading to a shift in goals. In a nutshell, SCCT posits that the choice goals that adolescents develop (e.g., the types of occupations they expect to pursue) are partly determined by their interests. That is, all else being equal, they tend to become oriented toward career paths representing activities in which they are most interested. SCCT shares this basic prediction with Holland's (1997) theory, another influential model of career choice. However,

SCCT offers a more detailed explanation of the processes through which interests emerge and change. It also specifies that, if interests change as a result of disconfirming efficacy experiences or shifting outcome expectations, one's choice goals will also likely change.

It should also be emphasized that, as shown in Figure 9.2, choice goals are sometimes influenced more directly and potently by self-efficacy beliefs, outcome expectations, and other contextual variables than they are by interests. Interests are expected to exert their greatest impact on academic and occupational choice under supportive environmental conditions—that is, conditions in which people are relatively free to pursue their interests. However, many adolescents and young adults are not able to follow their interests either unfettered by obstacles or with the full support of important others. The choice-making of these persons is constrained by such experiences as economic need, family pressures, or educational limitations. In such instances, adolescents and young adults may need to compromise their interests and, instead, make their choices largely on the basis of such pragmatic considerations as the type of work that is available to them, their self-efficacy beliefs (can I do this type of work?), and outcome expectations (will the job pay enough to make it worthwhile?). Cultural values (e.g., the degree to which one's choices may be made by elder family members rather than by the individual alone) may also limit the role of personal interests in career choice.

SCCT posits conditions that increase the probability that people will be able to pursue their interests as well as conditions where interests may need to be compromised in making career-related choices. Collectively labeled *contextual affordances* (Vondracek, Lerner, & Schulenberg, 1986), these conditions refer to the levels of support (e.g., family financial and emotional support), barriers (e.g., lack of finances, inadequate levels of education, cultural preferences), and opportunities available to the individual. Simply put, SCCT hypothesizes that interests will be a more potent predictor of the types of choices adolescents and young adults make under supportive environmental conditions than under more restrictive environmental conditions. Under the latter conditions, one's interests may need to be bypassed or compromised in favor of more pragmatic, pressing, or culturally acceptable considerations.

SCCT's Performance Model

SCCT's performance model is concerned with predicting and explaining two primary aspects of performance: the *level of success* that people attain in educational and occupational pursuits and the degree to which they *persist* in the face of obstacles. Because the focus of this book is on adolescence and because educational attainment is so important to

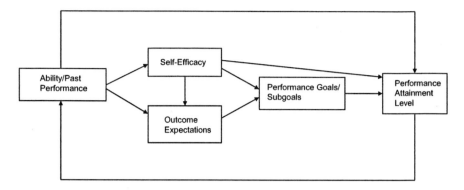

Source: Lent, Brown, and Hackett (1993), Reprinted with permission.

Figure 9.3.   Model of task performance.

expanding or limiting the types of choices available at this stage of the career development process, we will focus on the predictions that SCCT makes about academic performance and persistence.

As Figure 9.3 illustrates, success and persistence are assumed to be influenced by several key variables: ability, self-efficacy, outcome expectations, and performance goals. Ability (as reflected by past achievement and aptitudes) is assumed to affect performance via two primary pathways. First, ability influences performance and persistence directly. Students with higher scholastic aptitude tend to perform better in school than do those with lesser scholastic aptitude, and those with higher aptitude in a particular subject will tend to do better and persist longer in that subject than will students with lesser aptitude in that subject. (Ability or aptitude may be thought of as a composite of innate potential and acquired knowledge.) Second, ability is hypothesized to influence performance and persistence indirectly though the intervening paths of self-efficacy and outcome expectations.

Simply put, performance is assumed to involve both ability and motivational components (Russell, 2005), and, taking its lead from general social cognitive theory, SCCT emphasizes the motivational roles of self-efficacy, outcome expectations, and performance goals. Specifically, SCCT suggests that self-efficacy and outcome expectations work in concert with ability, in part by influencing the types of performance goals that people set for themselves. Controlling for level of ability, students with higher self-efficacy and more positive outcome expectations about the value of educational attainment will be more likely to establish higher performance goals for themselves (e.g., take on more challenging course work), to organize their skills more effectively, and to persist longer in the face of academic setbacks. As a result, they may achieve higher levels of educational success than would those with lower self-efficacy and less positive outcome expectations. In this sense, the social cognitive factors may enable students to make the best possible use of their abilities.

Because some prior critics of the theory have somehow assumed that our performance model ignores the important role of aptitude in the performance process (e.g., Achter & Lubinski, 2005; Gottfredson, 2005), we want to emphasize that self-efficacy is seen as complementing, not substituting for, aptitude. Self-efficacy should not be pictured as the "little blue engine" (the subject of a popular children's story), mechanically chanting "I think I can, I think I can" as it chugs along, oblivious to task requirements or environmental barriers. Indeed, social cognitive theory, in which SCCT is anchored, does not assume that self-efficacy will compensate for inadequate academic ability. It does, however, predict that the performance of individuals at the same ability level will be facilitated by stronger versus weaker self-efficacy beliefs (Bandura, 1986). For example, academically able adolescents who underestimate their academic talents, compared to their equally able peers with more optimistic self-efficacy beliefs, are likely to set lower goals for themselves, experience undue performance anxiety, give up more quickly in the face of obstacles, challenge themselves less academically and, consequently, experience less academic success.

Social cognitive theory posits that large overestimates of self-efficacy can also be self-defeating. Students whose self-efficacy drastically overshoots their relatively weak academic skills are likely to set unrealistic academic goals and to take on academic tasks that are beyond their current grasp, creating a situation where failure and discouragement is likely. Self-efficacy beliefs that modestly exceed current capabilities are probably optimum (Bandura, 1986, 1993). Such beliefs are likely to lead students to set challenging (but not too challenging) academic goals and to engage in academic activities that stretch their skills and that further strengthen their feeling of personal academic efficacy and expectations for positive outcomes.

There is one final set of assumptions that deserves emphasis, particularly from the perspective of efforts to promote robust but realistic self-efficacy beliefs. As discussed earlier, efficacy beliefs are developed from, and can be modified by, four primary sources of efficacy information: (a) performance accomplishments, (b) vicarious experiences, (c) social persuasion, and (d) physiological and affective states. While performance accomplishments are ordinarily expected to importantly affect self-efficacy, the information provided by an accomplishment must be cognitively processed in such a way that it will actually be perceived and remembered as a success experience by the person. Attributing a performance accomplishment in a specific domain to such factors as hard work, luck, or task ease will likely diminish its impact on the individual's sense of personal efficacy compared to an attribution based on personal ability. Attributing successes to *improving* ability may be especially valuable because such attributions imply that ability is by nature acquirable and incremental versus inherent and static (cf. Bandura, 1993).

Social cognitive theory thus cautions that performance successes (and favorable information conveyed by the other three efficacy sources) may not be sufficient to promote robust efficacy estimates. Attention must also be paid to the cognitive processes, or filters, through which students interpret the quality of their performances. Successful performance on a math test, for example, is not likely to translate into higher math self-efficacy if this success is discounted by the student as being due to an exceptionally easy test, good luck, or hard work. Such attributions tend to undermine self-efficacy in the face of success. We do not want to imply that attributing success to hard work is necessarily maladaptive; such attributions can, in fact, motivate further hard work, which facilitates academic success. But thinking that success is only due to effort and not to growing ability will likely leave the student's self-efficacy beliefs unchanged. The result might be that the student will set less challenging goals than will another student who perceives that he or she is developing increased knowledge and skill. In the end, the student who attributes success only to effort may foreclose potentially rewarding career pursuits because of self-efficacy beliefs that do not match up well with his or her abilities and because of thoughts that it will take too much continued effort to be successful.

EMPIRICAL SUPPORT FOR SCCT

A substantial body of research has accumulated suggesting that SCCT and its major constructs offer a useful explanatory framework for educational and vocational interest development, choice-making, and performance. Sufficient data have, in fact, accumulated to yield several meta-analyses relevant to SCCT, especially its hypotheses regarding interest and choice—developmental processes that are central to the adolescent and young adult years (Lent et al., 1994; Multon, Brown, & Lent, 1991; Rottinghaus, Larson, & Borgen, 2003; Sadri & Robertson, 1993; Stajkovic & Luthans, 1998). In the remainder of this section, we will summarize the primary findings that have been derived from these meta-analyses as well as from a review of selected individual studies that may refine the meta-analytic results.

Meta-analysis is a potent research strategy that can be used, after a sufficient body of research has emerged on a specific hypothesis, to integrate findings and draw conclusions about the strength of hypothesized relations among variables. The primary yield from most meta-analyses is an effect size that provides a quantitative estimate of the size or strength of relations among variables. The two most common meta-analytic effect sizes are the standardized mean difference between groups (usually labeled d) and the bivariate correlation (r), with the latter being more frequently used to estimate the strength of relations hypothesized by SCCT.

Meta-analyses of SCCT's interest model have revealed substantial support for its major hypotheses. Lent et al. (1994) reported that self-efficacy beliefs and outcome expectations each accounted for substantial variance in vocational and educational interests and that the relation of ability and prior performance to interests was fully mediated by self-efficacy beliefs (i.e., a null relation was reported between ability and interests after controlling for self-efficacy beliefs). Overall effect size estimates for self-efficacy beliefs and outcome expectations were .52 and .53, respectively, suggesting that each accounts for a little over 25% of the variance in vocational and academic interests. (A correlation of .50 or greater is typically assumed to reflect a large effect size in the social sciences.) A more recent meta-analysis of 53 samples, including over 37,000 adolescent and adult participants, replicated the finding of Lent et al. (1994) that self-efficacy is strongly related to interests (overall $r = .59$) (Rottinghaus et al., 2003).

Meta-analyses have also supported SCCT's choice hypotheses. Lent et al. (1994), for example, found that career-related choices were strongly predicted by interests ($r = .60$) and that the influence of self-efficacy beliefs and outcome expectations on choices was largely, but not completely, indirect through their relation to interests. Consistent with SCCT's assumptions about the importance of contextual and cultural influences, some recent research also suggests that interests may play a smaller role in the choice making process of particular racial/ethnic minority group members. Specifically, Castelino (2004) and Tang, Fouad, and Smith (1999) each found that interests seemed to be largely bypassed in favor of self-efficacy and family influences in terms of predicting career-related choice in samples of Asian American adolescents and young adults. Particularly among the less acculturated (i.e., those who adhere more to their culture of origin than to U.S. cultural values), there was a marked tendency for participants to choose a career path that they thought they could do and that was valued by their parents rather than one that necessarily fit their personal interests.

Although insufficient to meta-analyze, other studies on the role of contextual affordances (barriers and supports) in choice-making are largely consistent with SCCT's hypotheses that interests will relate more strongly to choices under favorable environmental conditions. For example, Lent et al. (2001) found that math and science interests were related more strongly to intentions to engage in math and science pursuits under low barrier ($r = .76$) than under high barrier conditions ($r = .43$). The importance of support to career choice making and success has been underscored by a number of qualitative (e.g., Lent et al., 2002; Richie, Fassinger, Prosser, & Robinson, 1997) and quantitative (e.g., Lent, Brown, & Hackett, 2000) studies and has also been found to be a critical component of successful career choice counseling interventions (Brown & Ryan Krane, 2000).

Meta-analyses relevant to SCCT's performance model predictions have highlighted the hypothesized linkage of self-efficacy to indicators of academic and occupational performance. Findings have shown that self-efficacy is a useful predictor of both academic (Multon et al., 1991) and occupational (Sadri & Robertson, 1993; Stajkovic & Luthans, 1998) performance and that certain factors affect the strength of self-efficacy-performance relations. For example, self-efficacy has been found to be more strongly related to academic performance in older (i.e., high school and college) than younger (elementary and middle school) students and in lower versus higher achieving students (Multon et al., 1991). The finding that self-efficacy beliefs relate more strongly to academic performance in older students may, in part, be due to a tendency for self-efficacy beliefs to become more refined and ability-consonant with age (Tracey & Ward, 1998). Such findings emphasize the importance of helping adolescents develop accurate but challenging self-efficacy beliefs in areas of academic talent. The findings that the self-efficacy-performance relation is stronger in lower than higher achieving students highlights the importance of helping less successful students build a more robust sense of self-efficacy in particular academic areas.

It is important to reiterate an earlier caveat: self-efficacy may facilitate the performance of lower achieving students, but these beliefs are not expected to wholly compensate for or cover up substandard levels of ability. In fact, Kinsman (1993) found that self-efficacy explained virtually no variance in the performance of high school freshmen deemed most at risk for academic failure. Thus, academic skill development rather than (or in addition to) self-efficacy promotion should be the primary intervention target for the least able students. For most other students, the data suggest that efficacy enhancement can be facilitative of school performance, as long as it works to foster reasonably accurate but optimistic (i.e., not falsely high) self-appraisals of academic capabilities.

Finally, meta-analyses have also been used to summarize data on the sources of information, or learning experiences, from which self-efficacy beliefs are assumed to derive. Of the hypothesized sources, domain-specific performance accomplishments typically show the strongest relations with self-efficacy in corresponding domains (e.g., successful performance in math-related classes is associated with higher math self-efficacy). The other (vicarious, persuasion, affective) sources have also been found to relate to domain-specific self-efficacy, although generally to a more modest degree than personal accomplishments (Lent et al., 1994).

In summary, meta-analyses relevant to SCCT's hypotheses suggest that:

1. Interests are strongly predicted by self-efficacy beliefs and outcome expectations.

2. An adolescent's ability and performance accomplishments in a specific domain (e.g., mathematics) are likely to lead to interests in that domain (e.g., occupations involving mathematics) to the extent that they foster a growing sense of self-efficacy and positive outcome expectations.

3. Self-efficacy and outcome expectations relate to career choices, especially among more "Westernized" adolescents, largely (though not completely) through their linkages to interests.

4. Past performance promotes future performance through the exercise of people's abilities as well as through self-efficacy beliefs. The latter serves to facilitate performance in domains of adequate ability through goal setting (higher self-efficacy is associated with more challenging goals), skills organization, and persistence in the face of setbacks.

5. Self-efficacy may derive most strongly from personal performance accomplishments but is also responsive to vicarious experience, social encouragement and discouragement, and affective or physiological states.

SOME PRACTICAL IMPLICATIONS OF SCCT

SCCT has the practical goals of (a) helping children and adolescents to develop career-related interests and talents that create as wide a range as possible of later educational and work options and (b) assisting students, by late adolescence or young adulthood, to select (and pursue) choice options that are consistent with their work personalities (e.g., interests, values, skills) and that are, as much as possible, unconstrained by environmental barriers. SCCT further posits that these goals might be most efficiently and effectively reached by aiding children and adolescents to (a) identify academic and non-academic areas of particular strength, (b) acquire self-efficacy beliefs in areas of strength that are commensurate with ability but are sufficiently challenging to foster further skill development, (c) gather information on occupational pursuits so that outcome expectations are as reality-based as possible, and (d) foster environments that will support the individual's choice and help him or her overcome barriers that might stand in the way. In the remainder of this section, we summarize some strategies that might be helpful in identifying strengths, enhancing efficacy and outcome expectations, and creating facilitative choice-making environments. (Also see Lent, Hackett, and Brown, 1999, regarding applications of SCCT to the school-to-work transition process; and Betz, this volume, on methods for using self-efficacy and interest information together in career counseling.)

Identifying Strengths

Helping children and adolescents to identify areas of talent is a critical step toward their developing realistic aspirations and (eventually) making aspiration-congruent occupational choices. SCCT posits a number of ways that this might be accomplished, such as reviewing past success experiences and trying to ensure that these experiences are, in fact, interpreted by the child or adolescent as successes. Two particularly compelling ways to ensure success perceptions are helping individuals to realize that progress, rather than "perfect" performance, is an important index of talent and to attribute successes to skills and talent rather than to task ease, luck, or (only) hard work. (See Brown and Lent, 1996, regarding ideas for reviewing past successes, organizing novel success experiences, and dealing with performance attributions.)

Another important issue and one we have not yet mentioned, but about which parents, teachers, and counselors need to be fully cognizant, is the type of social comparisons that adolescents make with their peers. Children and adolescents actively compare their performance in different activity domains to their peers and use this information to develop standards for their own performance. Performing worse than one's peers leads to lower perceptions of ability; performing as well as or better than one's peers leads to higher ability percepts. Although such comparison processes can provide useful information in identifying areas of talent, they clearly rely on context-specific information.

For example, adolescents attending selective, high-performing schools and school districts may disparage their performance in an academic domain even though they might be quite capable relative to national norms. Likewise, a student at the same level of ability attending a school with less academically successful peers may overestimate his or her academic abilities. Being either a "small fish in a big pond" or a "big fish in a small pond" can have its downsides. The first student may eliminate from consideration career pursuits in which he or she could be successful because of unrealistically low self-efficacy, whereas the second student may attempt entry into educational or occupational options for which his or her capabilities are less than adequate, reflecting unrealistically high self-efficacy. As counselors, we have seen many students whose performance standards, based on skewed comparison information, have led them prematurely to rule out potentially satisfying choice options or to rule in options for which they may presently be ill-equipped.

Parents, teachers, and counselors may therefore wish to assist adolescents to access information that they can use to develop reasonably accurate competency judgments. Such information may include national rather than local norms on standardized achievement tests, careful review of past performance accomplishments (e.g., grades in different academic subjects, extracurricular achievements), and volunteer, job shadowing, and other experiences in which the student can get first-hand knowledge of the types and levels of skills needed for success in occupational areas that interest them. The goal of such activities would not necessarily be to disparage aspirations for occupations that seem out of reach of one's current capabilities. Such information could rather be used as the basis for designing novel experiences to boost self-efficacy (in the case of unrealistically low self-efficacy) or to prepare students for shocks that may be encountered in competing at a higher level than they have previously encountered (in the case of unrealistically high self-efficacy).

Building Talent-Congruent but Challenging Efficacy Beliefs

In addition to helping students to identify particular areas of competence and interest, it is valuable to help nurture self-efficacy beliefs that are at once ability-congruent and challenging. The four sources of efficacy information can be used to structure such interventions. Helping adolescents to set specific, attainable, but challenging performance goals is one way to promote further performance accomplishments and, hence, skill development. Such goals allow for incrementally-graded success experiences and can foster a sense of efficacy, particularly where students are helped to view progress, rather than ultimate goal attainment, as the guidepost for success. Such goals also enable individuals to view some substandard performance or lack of goal attainment as a normal part of skill development (e.g., even the best hitters in baseball strike out and get on base only part of the time). It is also important to attend to how students process new (as well as previous) success experiences. As we have discussed previously, objective success experiences (e.g., getting a B in a class when all prior grades received in the subject had been substantially lower) may not influence the student's self-efficacy beliefs if he or she attributes the success only to task ease, luck, or hard work. Thus, efforts at promoting self-efficacy beliefs might encourage students to entertain and practice more self-enhancing performance attributions (e.g., attributing the B to developing capabilities in the subject area).

Useful intervention elements can also be fashioned from the other three sources of efficacy information. For example, modeling can be used to assist students to explore academic and career domains that they might not have previously encountered or been encouraged to consider. Adolescents are more likely to identify with models whom they perceive to be similar to themselves along such dimensions as gender, race/ethnicity, and age. Exposure to similar, credible models (especially those who have coped successfully with the same challenges that the observer is currently facing) may be exceptionally inspiring for the student, especially those whose family environments provide them with limited access to successful models in career areas in which the student has talent and interest. Social support and persuasion can be used to encourage students to attempt new efficacy-challenging tasks, to persist despite setbacks, and to interpret their performances favorably, for example, by focusing on progress (e.g., getting a B) rather than ultimate success (consistent A-level performance) and by encouraging students to view progress as reflective of growing talent.

Nurturing Accurate Outcome Expectations

Sustained interests in different occupational pursuits is affected not only by robust, skill-correspondent self-efficacy beliefs, but also by accurate and positive information about the likely outcomes of particular occupational paths. Interests, as we noted earlier, are not likely to bloom, even when a person's odds of occupational success are high, in the presence of negative or neutral outcome expectations. It is therefore important that students base their outcome expectations on accurate and up-to-date occupational information rather than on information gleaned, for example, from media portrayals or other sources of potentially inaccurate and biased information. In fact, in their meta-analysis of career choice counseling, Brown and Ryan Krane (2000) identified career information search as an important ingredient of effective interventions. The amount of client effort devoted to information gathering was, on average, very highly correlated with the outcome of career choice counseling ($r = .82$).

There are excellent print and internet-based sources of information that can be accessed to gather career information (see Gore & Hitch, 2005, for a review of useful sources). Informational interviews with job incumbents, job shadowing, and other more direct methods of gathering information have also been found to be helpful. Because such information gathering can produce a vast array of data, it is also helpful to provide students with ways to organize and weigh these data in relation to personal work values. For example, a decisional grid or balance sheet can be created where different occupational options are rated in terms of how well each meets criteria that are particularly important to the individual such as the potential to help others, to be "looked up to," to work independently, or to make a large salary. Fit of different options to culturally relevant values and to the wishes of significant others can also be considered here.

Overcoming Barriers to, and Building Supports for, Career Plans

Data relevant to SCCT's choice hypotheses suggests that it is important to help students, as they contemplate potential career choices, to consider potential environmental, familial, and personal barriers to implementing their choices and to consider strategies to prevent or manage such barriers. At least equally important is to help students consider the supports that they have available for implementing their choices and how to locate additional supports that may be needed. Support, in and of itself, makes it more likely that people will be able to transform their interests into goals and their goals into actions. Support-seeking also represents a potent way to cope with the career-limiting influences of environmental barriers. Findings suggest, for example, that levels of support received from families, friends, teachers, and others are important in enabling highly successful career women to overcome barriers to occupational success (Richie et al., 1997) and to help academically at-risk students to overcome barriers to educational success (Lent et al., 2002; see also Arbona, 2005).

In helping students build support for their career plans, it is important for teachers and counselors to keep in mind the findings cited earlier on potential racial/ethnic differences in the role of interests in the choice-making process. In certain cultural contexts, young people's choices may be influenced more by family wishes (and by self-efficacy) than by interests. Thus, counselors and teachers must remain sensitive to the possibility that the aspirations they would like to support in a particular student, even though congruent with the student's self-efficacy and outcome expectations, may conflict with the wishes of his or her influential family members. Due to cultural considerations and other factors (e.g., financial limitations), individuals are not always free to pursue their preferred options.

One strategy we have used to navigate such complexities while helping adolescents make maximally informed career decisions is to use a balance sheet procedure that invites them first to consider how well different choice options match up with their interests and other important considerations, and second, to list gains and losses they and significant others would experience if they were to select each option. We base this strategy on data showing that post-decisional regret is typically lower and satisfaction and choice persistence are higher if a decision is based on a full consideration of gains and losses (Janis & Mann, 1977). Once students list gains and losses, we invite them to rate how likely each loss (representing a potential barrier) is to actually occur and what strategies they might use to deal with it. Although we have no data other than clinical experience on the effectiveness of this strategy, our desire in developing it was to help students to consider as fully as possible (and to prepare for) the implications of their choices, including potential conflicts with the occupational wishes of their parents and cultures. Where such conflicts are identified, further dialogue is sought with the student (and possibly his or her family members) to negotiate the best possible resolution for the student and family system.

CONCLUSION

We have outlined a social cognitive theory of career and educational interest development, choice-making, and performance. In doing so, we tried to provide both an overview of the theory and its research base and suggestions for parents, teachers, counselors, and others who wish to help adolescents prepare to make satisfying career decisions. To this point, much of the research base on SCCT, although extensive, has been directed toward testing basic hypotheses. Intervention studies have been less common but are increasing in frequency (e.g., Betz & Schifano, 2000; Luzzo, Hasper, Albert, Bibby, & Martinelli, 1999), as are applications of social cognitive theory and, particularly, SCCT to career education (McWhirter, Rasheed, & Crothers, 2000; Prideaux, Patton, & Creed, 2002) and school-to-work transition (Lent et al., 1999; Pinquart, Juang, & Silbereisen, 2003). Our hope is that more such work will soon appear, offering additional theory-based ideas for furthering the career development of adolescents and young adults, particularly those who encounter academic difficulties or other barriers to their choice-making.

REFERENCES

Achter, J. A., & Lubinski, D. (2005). Blending promise with passion: Best practices for counseling intellectually talented youth. In S. D. Brown & R. W. Lent (Eds.), *Career development and counseling: Putting theory and research to work* (pp. 600-624). New York: Wiley.

Arbona, C. (2005). Promoting the career development and academic achievement of at-risk youth: College access programs. In S. D. Brown & R. W. Lent (Eds.), *Career development and counseling: Putting theory and research to work* (pp. 525-550). New York: Wiley.

Bandura, A. (1986). *Social foundations of thought and action: A social cognitive theory.* Englewood Cliffs, NJ: Prentice-Hall.

Bandura, A. (1993). Perceived self-efficacy in cognitive development and functioning. *Educational Psychologist, 28,* 117-148.

Bandura, A. (1997). *Self-efficacy: The exercise of control.* New York: Freeman.

Betz, N. E. (1989). Implications of the null environment hypothesis for women's career development and for counseling psychology. *The Counseling Psychologist, 17,* 136-144.

Betz, N. E., & Schifano, R. S. (2000). Evaluation of an intervention to increase realisitic self-efficacy and interests in college women. *Journal of Vocational Behavior, 56,* 35-52.

Brown, S. D., & Lent, R. W. (1996). A social cognitive framework for career choice counseling. *Career Development Quarterly, 44,* 354-366.

Brown, S. D., & Ryan Krane, N. E. (2000). Four (or five) sessions and a cloud of dust: Old assumptions and new observations about career counseling. In S. D. Brown & R. W. Lent (Eds.), *Handbook of counseling psychology* (3rd ed., pp. 740-766). New York: Wiley.

Castelino, P. (2004). *Factors influencing career choices of South Asian-Americans: A path analysis.* Unpublished doctoral dissertation, Loyola University Chicago.

Gore, P. A., Jr., & Hitch, J. L. (2005). Occupational classification and sources of occupational information. In S. D. Brown & R. W. Lent (Eds.), *Career development and counseling: Putting theory and research to work* (pp. 382-413). New York: Wiley.

Gottfredson, L. (2005). Using Gottfredson's Theory of Circumscription and Compromise in career guidance and counseling. In S. D. Brown & R. W. Lent (Eds.), *Career development and counseling: Putting theory and research to work* (pp. 71-100). New York: Wiley.

Hackett, G., & Betz, N. E. (1981). A self-efficacy approach to the career development of women. *Journal of Vocational Behavior, 18,* 326-336.

Hansen, J. C. (2005). Assessment of interests. In S. D. Brown & R. W. Lent (Eds.), *Career development and counseling: Putting theory and research to work* (pp. 281-304). New York: Wiley.

Holland, J. L. (1997). *Making vocational choices: A theory of vocational personalities and work environments* (3rd ed.). Odessa, FL: Psychological Assessments.

Janis, I. L., & Mann, L. (1977). *Decision making: A psychological analysis of conflict, choice, and commitment.* New York: Free Press.

Kinsman, C. (1993). *An investigation of the relationship among self-efficacy beliefs, goal setting, and academic performance of students in a transition to high school program.* Unpublished doctoral dissertation, Loyola University Chicago.

Lent, R. W., Brown, S. D., Brenner, B., Chopra, S. B., Davis, T., Talleyrand, R., & Suthakaran, V. (2001). The role of contextual supports and barriers in the choice of math/science educational options: A test of social cognitive hypotheses. *Journal of Counseling Psychology, 48*, 474-483.

Lent, R. W., Brown, S. D., & Hackett, G. (1994). Toward a unifying social cognitive theory of career and academic interest, choice, and performance [Monograph]. *Journal of Vocational Behavior, 45*, 79-122.

Lent, R. W., Brown, S. D., & Hackett, G. (2000). Contextual supports and barriers to career choice: A social cognitive analysis. *Journal of Counseling Psychology, 47*, 36-49.

Lent, R. W., Brown, S. D., Talleyrand, R., McPartland, E. B., Davis, T., Chopra, S. B. et al. (2002). Career choice barriers, supports, and coping strategies: College students' experiences. *Journal of Vocational Behavior, 60*, 61-72.

Lent, R. W., Hackett, G., & Brown, S. D. (1999). A social cognitive view of school-to-work transition. *The Career Development Quarterly, 44*, 297-311.

Luzzo, D. A., Hasper, P., Albert, K. A., Bibby, M. A., & Martinelli, E. A. (1999). Effects of self-efficacy-enhancing interventions on the math/science self-efficacy and career interests, goals, and actions of career undecided college students. *Journal of Counseling Psychology, 46*, 233-243.

McWhirter, E. H., Rasheed, S., & Crothers, M. (2000). The effects of high school career education on social-cognitive variables. *Journal of Counseling Psychology, 47*, 330-341.

Multon, K. D., Brown, S. D., & Lent, R. W. (1991). Relation of self-efficacy beliefs to academic outcomes: A meta-analytic investigation. *Journal of Counseling Psychology, 38*, 30-38.

Pinquart, M., Juang, L. P., & Silbereisen, R. K. (2003). Self-efficacy and successful school-to-work transition: A longitudinal study. *Journal of Vocational Behavior, 63*, 329-346.

Prideaux, L., Patton, W., & Creed, P. (2002). Development of a theoretically derived school career program: An Australian endeavor. *International Journal for Educational and Vocational Guidance, 2*, 115-130.

Richie, B. S., Fassinger, R. E., Prosser, J., & Robinson, S. (1997). Persistence, connection, and passion: A qualitative study of the career development of highly achieving African American-Black and White women. *Journal of Counseling Psychology, 44*, 133-148.

Rojewski, J. W. (2005). Occupational aspirations: Constructs, meanings, and application. In S. D. Brown & R. W. Lent (Eds.), *Career development and counseling: Putting theory and research to work* (pp. 131-154). New York: Wiley.

Rojewski, J. W., & Kim, H. (2003). Career choice patterns and behavior of work-bound youth during early adolescence. *Journal of Career Development, 30*, 89-108.

Rojewski, J. W., & Yang, B. (1997). Longitudinal analysis of select influences on adolescents' occupational aspirations. *Journal of Vocational Behavior, 51*, 375-410.

Rottinghaus, P. J., Larson, L. M., & Borgen, F. H. (2003). The relation of self-efficacy and interests: A meta-analysis of 60 samples. *Journal of Vocational Behavior, 62*, 221-236.

Russell, J. E. A. (2005). Work performance and careers. In S. D. Brown & R. W. Lent (Eds.), *Career development and counseling: Putting theory and research to work* (pp. 203-224). New York: Wiley.

Sadri, G., & Robertson, I. T. (1993). Self-efficacy and work-related behavior: A review and meta-analysis. *Applied Psychology: An International Review, 42*, 139-152.

Stajkovic, A. D., & Luthans, F. (1998). Self-efficacy and work-related performance: A meta-analysis. *Psychological Bulletin, 124*, 240-261.

Tang, M., Fouad, N. A., & Smith, P. L. (1999). Asian Americans' career choices: A path model to examine factors influencing their career choices. *Journal of Vocational Behavior, 54*, 142-157.

Tracey, T. J. G.,& Ward, C. C. (1998). The structure of children's interests and competence perceptions. *Journal of Counseling Psychology, 45*, 290-303.

U. S. Department of Education (2002). *National Education Longitudinal Study: 1988-2000*. Washington, DC: Office of Educational Research and Improvement.

U. S. Department of Labor (2002). *Occupational outlook handbook, 2002-2003*. Washington, DC: Bureau of Labor Statistics, Office of Occupational Statistics and Employment.

Vondracek, F. W., Lerner, R. M., & Schulenberg, J. E. (1986). *Career development: A life-span developmental approach*. Hillsdale. NJ: Erlbaum.

CHAPTER 10

DEVELOPING AND USING PARALLEL MEASURES OF CAREER SELF-EFFICACY AND INTERESTS WITH ADOLESCENTS

Nancy E. Betz

One of the most popular areas of application of Bandura's (1986) self-efficacy theory is to the field of career development and career counseling. Going back to the writings of Frank Parsons in 1909, the field of career psychology includes as one of its most important objectives understanding and facilitating the career decision-making processes, including educational decisions, undertaken by adolescents and young adults. Called by theorist Donald Super (1957) the "Exploration" stage of career development, the adolescent years are those in which the young person arrives at a sense of his/her identity as far as educational and career options. This "identity" includes the critically important variables of preferences for career activities and self-concept regarding one's vocational abilities. It also includes the variables of objectively measured aptitudes and abilities, as well as work needs and values, but these will not be discussed in this chapter. Readers are referred to Walsh and Betz (2001) for an overview of the use of these variables in vocational assessment.

Self-Efficacy Beliefs of Adolescents, 225–244

The first of these individual differences variables, preferences for educational and career activities, has long been studied and measured using the concept of vocational interests. Vocational interest measures are taken by literally millions of students and adults each year, and are a fundamental basis of career counseling methods. Inventories such as the Strong Interest Inventory (Donnay, Morris, Schaubhut, & Thompson, 2005; Harmon, Hansen, Borgen, & Hammer, 1994), the Kuder Career Search (Zytowski, 1997), the ACT UNIACT Interest Inventory (Prediger & Swaney, 1995), and the Campbell Interest and Skill Survey (CISS; Campbell, Hyne, & Nilsen, 1992) have proven to have widespread theoretical and practical uses in our field. The book *Occupational Interests: Their Meaning, Measurement, and Use in Counseling* (Savickas & Spokane, 1999) provides an excellent review of current issues in research and practice.

Historically, both the measurement of vocational interests and the interpretation of vocational interest inventories were focused on three major types of scales. Empirical interest scales, often referred to descriptively as occupational scales, were originally developed by E. K. Strong, Jr. (1927) in the Strong Vocational Interest Blank and are used commonly today in such inventories as the Strong Interest Inventory (SII; Harmon et al., 1994), the Kuder Occupational Interest Survey (Kuder & Zytowski, 1991), and the CISS (Campbell et al., 1992). Occupational scales assess the similarity of the person's activity preferences to those of people in specific occupations—for example, physician, psychologist, or banker. This comparison is usually made in reference to a specific gender—for example, female lawyers or male lawyers.

Basic Interest Scales were originated by Kuder (1964) in the Kuder Preference Record and were introduced to the Strong Interest Inventory in 1968. Basic interest scales describe activity areas that can be associated with one or more specific occupations, college subjects, or leisure pursuits. Basic interests appearing on virtually all major inventories include Mathematics, Science, Outdoors/Nature, Music, Art, Writing, Social Service, Sales, and Mechanical Activities and Computer Activities. Others that have been included are Athletics, Domestic Arts, and Religious Activities. Basic Interest scales are central features of the Strong Interest Inventory and Strong Interest Explorer (Morris, Chartrand, & Donnay, 2002), the Kuder Career Search (Zytowski, 1997), and the ACT Testing programs (Prediger & Swaney, 1995) among others.

Most general in focus are the broad occupational orientations exemplified by Holland's (1997) theory, as measured by the scales of the Self-Directed Search (Holland, 1994; see also Wall and Baker, 1997) and the General Occupational Themes of the Strong Interest Inventory. Comparable in generality and similar in content are the eight fields of Roe's (1956) theory, the Kuder Career Search (Zytowski, 1997), and the ACT

Testing Program (Prediger & Swaney, 1995). All systems include such broad areas as social, scientific, artistic, business/sales, outdoor/technical, and business detail. For example, Roe's eight fields were technical, outdoor, science, general culture, arts and entertainment, service, business, and organization. The six Kuder Career Clusters (Zytowski, 1997) are art/communication, business detail, outdoor/mechanical, sales/management, science/technology, and social/personal. The World of Work Map, used by ACT in the Career Exploration Program (see Prediger & Swaney, 1995) contains Business Contact, Business Operations, Technical, Science, Arts, and Social Service, within which are grouped more than 500 occupational titles and 565 Occupational Groups (cf. Prediger & Swaney, 1995). Assessment of these types is accompanied by some means of matching people to college majors or occupations congruent with these broad interest orientations.

Although interest measurement has been a hallmark of career psychology for almost 90 years now, the use of measures of self-concepts of vocationally relevant abilities is a more recent addition to our assessment procedures, and this area has been greatly advanced by self-efficacy theory. Beginning with Hackett and Betz's (1981) original theoretical integrations of self-efficacy and career development theories, and the first empirical study of what was called "occupational self-efficacy" (Betz & Hackett, 1981), the promise of self-efficacy theory for career assessment and exploration became increasingly clear.

More specifically, Bandura's use of the concepts of "approach" versus "avoidance" behavior as one of the major consequences of self-efficacy expectations is one of the simplest, yet one of the most profound, in its impact on career counseling. In the context of career development in particular, approach behavior describes what we will try, whereas avoidance behavior refers to things we will not try. It thus encompasses both the content of career choice, that is, the types of educational majors and careers we will attempt, and the process of career choice, that is, the career exploratory and decision-making behaviors essential to making good choices. Avoidance is a pernicious phenomenon because when we avoid something we give ourselves no chance to learn it—to master it. A student who is "computer phobic," for example, will avoid using computers as much as possible and never become competent in or comfortable with their use. Students who fear mathematics will likely avoid taking math courses and never learn the subject matter—their low self-efficacy will be an accurate assessment of their capabilities.

Performance is also crucial to career development in that it requires successful completion of educational and/or training coursework and programs. Low self-efficacy may interfere with exam performance by causing negative self-talk or anxiety responses that interfere with an effective

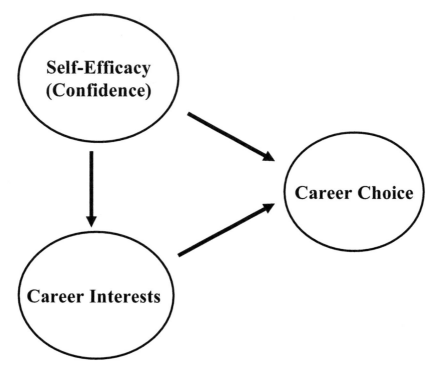

Figure 10.1.   Simplest model of relationship of career self-efficacy
(confidence) and interests to career choices.

focus on the task at hand. Low self-efficacy may be, in effect, a self-fulfilling prophecy. Finally, strong expectations of self-efficacy are important to
persistence in pursuit of one's educational and career goals in the face of
obstacles, occasional failures, and dissuading messages from the environment such as gender- or race-based discrimination or harassment.

Although interests and self-efficacy arrived separately on the "stage" of
career psychology, they are increasingly being integrated in both career
research, assessment, and counseling. Beginning with the research of Betz
and Hackett (1981), it became clear that both interests and self-efficacy
were necessary for perception of a major or occupation as a viable option
to pursue. A simple model based on the findings of Betz and Hackett
(1981) is presented in Figure 10.1. This model was later presented in
modified form by Donnay & Borgen (1999) and as part of a considerably
expanded model by Lent, Brown, and Hackett (1994). According to the
model shown in Figure 10.1, neither interests nor confidence (self-efficacy) alone is sufficient to lead to a choice of a career in that domain, but
rather both must be present. For example, choice of a career in science

requires both interests in science and confidence in one=s abilities to learn and perform scientific activities. Further, because we have means of increasing self-efficacy or confidence via interventions based on Bandura=s theory, joint use of interest and efficacy measures in career assessment and counseling can be used to identify potential career options previously avoided because of lack of confidence.

APPLICATIONS TO BROAD VOCATIONAL DIMENSIONS

To study and apply the model shown in Figure 10.1, measures of self-efficacy with respect to the interest domains were needed. Not surprisingly, the first major focus of such measurement was the six broad interest themes of Holland=s vocational theory (Holland, 1997). Table 10.1 provides brief definitions of each theme and examples of behavioral items that are used in the assessment of self-efficacy with respect to that domain. Although Holland interest measures have been available for

Table 10.1. Brief Definitions of the Holland (1997) Vocational Themes and Sample Items from the Skills Confidence Inventory

Holland Vocational Themes	Sample Items
Realistic Theme (Involves working with hands, skilled trades, outdoor activities, mechanical activities)	Build a doll house Learn to do auto maintenance
Investigative Theme (Scientific activities, intellectual pursuits)	Perform a scientific experiment Solve abstract puzzles
Artistic Theme (Activities in the areas of music, art, drama, writing)	Design sets for a play Write a play or short story
Social Theme (Helping, Teaching, and/or counseling people)	Help others solve their problems Teach children
Enterprising Theme (Leadership, sales, politics, business management)	Sell a product to a customer Start a business
Conventional Theme (Organizing and processing data, finance, computing)	Keep financial records for an organization Manage computer systems

Note: Brief definitions of Holland themes are adapted from descriptions of Holland (1997) and from the descriptions of the General Confidence (Holland) Themes from the Skills Confidence Inventory (Betz, Borgen, & Harmon, 2005).

many years (notably the Vocational Preference Inventory [Holland, 1985], Self-Directed Search [Holland, 1994], and Strong Interest Inventory [SII; Harmon et al., 1994]), measures of self-efficacy with respect to the Holland themes are more recent in arrival.

One of the first studies using self-efficacy measures of the Holland themes was that of Lapan, Boggs, and Merrill (1989) who asked college students to rate their self-efficacy with respect to occupations representing the six Holland theme areas and with respect to the occupational group as a whole (e.g., Ajobs which involve science and science-related activities@ for Investigative; Lapan et al., 1989, p.177). Lenox and Subich (1994) developed measures of self-efficacy with respect to Holland=s themes. Six 5-item scales were developed using activities representing each theme. Both Lapan et al. and Lenox and Subich reported that women had lower Realistic and Investigative self-efficacy than did men and that self-efficacy was moderately related to interests.

The Skills Confidence Inventory (SCI; Betz, Harmon, & Borgen, 1996), a measure of self-efficacy for the six Holland themes, was designed to be used jointly with the General Occupational (Holland) Themes from the Strong Interest Inventory. Normed on over 1800 college students and employed adults, the Skills Confidence Inventory was shown to possess high levels of internal consistency, test-retest reliability, and predictive validity (Betz, Harmon, et al., 1996). There were significant gender differences among college students, with college men reporting significantly higher confidence on the Realistic, Investigative, Enterprising, and Conventional themes and college women reporting higher self-efficacy only on the Social theme.

Although there are a number of studies of the validity of the Skills Confidence Inventory, probably the largest scale validity study was that of Donnay and Borgen (1999), who used scores on the six Holland interest themes of the Strong Interest Inventory and the six Holland confidence themes of the Skills Confidence Inventory (Betz, Borgen, & Harmon, 2005; Betz, Harmon et al., 1996) to predict the occupation of 1,105 adults employed in 21 occupational groups. Using discriminant analysis in both a validation and a cross-validation sample, Donnay and Borgen found significant incremental validity for the confidence (self-efficacy scales) beyond that accounted for by the interest scales. In percentage of variance terms, the interest scales accounted for 79% of the differences among the 21 occupational groups, the confidence scales accounted for 82% of occupational differences, and the combined interests and confidence scales accounted for 91% of occupational differences.

Isaacs, Borgen, Donnay, and Hansen (1997) investigated the extent to which self-efficacy added to the prediction of college major when interests are controlled. Using the Holland interest themes from the SII and the

High Interest/ High Confidence for Investigative (High Priority)	High Interest/ Low Confidence for Realistic (Could consider if confidence can be increased)
Low Interest/ High Confidence for Social and Conventional (Interests must be increased – not optimal)	Low Interest/ Low confidence for Enterprising (Low Priority)

Figure 10.2.   Cross-classification of interest scores and confidence scores for Karen.

General Confidence (Holland) themes from the Skills Confidence Inventory, they found that self-efficacy and the combined synergistic effect of interest and self-efficacy added to the prediction of the Holland theme of the college major. Given findings of the predictive utility of both interests and self-efficacy, it is appropriate that means for joint use of such measures in career counseling are now increasingly available.

Generally speaking, such joint use, regardless of the specific measures utilized, may be based on a cross-classification of interests and confidence, with each cell of the cross-tabulation having unique implications for career exploration. In the simplest example, both interests and confidence are classified as high or low, yielding a 2 x 2 cross-tabulation. See Figure 10.2 for an example of such a cross classification (and see Betz, Harmon et al., 1996; Harmon et al., 1996, for extended discussions and case examples of the joint use of interest and confidence measures in career counseling).

Figure 10.2 shows a sample cross classification for a student named Karen, who sought career testing from the author. Holland themes for which Karen's interests and confidence are both high are shown in the upper left quadrant. These themes constitute high priorities for occupational exploration. This is done by finding educational majors or occupations which share the Holland theme on which the student has both high interests and high confidence. For Karen, Investigative is the only theme with high interest and high confidence. Investigative is associated with

occupations in the sciences, so this would provide a first step in exploration. If instead of the Investigative code shown for Karen, other themes
were found in the high interest/high confidence quadrant, occupations
corresponding to those Holland theme areas would be suggested. Examples are as follows: the Conventional is associated with Accountant; Social
with Counselor or Social Worker; Artistic with Artist or Musician or
Writer; Enterprising with Business Manager and Salesperson; and Realistic with Mechanic, Engineer, or Forester. Most majors and occupations
have more than one descriptive Holland code (for example, Realistic/
Investigative is the typical code for engineering occupations), so a Holland theme code book (see the Dictionary of Holland Occupational
Codes, Gottfredson & Holland, 1989, or the Holland College Majors
Finder, Rosen, Holmberg, & Holland, 1989) is used to find matching
majors or occupations.

Holland themes for which there is some interest but low confidence,
shown as the upper right quadrant, may well be possible options if confidence can be increased using Bandura=s (1986) four sources of efficacy
information. Since Bandura's theory contains within it the means of intervention (the four sources of efficacy information, uses of which are
described below), the area of high interest-low confidence is that which
provides a particularly promising means of widening vocational options
by increasing self-efficacy. In the case shown in Figure 10.2, Realistic
(associated with outdoor and technical activity areas) is in this quadrant—
Karen has some interest in this area, although she lacks confidence.
Because IR is the code associated with a large array of engineering and
technical occupations, increasing Karen's confidence in Realistic activities
has the potential of expanding her range of occupational options to
include those. This will be discussed further later in the chapter.

The third quadrant of the cross classification, areas of low interest but
higher confidence, may provide options if interests can be strengthened.
There is an increasing body of research which has examined the importance of interests to intrinsic motivation (Renninger, 2000) which is, in
turn, essential to student learning and achievement (Hidi, 2000; Hidi &
Harackiewicz, 2000). Other researchers are examining ways of enhancing
or triggering interest development through the vehicle of "situational
interests" (Renninger & Hidi, 2002). For example, Hoffman & Haussler
(1998) described three different approaches to triggering interests in a
physics course: emphasis on physics as a scientific enterprise, emphasis
on the usefulness of physics in helping mankind, and the impact of physics on society. Different students responded more or less positively to each
approach, and altogether the interests of many more students were stimu-
lated when alternative stimulus triggers were used. Though research on
interest development is beyond the scope of this chapter, it is a promising

Table 10.2.   Sample Items and Parallel Interest Scale for the Expanded Skills Confidence Inventory—High School

Confidence Scale	Sample Items-ESCI High School	Parallel Interest Scale
Mechanical	Assemble an entertainment center	Construction and engineering
Mathematics	Calculate a shooting percentage in basketball	Working with numbers
Science	Study the way the human mind works	Health and science
Creative production	Produce a music video	Music and arts
Writing	Write a weekly column for the school newspaper	Writing/mass communication
Cultural sensitivity	Help educate family members about other races or religions	Cultural relations
Helping	Volunteer in a nursing home or hospital	Helping others
Teaching/training	Lead a scout troop or church group for kids	Teaching and training
Public speaking and leadership	Speak at your class graduation	Law and politics
Sales and organizational management	Raise money for your club or team	Business, sales, marketing
Office Services	Be in charge of banquet arrangements for a school prom or club/team	Office and project management
Using technology	Help a teacher with the class computers	Working with computers
Nature	Manage the landscaping for a city park	Plants and animals
Outdoor/physical	Work as a forest ranger	Protective services

Note: As taken from Betz and Wolfe, 2005.

avenue for further research. And finally, the last quadrant in the cross classification, areas of low interest and low confidence, is generally considered low in priority for exploration.

These interpretive principles, that is, conjoint interpretation of interests and confidence, can be used with any interest measure for which there is a parallel confidence measure. Other inventories providing measures of both interests and skills confidence for broad occupational orientations include the seven dimensions of the Campbell Interest and Skill

Survey (Campbell et al., 1992). The dimensions are Influencing, Organizing, Helping, Creating, Analyzing, Producing, and Adventuring. The Kuder Task Specific Self-Efficacy Scale (Kelly, 2002; Lucas, Wanberg, & Zytowski, 1997) assesses confidence with respect to the 10 Activity Reference areas measured by the Kuder Career Search. These include Nature, Mechanical, Computations, Art, Human Services, Office Detail Sales/ Management, Science/Technical, Communications, and Music. The substantive overlap of these sets of scales with the six Holland themes may be noted.

Although measures of confidence with respect to the broad domains of vocational activity have been useful, it has also been useful to focus on more specific, occupationally relevant domains of behavior—those analogous in specificity to the basic interest domains of vocational interest measurement. These domains are more amenable to the assessment of self-efficacy because they describe homogenous activity dimensions. The Expanded Skills Confidence Inventory (Betz et al., 2003) was developed to measure confidence with respect to 17 basic domains of vocational activity parallel to several Basic Interest scales of the Strong Interest Inventory. These domains were selected to represent activities important across occupations, including Leadership, Public Speaking, Writing, Mathematics, Science, Helping, and Creative Production. Other confidence scales reflect new emphases within institutions such as schools and colleges, as well as business organizations, on high technology and on fostering cooperation and diversity among group members (e.g., Using Technology, Cultural Sensitivity, and Teamwork).

The Expanded Skills Confidence Inventory was normed with samples of 934 college students and 972 employed adults. Scores were found to have incremental predictive validity (beyond interests) in the prediction of students' choices of college major and career (Rottinghaus, Betz, & Borgen, 2003). In the study of Paulsen and Betz (2004) six Basic Confidence Scales—Mathematics, Science, Writing, Using Technology, Leadership, and Cultural Sensitivity—predicted 49% of the variance in students' confidence in their career decision making skills.

A version of the inventory for use with high school students was developed by Betz and Wolfe (2005). It has 14 confidence scales designed to be parallel to the 14 basic interest scales of the Strong Interest Explorer. The scales of the Expanded Skills Confidence Inventory-High School (ESCI-HS), sample items, and the parallel Strong Interest Explorer scale are shown in Table 10.2. The revised inventory was studied in samples of 154 freshman college students and 85 students from an inner city high school, 71% of whom were African American. This pair of inventories (the ESCI-HS and the Explorer) provides parallel assessment of 14 highly relevant dimensions of vocational choice.

INTERVENTIONS

Once means of assessing both interests and self-efficacy are available, which is now the case, assessment results can be used in career counseling to indicate domains of behavior where an increase in self-efficacy might be beneficial to the student or client's future educational and career development, so a plan for the intervention(s) should be made. Interventions are based on Bandura's four sources of efficacy information and should therefore ideally include enactive mastery experiences, vicarious learning or modeling, managing anxiety, and providing support and encouragement. Mastery experiences have been found to be the most powerful type of intervention, but encouragement and support can always be provided by parents and teachers as well as counselors, so focusing on at least these two may provide a first step in designing the intervention. It should be noted that although interventions would typically be designed by counselors or teachers, parents and friends can also play an important role in encouraging and supporting the young person as he/she undertakes confidence-building experiences.

In planning mastery experiences, opportunities should be sought where at first success is virtually ensured. Only after some success experiences should more difficult challenges be faced. Summer or after-school programs or community or technical colleges offering entry level or remedial courses and programmed learning materials may be good sources for such learning. Those doing the instruction must expect and ensure success rather than failure—thus, mastery-oriented education rather than evaluations made by comparing one to others is ideal.

In using modeling the counselor or teacher would need to locate people who have succeeded in the area in which the student or client lacks self-efficacy. It is helpful, though not essential, if these models are the same race and gender of the individual, and this may be especially true if the domain of behavior is nontraditional for that person's gender. For example, a woman teaching automobile maintenance and repair or carpentry to girls will provide helpful modeling effects because these are traditionally male domains. Similarly, a man teaching parenting skills to young men would provide the additional benefit of modeling a nontraditional competency. Models can be in person or on film or television, in books, or other media. For example, a book on the life of a female astronaut or scientist could be a useful model for a young girl considering these fields.

The third component of the intervention is anxiety management. Learning new things may be associated with anxiety, particularly if these are gender nontraditional domains. If a domain like math has been associated with males, and if a female student has internalized a message of "girls can't do math," anxiety will likely accompany new learning efforts. Thus anxiety management may also be appropriate. Relaxation training and learning to consciously focus self-talk on the task rather than the self can be helpful.

Finally, the counselor, teacher, and/or parent can serve as a student's or client's cheerleader as the students try new things. This role includes generally encouraging the student that she CAN do it, and more specifically reinforcing effort as she tries new things. Helping students set goals, reinforcing them when they are achieved, and helping them to try again when they have temporarily faltered is also important. Finally the counselor can counteract negative societal beliefs that the clients have internalized.

Evidence of the effectiveness of a self-efficacy theory-based intervention in increasing Holland theme self-efficacy was provided by Betz and Schifano (2000)—the intervention was designed to increase self-efficacy regarding Holland's Realistic theme in college women. The Realistic theme is important along with the Investigative theme for choosing a large array of engineering and technical fields in which women continue to be underrepresented. The Realistic theme is the theme where gender differences remain most persistent. We were interested in whether a group intervention to increase Realistic self-efficacy in women could be designed, with the potential to increase their willingness to consider occupations in these areas.

In the intervention, college women selected to be low in Realistic self-efficacy but to have at least moderate levels of Realistic interests were given a group intervention that included Bandura's sources of efficacy information and included the following content areas: hand tool identification and usage; building and repairing useful objects such as bookcases, lamps, and sink drain pipes; and architectural design and engineering. During the instruction, periodic breaks for structured relaxation exercises, positive self-talk, and group support were taken. The modeling component was met by having the chief university architect, a woman, take the young women on a "hard hat" tour of major construction sites on campus, teaching them about the process of designing and constructing large buildings. The intervention ended with a "test" on which each young woman was given a broken lamp to repair, and then, when she had accomplished the task, was given a brand new light bulb to serve as a test of her success (or failure)—the light-turned-on was a literal as well as figurative symbol of her success, which fortunately occurred in all cases.

The intervention, as opposed to the control condition, led to significant increases in Realistic self-efficacy. An example of the effectiveness of the treatment is shown in Figure 10.3. As shown, no pretest treatment group participants had high Realistic confidence, but 62% of the posttest treatment group did. Since they had Realistic interests upon entering the

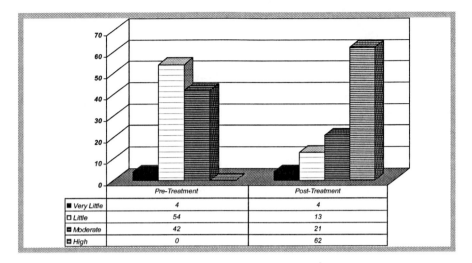

	Pre-Treatment	Post-Treatment
■ Very Little	4	4
□ Little	54	13
▣ Moderate	42	21
▣ High	0	62

Figure 10.3   Percentages of realistic confidence before and after treatment.

treatment program, our ability to increase their Realistic confidence means that these Realistic theme areas could now be included among their career options.

Case Example

Two successful interventions in individual career counseling area shown in Figures 10.2 and 10.4. The case previously shown in Figure 10.2 was that of Karen, a young woman with high interests in both Realistic and Investigative areas but low confidence in Realistic areas, the same theme area described in the Betz and Schifano (2000) intervention study. As shown in Figure 10.2, Realistic areas could add to Karen's career options if her confidence in the area could be increased. Accordingly, an intervention was implemented in which Karen took beginning level classes in electronics, mechanics, and computer programming; visited a facility employing a number of women engineers; and received help with anxiety management and social support. Karen's confidence improved such that she decided to pursue a degree in electrical engineering.

The second case (Figure 10.4) is that of a college student named Richard, who had changed majors several times and simply could not decide on a satisfactory major. The results of assessment using interests and self-efficacy with regard to the six Holland theme areas (the Strong Interest Inventory and the Skills Confidence Inventory) are summa-

High Interest/ High Confidence for No Themes	High Interest/ Low Confidence for Enterprising (Could consider if confidence can be increased)
Low Interest/ High Confidence for Realistic (Interests must be increased – not optimal)	Low Interest/ Low confidence for Investigative, Artistic, and Social (Low Priority)

Figure 10.4.   Percentages of realistic Cross classification of interest scores and confidence scores for Richard.

rized in Figure 10.4. These assessment data indicated that Richard had only one area of high interest, that of Enterprising, which would suggest careers in business management or sales or involving leadership activity of some type. But Richard was very low in self-efficacy with regard to this area—he was socially unskilled and unassertive. He had no Holland theme areas where he reported both high interest and high confidence, the upper left quadrant, so his perceived career options were very limited.

After obtaining the results of this assessment the counselor wondered whether it might be possible to increase Richard's self-efficacy with regard to Enterprising skills in particular and social skills more generally. The first step was training in communication skills and public speaking skills. The Counseling Center offered a social skills group for college students, and the community adult education program offered a course entitled "Practically Painless Public Speaking." Richard's counselor convinced him to enroll in both and provided constant support and "cheerleading" for him as he went through these courses. She taught him how to do progressive muscle relaxation and to use it whenever he felt threatened or frightened by new experiences. Richard met other "kindred" fearful students and adults and learned that he was not alone in his feelings of incompetence. The cumulative effects of this intervention were that Richard was able to declare a major in business and feel reasonably confident that he could succeed there. The intervention also greatly improved Richard's social skills with his peer group.

Gender Traditionality Issues in Conjoint Occurrences

Betz, Borgen, et al. (1996) examined the pattern of interest and skills confidence scores in a sample of 358 college students. Although most participants had congruent levels of interest and skills confidence, a sizable portion of individuals were high on one and low on the other within at least one occupational domain. Based on research examining the effects of stereotypic gender role socialization experiences (e.g., see Betz, 1993; Matlin, 1999), it was postulated that competencies in gender traditional areas might be encouraged by parents and teachers, but that parallel interests might not also develop. Thus, a girl might be socially skilled but have no interest in a social service/helping occupation. Conversely, a boy might be taught to be competent in mechanical activities yet have no interest in becoming an engineer. In fact, Betz, Borgen, et al. (1996) found that high confidence/low interest patterns occurred more frequently in gender-stereotypic areas. For example, 30% of the high confidence-low interest patterns were in the Realistic domain for men, but these patterns were only 11% among women. In contrast, 32% of high confidence/low interest patterns for women were in the Social theme, compared to 17% among men. Conversely, high interest-low confidence patterns occurred more frequently in gender nontraditional areas.

Rottinghaus et al. (2003) classified scores on the Basic Interest scales of the Strong and the Basic Confidence Scores of the Expanded Skills Confidence Inventory into thirds, yielding a 3 x 3 category system providing percentages of participants who fell into each of the resulting nine cells (high, medium, and low confidence crossed with high, medium, and low interest). The percentages of male and female students classified into on-diagonal or off-diagonal cells were calculated. On-diagonal cells are those where interest and confidence are both High, both Medium, or both Low, whereas off-diagonal cells are those in which interest is higher than confidence, or confidence is higher than interest. It was hypothesized that within gender non-stereotypic domains, there would be more frequent occurrence of higher interest with lower confidence, and on gender stereotypic domains there would be a relatively greater occurrence of higher confidence but lower interest. The data supported these hypotheses, especially with respect to male stereotypic behavior domains. For male stereotypic domains, the percentage of higher interest than confidence ranged from 11% to 15% for men but from 24% to 28% for women. Conversely, the percentages of higher confidence than interest are higher for men (24% to 41%) than for women (13% to 24%) on these domains. Results for Mechanical Activities are shown in Figure 10.5. Note that 27% of women report

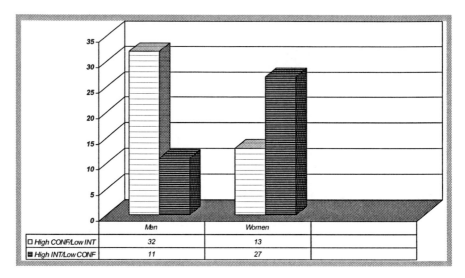

Figure 10.5.   Percentages of Patterns of Confidence and Interests for Mechanical by Gender.

more interest than confidence on Mechanical Activities—these are women who might try mechanical activities and majors/careers in fields like Engineering if confidence could be increased. Conversely, 32% of men have higher confidence than interest in this area. It is likely that gender stereotypic socialization has led to competencies in this area, but interests have not also developed.

The pattern is similar though less striking for the traditionally female domains. For Helping/Social Service, Teaching, and Office Services, men can be found more often in the higher interest/lower confidence cells and less often in the higher confidence/lower interest cells. As shown in Figure 10.6 for Social Service, 35% of young women feel confident in their Helping competencies but are not interested in Social Service activities. This is in contrast to 13% of young men. In contrast, 39% of young men versus 20% of women are interested in social service but lack confidence in their ability to succeed in those tasks. When the inevitable peer ridicule that will accompany preferences for gender-atypical choices is added to the lack of confidence, the need for support from adults is clear.

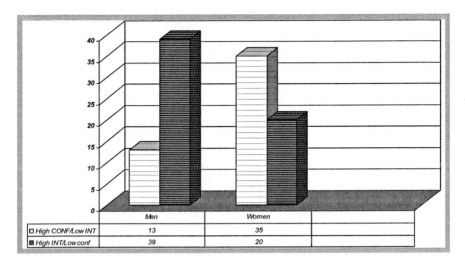

Figure 10.6.   Percentages of patterns of confidence and interests for social service by gender.

SUMMARY

Assessments in career counseling, and in career counseling interventions, now increasingly include as standard "ingredients" the examination of the client's self-efficacy with respect to the vocational domains in which he/she expresses an interest. Because of the comprehensive implications for intervention contained in the theory, the potential of self-efficacy constructs to help young people increase their career options and to achieve success in implementing the necessary educational objectives to reach their goals is significant.

For young people especially, this theory is very important because it takes an explicitly developmental position. In other words, we make the assumption that adolescents are still exploring and developing their interests and self-perceived competencies and that counseling and interventions that can stimulate them to explore new areas is both appropriate and important. Later in life, competencies especially may be more fully developed (not to say that you "can't teach an old dog new tricks"), but the potential growth for young people is especially great. Young people may also be lacking basic occupational information and decision making skills, so these too are an important focus of career education and counseling. But the enhancement of interests and self-perceived competencies in adolescence may have important implications for the subsequent quality of educational and occupational decision making and achievement.

REFERENCES

Bandura, A. (1986). *Social foundations of thought and action*. Englewood Cliffs, NJ: Prentice Hall.

Betz, N. E. (1993). Issues in the use of ability and interest measures with women. *Journal of Career Assessment, 1*, 217-232.

Betz, N. E., Borgen, F. H., & Harmon, L. (1996). *Skills Confidence Inventory: Applications and technical guide*. Palo Alto, CA: Consulting Psychologists' Press.

Betz, N. E., Borgen, F., & Harmon, L. (2005). *Skills Confidence Inventory Manual: Research, development, and strategies for interpretation*. Mountain View, CA: CPP.

Betz, N. E., Borgen, F. H., Rottinghaus, P., Paulsen, A., Halper, C., & Harmon, L. W. (2003). The Expanded Skills Confidence Inventory: Measuring basic dimensions of vocational activity. *Journal of Vocational Behavior, 62*, 76-100.

Betz, N. E., & Hackett, G. (1981). The relationship of career-related self-efficacy expectations to perceived career options in college women and men. *Journal of Counseling Psychology, 28*, 399-410.

Betz, N. E., Harmon, L. W., & Borgen, F. H. (1996). The relationship of self-efficacy for the Holland themes to gender, occupational group membership, and vocational interests. *Journal of Counseling Psychology, 43*, 90-98.

Betz, N. E., & Schifano, R. (2000). Increasing Realistic self-efficacy and interests in college women. *Journal of Vocational Behavior, 56*, 35-52.

Betz, N. E., & Wolfe, J. B. (2005). *Measuring confidence for basic domains of vocational activity in high school students. Journal of Career Assessment, 13*, 251-270.

Campbell, D. P., Hyne, S. A., & Nilsen, D. L. (1992). *Manual for the Campbell Interest and Skills Survey: CISS*. Minneapolis: National Computer Systems.

Donnay, D. A. C., & Borgen, F. H. (1999). The incremental validity of vocational self-efficacy: An examination of interest, self-efficacy, and occupation. *Journal of Counseling Psychology, 46*, 432-447.

Donnay, D. A. C., Morris, M., Schaubhut, N., & Thompson, R. (2005). *Strong Interest Inventory Manual: Research, development, and strategies for interpretation*. Mountain View, CA: CPP, Inc.

Gottfredson, G. D., & Holland, J. L. (1989). *Dictionary of Holland occupational codes (2nd ed.)*. Odessa, FL: PAR.

Hackett, G., & Betz, N. (1981). A self-efficacy approach to the career development of women. *Journal of Vocational Behavior, 18*, 326-339.

Harmon, L. W., Hansen, J. C., Borgen, F. H., & Hammer, A. L. (1994). *Strong Interest Inventory: Applications and technical guide*. Stanford, CA: Stanford Press.

Hidi, S. (2000). An interest researcher's perspective on the effects of extrinsic and intrinsic factors on motivation. In C. Sansone & J. M. Harackiewicz (Eds.), *Intrinsic and extrinsic motivation: The search for optimum motivation and performance* (pp. 309-339). New York: Academic Press.

Hidi, S. & Harackiewicz, J. (2000). Motivating the academically unmotivated: A critical issue for the 21st century. *Review of Educational Research, 70*, 151-179.

Hoffman, L. & Haussler, P. (1998). An intervention project promoting girls' and boys' interest in physics. In L. Hoffman, A. Krapp, K. Renninger, & J. Baumert (Eds.), *Interest and learning: Proceedings of the Second Conference on Interest and Gender* (pp. 301-316). Kiel, Germany, IPN.

Holland, J. L. (1985). *Vocational Preference Inventory.* Odessa, FLA: PAR.

Holland, J. L. (1994). *Self-directed search.* Odessa, FL: PAR.

Holland, J. L. (1997). *Making vocational choices: A theory of vocational personalities and work environments* (3rd ed.). Odessa, FL: Psychological Assessment.

Isaacs, J., Borgen, F. H., Donnay, D. A. C., & Hansen, T. A. (1997). *Self-efficacy and interests: Relationships of Holland themes to college major.* Poster presented at the annual meeting of the American Psychological Association, Chicago.

Kelly, K. R. (2002). Concurrent validity of the Kuder Career Search Activity Preference Scales and career clusters. *Journal of Career Assessment, 10,* 127-144.

Kuder, F. (1964). *Manual for the Kuder General Interest Survey.* Chicago: Science Research Associates.

Kuder, F ., & Zytowski, D. (1991). *Kuder Occupational Interest Survey Form DD. General manual* (3rd ed.). Monterey, CA: CTB McGraw Hill.

Lapan, R. T., Boggs, K. R., & Morrill, W. H. (1989). Self-efficacy as a mediator of investigative and realistic general occupational themes on the Strong Interest Inventory. *Journal of Counseling Psychology, 36,* 176-182.

Lenox, R., & Subich, L. (1994). The relationship between self-efficacy beliefs and inventoried vocational interests. *Career Development Quarterly, 42,* 302-313.

Lent, R. W., Brown, S. D., & Hackett, G. (1994). Toward a unifying social cognitive theory of career and academic interest, choice, and performance. *Journal of Vocational Behavior, 34,* 79-122.

Lucas, J. L., Wanberg, C. R., & Zytowski, D. G. (1997). Development of a career task self-efficacy scale: The Kuder Task Self-Efficacy Scale. *Journal of Vocational Behavior, 50,* 432-459.

Matlin, M. W. (1999). *The psychology of women* (4th ed.). Belmont, CA: Wadsworth.

Morris, M., Chartrand, J., & Donnay, D. (2002). *Reliability and validity of the Strong Interest Explorer.* Palo Alto, CA: Consulting Psychologists Press.

Parsons, F. (1909). *Choosing a vocation.* Boston: Houghton Mifflin.

Paulsen, A., & Betz, N. (2004). Basic confidence predictors of career decision self-efficacy. *Career Development Quarterly, 52,* 353-361.

Prediger, D. J ., & Swaney, K. B. (1995). Using UNIACT in a comprehensive approach to assessment for career planning. *Journal of Career Assessment, 3,* 429-452.

Renninger, K. A. (2000). How might the development of individual interests contribute to the conceptualization of intrinsic motivation? In C. Sansone & J.M. Harackiewicz (Eds), *Intrinsic and extrinsic motivation: The search for optimal motivation and performance* (pp. 373-404). New York: Academic Press.

Renninger, K. A. & Hidi, S. (2002). Student interest and achievement: Developmental issues raised by a case study. In A. Wigfield & J. Eccles (Ed.), *Development of achievement motivation* (pp. 173-195). San Diego: Academic Press.

Roe, A. (1956). *The psychology of occupations.* New York: Wiley.

Rosen, D., Holmbers, K., & Holland, J. L. (1989). *Holland Self-Directed Search: The college majors finder.* Odessa, FL: Psychological Assessment Resources.

Rottinghaus, P., Betz, N., & Borgen, F., (2003). Validity of parallel measures of vocational interests and confidence. *Journal of Career Assessment, 11,* 355-378.

Savickas, M. L., & Spokane, A. R. (Eds.) (1999). *Vocational interests: Their meaning, measurement and counseling use.* Palo Alto, CA: Davies-Black.

Strong, E. K., Jr. (1927). *Strong Vocational Interest Blank for Men*. Stanford, CA: Stanford University Press.

Super, D. E. (1957). *The psychology of careers*. New York: Harper.

Wall, J. E., & Baker, H. E. (1997). The interest finder: Evidence of validity. *Journal of Career Assessment, 5,* 255-273.

Walsh, W. B., & Betz, N. E. (2001). *Tests and assessment* (4th ed.). Upper Saddle River, NJ: Prentice Hall.

Zytowski, D. G. (1997). *Kuder Career Search Schedule: Users Manual*. Ames, IA: National Career Assessment Services.

CHAPTER 11

CULTURE AND SELF-EFFICACY IN ADOLESCENTS

Gabriele Oettingen and Kristina M. Zosuls

The goals set by individuals at different times in their lives reflect the developmental tasks of those particular periods in the lifespan (Havighurst, 1972). Robert Havighurst proposed that a combination of cultural and biological demands as well as individual contexts create developmental tasks and that the way in which an individual meets these demands influences that individual's well-being and success with future tasks. A key task for adolescents is to form an identity that they will carry over into adulthood (Aquino & Reed, 2002; Arnett, 2002; Harter, Waters, Whitesell, & Kastelic, 1998). According to Havighurst (1972), this overarching responsibility includes mastering educational and vocational demands, establishing mature relationships with peers, and becoming a socially responsible member of society. At this crossroad, adolescence may be thought of as a time during which the role of the individual changes from being the recipient of one's culture to becoming an agent carrying that culture.

The competencies adolescents develop when solving their developmental tasks are rooted in the demands of the respective culture. Thus the types of competencies developed by adolescents may differ across cultures. However, adolescents of all cultures eventually develop competen-

Self-Efficacy Beliefs of Adolescents, 245–265

cies in mastering the transition from being shaped by the culture to yielding to the demands of the culture. They increasingly are responsible for acting in line with what is expected from them culturally and what is necessary to optimize their physical and mental well-being (Grigorenko & O'Keefe, 2004).

In this chapter, we investigate the role that self-efficacy beliefs play in adolescents successfully solving this transition. We first provide an overview of how adolescents' efficacy beliefs differ between Asian and Western cultures. We then argue that cultures, by affecting their institutions (e.g., family, school) as well as by affecting the selection and weighting of the sources of self-efficacy appraisal, shape efficacy beliefs. We conclude with the contention that, in modern cultures where norms no longer play a central role in guiding action, efficacy beliefs become pivotal for adolescents' successful transition into adulthood.

ADOLESCENTS' SELF-EFFICACY IN ASIAN VERSUS WESTERN CULTURES

Expectations and Self-Efficacy

Following the neo-behaviorist tradition of Edward Chace Tolman (1932), the concept of *expectation* has been the most powerful cognitive variable predicting motivation and performance. Expectations—subjective judgments about how likely it will be that certain future events will occur or not occur—are based on past experiences and thus reflect a person's performance history (Bandura, 1977; Mischel, 1973). Expectancy judgments may be *self-efficacy beliefs*, defined as individuals' judgments of their capability to execute a certain behavior required for a desired outcome, or *outcome expectations*, defined as individuals' beliefs that a certain behavior will actually result in a desired outcome (Bandura, 1997). Expectancy judgments may also be conceptualized as *general expectations*, that is, expectations as to whether a desired outcome will or will not occur (Heckhausen, 1991; Oettingen, 1995). No matter how expectancy judgments are conceived, a strong body of literature shows that optimistic, positive expectations of success foster effort and persistence and, ultimately, successful performance. Findings on the beneficial effects of optimistic expectations emerge in various life domains, such as in school, work, and sports, in the interpersonal domain, and in the domain of physical and mental health (see Bandura, 1997; Scheier & Carver, 1992; Seligman, 1991; Taylor & Brown, 1988).

Among the various forms of expectancy judgments, efficacy beliefs have emerged as the most important predictor of motivation and performance (Schunk & Pajares, 2002). Research has supported a consistent link between strong efficacy beliefs and achievement (Multon, Brown, & Lent, 1991; Robbins et al., 2004). Children and adolescents who have strong efficacy beliefs exert more effort and exhibit greater persistence. They also show a higher level of engagement in learning and employ more effective problem solving and learning strategies. Finally, they are plagued by fewer negative emotional reactions in the face of obstacles and are more likely to take on challenging activities and goals (Pajares & Miller, 1994, 1995; Pintrich, 2003; Zimmerman, 2000; see also Bandura, 1997). All of these attributes foster motivation and successful performance, and thereby successful mastery of impending developmental tasks.

Developmental Task: School Achievement

Despite these findings, a growing body of research reveals cultural differences in mean levels of self-efficacy and in the relationship between self-efficacy and achievement. Culturally-based differences in academic self-efficacy may have their origins in the respective cultural values stemming from historical, sociopolitical, and economic influences. These values are particularly salient in the developmental tasks arising in school. Adolescents spend more time in school than in other places outside the home, and most developmental tasks with which adolescents are confronted in school need to be solved in school. Consequently, schools have a considerable impact on adolescent development (Eccles, 2004; Eccles & Wigfield, 2002). Characteristics at the classroom, school, district, and community levels influence student performance (see Williams, 1998) and thus academic self-efficacy. Thereby, adolescents' own interpretations of their experiences in school are critical mediators between school characteristics and students' academic-related thoughts, feelings, and behaviors (Eccles, 2004).

In some East Asian cultures, school features such as high achievement standards, an emphasis on hard work and effort (versus ability), and performance feedback focusing on weaknesses have been considered to influence the efficacy beliefs of children and adolescents. Salili, Chiu, and Lai (2001) observed that a sample of Hong Kong high school students scored lower on self-efficacy than did immigrant Chinese Canadian and European Canadian high school students. Comparing the two groups of Canadian students, the authors reported that although the immigrant Chinese Canadian students spent more time studying and attained higher grades than did their European Canadian counterparts, the Chinese Canadian students did not differ significantly from the European Canadian students in self-efficacy. The authors suggested that the difference in level of self-efficacy between Hong Kong and Canadian students of both ethnicities was likely due to differences in criteria for success in the two contexts. Hong Kong high schools set extremely high standards of achievement and are geared toward the brightest and highest achievers. Students in Hong Kong are typically given large amounts of homework and are seldom praised for good work, but they are frequently admonished for poor performance. Thus, the academic context in Hong Kong appears to give the average student fewer experiences that would be conducive to the development or maintenance of strong efficacy beliefs.

Self-efficacy may not be as strong in cultures that place little emphasis on self-reliance and agency (Skinner, Schindler, & Tschechne, 1990). However, Karasawa, Little, Miyashita, Mashima, and Azuma (1997) found that Japanese children exhibited action-control beliefs about school performance in general that are similar to those of children from Western cultures. But Japanese students had relatively independent conceptions of personal agency related to *effort* and *ability* compared to American, Russian, and German students. Compared to children in these cultures, Japanese children had lower agency beliefs related to ability and higher agency beliefs related to effort. These results are supported by other researchers who have found a consistent tendency among Asian students to attribute successes and failures to effort rather than to ability, in contrast to students from Western countries who tend to make more ability-based attributions (Holloway, 1988; Yan & Gaier, 1994). The authors concluded that these differences in the Japanese children may stem from a number of sources. Japanese students are typically assigned materials and given feedback that emphasizes effort rather than ability. Furthermore, performance feedback is typically highly private and therefore may impede social-comparison processes that might otherwise promote assessment of ability (Karasawa et al., 1997).

Other measures of efficacy-related beliefs have also shown lower scores among children and adolescents from Asian cultures. Despite outperforming non-Asian American students on a verbal task, Asian American high school students exhibit weaker efficacy beliefs and higher levels of fear of failure than do non-Asian students (Eaton & Dembo, 1997). Apparently, values derived from high parental expectations play a greater role in the motivation and achievement behavior of Asian American students than of non-Asian students. Familial aspirations have also been found related to differences in English achievement between first-generation and third-generation high school students (Urdan, 2004). When controlling for perceived family aspirations, the better performance of first-generation students (from Asian and Latin American cultures) compared to third-generation students disappeared. This implies that the stronger achievement of the first-generation students was partly due to the perceived demands of their families, which were less acculturated than were their third-generation counterparts.

Developmental Task: Entering Professional Life

Efficacy beliefs steer occupational considerations and related life choices (Bandura, Barbaranelli, Caprara, & Pastorelli, 2001). Furthermore, cultural differences in self-efficacy regarding career decision-making should reflect the way in which adolescents and young adults are expected to solve this developmental task. In a study comparing Taiwanese and American students, Mau (2000) observed that Taiwanese students scored significantly lower on a measure of career decision-making self-efficacy (assessing beliefs that one can successfully set vocational goals, seek occupation-related information, plan, solve problems, overcome obstacles, and appraise one's performance). This difference in self-efficacy may reflect differences in the ways in which adolescents and young adults make their career decisions in Asian versus Western cultures. American students are actively encouraged to make their own career decisions, and thus they need to develop competence in establishing a career path. In contrast, in many Asian cultures, students conform to familial and societal norms and often follow a career track that is more clearly laid out for them. Thus career decision-making self-efficacy may be far less relevant in Taiwan and in other Asian cultures compared to many Western cultures.

Developmental Task: Emotional Independence

Although we have focused on cultural differences in level and predictive value of self-efficacy related to developmental tasks in the achievement and vocational domains, culture should influence adolescents' self-efficacy in a number of other domains relevant to their development, including physical and mental health. Indeed, research suggests that self-efficacy may be less important for mental health in some Asian cultures. Stewart et al. (2004) found that generalized self-efficacy was a weaker predictor of depressive symptoms in Hong Kong adolescents than in American adolescents. Self-efficacy was also lower among Hong Kong adolescents, supporting the findings reported earlier. Stewart et al. posited that in cultures that place strong value on obedience and respect for authority, young people may be less attendant to their efficacy beliefs and other expectancy judgments. The researchers also found higher levels of depressive symptoms among the Asian adolescents and suggested that these same cultural norms may decrease vulnerability to acting out but increase vulnerability to depressed mood.

SUMMARY

The research reviewed above suggests that adolescents raised in Asian cultures hold weaker efficacy beliefs than do adolescents raised in Western cultures. These findings pertain to self-efficacy for mastering developmental tasks in three domains: achievement, vocation, and emotional independence. We called particular attention to the academic domain, in which Asian adolescents reported lower self-efficacy than did adolescents in Western cultures despite having more successful mastery of respective developmental tasks. The observed differences in self-efficacy may originate in the values of the cultures themselves. Specifically, cultural values may influence the formation of self-efficacy through its influence on the proximal context and on the psychological processes of efficacy appraisal. It is this influence we now address.

SELF-EFFICACY AND CULTURAL VALUES

In this section, we first specify three critical dimensions of cultural values and then describe how they might exert their influence on the school environment and on selecting and weighting the sources that are responsible for efficacy appraisal. We then present studies with children and adolescents in East and West Germany before and after unification that support our reasoning.

Three Dimensions of Cultural Values

Material factors in the environment—in particular, value systems—exert influence on adolescents' development within different cultures (Greenfield, Keller, Fuligni, & Maynard, 2003). Attempts to empirically investigate cultural differences have identified a number of dimensions of cultural values (Hofstede, 1997; Triandis, 1989). Geert Hofstede analyzed cultural value systems in matched samples of employees in the same multinational business in more than forty countries and identified various dimensions of cultural differences, among them individualism/collectivism, power distance, and uncertainty avoidance. These dimensions have provided a useful framework for examining how cultural values are expressed in major societal systems and institutions and thereby affect efficacy beliefs.

The *individualism/collectivism* dimension has received the most attention in cross-cultural research (e.g. Triandis, 1989; see also the dimension of independence versus interdependence, Markus & Kitayama, 1991). Collectivist cultures promote the view that people belong to in-groups that demand lasting loyalty and from which members cannot easily free themselves. In return, people receive protection from the in-group. In contrast, individualist cultures promote the view that people look primarily after their own welfare and their immediate family's interests. They value an autonomous definition of the self and individual goals more than group goals (Triandis, McCusker, & Hui, 1990).

In cultures with large disparity in power, or *power distance*, people are expected to accept inequality in power. This is especially true for the less powerful members of the culture. People in cultures with small power distance value a more equal distribution of power.

People in cultures of strong *uncertainty avoidance* are easily distressed by new, unstructured, unclear, or unpredictable situations. They try to avoid these situations by maintaining strict codes of conduct and a belief in absolute truths. Members of such cultures tend to be compulsive, security seeking, intolerant, aggressive, and emotional. In contrast, people in cultures of weak uncertainty avoidance value being relaxed, tolerant, risk accepting, and contemplative.

How Do Cultural Values Affect Self-Efficacy Appraisal?

We assume that culture reveals its effect on the efficacy beliefs of adolescents by affecting the systems and institutions in which adolescents are embedded: the family, the school, and the community. Hofstede (1986) posited that because families and schools are fundamental institutions of virtually all societies, they both reflect the social role patterns of a given culture and are important means by which cultures are transmitted from one generation to the next. These contexts also provide sources of efficacy appraisal. Understanding how cultural values affect these major societal systems may clarify the processes that make adolescents' self-efficacy appraisals vary across cultures. Thus, we now examine how the three dimensions of cultural values described above may affect the institutions of family and school.

Cultural Values Affect Educational Context

Hofstede (1986, 1997; see also Triandis, 1989; Triandis et al., 1990) contended that families in cultures high on collectivism teach their adolescents to love and respect the needs of their in-group. In school, adolescents pursue performance goals demonstrating required competencies more than learning goals of expanding one's competencies (Ames, 1992; Dweck & Leggett, 1988; Nicholls, 1984). They create a social reality that makes their performance outcomes noticeable to their collective. In cultures high on individualism, adolescents are expected to learn how to learn, and performance outcomes are seen as instrumental to realizing one's individual potential rather than meeting the approval of one's in-group.

Hofstede's (1986, 1997) ideas on how power distance or power disparity affects family and school life focus on adolescents' relation to authority. In cultures with a large power differential, adolescents are taught to obey their parents and to treat them as superiors. Education is teacher-centered (Stipek, 1988), and the curriculum is supposed to reflect the wisdom of the educators, who are not to be contradicted or criticized. In contrast, in cultures with a small power differential, adolescents are encouraged to express their views freely in the family and to treat parents as equals. Education in school is child-centered (Stipek, 1988, 1991). Teachers expect students to initiate communication, speak up and criticize, and to find their own direction and pace of learning.

Hofstede (1986, 1997) speculates that in families and schools of cultures adhering to values of strong uncertainty avoidance, foreign influences are experienced as a source of high threat and stress, and emotional reactions and self-righteousness are prevalent. Teachers are expected to have the right answers and to speak in a formal manner (Stroebe, 1976). Intellectual disagreement is interpreted as personal offense. Adolescents adapt to highly structured, unidimensional teaching strategies (Rosenholtz & Rosenholtz, 1981; Rosenholtz & Simpson, 1984) where materials are predefined and explicit. Rules are readily embraced. In contrast, adolescents in cultures of weak uncertainty avoidance are curious about new and foreign experiences and respond reflectively rather than emotionally to ambiguities (see also Sorrentino, Raynor, Zubek, & Short, 1990). Teachers are not expected to be all-knowing, and they take intellectual disagreements as challenges. Adolescents deal effectively with multidimensional teaching strategies that entail only partially-structured learning materials, general instructions, and flexible, individualized pacing.

Cultural Values Affect Selecting and Weighting of Efficacy Sources

To understand how cultural values may influence self-efficacy beliefs, it is necessary to explore the processes of efficacy appraisal. Bandura (1997) has specified four information sources of efficacy information, the first of which is *mastery experience*. Success fosters a strong sense of efficacy, particularly when achieved in the face of adversity. Failures result in a weak sense of efficacy, especially when experienced early and frequently and cannot be attributed to lack of effort or unfavorable circumstances. The second source of efficacy appraisal is the *vicarious experience* by which attainments achieved by similar others are modeled. Successes attained by similar others raise the observer's sense of efficacy, but failures diminish it. The achievements of similar others may also influence efficacy appraisal by providing a standard of comparison against which one's actions can be judged. Achievements such as school grades are judged relatively, and one's own efficacy is inferred by comparing one's attainments to those of one's peers. Performance evaluations by others, or *social persuasions*, can also influence one's sense of efficacy. Active attempts at persuasion are particularly effective when communicators are endowed with competence and authority. A fourth information source results from the *physiological reactions* that one experiences when confronted with difficult performance situations. For example, feeling one's heart beating during an important test would indicate a low level of self-efficacy, whereas "staying cool" would be a sign of high self-efficacy.

People may not always have access to all of the sources of efficacy appraisal. The opportunity for vicarious experiences, for example, may be limited because there are few competent models available. Moreover, individuals may sample selectively and weight and integrate the information available in their preferred manner. The persuasive efforts of others may be readily embraced if the feedback is positive but may be defensively disregarded if negative. These considerations imply that forming beliefs of personal efficacy is a complex appraisal process that entails selecting, weighting, and integrating information from multiple sources. It is in this appraisal process that culture may play its influential role. Thus, cultural values may affect not only the type of information provided by the various sources, but also which information is selected and how it is weighted and integrated in efficacy judgments.

Selecting, Weighting, and Integrating Cultural Information

In collectivist cultures, adolescents should be sensitive to feedback from the in-group so that they may adjust their behavior to meet the norms of the group (Kitayama, Markus, Matsumoto, & Norasakkunkit, 1997). Evaluation by in-group members should be the source of efficacy information that is predominantly selected and weighted, with modeling by other in-group members also being influential. To the contrary, adolescents in individualist cultures should focus their self-appraisals of efficacy on information concerning their personal performance attainments (e.g., improvements or declines; see Rosenholtz & Rosenholtz, 1981). Further, whereas adolescents in individualist cultures may be more in tune with their private emotional states, adolescents socialized in collectivist cultures should direct their emotional responses more to the preference of their in-group (Markus & Kitayama, 1991).

Under conditions of a large power differential, evaluations of authorities such as parents and teachers should be especially selected and weighted in efficacy appraisal. In addition, parents and teachers should be readily taken as models and as convincing persuaders. Finally, unquestioned authority of teachers may heighten negative emotional arousal, thus leading emotional states to become prevalent sources of information for self-efficacy judgments. In contrast, in cultures of low power differential, adolescents become creators of their own development, sampling information comparatively free of authorities' influences.

In cultures of strong uncertainty avoidance, teachers give regular and frequent feedback on the same assignments. In this monolithic structure, students know where they stand in the social comparative judgment of their own efficacy. Moreover, the verbal communications of important persuaders such as teachers, parents, and peers are phrased unambiguously and reflect a high degree of social consensus. Adolescents of families and schools in less uncertainty avoidance cultures face more ambiguity when it comes to appraising their efficacy. Social ranking by performance attainment is less possible because of individualized instruction. Hence, inferences from performance attainments as well as from vicarious experiences provide leeway for personal interpretation. This permits self-enhancing attributions and judgments of capability linked to relatively stronger efficacy beliefs (Bandura, 1986; Taylor, 1989).

Summary

To explore why the self-efficacy beliefs of adolescents from Asian cultures are weaker than those of adolescents from Western cultures, we have considered how cultural values as defined by Hofstede (1997) may affect both the features of the proximal cultural environment (i.e., its institutions such as the family and the school) and the psychological processes of efficacy appraisal (i.e., performance experience, vicarious performance, persuasion, and physiological processes). We hypothesize that valuing collectivism, large power distance, and high uncertainty avoidance will lead to comparatively weak efficacy beliefs because self-efficacy is appraised by selecting and weighting information provided by the in-group, by a respected authority, and by unambiguous norms and rules. To the contrary, we hypothesize that valuing individualism, small power distance, and low uncertainty avoidance will lead to comparatively strong efficacy beliefs, because self-efficacy is appraised by selecting and weighting information provided by various past accomplishments, by messages from a variety of individuals without overwhelming authority, and by ambiguous contexts allowing for multiple interpretations. We will discuss findings supporting these hypotheses as well as the contention that both the educational environment and the selecting and weighting of the different information sources underlie the relation between cultural values and efficacy beliefs. These findings are derived from an experiment of culture in East and West Berlin.

AN EXPERIMENT OF CULTURE: EAST AND WEST BERLIN

East and West Berlin before unification were ideal settings in which to investigate the relation between sociocultural values and efficacy beliefs. Over centuries, East and West Berlin shared a cultural and historical background as well as one political system. But between 1945 and 1990, East Berliners and West Berliners lived under the different political systems of communism and social-capitalism. Possible differences between East and West Berlin can therefore be readily interpreted as stemming from these political system differences and their economic, social-structural, and educational consequences. The effects of political system differences on the educational context are of particular relevance for academic self-efficacy.

East and West Berlin Schools

East and West Berlin schools before unification differed in cultural values and educational contexts. Values in East Berlin were more directed toward collectivism, large power distance, and uncertainty avoidance. In East Berlin, the educational program, guided by official party doctrine, aimed to develop harmonious socialistic personalities by teaching all students to evaluate themselves "adequately," that is, consistent with the authorities' evaluations of their competence and personal attributes (Franz, 1987; Waterkamp, 1990). In school, performance feedback was given to each child by the teacher and by the "class collective" from first grade on. Further, performance evaluations were publicized and children were asked to critically evaluate themselves in front of the entire class. A strictly uni-dimensional style of teaching (Rosenholtz & Rosenholtz, 1981) was practiced in which children in a given grade level were confronted with the exact same materials, tasks, and tests and were bound to the same pacing, irrespective of their potential or interests. This structure facilitated differential evaluation by the teachers and by the class collective, making a child's performance rank highly salient. Finally, the school and leisure domains overlapped considerably (i.e., children from one classroom met again in the same constellation in the afternoon), making it even more difficult to change their social realities. Because it favored public performance evaluations and standardized teaching strategies, the East Berlin school context should have fostered children's precise estimation of their potential and discouraged self-serving, overly positive self-evaluations.

In contrast, West Berlin schools did not focus on self-evaluations and favored more vague and private performance evaluations starting as early as Grade 2. In addition, in West Berlin, more individualized and multidimensional teaching styles prevailed. Finally, school and leisure time were less likely to overlap in West Berlin. Thus, children were given more interpretative leeway in forming their subjective senses of efficacy.

East and West Berlin: A Cross-Sectional Study

In June 1990, before unification of the two Germanys, we assessed the efficacy beliefs and recorded the mathematics and verbal grades of more than 300 East Berlin children from two schools, Grades 2 to 6 (Oettingen, Little, Lindenberger, & Baltes, 1994). We compared the data to a matched study in West Berlin conducted in 1991 involving over 500 children. As measured by the Control, Agency, Means-ends Instrument (CAMI; Skinner, Chapman, & Baltes, 1988), East Berlin children had a lower sense of academic self-efficacy than did West Berlin children. That is, they had less confidence in their ability to exert effort in school, they considered themselves to be less smart, and they thought they would have less luck. The differences began in the third grade and were also evident in Grades 4 through 6. At the same time, East Berlin children conformed more readily to their teachers' performance evaluations than did West Berlin children, as indicated by stronger correlations between their self-efficacy and the course grades they received from their teachers (Oettingen et al., 1994).

In 1991, one year after the first assessment, but still before the East Berlin school system adopted West Berlin's educational policies, we returned to the East Berlin schools in an effort to replicate the findings (Oettingen & Little, 1993). At this point, we also administered Raven's Progressive Matrices test. We hypothesized that the observed differences between East and West Berlin children's self-efficacy and conformity would be due to the children with lower Raven scores because once they enter school, they are more frequently confronted with negative performance feedback that contradicts their naïve optimism. Therefore, the children with lower scores on the Raven test may have needed to revise their initial naïve performance optimism to a greater extent than would the children who obtained higher scores. Moreover, because of the initial negative performance feedback, lower scoring children should more readily accept future failure feedback than higher scoring children. Most importantly, this effect should be particularly pronounced in school systems aiming at "adequate" self-evaluation, that is, more in East Berlin than in West Berlin. Our hypotheses were confirmed. We observed that the differences in mean levels of self-efficacy and in conformity of efficacy appraisal were particularly due to the children with lower Raven scores (Oettingen & Little, 1993).

Implications of This Study

As we have shown, a growing body of literature suggests that a strong sense of efficacy promotes cognitive and self-regulatory learning skills. It also reduces fear of failure, raises aspirations, and fosters effortful action and successful behavior. A weak sense of efficacy achieves the contrary. Accordingly, East Berlin children who had lower self-efficacy than West Berlin children should have suffered comparatively more from the cognitive, affective, and behavioral disadvantages linked to this weak sense of efficacy.

Moreover, findings on the correlation between self-efficacy and teacher evaluations suggested that the East Berlin children with lower Raven scores accepted the public and unambiguous feedback of their teachers more readily than did their West Berlin counterparts. Because the feedback was highly veridical in East Berlin, it should have contradicted the naïve optimism of the children with low Raven scores, thus leading to a weak sense of efficacy. Consequently, the East Berlin children with low scores on this measure should have particularly suffered from the problematic consequences of a low self-efficacy. For example, they may have suffered from fear of failure and may have exerted little effort and persistence. This, in turn, should have reduced the successful mastery of impending developmental tasks. In summary, our findings suggest that the East Berlin educational background provided a disadvantage for the children with low Raven scores. Regrettably, these are precisely the children who would have benefited most from the motivational advantages of a strong sense of efficacy.

East Berlin in Transition: A Longitudinal Study

Our hypothesis that the political system and the respective educational goals and practices influenced the development of children's sense of efficacy would be further supported, if, after East Berlin adopted the West Berlin school system in the fall of 1991, the East Berlin data pattern began to resemble that of the West Berlin sample. Indeed, in the spring of 1992, after East Berlin students had been taught according to the West Berlin educational model for one year, the East Berlin children's level of agreement between their perceived self-efficacy and their teachers' performance evaluations decreased to that of West Berlin students (Little, Lopez, Oettingen, & Baltes, 2001). It seems, then, that surrendering the educational goal of receiving "adequate" self-evaluation lessened East Berlin students' agreement with the teachers' performance judgments. It may also be that, after the fall of the wall, a diminished respect for the authorities' evaluations lessened students' readiness to give in to the teachers' evaluations. In contrast, the level of self-efficacy did not change. After one year of being taught under the West Berlin educational model, East Berlin children still believed less in their capability to exert effort, to be smart, and to have luck in school than did their West Berlin counterparts.

Unlike conformity, the level of self-efficacy does not only depend on the teachers' performance evaluations. The other three information sources of efficacy appraisal may explain why the level of self-efficacy did not increase to the West Berlin level at the same time. However, we expect that, in time, the level of East Berlin students' beliefs will eventually parallel those in West Berlin.

Supportive Evidence in Adolescents

How well do the differences in the political systems and their consequences serve as an explanation for the observed differences in East and West Berlin children's sense of efficacy and in the students' conformity with the teacher evaluations? We found similar patterns of results from studies conducted by other researchers, with different samples, in different places, and with different instruments.

Hannover (1995) found that adolescents with low academic performance from various schools in East Germany were less convinced of their academic potential than were adolescents in a West German comparison group, but there was no difference among students with strong academic performance. Also, East German youngsters conformed more readily to their teachers' evaluations than did their West German peers. Ettrich,

Krause, Hofer, and Wild (1996) demonstrated the lessening of East Berlin adolescents' conformity level to the West Berlin level after the introduction of the West Berlin school system. East German and West German adolescents who were tested in 1993 (i.e., after the East Germans had been taught according to the West German model for two years) no longer showed differences in conformity. However, as we observed in our younger participants, the East German adolescents continued to evince a lower sense of efficacy than did West German adolescents.

Supporting the notion that different cultural values were endorsed by former East German and West German adolescents, Reitzle and Silbereisen (2000) found that, in 1991 (during the immediate aftermath of the unification of Germany), East German adolescents endorsed a higher degree of collectivist values such as politeness, family safety, respect for tradition and social order than did West German adolescents, and they were less likely to endorse individualistic values such as social power (control or dominance over others) and freedom. By 1996, these differences were attenuated. More in line with the values endorsed by West German adolescents, East German adolescents showed less of an emphasis on collectivist values.

Summary

In line with the East Berlin political system reinforcing comparatively stronger values of collectivism, power distance, and uncertainty avoidance, East Berlin's educational goals were geared towards adequate self-evaluation, and teaching strategies were strictly unidimensional. The differences in cultural values, as well as in the proximal contexts, should have facilitated self-efficacy appraisal based on unambiguous and public performance evaluations by teachers and by peers. Our findings that East Berlin students had both a weaker sense of efficacy and higher conformity than did West Berlin students are consistent with these postulations.

These findings also shed light on the question of why a comparatively lower sense of efficacy is often observed in Asian adolescents compared to Western adolescents. Asian cultures have been characterized by stronger values of collectivism and norm-orientation (Hofstede, 1997; Markus & Kitayama, 1998; Triandis, 1989; and see Kim & Park, this volume) that are expressed in the family and in school contexts. These values are readily embraced by these adolescents. However, the superb mastery of impending developmental tasks in the Asian adolescents despite their relatively weak efficacy beliefs remains a puzzle. We try to shed light on this puzzle by speculating about the action-guiding function of norms versus efficacy beliefs in different cultural contexts.

ACTION-GUIDING FUNCTION OF
SELF-EFFICACY ACROSS CULTURES

One could argue that in modern cultures that value individualism, small power distance, and weak uncertainty avoidance, as opposed to collectivism, large power distance, and strong uncertainty avoidance valued in traditional cultures, self-efficacy is important for guiding action. This is because, in more modern cultures, norm-oriented rituals that traditionally have provided assurance and boundaries for acting (by determining who interacts with whom, when, where, and how) are fading (see Boesch, 1982). What, then, provides the basis for action in modern societies? We suggest that, in modern societies, efficacy beliefs are taking over the function of norms and rituals (Oettingen, 1997). Specifically, by reflecting performance histories, self-efficacy provides the necessary assurance to act and shows the boundaries of acting.

These contentions are in line with the findings provided in the first part of our chapter. Although adolescents in Asian cultures tend to show lower self-efficacy, they surpass Western peers in academic performance (Eaton & Dembo, 1997). Assuming that Asian cultures adhere to values of collectivism, large power distance, and strong uncertainty avoidance (Hofstede, 1997; Markus & Kitayama, 1998; Triandis, 1989) expressed in comparatively stronger norm-orientation in family and school contexts, we now understand why adolescents in Asian cultures perform well despite relatively weak efficacy beliefs. They are led by the norms of their cultures more so than are adolescents in Western cultures, where adolescents largely rely on their subjective sense of efficacy.

CONCLUSION

We have argued that adolescents solve developmental tasks related to the transition from being the recipient of culture to becoming the carrier of culture. We have also argued that self-efficacy is a critical variable in determining the mastery of this transition. Though adolescents of all cultures are confronted with this transition, research has yielded consistent findings that, despite outperforming their Western counterparts in many critical developmental tasks, adolescents socialized in Asian cultures show weaker self-efficacy than do adolescents socialized in Western cultures.

To solve this puzzle, we analyzed how cultural values affect self-efficacy beliefs. We have argued that cultural values determine the proximal contexts of a culture (i.e., its institutions such as the family or school) on the one hand and the psychological processes of efficacy appraisal on the other (i.e., which sources are selected and how they are weighted). Our findings from our East German and West German students before and after unification are in line with our hypotheses that children and adolescents in sociocultural contexts that value norms (i.e., valuing collectivism, large power distance, and strong uncertainty avoidance) have lower self-efficacy and are more compliant with the authorities' evaluations than are children and adolescents in sociocultural contexts that value norms to a lesser extent (i.e., valuing individualism, small power distance, and weak uncertainty avoidance).

We also asked why comparatively weak efficacy beliefs in adolescents from Asian cultures should be consistent with comparatively higher performance. In cultures with a strong norm-orientation, which is the case in many Asian cultures, adolescents take family and school norms as a guide for action and thus can excel in mastering their developmental tasks despite a relatively weak subjective sense of efficacy. In Western cultures, however, as norm-orientation decreases, self-efficacy becomes more critical for adolescents to solve their developmental tasks. Thus, in cultures in which norm-orientation is deteriorating, strong self-efficacy is a particularly important cognition for shaping successful development across the lifespan.

REFERENCES

Ames, C. (1992). Classrooms: Goals, structures, and student motivation. *Journal of Educational Psychology, 84,* 261-271.

Aquino, K., & Reed, A. R., II. (2002). The self-importance moral identity. *Journal of Personality and Social Psychology, 83,* 1423-1440.

Arnett, J. J. (2002). The psychology of globalization. *American Psychologist, 57,* 774-783.

Bandura, A. (1977). Self-efficacy: Toward a unifying theory of behavioral change. *Psychological Review, 84,* 191-215.

Bandura, A. (1986). *Social foundations of thought and action: A social cognitive theory.* Englewood Cliffs, NJ: Prentice Hall.

Bandura, A. (1997). *Self-efficacy: The exercise of control.* New York: Freeman.

Bandura, A., Barbaranelli, C., Caprara, C. V., & Pastorelli, C. (2001). Efficacy beliefs as shapers of children's aspirations and career trajectories. *Child Development, 72,* 187-206.

Boesch, E. E. (1982). Ritual und psychotherapie [Ritual and psychotherapy]. *Zeitschrift für Klinische Psychologie und Psychotherapie, 30,* 214-234.

Dweck, C. S., & Leggett, E. L. (1988). A social-cognitive approach to motivation and personality. *Psychological Review, 95,* 256-273.

Eaton, M. J., & Dembo, M. H. (1997). Differences in the motivational beliefs of Asian American and non-Asian students. *Journal of Educational Psychology, 89,* 433-440.

Eccles, J. (2004). Schools, academic motivation, and stage-environment fit. In R. M. Lerner & L. Steinberg (Eds.), *Handbook of adolescent psychology*, (2nd ed., pp. 125-153). Hoboken, NJ: Wiley.

Eccles, J. S., & Wigfield, A. (2002). Motivational beliefs, values, and goals. *Annual review of Psychology, 53*, 109-132.

Ettrich, K. U., Krause, R., Hofer, M., & Wild, E. (1996). Der Einfluß familienbezogener Merkmale auf die Schulleistungen ost- und westdeutscher Jugendlicher [The influence of family-related characteristics on the achievement of young people in East and West Germany]. *Unterrichtswissenschaft, 24*, 106-127.

Franz, S. (1987). *Unsere Schüler zur Selbsteinschätzung befähigen* [Teaching self-evaluation to our students]. Berlin: Volk und Wissen.

Greenfield, P. M., Keller, H., Fuligni, A., & Maynard, A. (2003). Cultural pathways through universal development. *Annual Review of Psychology, 54*, 461-490.

Grigorenko, E. L., & O'Keefe, P. A. (2004). What do children do when they cannot go to school? In R. J. Sternberg & E. L. Grigorenko (Eds.), *Culture and competence: Contexts of life success* (pp. 23-54). Washington, DC: APA.

Hannover, B. (1995). Self-serving biases and self-satisfaction in East versus West German students. *Journal of Cross-Cultural Psychology, 26*, 176-188.

Harter, S., Waters, P. L., Whitesell, N., Jr., & Kastelic, D. (1998). Level of voice among female and male high school students: Relational context, support, and gender orientation. *Developmental Psychology, 34*, 892-901.

Havighurst, R. J. (1972). *Developmental tasks and education.* New York: David McKay. (Original work published 1948)

Heckhausen, H. (1991). *Motivation and action.* Heidelberg, Germany: Springer.

Hofstede, G. (1986). Cultural differences in teaching and learning. *International Journal of Intercultural Relations, 10*, 301-320.

Hofstede, G. (1997). *Cultures and organizations: Software of the mind.* New York: McGraw-Hill.

Holloway, S. D. (1988). Concepts of ability and effort in Japan and the United States. *Review of Educational Research, 58*, 327-345.

Karasawa, M., Little, T. D., Miyashita, T., Mashima, M., & Azuma, H. (1997). Japanese children's action-control beliefs about school performance. *International Journal of Behavioral Development, 20*, 405-423.

Kitayama, S., Markus, H. R., Matsumoto, H., & Norasakkunkit, V. (1997). Individual and collective processes in the construction of the self: Self-enhancement in the United States and self-criticism in Japan. *Journal of Personality and Social Psychology, 72*, 1245-1267.

Little, T. D., Lopez, D. F., Oettingen, G., & Baltes, P. B. (2001). A comparative-longitudinal study of action-control beliefs and school performance: On the role of context. *International Journal of Behavioral Development, 25*, 237-245.

Markus, H. R., & Kitayama, S. (1991). Culture and the self: Implications for cognition, emotion, and motivation. *Psychological Review, 98*, 224-253.

Markus, H. R., & Kitayama, S. (1998). The cultural psychology of personality. *Journal of Cross Cultural Psychology, 29*, 63-87.

Mau, W. (2000). Cultural differences in career decision-making styles and self-efficacy. *Journal of Vocational Behavior, 57*, 365-378.

Mischel, W. (1973). Toward a cognitive social learning reconceptualization of personality. *Psychological Review, 80*, 252-253.

Multon, K. D., Brown, S. D., & Lent, R. W. (1991). Relation of efficacy beliefs to academic outcomes: A meta-analytic investigation. *Journal of Counseling Psychology, 38*, 30-38.

Nicholls, J. G. (1984). Achievement motivation: Conceptions of ability, subjective experience, task choice, and performance. *Psychological Review, 91*, 328-346.

Oettingen, G. (1995). Explanatory style in the context of culture. In G. M. Buchanan & M. E. P. Seligman (Eds.), *Explanatory style* (pp. 209-224). Hillsdale, NJ: Erlbaum.

Oettingen, G. (1997). Culture and future thought. *Culture & Psychology, 3*, 353-381.

Oettingen, G., & Little, T. D. (1993). Intelligence and performance-related efficacy beliefs in East and West Berlin children. *Zeitschrift fuer Sozialpsychologie, 24*, 186-197.

Oettingen, G., Little, T. D., Lindenberger, U., & Baltes, P. B. (1994). Causality, agency, and control beliefs in East versus West Berlin children: A natural experiment on the role of context. *Journal of Personality and Social Psychology, 66*, 579-595.

Pajares, F., & Miller, M. D. (1994). Role of self-efficacy and self-concept beliefs in mathematical problem solving: A path analysis. *Journal of Educational Psychology, 86*, 193-203.

Pajares, F., & Miller, M. D. (1995). Mathematics self-efficacy and mathematics performance: The need for specificity of assessment. *Journal of Counseling Psychology, 42*, 190-198.

Pintrich, P. R. (2003). A motivational science perspective on the role of student motivation in learning and teaching contexts. *Journal of Educational Psychology, 95*, 667-686.

Reitzle, M., & Silbereisen, R. K. (2000). Adapting to social change: Adolescent values in Eastern and Western Germany. In J. Bynner & R. K. Silbereisen (Eds.), *Adversity and challenge in life in the new Germany and in England* (pp. 123-152). Houndmills, England: Macmillan.

Robbins, S. B., Lauver, K., Le, H., Davis, D., Langley, R., & Carlstrom, A. (2004). Do psychological and study skill factors predict college outcomes? A meta-analysis. *Psychological Bulletin, 139*, 261-288.

Rosenholtz, S. J., & Rosenholtz, S. H. (1981). Classroom organization and the perception of ability. *Sociology of Education, 54*, 132-140.

Rosenholtz, S. J., & Simpson, C. (1984). The formation of ability conceptions: Developmental trend or social construction? *Review of Educational Research, 54*, 31-63.

Salili, F., Chiu, C., & Lai, S. (2001). The influence of culture and context on students' motivational orientation and performance. In F. Salili, C. Chi, & Y. Hong (Eds.), *Student motivation: The culture and context of learning* (pp. 221-247). New York: Kluwer Academic/Plenum Publishers.

Scheier, M. F., & Carver, C. S. (1992). Effects of optimism on psychological and physical well-being: Theoretical overview and empirical update. *Cognitive Therapy and Research, 16*, 201-228.

Schunk, D. H., & Pajares, F. (2002). The development of academic self-efficacy. In A. Wigfield & J. Eccles (Eds.), *Development of achievement motivation* (pp. 16-31). San Diego: Academic Press.

Seligman, M. E. P. (1991). *Learned optimism*. New York: Knopf.

Skinner, E. A., Chapman, M., & Baltes, P. B. (1988). Control, means-ends, and agency beliefs: A new conceptualization and its measurement during childhood. *Journal of Personality and Social Psychology, 54*, 117-133.

Skinner, E. A., Schindler, A., & Tschechne, M. (1990). Self-other differences in children's perceptions about the causes of important events. *Journal of Personality and Social Psychology, 58*, 144-155.

Sorrentino, R. M., Raynor, J. O., Zubek, J. M., & Short, J.-A. C. (1990). Personality functioning and change. Informational and affective influences on cognitive, moral, and social development. In E. T. Higgins & R. M. Sorrentino (Eds.), *Handbook of motivation and cognition: Foundations of social behavior* (Vol. 2, pp. 193-228). New York: Guilford.

Stewart, S. M., Kennard, B. D., Lee, P. W. H., Hughes, C. W., Mayes, T. L., Emslie, G. J., et al., (2004). A cross-cultural investigation of cognitions and depressive symptoms in adolescents. *Journal of Abnormal Psychology, 113*, 248-257.

Stipek, D. J. (1988). *Motivation to learn: From theory to practice*. Englewood Cliffs, NJ: Prentice Hall.

Stipek, D. J. (1991). Characterizing early childhood education programs. *New Directions for Child Development, 53*, 47-55.

Stroebe, W. (1976). Is social psychology really that complicated? A review of Martin Irle's Lehrbuch der Sozialpsychologie. *European Journal of Social Psychology, 6*, 509-511.

Taylor, S. E. (1989). *Positive illusions: Creative self-deception and the healthy mind*. New York: Basic Books.

Taylor, S. E., & Brown, J. D. (1988). Illusion and well-being: A social psychological perspective on mental health. *Psychological Bulletin, 103*, 193-210.

Tolman, E. C. (1932/1967). *Purposive behavior in animals and men*. New York: Appleton-Century-Crofts.

Triandis, H. C. (1989). The self and social behavior in different cultural contexts. *Psychological Review, 96*, 506-520.

Triandis, H. C., McCusker, C., & Hui, C. H. (1990). Multimethod probes of individualism and collectivism. *Journal of Personality and Social Psychology, 59*, 1006-1020.

Urdan, T. (2004). Predictors of academic self-handicapping and achievement: Examining achievement goals, classroom goal structures, and culture. *Journal of Educational Psychology, 96*, 251-264.

Waterkamp, D. (1990). Erziehung in der Schule [Education in the school]. In Bundesministerium für innerdeutsche Beziehungen (Ed.), *Vergleich von Bildung und Erziehung in der Bundesrepublik Deutschland und in der Deutschen Demokratischen Republik* (pp. 261-277). Cologne, Germany: Wissenschaft und Politik.

Williams, W. M. (1998). Are we raising smarter children today? School- and home-related influences on IQ. In U. Neisser (Ed.), *The rising curve: Long-term changes in IQ and related measures.* Washington, DC: American Psychological Association Books.

Yan, W., & Gaier, E. L. (1994). Causal attributions for college success and failure: An Asian-American comparison. *Journal of Cross-Cultural Psychology, 25*, 146-158.

Zimmerman, B. J. (2000). Self-efficacy: An essential motive to learn. *Contemporary Educational Psychology, 25*, 82-91.

CHAPTER 12

FACTORS INFLUENCING ACADEMIC ACHIEVEMENT IN RELATIONAL CULTURES

The Role of Self-, Relational, and Collective Efficacy

Uichol Kim and Young-Shin Park

The twentieth century has often been called the Pacific Era to characterize the phenomenal achievements in economics, education, and nation building. At the turn of the century, East Asian societies were far behind in science and technology, lacking educational, economic, and political infrastructure and experiencing national turmoil. Despite limited natural resources, East Asian countries were able to design educational, political, and economic policies to kinetically transform latent human resources and become leading nation states. Currently, Japan has the second largest economy in the world, and China has the fastest growing.

In 1960, South Korea had all the problems of a resource-poor, low-income, under-developed nation. Literacy rates and educational levels were low, and it was one of the poorest countries in the world, with a per

Self-Efficacy Beliefs of Adolescents, 267–285

capita gross national product (GNP) of $82. From 1965, the economy grew over 8% a year and per capita GNP increased to $1,640 in 1981 and $10,307 in 1997. Although South Korea suffered a severe economic crisis in 1998, the economy recovered, and the per capita GNP in 2004 was $14,100, the literacy rate 98%, and high school enrollment 99%. This economic miracle is closely tied to the educational aspiration and investment made by South Korean adolescents and their parents (Park & Kim, 2004).

In international studies of academic achievement, East Asian students are regularly ranked at the top (National Center for Educational Statistics, 2000, TIMSS; Organisation for Economic Co-operation and Development, 2003, PISA). In a 39-nation study of students in Grade 8 (TIMSS), Singapore, South Korea, Taiwan, Hong Kong, and Japan were the top performers in mathematics and science. In a 31-nation study of students in Grade 9 (PISA), Japan obtained the top scores in mathematics. South Korea was the top performer in science and near the top in reading literacy (South Korea ranked 6 and Japan 8).

Students from the United States performed below their East Asian counterparts. In the TIMSS, they ranked 19 in mathematics and 18 in science; in PISA, they ranked 14 in science, 15 in reading, and 19 in mathematics literacy. Although South Korea spends less than half what the USA pays per student and class size is almost twice as large, South Korean students outperform American students in international studies. These results notwithstanding, American students had higher self-esteem than did East Asian students. They ranked first in self-concept for science and fourth in mathematics (TIMSS). In contrast, East Asian students had low self-esteem in both subjects (South Korea ranked 32 in mathematics and 21 in science; Japan ranked 34 and 16; Taiwan ranked 30 and 18). These results baffle many psychologists and educators.

As regards motivation to study mathematics, 41% of American students strongly endorsed a personal motivation to study in school ("to get the desired job") whereas only 10% of South Korean students and 12% of Japanese students endorsed it. Instead, South Korean students endorsed *relational* motivation (62% reported that they study "to please their parents") and social motivation (85% reported that they study to "enter a desired university") (TIMSS). American students who attributed their success to effort had lower mathematics scores, but the reverse was the case for South Korean students, who believed that they had to expend a lot of effort to do well in mathematics.

American and South Korean students also had different life goals: 64% of American students agreed or agreed strongly that "enjoying life is more important than preparing for life," compared to only 32% of South Korean students. As regards the effort needed to do well in mathematics ("how much effort do you need to succeed in math"), 8% of American students replied *a lot of effort*, compared to 36% of South Korean students. Clearly, South Korean students differ from American students in terms of life goals, self-esteem, and motivation.

Berliner and Biddle (1995) defended the performance of American students and of the educational system contending that (a) the level of achievement of American students has been relatively stable over time, (b) American youngsters are out-achieving their parents substantially, (c) American students stack up very well compared to other nations, and (d) the educational crisis in the United States is a myth. However, the performance of East Asian students has been increasing at a much more rapid rate, and they are out-achieving their parents by a higher margin than are American students (Park & Kim, 2004). Berliner and Biddle may be correct that the educational system is not the main reason behind the "manufactured crisis." American universities are consistently ranked as the best in the world, and within the United States there are variations in academic achievement across diverse ethnic groups. Asian American students are consistently the top performers on standardized tests and in high school and college grade point average (Hsia, 1988). More Asian Americans receive high school diplomas or college degrees than does any other group (Sue & Okazaki, 1990). The academic achievement of Asian American students in the United States parallels the educational success achieved by students in East Asia.

TRADITIONAL APPROACHES

Psychology developed as a branch of the natural sciences, adopting their method and epistemology. To create an "objective" science, early psychologists opted not to study subjective aspects such as consciousness, meaning, intentions, and agency, and they seldom attended to the influence of context and culture. Although early psychologists such as Wilhelm Wundt and William James considered the concept of agency central to human functioning, it was lost in the behaviorist onslaught of the early twentieth century. Instead, the goal of behaviorist psychologists was to examine the relationships between stimulus, response, and reinforcement (see Figure 12.1). Aspects not directly observable—such as consciousness, agency, meaning, or intentions—were considered noise and eliminated from research designs. Mind was viewed as a black box, and human beings as passive and reactive organisms. As Bandura (1999) accurately critiqued, for these psychologists, "brains [were] merely repositories for past stimuli inputs and conduits for external stimulations, but they can add nothing to their performance" (p. 22).

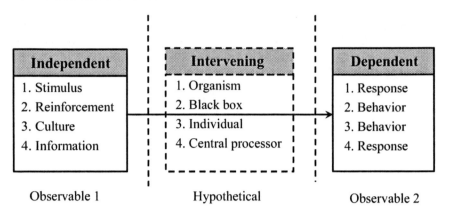

Independent	Intervening	Dependent
1. Stimulus	1. Organism	1. Response
2. Reinforcement	2. Black box	2. Behavior
3. Culture	3. Individual	3. Behavior
4. Information	4. Central processor	4. Response

Observable 1   Hypothetical   Observable 2

Source: Adapted from Kim (1999).

Figure 12.1.

The Information Processing approach subsequently replaced the black box with a central processor that performs multiple, complex, and dynamic operations using preordained rules (Bandura, 1999). As Shweder (1991) noted, "epistemologically speaking, knowledge-seeking in general psychology is the attempt to get a look at the central processing mechanism untainted by content and context" (p. 80). In cross-cultural psychology, culture is viewed as a quasi-independent variable because researchers cannot control or manipulate culture. Behavior is treated as the dependent variable (Triandis, 1980).

Lewis Terman developed the Stanford-Binet Intelligence Quotient (IQ) Test to assess native intelligence. Gould (1981) contended that IQ tests have since been used to document individual, gender, and race differences in the belief that "the social and economic differences between human groups—primarily races, classes, and sexes—arise from inherited, inborn distinctions and that society, in this sense, is an accurate reflection of biology," and psychologists claimed that "worth can be assigned to individuals and groups by *measuring intelligence as a single quantity*" (p. 201). Results from IQ tests were initially used to inform American policies such as forced sterilization, segregation of races, and restriction of immigration (Chorover, 1980).

When the first IQ test was published in 1916, girls of all ages outscored boys by an average of 2%-4%. Soon after Terman deleted, revised, or added items, this difference began to favor boys (Kamin, 1974). Asian Americans were viewed as a "kind of inferior species, who could be used for unskilled labor and menial jobs but could never be accepted as equals into the white community" (Vernon, 1982, p. 2). When the number of Chinese immigrants began to increase, the U.S. Congress passed the 1882 Chinese Exclusion Act that barred immigration from China. In 1924, the National Origins Act was passed barring immigration from Asia, with the exception of Filipino immigrants, who were barred in 1934 (Kim, 1992). These laws were a result of fears that the "genetically inferior" Asian race would pollute the genetic pool and lead to nation degeneracy, even though Asian Americans had IQ scores comparable to those of European Americans (Chorover, 1980; Vernon, 1982).

In their recent study of 60 nations, Lynn and Vanhanen (2002) found that East Asians had the highest IQ (106 for South Koreans, 105 for Japanese, 104 for Taiwanese, and 103 for Singaporeans). Europeans and Americans had lower scores (98 for the USA, 100 for United Kingdom, and 102 for Germany). Lynn and Vanhanen concluded that IQ scores reflect the superiority of the Mongolian race. Ironically, although East Asians were discriminated as genetically inferior 80 years ago, they are now touted as a genetically superior race.

Traditional psychological theories assume that differences in academic performance can be explained either by innate ability, personality, or environmental factors. As Bandura (1999) pointed out, "it is ironic that a science of human functioning should strip people of the very capabilities that make them unique in their power to shape their environment and their own destiny" (p. 21). Indeed, "psychology has undergone wrenching paradigm shifts" and "in these transformations, the theorists and their followers think, argue and act agentically, but their theories about how other people function grant them little, if any, agentic capabilities" (p. 21). Bandura's (1997) social cognitive theory represents the *transactional* approach in which the concept of agency, meaning, and intention are central to human functioning.

TRANSACTIONAL APPROACH

Human beings have changed little biologically during the past 7,000 years, but social and cultural changes from the early Stone Age to the current Information Age have been dramatic. Cultural transformations during the last 7 millennia have changed the way people understand and manage their world (Bandura, 1997; Kim, Helgesen, & Ahn, 2002). Modern nations did not evolve logically, sequentially, or evolutionarily. Rather, they arose out of a clash of ideas. Individuals and groups have been able to integrate these ideas into cultural forms (Kim, Aasen, & Ebadi, 2003). Individuals, cultures, and nations undergo changes through dialectical transformation. Biological approaches such as Darwinian Evolutionary Theory assume that human biology is the source of all behavior and that human beings have evolved and survived as *homo sapiens* because they were able adapt to their ecology. But humans have survived not because of their biological makeup but because they have been able to overcome their instincts. As a relatively weak species physically, humans were at the constant mercy of predators and of a harsh environment. Although it is a natural instinct to fear fire, humans harnessed the power of fire for protection and learned to cook food, which increased the kinds and types of foods they could consume. Fire enabled them to transform clay and iron into cups, utensils, houses, and weapons. How were they able to make tools that do not exist in nature? They were able to do so by engaging reflective and generative capabilities (Bandura, 1997).

Human beings are motivated by a desire to control events that affect their lives (Bandura, 1997). The methods by which they can exert control over the environment can be direct or indirect and controlled by an individual or in collaboration with others (Bandura, 1997). Direct control can be viewed as *primary* or *collective*. Primary control refers to exerting direct control over the environment to achieve a desired outcome. When people work together in managing their environment (democracy), this is collective control. Indirect control can be *secondary* or *proxy*. Secondary control refers to accepting a given environment and regulating oneself to adapt to it. Proxy control refers to obtaining assistance from others in managing one's environment. The effectiveness of each type of control depends on the context, individual, organizations, and cultures. When all four can be coordinated and integrated, better outcomes are obtained.

In the transactional model, subjective qualities such as intention, meaning, belief, and agency are central concepts that link a situation or event with behavior (see Figure 12.2) (Bandura, 1997). In this model, it is impor-

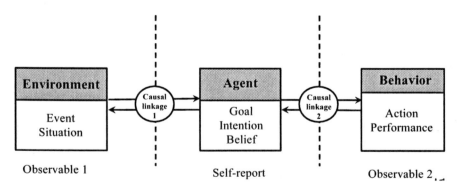

Source: Adapted from Kim (1999).

Figure 12.2.

tant to examine how an individual perceives or interprets a particular event or situation (Causal linkage 1). This information can be obtained through self-report. The second step involves assessing individuals' performance (Causal linkage 2). In a study of management effectiveness, Bandura (1997) told one group that they did much better than average and another group that they did much worse. Positive feedback increased self-efficacy, and negative feedback decreased it (Causal linkage 1). In the second phase, he measured analytical skills and management effectiveness. Participants with high self-efficacy were more likely to use their analytical ability efficiently to perform well (Causal linkage 2). The reverse was true for those who were provided negative feedback. They had lower self-efficacy, used their analytical ability poorly, and achieved less.

The causal pathway can be reversed. If poor performing participants in Trial 1 are given positive feedback in Trial 2, their self-efficacy increases and their performance improves. The rise or fall in performance can be systematically linked to the rise or fall in self-efficacy. Successful performance increases self-efficacy, which can motivate individuals to seek more challenging goals. Successful mastery experiences can also lead to *transformative* changes in other aspects of one's life. Bandura (1997) found that some individuals who mastered their snake phobia were able to reduce their social timidity, increase their boldness, boost their self-expressiveness, and increase their desire to overcome other fears.

At the cultural level, differences in academic achievement can be attributable to cultural systems that promote self-, relational, and collective efficacy. Culture is defined as the collective utilization of natural and human resources to achieve desired outcomes (Kim, 2001). Differences in cultures exist because individuals have different goals, utilize different methods and resources to attain them, and attach different meanings to them. Culture is an emergent property of individuals and of groups interacting with their natural and human environment. Following this line of thought, East Asian adolescents are high achievers because educational attainment is highly valued, persistent effort is emphasized, and people work together to achieve this goal.

EDUCATIONAL ACHIEVEMENT

China, Japan, and South Korea share a Confucian heritage in which education and self-cultivation are viewed both as ends and as means to those ends (Kim & Park, 2003). In contrast to the Western emphasis on individualism, Confucianism focuses on emotions that bind individuals and family members. In fact, the Chinese, Japanese, and South Korean word for human being can be translated literally as "human between." It is not what happens within an individual but between individuals that makes one human (Kim, 2001). Mencius observed that "if you see a child drowning and you don't feel compassion, then you are not a human being." It is compassion that helps individuals relate to the child and propels them to take the necessary action to save that child. Human essence is essentially relational and can be defined in terms of emotions that bind people. Parental love, care, and devotion are viewed as necessary and essential for a newborn child to mature and succeed in life.

Confucius (1979) articulated the need to cultivate oneself so as to achieve harmony with others. Self-cultivation involves self-examination and learning from others. In Confucian societies, individuals of merit were selected through national examinations to lead and to serve the public, and successful candidates were given official government positions. In return for their service, they were given a large tract of land for three generations. Success in national examinations was an indication of their knowledge, wisdom, and moral integrity. Social, economic, and political benefits were also provided. Educational success became a vehicle for fulfilling one's filial piety. Since education was the most viable means of personal growth, social mobility, social recognition, and economic security, it became not only a means to an end, but an end in itself.

The educational attainment of East Asian students has been well documented (Hess, Azuma, Kashiwagi, Holloway, & Wenegrat, 1987; Hess et al., 1986; Park & Kim, 2004; Stevenson, Azuma, & Hakuta, 1986; Stevenson & Lee, 1990). Researchers have suggested that the main factor responsible for high performance rests in socialization practices that promote and maintain a strong relational and emotional bond between parents and children. It is the role of parents to provide a positive family environment for their children and to pressure them to succeed. Children learn to discipline themselves and to develop their academic skills with the help of parents. This socialization promotes the development of proxy control. A second major factor is the emphasis on discipline and on self-regulation, especially the belief of persistent effort. The third major factor is a compatibility of values between the family and the school that promotes collective efficacy. It is because Asian Americans have been able to cultivate these values that they have such strong academic achievement (Hsia, 1988; Sue & Okazaki, 1990).

Interdependence and Proxy Control

Parental devotion, sacrifice, and support are important features of the traditional socialization practices that still remain in modern East Asia (Azuma, 1986; Ho, 1986; Park & Kim, 2004). In East Asia, a mother remains close to her child to make the child feel secure, to minimize the boundary between them, and to meet the child's needs. Children's emotional and physical dependency needs are satisfied by their mother's indulgent devotion, even if that means a tremendous sacrifice on her own part.

A mother's job is to use this relationship to encourage the child's self-discipline and success in school. She becomes a mediator between the home and the school by socializing appropriate values and norms. As children grow, they are expected to extend and transfer their interdependent identification and loyalty from their mothers to their teachers. The relationship between teachers and students is an extension of the mother-child relationship. Children are motivated to please their teacher, and their attention is focused on the teacher. Even with class sizes as large as 40, East Asian students are more attentive, less disruptive, and more devoted to doing their schoolwork and homework than are American students (Hess et al., 1986; Park & Kim, 2004; Stevenson et al., 1986; Stevenson & Lee, 1990).

In East Asia, a typical school climate is one that pressures the student to strive for personal excellence and encourages group cooperation. Teachers assume that children come to school motivated to learn regardless of the task assigned: "When a teacher wants to motivate a child or punish an inadequate piece of work that the child has produced, she/he will often refer to the feelings of parents, possibility of shame by the group of which the child is a member, or the teacher's own disappointment" (Hess et al., 1987, p. 437). Parents socialize their children to contribute to the group and to emphasize collective goals, and "the emphasis on individual effort includes a sense of responsibility to the group to which one belongs" (Holloway, Kashiwagi, & Azuma, 1986, p. 272). Success is collectively defined and rewards are equally shared.

Compared to European American parents, Asian American parents promote a strong sense of interdependence and proxy control. Asian American parents are more willing than are European American parents to devote resources to their children to ensure the best possible education for them. Although the median income of Asian Americans is lower than that of European Americans for college-bound seniors ($25,400 to $32,900), they devote a relatively larger portion of their income to educate their children. They provide a supportive and structured home environment, they value a team approach, and they try to assert their influence on their children's educational and career choices. They also assign fewer household chores than do European American parents. They stress the importance of respecting one's parents and teachers and accepting teacher authority. Finally, Asian American students associate excellence in their performance with their parents' honor, pride, and happiness (Lee & Rong, 1988; Pang, 1991; Schneider & Lee, 1990; Slaughter-Defoe, Nakagawa, Takanishi, & Johnson, 1990; Yao, 1985).

Self-Regulation

The second factor responsible for the high performance of East Asian students is the emphasis on discipline and self-regulation, especially the emphasis on persistent effort. In East Asia, self-cultivation and effort (an internal and changeable attribution) rather than innate ability (an internal and determined attribution) is believed to be the key to success (Hess et al., 1987; Kim & Park, 2003; Stevenson et al., 1986; Stevenson & Lee, 1990; Yu & Yang, 1994). Academic excellence provides evidence that a child has developed a moral character through perseverance and persistence.

Paralleling results obtained in East Asia, Asian Americans view effort as a key to success. European American students, parents, and teachers are more likely to attribute failure to innate ability, whereas Asian Americans attribute both success and failure to effort. Asian Americans are also more likely to place greater value on education, attribute success in life to educational performance, and have higher performance expectations than do European Americans. Because they value effort and high achievement, Asian American students study more hours than do European American students (Mizokawa & Ryckman, 1990; Schneider & Lee, 1990; Slaughter-Defoe et al., 1990; Yao, 1985).

Collective Control

There is a greater congruence of values emphasized in the family, school, and society in East Asia than there is in the West, where individualistic values are often in conflict with a relatively hierarchical classroom structure, curriculum, and teacher-student relationship (Farkas, Grobe, Sheehan, & Shuan, 1990). In addition, students, parents, teachers, and administrators often hold different views about the meaning of success and of the factors that lead to it. In East Asia, students, parents, and teachers unanimously agree that academic achievement is the primary goal of children and of adolescents, and they work together toward this goal. There is greater agreement among all parties about the goals of education and of the method to achieve it. This collective agreement promotes collective efficacy and is a key factor in motivating students to attain a high level of achievement (Park & Kim, 2004).

The institutional structure, administration, and curricula of the American public school system are more compatible for Asian American students than for other ethnic groups, including European Americans (Farkas et al., 1990). Researchers have found that Asian American parents and students hold compatible and supportive values in placing a high premium on education, attributing success in life to educational performance, emphasizing effort as a key to success, and having high performance expectations (Mizokawa & Ryckman, 1990; Schneider & Lee, 1990; Slaughter-Defoe et al., 1990; Yao, 1985). Even European American students and teachers expect higher performance levels from Asian American students. In the United States, there appears to be a consistent agreement at home and in school that Asian Americans should be high achievers.

Farkas et al. (1990) investigated the student characteristics that account for academic success (coursework mastery and course grade) with a sample of European American, Asian American, and African American students. Students' basic cognitive skills and noncognitive skills rated by teachers (students' work habits measured by absenteeism, homework completed, class participation, effort, and organization) predicted coursework mastery, which in turn predicted obtained grades. Work habits explained most of the variance in grades, followed by coursework mastery and basic skills. Asian American students performed a full letter grade better than did European American students, and noncognitive performance explained most of the variance. The researchers concluded that "any individual or group possessing strong basic skill performance as well as a reputation for good citizenship can achieve unusually high course grades" and "Asian students have done just this" (p. 140). The relational orientation of Asian Americans, the emphasis on effort, and high academic expectations provide the necessary ingredients in promoting high achievement.

South Korean Studies

In 1998, a cross-sectional study was conducted in South Korea to examine the factors that influence academic achievement (Park et al., 2000). Over 3,000 elementary, middle, and high school students completed an instrument that included social support received from father, mother, friends, and teachers; life-satisfaction scale; and self-efficacy, relational self-efficacy, and self-efficacy for promoting social harmony. For elementary school students, self-efficacy had a direct effect on life-satisfaction and on academic achievement. Support received from parents, teachers,

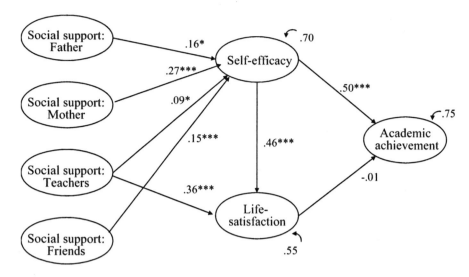

Note: *p < .05, **p < .01, ***p < 001.
Source: Adapted from Park et al. (2000).

Figure 12.3.

and friends had a direct effect on self-efficacy, and support received from teachers had a direct effect on life-satisfaction (see Figure 12.3).

Middle school students had a similar pattern. Self-efficacy had a direct effect on life-satisfaction and on academic achievement. Life-satisfaction had a direct effect on academic achievement. Support received from parents and friends had a direct effect on self-efficacy, and support received from mother and teachers had a direct effect on life-satisfaction (see Figure 12.4).

For high school students, the role of parents was more dominant and the influence of teachers was minimal. As in the other samples, self-efficacy had a direct effect on life-satisfaction and on academic achievement. Life-satisfaction had a direct effect on academic achievement. Support received from parents and friends had a direct effect on self-efficacy, and support received from parents had a direct effect on life-satisfaction (see Figure 12.5).

These results document the mediating role that self-efficacy plays in influencing life-satisfaction and academic achievement of South Koreans adolescents. Also, the social support received from significant others raises the self-efficacy of adolescents. Parents played a central role in raising their students' self-efficacy at each academic level, as well as the life-satisfaction of high school students. Social support received from friends

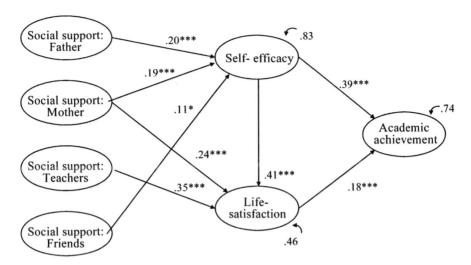

Note: *p < .05, **p < .01, ***p < .001.
Source: Adapted from Park et al. (2000).

Figure 12.4

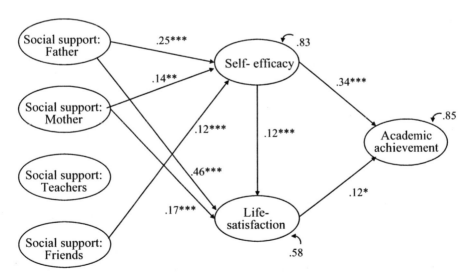

Note: *p < .05, **p < .01, p. < .001.
Source: Adapted from Park et al. (2000).

Figure 12.5.

increased self-efficacy. The role of teachers was important for elementary students but not for high school students.

In a longitudinal study that tracked students from Grade 6 to Grade 9 to Grade 11, Park, Kim, and Chung (2004) examined the influences that South Korean parents have on the academic achievement of adolescents, as well as the mediating role that self-efficacy plays on achievement motivation. Variables assessing parents-adolescent relationship were social support received from parents, sense of indebtedness to parents, and parental pressure for academic achievement. Other variables in the study included self-efficacy, achievement motivation, study time, and academic achievement. Path analysis results revealed that the grade obtained in 9th grade was the most powerful predictor of the grade obtained in 11th grade. Self-efficacy for self-regulated learning, achievement motivation, and study time had a direct effect on academic achievement. Self-efficacy for self-regulated learning had a direct effect on achievement motivation. Parental support and parental achievement pressure had a direct effect on self-efficacy for self-regulated learning. Parental achievement pressure and a sense of indebtedness to parents had a direct effect on achievement motivation (see Figure 12.6).

These results suggest that parental and relational factors increase academic achievement through self-efficacy for self-regulated learning and achievement motivation. In other words, close parent-child relationships and social support are important factors in raising the self-efficacy and achievement motivation of South Korean adolescents, which in turn increase academic achievement.

DISCUSSION

Consistent with Confucian values, East Asians view education as an important life goal and persistent effort and discipline as the means to that goal. The sacrifice and support provided by parents are viewed as essential ingredients for success. Emotional support in the form of encouragement, praise, security, and understanding are valued. East Asians believe that ability can be acquired and personality can be polished through persistent effort and with the support of significant others. This pattern of results has also been found for Asian Americans.

These results point to the limitation of traditional psychological theories. Those that emphasize biology (innate ability, intelligence), individualistic values (intrinsic motivation, ability attribution, self-esteem), or structural features (high educational spending, small class size, individualized instruction) have difficulty explaining the high performance of East Asian students. Few East Asians emphasize innate ability. Instead,

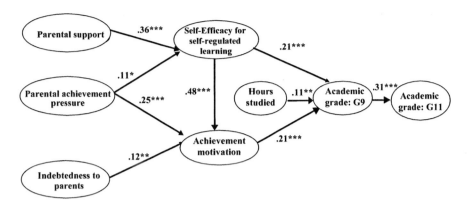

Note: *p < .05, **p < .01, ***p < .001.
Source: Adapted from Park et al. (2004).

Figure 12.6.

they believe that self-regulation is the most important factor leading to success or failure.

Most developmental theories do not examine the influence of parents on child or adolescent development. Although attachment theories include the role of parents, these theories assume that separation and individuation are necessary for successful maturation (Rothbaum, Weisz, Pott, Miyake, & Morelli, 2000). In East Asia, parental support and influence are strong during childhood and adolescence, and they persist into adulthood. Close in-group members are highly influential, whereas professional relationships are not. Support from teachers is important when children are young, but teachers' influence decreases as children become older. Emotional support rather than informational support is found to be the most influential factor. East Asians attribute their success to persistent effort and attribute failure to a lack of effort. In East Asia, it is considered appropriate for children to feel indebted to their parents for their devotion, sacrifice, support, and affection. A sense of indebtedness is viewed as a positive interpersonal effect that promotes filial piety, academic achievement, and harmony.

Results from the South Korean studies earlier reviewed affirm the important mediating role that self-efficacy plays in influencing academic achievement and life-satisfaction. Social support received from parents, achievement pressure, and a sense of indebtedness raise self-efficacy, which in turn raises academic achievement and life-satisfaction. These results are consistent with those obtained in Europe and in the United

States (Bandura, 1997), supporting the validity and usefulness of Bandura's social cognitive theory.

East Asian students become high achievers because they live in a culture in which education is valued and self-, proxy, and collective efficacy for academic achievement is high. Children are taught to discipline themselves to become high achievers. Many high school students study from 14 to 16 hours daily, and parents play a key role in providing emotional, informational, and financial support to ensure that their children succeed in school. Parents set high goals for their children and pressure them to excel. They provide a good study environment so that children can focus their attention on academic work. Peers view educational success as the most important goal in life, and schools and teachers provide adolescents with the necessary academic skills and guidance. It is the joint effort of adolescents, parents, teachers, and society that is responsible for promoting high self-, relational, and collective efficacy for academic achievement.

The ingredients necessary for academic success do not exist only in East Asian countries. Asian Americans possess these ingredients and are high achievers. Compared with Asian Americans, European American and African American adolescents and parents have lower expectations and do not invest as much time and effort in their academic work (Hsia, 1988; Lee & Rong, 1988; Pang, 1991; Schneider & Lee, 1990; Slaughter-Defoe et al., 1990; Yao, 1985). High governmental spending, small class sizes, and individualized instruction will have limited impact if adolescents and parents have low expectations and do not invest in education.

Although South Korean students are high achievers, there are costs. In 1996, when students were asked to describe the most stressful aspect of their lives, 28% reported pressure to achieve academically, followed by human relationships (20%) and family life (15%) (Park & Kim, 2004). During the economic crisis of 1999, 44% of students reported pressure to achieve academically as being the most stressful. Even with the pressure and stress, when students succeed academically, they are given social, relational, and economic rewards, and many feel it is worth the investment.

But South Korean society is not prepared to deal with adolescents who cannot adjust to the rigid school system, cope with the pressure to achieve, fail to do well academically, or engage in delinquent behavior. The rates of students who refuse to attend school, delinquency, and school violence have been increasing in recent years. Nearly half of the teachers and students feel that teachers and administrators have lost some of the leadership and authority to teach and regulate students, and half of the primary, middle, and high school students report experiencing school violence (Park & Kim, 2004). Students, teachers, and parents report low self-efficacy in dealing with school violence, and they are unable to stem the rising tide. South Korean society has been able to foster the development of self-, proxy, and collective control in promoting high academic achievement, but it has yet to develop the necessary control in stemming the rising dropout rate, delinquency, and school violence.

REFERENCES

Azuma, H. (1986). Why study child development in Japan? In H. Stevenson, H. Azuma, & K. Hakuta (Eds.), *Child Development and Education in Japan* (pp. 3-12). New York: Freeman.

Bandura, A. (1997). *Self-efficacy: The exercise of control*. New York: Freeman.

Bandura, A. (1999). Social cognitive theory: An agentic perspective. *Asian Journal of Social Psychology, 2*, 21-42.

Berliner, D. C., & Biddle, B. J. (1995). *The manufactured crisis: Myths, fraud, and the attack on America's public schools*. Reading, MA: Addison-Wesley.

Chorover, S. L. (1980). *From genesis to genocide: The meaning of human nature and the power of behavior control*. Cambridge, MA: MIT press.

Confucius (1979). *The Analects*. Translated by D. C. Lau. New York: Penguin Books.

Farkas, G., Grobe, R. P., Sheehan, D., & Shuan, Y. (1990). Cultural resources and school success: Gender, ethnicity, and poverty groups within an urban school district. *American Sociological Review, 55*, 127-142.

Gould, S. J. (1981). *The mismeasure of man*. New York: Norton.

Hess, R., Azuma, H. M., Kashiwagi, K., Dickson, W. P., Nagano, S. Holloway, S., Miyake, K., et al. (1986). Family influence on school readiness and achievement in Japan and the United States: An overview of a longitudinal study. In H. W. Stevenson, H. Azuma, & K. Hakuta (Eds.), *Child development and education in Japan* (pp. 147-166). New York: Freeman.

Hess, R. D., Azuma, H., Kashiwagi, K., Holloway, S. D., & Wenegrat, A. (1987). Cultural variations in socialization for school achievement: Contrasts between Japan and the United States. *Journal of Applied Developmental Psychology, 8*, 421-440.

Ho, D. Y. F. (1986). Chinese patterns of socialization: A critical review. In M. H. Bond (Ed.), *The psychology of the Chinese people* (pp. 1-37). Oxford: Oxford University Press.

Holloway, S., Kasgiwagi, K., & Azuma, H. (1986). Causal attributions by Japanese and American mothers and children about performance in mathematics. *International Journal of Psychology, 21*, 269-286.

Hsia, J. (1988). *Asian Americans in higher education and work*. Hillsdale, NJ: Lawrence Erlbaum Associates.

Kamin, L. J. (1974). *The science and politics of I.Q.* New York: Penguin Books.

Kim, H. C. (Ed.). (1992). *Asian Americans and the Supreme Court: A Documentary History*. New York: Greenwood.

Kim, U. (2001). Culture, science and indigenous psychologies: An integrated analysis. In D. Matsumoto (Ed.), *Handbook of culture and psychology* (pp. 51-76). Oxford: Oxford University Press.

Kim, U., Aasen, H. S., & Ebadi, S. (2003). *Democracy, human rights and Islam in modern Iran: Psychological, social and cultural perspectives.* Bergen: Fagbokforlaget.

Kim, U., Helgesen, G., & Ahn, B. M. (2002). Democracy, trust and political efficacy: Comparative analysis of Danish and South Korean political culture. *Applied Psychology: An International Review, 51,* 317-352.

Kim, U., & Park, Y. S. (2003). An indigenous analysis of success attribution: Comparison of South Korean students and adults. In K. S. Yang, K. K. Hwang, P. Pedersen, & I. Daibo (Eds.), *Progress in Asian social psychology: Conceptual and empirical contributions* (pp. 171-195). New York: Preager.

Lee, E. S., & Rong, X. L. (1988). The educational and economic achievement of Asian Americans. *Elementary School Journal, 88,* 545-559.

Lynn, R., & Vanhanen, T. (2002). *IQ and the Wealth of Nations.* Westport, CT: Praeger.

Mizokawa, D. T., & Ryckman, D. B. (1990). Attributions of academic success and failure: A comparison of six Asian-American ethnic groups. *Journal of Cross-Cultural Psychology, 21,* 434-451.

National Center for Educational Statistics. (2000). *Mathematics and science in eighth grade: Findings from the Third International Mathematics and Science Study.* Washington, DC: U.S. Department of Education.

Organisation for Economic Co-operation and Development. (2003). *Education at a glance: OECD indicators.* Paris: OECD.

Pang, V. O. (1991). The relationship of test anxiety and math achievement to parental values in Asian-American and European-American middle school students. *Journal of Research and Development in Education, 24,* 1-10.

Park, Y. S., & Kim, U. (2004). *Adolescent culture and parent-child relationship in South Korea: Indigenous psychological analysis* [in Korean]. Seoul: Kyoyook Kwahaksa.

Park, Y. S., Kim, U., & Chung, K. (2004). Longitudinal analysis of the influence of parent-child relationship on adolescents' academic achievement: With specific focus on the mediating role of self-efficacy and achievement motivation. *Korean Journal of Psychological and Social Issues, 10,* 37-59.

Park, Y. S., Kim, U., Chung, K. S., Lee, S. M., Kwon, H. H., & Yang, K. M. (2000). Causes and consequences of life-satisfaction among primary, junior high, senior high school students. *Korean Journal of Health Psychology, 5,* 94-118.

Rothbaum, F., Weisz, J., Pott, M., Miyake, K., & Morelli, G. (2000). Attachment and culture: Security in the United States and Japan. *American Psychologist, 55,* 1093-1104.

Schneider, B. & Lee, Y. (1990). A model for academic success: The school and home environment of East Asian students. *Anthropology and Education Quarterly, 21,* 358-377.

Shweder, R. A. (1991). *Thinking through cultures: Expeditions in cultural psychology.* Cambridge, MA: Harvard University Press.

Slaughter-Defoe, D. T., Nakagawa, K., Takanishi, R., & Johnson, D. J. (1990). Toward cultural/ecological perspectives on schooling and achievement in African- and Asian-American children. *Child Development, 61,* 363-383.

Stevenson, H., Azuma, H., & Hakuta. K. (Eds.). (1986). *Child development and education in Japan*. New York: W. H. Freeman.

Stevenson, H., & Lee, S. Y. (1990). Context of achievement: A study of American, Chinese and Japanese children. *Monographs of the Society for Research in Child Development, 55*(1-2, Serial No. 221).

Sue, S., & Okazaki, S. (1990). Asian-American educational achievements: A phenomenon in search of an explanation. *American Psychologist, 45*, 913-920.

Triandis, H. (Ed.). (1980). *Handbook of cross-cultural psychology*. Boston: Allyn & Bacon.

Vernon, P. E. (1982). *The abilities and achievements of Orientals in North America*. New York: Academic.

Yao, E. L. (1985). A comparison of family characteristics of Asian-American and Anglo-American high achievers. *International Journal of Comparative Sociology, 26*, 198-207.

Yu, A. B., & Yang, K. S. (1994). The nature of achievement motivation in collectivistic societies. In U. Kim, H. C. Triandis, C. Kagitcibasi, S. C. Choi, & G. Yoon (Eds.), *Individualism and collectivism: Theory, method, and applications* (pp. 239-250). Thousand Oaks, CA: Sage.

CHAPTER 13

ASKING THE RIGHT QUESTION

How Confident Are You That You Could Successfully Perform These Tasks?

Mimi Bong

Self-efficacy refers to "the conviction that one can successfully execute the behavior required to produce the outcomes" (Bandura, 1977, p. 79). Since its initial conception, researchers and practitioners in education have been paying close attention to the utility of self-efficacy in explaining and predicting students' academic functioning in school. Their efforts have been justified. It has been repeatedly demonstrated that students with a strong sense of efficacy are motivated to engage in challenging tasks (Bandura & Schunk, 1981), invest greater effort in assigned tasks (Salomon 1984; Schunk, 1983), set higher goals (Schunk & Swartz, 1993), persist longer in the face of occasional setbacks (Lent, Brown, & Larkin, 1984; Schunk, 1982), express lower levels of anxiety (Bandura, Pastorelli, Barbaranelli, & Caprara, 1999; Pajares, Miller, & Johnson, 1999), use more effective learning strategies (Zimmerman, Bandura, & Martinez-Pons, 1992; Zimmerman & Kitsantas, 1999), and achieve at higher levels (Pajares et al., 1999; Pietsch, Walker, & Chapman, 2003) compared to those with low self-efficacy.

Self-Efficacy Beliefs of Adolescents, 287–305
Copyright © 2006 by Information Age Publishing

Academic self-efficacy, in particular, refers to students' subjective conviction that they can successfully carry out given school and classroom tasks at desired levels (Schunk, 1991). Though little disagreement exists regarding this conceptual definition, considerable variations exist in the ways it is translated to form particular self-efficacy items and scales. Children and adolescents must learn and perform a variety of tasks in a variety of domains, so the sheer number of measurement instruments in the academic self-efficacy literature alone is not a problem. The problem, however, is in the nature of the questions and statements included in those instruments. Some of the purported self-efficacy scales are not consistent with Bandura's (1997) prescriptions and assess something other than self-efficacy. Studies relying on these "pseudo" self-efficacy scales run the risk of reaching faulty conclusions. Researchers hence erroneously conclude at times that self-efficacy is not a significant predictor of student motivation or that other constructs better predict student achievement.

Reasons for such misguided practice seem to fall into one of three main categories, which are not mutually exclusive. The first is the confusion with other constructs referring to the self, the second is the lack of accurate understanding in the context-specific and generative nature of self-efficacy, and the third is the failure to ensure correspondence between self-efficacy and its prediction target. The purpose of this chapter is to examine these common sources of mistakes in assessing adolescents' self-efficacy and the likely impact these less-than-optimal procedures might have had on relevant results. A number of theoretical and practical issues in self-efficacy item and scale construction are then discussed, followed by guidelines on how best to operationalize self-efficacy in academic settings.

COMMON SOURCES OF MISTAKES IN SELF-EFFICACY ASSESSMENT

Confusion Between Self-Efficacy and Other Self-Referent Constructs

Perhaps due to its relatively short history, self-efficacy is often inappropriately equated with other constructs referring to the self that have existed longer in the literature (see, for example, Thomas, Iventosch, & Rohwer, 1987; Wilhite, 1990). One such construct is self-esteem, which refers to one's evaluative orientations toward the self (Damon & Hart, 1982) and represents a person's general sense of worth and overall feelings of adequacy across different areas in life (Byrne, 1996; Pelham,

1995). In achievement situations, self-esteem embodies students' judgments of their own worth and feelings of self-satisfaction as a student.

Despite the unique function of self-esteem in adolescents' mental and psychological health, drawing a parallel between self-esteem and self-efficacy cannot be justified theoretically or empirically. The most common mistake is to assess self-efficacy as a domain-specific form of self-esteem. Investigators who commit this error conceptualize self-esteem as a global index of perceived self-worth spanning across many disparate domains and self-efficacy as similar emotional reactions toward the self but in specific domains. However, self-esteem need not be detached from a functional domain, nor is there a part-whole relationship between self-efficacy and self-esteem (Bandura, 1997).

When judging self-esteem, the competencies deemed important and the standards used to evaluate them likely differ across individuals (James, 1980, as cited in Pelham, 1995). For adolescents who consider mathematics an important domain, their self-worth as students would partly depend on their mathematics competencies (but see Marsh, 1995). They may gauge these competencies against personal criteria or adopt socially accepted indicators of success such as obtained grades. Students' feelings of self-worth also may be global in nature or tied to a specific domain. Therefore, items such as "I am happy with the way I am in math" or "Everything I do goes wrong in math" are self-esteem statements as much as are items such as "I like myself the way I am" or "I believe I am a good student" (see the Perceived Competence Scale for Children; Harter, 1982). The former represent mathematics self-esteem and the latter represent global academic self-esteem. None of these items represents self-efficacy.

Self-concept, another construct frequently confused with self-efficacy, refers to "a person's perception of himself" formed through experiences with the environment and influenced by environmental reinforcements and significant others (Shavelson, Hubner, & Stanton, 1976). Academic self-concept refers specifically to individuals' knowledge and perceptions about themselves in achievement situations (Byrne, 1984; Shavelson & Bolus, 1982; Wigfield & Karpathian, 1991).

In the past, self-concept was viewed as a global construct like general self-esteem. For example, the original version of the Piers-Harris Children's Self-Concept Scale (PHCSCS) operationally defined self-concept as a composite score derived from multiple scales tapping such diverse contents as behavior, general and academic status, physical appearance and attributes, anxiety, popularity, and happiness and satisfaction (Piers & Harris, 1964; see also Byrne, 1996). Harter (1982, 1990) criticized such practice, noting that global self-concept measures cannot reveal important distinctions children might make between different activity domains. Marsh and his colleagues also generated abundant empirical evidence that self-concepts of children and adolescents are differentiated into multiple domains even within the "academic" realm (Marsh, 1990, 1992; Marsh, Byrne, & Shavelson, 1988). Contemporary self-concept scales reflect this multidimensionality in students' academic self-concept.

Its domain-specificity notwithstanding, self-concept still differs from self-efficacy in several important ways. Most notably, adolescents' academic self-concept is about whether they believe they are good in certain domains based on their past experiences, whereas their academic self-efficacy is about whether they believe they can successfully perform present tasks under the given circumstances (Bong & Skaalvik, 2003; Skaalvik & Bong, 2003). Self-efficacy thus more narrowly focuses on the judgments of competence in specific performance situations over other competence-related information that may be available in one's self-schema (Bong & Clark, 1999). Pajares (1996) suggested that self-concept includes a self-efficacy component because it consists of competence judgments coupled with evaluative reactions and feelings of self-worth (see also Schunk, 1991).

Owing likely to these differences, findings from the self-esteem and self-concept research on the predictive and explanatory utility of these constructs for important student outcomes have been less than unequivocal. Proponents of the self-esteem movement argue that increasing students' self-esteem by praising them invariably would lead to improved school achievement, a claim still in search of empirical evidence (Dweck, 1999). The relations between academic self-concept and scholastic achievement had been similarly disappointing but became somewhat stronger once perceived competence was treated as the most critical element in one's academic self-concept (Hansford & Hattie, 1982; Wigfield & Karpathian, 1991).

In contrast, consistent support exists for the direct and mediating effects of self-efficacy on students' performance and persistence on diverse academic tasks (Multon, Brown, & Lent, 1991). Although perceived competence is an important ingredient in self-efficacy appraisal as well (Bong & Skaalvik, 2003; Pajares, 1996), assessing self-efficacy requires more than simply asking about one's generalized perceptions of competence in the given domain. Asking whether one has certain abilities or whether one is good at certain tasks differs from asking whether one can execute, with those recognized capabilities, the requisite course of action to meet a variety of situational demands for achieving successful performance (Bandura, 1997).

Lack of Accurate Understanding in the Context-Specific and Generative Nature of Self-Efficacy Judgments

Self-efficacy is sometimes confused with other self-referent constructs because of a failure to understand exactly what percepts of self-efficacy entail. Among the many distinctive attributes of self-efficacy, its context-specificity and generative nature as a predictive construct appear most frequently neglected in so-called "self-efficacy scales." The result is substantially reduced explanatory and predictive power for the constructs so assessed.

Context-specificity may be related to, but should not be confused with, domain-specificity, content-specificity, and measurement specificity. As I have noted, self-esteem and self-concept can each be domain-specific. Adolescents may form different ideas about their own personal worth and perceived competence in cognitive, social, and physical domains (Harter, 1998). Likewise, they may hold differentiated views of their capabilities across specific content areas such as English, history, and math (e.g., Byrne & Shavelson, 1986; Marsh, 1992). Although measures of these domain- and content-specific perceptions demonstrate improved explanatory utility compared to omnibus measures (Bandura, 1997), they are still inferior predictors of students' academic functioning than are context-specific self-efficacy beliefs (Pajares & Miller, 1994; Pietsch et al., 2003).

Some investigators mistakenly believe that assessing perceived competence at skill-specific levels automatically captures judgments of self-efficacy. Quite the contrary, self-efficacy can be assessed at varying levels of specificity depending on the researchers' explanatory and predictive goals (Bandura, 1997). Adolescents develop self-efficacy beliefs that are skill-specific, task-specific, or domain-specific. A study by Lau, Yeung, Jin, and Low (1999) showed that not all skill-specific measurements of self-perceived capabilities embody self-efficacy. The researchers assessed Hong Kong students' perceptions of competence in listening, speaking, reading, and writing in English as their second language. As Table 13.1 presents, the skill-specific self-concept items do not directly tap the set of component skills that define proficient performance in each skill area. They focus instead on the overall feelings of competence, adequacy, and affective reactions regarding the skills. Also listed in Table 13.1 are examples of self-efficacy items that can be readily developed out of the skill definitions provided by the authors. Although the two constructs tap the same level of measurement specificity, it is not difficult to identify markedly different characteristics of the proposed self-efficacy items from the skill-specific self-concept items.

Table 13.1.   Skill-Specific Self-Concept and Self-Efficacy Items

Skill Area	Definition of Skills	Possible Self-Efficacy Items	Self-Concept Items
Listening in English	Understanding English speeches in formal and social situations and in academic and non-academic contexts	I'm confident I can understand English speeches in formal situations. I'm confident I can understand English speeches in social situations. I believe I can understand English speeches successfully in academic contexts. I believe I can understand English speeches successfully in non-academic contexts.	Compared to other students I'm good at (listening/speaking/reading/writing) in English. I'm hopeless when it comes to (listening/speaking/reading/writing) in English. I have always done well in (listening/speaking/reading/writing) in English.
Speaking in English	Activities such as delivery of a talk or having a conversation with another person in class and out of class	I believe I can successfully deliver a talk in English. I'm confident I can carry out a conversation with another person in English in class. I'm confident I can carry out a conversation with another person in English outside class.	Work in (listening/speaking/reading/writing) in English is easy for me. I get good marks in (listening/speaking/reading/writing) in English. I learn things quickly in (listening/speaking/reading/writing) in English.
Reading in English	Comprehension of written prose, understanding of vocabulary, and study for academic and non-academic purposes	I believe I can successfully comprehend written prose in English. I'm confident I can understand the vocabulary while reading in English. I believe I can successfully read materials written in English for academic purposes. I believe I can successfully read materials written in English for non-academic purposes.	
Writing in English	Written work leading to essays, reports, and all other work in the written form as required academically in their respective disciplines at the university	I'm confident I can write essays in English. I'm confident I can write reports in English. I believe I can successfully produce written work in English as required academically at my university.	

Note.   Definitions of skills and skill-specific self-concept items are from Lau, Yeung, Jin, and Low (2000), Study 2. The skill-specific self-concept items were developed for Hong Kong students, for whom English was a second language.

First and foremost, the primary emphasis of the self-efficacy items is on the self-judged confidence regarding whether one can successfully execute the required behavior under the specified circumstances. By explicitly telling the respondents what constitutes a successful performance in each skill area, errors of prediction due to misinterpretation of the items are minimized. Second, the self-efficacy items make no reference to the emotional reactions that may arise as a result of the self-appraised proficiency. Affective responses are important psychological outcomes of perceived self-efficacy, but they are not constituents of efficacy beliefs (Bong & Clark, 1999; Bong & Skaalvik, 2003; Pajares, 1996). Third, relative superiority or inferiority of the skills compared to others is less consequential in shaping one's self-efficacy than are perceived capabilities to meet the designated criteria for success (Bong & Clark, 1999; Bong & Skaalvik, 2003; Zimmerman, 1995).

The core in self-efficacy assessment, then, is to get to the very belief that individuals draw on when they are faced with situations that involve certain actions or performance (Pajares, 1996). People do not act in vacuum, nor do they act with only vague feelings about what they are generally like. Rather, they proceed with more or less concrete ideas about where they stand in reference to the performance goals, taking into account all known factors that might moderate their capabilities to realize desired outcomes. To accurately assess these beliefs means to envisage and reflect all necessary competencies and situational constraints in the assessment instrument. Context-specific self-efficacy measurement thus requires that important features of the tasks and situations that could wield tangible influence on performance outcomes be clearly spelled out in the items (Bandura, 1997). This helps respondents to evaluate their self-efficacy more accurately, which consequently predicts their ensuing thought patterns, emotional reactions, and performance quality with increased precision (Mischel, 1977).

Just as ignoring the context-specific nature of efficacy expectations is highly problematic, failing to reflect the generative property of such expectations can also seriously restrict the prediction afforded by the assessed beliefs. These situations occur when respondents are asked only to appraise their capabilities to perform a set of highly particularized constituent skills. Yet successful academic performance often calls for more than errorless execution of the component skills. When investigators want to predict the quality of students' everyday writing from their writing self-efficacy, they are well advised to incorporate not only the specific component skills required in writing (e.g., use of correct punctuation, use of correct plurals, prefixes, and suffixes) but also the common tasks (e.g., get your points across in your writing) and situations (e.g., write a letter to a friend, write a 1-page summary of a book you read, write a 2-page report for a class) that necessitate competent execution of those subskills (Shell, Colvin, & Bruning, 1995; Shell, Murphy, & Bruning, 1989). The act of writing demands an adroit combination of the basic skills as well as successful adaptation to the complexities of the given writing situation.

Bandura (1997) warns against the "fragmentation and decontextualization of capabilities" because "the whole is greater than the sum of its parts" (p. 38). As illustrated in the writing example above, efficacy expectations formed in reference to separate performance contexts are comprised of qualitatively different elements. Therefore, the sum of self-efficacy beliefs toward particular subskills in writing is not necessarily identical to the beliefs toward writing itself (Bong & Skaalvik, 2003). Unlike other belief systems, self-efficacy as a context-specific and generative judgment mirrors the varying intricacies of the performance situations.

Failure to Ensure Correspondence Between Self-Efficacy and Prediction Target

Another related reason that many items and scales stray from the prerequisite conditions for self-efficacy scale construction can be traced to the degree of correspondence to their prediction target. Self-efficacy is a predictive construct of behavioral change that needs to be assessed prior to the outcomes of interest (Bandura, 1977; Zimmerman, 1995). When self-efficacy scales are developed without reference to a specific prediction target or when the chosen self-efficacy assessment tasks are not compatible with the performance outcomes they are meant to predict, their forecasting power diminishes (Pajares, 1996).

In the former situation where investigators develop self-efficacy scales with no specific aim of explaining or predicting any particular outcome, there is a danger of winding up with a compilation of generic items. Beliefs of self-efficacy, when assessed with these generic items, may be able to predict relevant outcomes to a certain degree but by no means with the level of accuracy that has been the hallmark of the self-efficacy research. A related problem that often arises is the blending of the predictor and the predicted. In Yeung et al. (2000, Study 2), for example, the following three items were used to measure students' self-efficacy in English reading: "How confident are you when you read English?" "How well do you read English?" and "How often do you read in English?" Among these three, only the first item may pass as a self-efficacy item. The other two tap students' expectations on likely consequences of their self-efficacy to read in English.

There are also situations in which self-efficacy items are developed with the purpose of predicting some concrete target yet fail to emulate the target's content, scope, or difficulty level to a sufficient degree. Pajares and Miller (1995) demonstrated this point empirically. They assessed participants' math self-efficacy with the Mathematics Self-Efficacy Scale (MSES). Each of the three subscales in the MSES measured students' subjective confidence in their ability to solve a set of mathematics problems, complete everyday mathematics tasks, or perform successfully in mathematics-related courses. All three subscale scores as well as a composite score based on the full MSES were positively and strongly correlated both with students' mathematics problem-solving performance and with their choice of mathematics-related majors. Nonetheless, students' self-efficacy scores estimated against the 18 specific mathematics problems emerged as the strongest predictor of their performance on the same set of problems. In contrast, students' choices of mathematics-related majors were best predicted by their self-efficacy expectations in these courses.

As this study illustrates, percepts of efficacy assessed in reference to outcomes that fall in the vicinity of the prediction target would still prove useful to a certain, sometimes even satisfactory, extent. However, as the study further demonstrated, the predictive utility of self-efficacy is maximized when these beliefs are estimated in reference to the tasks and contexts that best correspond to the criterial variable (Bandura, 1997; Pajares, 1996). Therefore, if researchers aim to capitalize on the power of self-efficacy to explain and predict adolescents' academic functioning, they must assess the beliefs that match the target of prediction.

ISSUES TO CONSIDER IN SELF-EFFICACY ITEM AND SCALE DEVELOPMENT

The following are some of the essential issues that should be considered when one wishes to develop self-efficacy items and scales in studies of adolescents' psychological and performance-related outcomes in achievement situations. It should be noted that this list is not meant to be exhaustive. Nonetheless, care was taken to incorporate most theoretical and practical issues deemed particularly important in the study of adolescents' functioning in school.

Levels of Specificity at Which Self-Efficacy is Assessed

As discussed earlier, self-efficacy is superior to other self-referent constructs in predicting achievement outcomes because efficacy beliefs are judgments of capability tailored to a specific outcome. When constructing self-efficacy assessment tools, one must determine the appropriate level of specificity at which percepts of efficacy should be tapped. This is a question that cannot be answered without careful analysis of the prediction target. If the goal is to predict students' levels of performance on some defined academic task, researchers must analyze the types of skills, knowledge, and potential constraints on performance involved in successful accomplishment of that task before creating a self-efficacy scale. If the goal is to predict cognitive and affective outcomes rather than performance attainments, investigators must still identify the tasks with which those outcomes are most likely triggered and the contexts within which they are most relevant (see Díaz, Glass, Arnkoff, & Tanofsky-Kraff, 2001).

Measurement specificity is not a sufficient condition for context-specificity, as I showed earlier with the study of skill-specific self-concept. Still, it is a necessary condition for ensuring context-specific judgments of competence. Pajares (1996) cautioned that self-efficacy should be assessed "as specifically as is relevant and useful" to the research question (p. 564). Self-efficacy expectations need not be microscopically assessed. Nor is it useful to use students' percepts of efficacy developed toward, for example, mathematics as a whole to predict performance on a set of fraction problems. If investigators wish to account for the performance variations among students' skills with fractions, they must solicit efficacy judgments about the same or similar types of fraction problems under study (e.g., Shih & Alexander, 2000). As Bandura (1986) cautioned, "the optimal level of generality at which self-efficacy is assessed varies depending on what one seeks to predict and the degree of foreknowledge of the situational demands" (p. 49).

Correspondence to the Prediction Target

Ascertaining context-specificity requires more than specificity of measurement. It also requires that efficacy expectations be estimated against the very skills, tasks, and situations that correspond to the key outcomes the researcher tries to predict. The value of assessing matching self-efficacy as a forebear of one's ensuing cognitive, affective, and behavioral repertoire is well described in the comments by Mischel (1977), who observed that

> if we want individuals to tell us about themselves directly, we have to ask questions that they can answer. If we ask people to predict how they will behave on a future criterion ... but do not inform them of the specific criterion measure that will constitute the assessment, we cannot expect them to be accurate. (p. 249)

In addition to ensuring that self-efficacy is assessed at the same level of specificity as the outcome of interest, it is imperative to sample a representative set of behaviors, tasks, and situations from a universe of possibly infinite variations of the requisite behaviors, tasks, and situations. The job of selecting archetypal items among the available pool of component skills and tasks requires expert knowledge of the essential capacities, scopes, and difficulty levels of diverse tasks as well as of the range of possible situations and restrictions in carrying out those tasks (Bandura, 1997).

Use of specific problems and tasks that appropriately match the target performance has the added advantage of more precisely demonstrating the impact of a changed sense of self-efficacy. Schunk and his colleagues successfully documented the effects of improved self-efficacy on specific types of mathematical operations among students with academic difficulties (Bandura & Schunk, 1981; Schunk, 1982, 1983; Schunk & Hanson, 1985; Schunk, Hanson, & Cox, 1987). In these studies, researchers used the same type of mathematics problems to assess self-efficacy and achievement before and after the implementation of remedial instructional programs. At program's end, participants displayed significant growth in their self-efficacy toward solving the problems, which resulted in significantly improved problem-solving performance. Self-efficacy assessment items that correspond to the criterial variable are the most sensitive measure of cognitive precursor to behavioral change.

Provision of Concrete Anchors for Self-Efficacy Judgments

One dilemma that researchers and practitioners sometimes face is whether to incorporate in a self-efficacy scale all problems and tasks that respondents will be asked to solve or perform. For instance, Schunk (1996) presented 31 pairs of fraction problems to gauge students' self-efficacy about their fraction skills, each of which shared the same form and operations with one of the 31 problems in the skills test. There is no doubt but that the 31 pairs of problems would more accurately capture subtle as well as obvious changes in students' efficacy expectations toward fractions. Unfortunately, some situations do not permit such a lengthy survey.

Presenting verbal descriptions of the problems in lieu of the actual problems provides a practical solution in some of those situations. Bong (2002) categorized 25 achievement test problems into 10 problem types and developed representative verbal descriptions for each type. Efficacy beliefs judged in reference to these verbal task descriptions were highly correlated with self-efficacy ratings made in reference to the actual test problems. The self-efficacy measures also displayed comparable utility for predicting students' mathematics test performance.

Researchers should be warned, however, that resorting to written descriptions instead of the actual problems may have hidden cost. Pajares et al. (1999) cautioned that the manner in which questions are posed makes a difference in how people appraise and report their perceived competence. Accordingly, using verbal problem descriptions may prove effective only in some situations. Bong (2002) showed that students provided similar yet slightly different estimates of their self-efficacy depending on whether they were presented with a set of actual test problems or with only written descriptions of the problems. The nature of these judgment discrepancies also differed across domains. Students made more conservative self-efficacy estimates when verbal task descriptions instead of particularized test problems were presented in English, whereas the opposite was true in mathematics. A perceived difficulty level of the written task "Read a given passage and determine its main theme" could vary considerably by the hypothesized length, style, topic, or vocabulary used. In comparison, a description of a mathematics task such as "Compute the mean, standard deviation, and variance using a frequency table" may convey a less ambiguous message to students.

Assessment of Self-Efficacy Toward Unfamiliar Tasks

There are situations in which researchers and teachers wish to assess a student's self-efficacy toward problems and tasks that are yet to be learned. Depending on the expected type and scope of the performance, self-efficacy for self-regulated learning, self-efficacy for academic achievement, or both could be assessed (e.g., Zimmerman et al., 1992). The self-efficacy subscale of the Motivated Strategies for Learning Questionnaire (MSLQ; Pintrich & De Groot, 1990) can be used to measure students' expectations of academic performance in a given course. Among the nine MSLQ self-efficacy items, three solicit students' judgments of their capabilities compared to those of their peers. Self-efficacy theorists maintain that efficacy beliefs are more heavily affected by one's mastery experiences and absolute criteria of success (i.e., being able to succeed) rather than by social comparison and normative criteria (i.e., being better than others) (Bandura, 1977; Bong & Clark, 1999; Bong & Skaalvik, 2003; Zimmerman 1995). There could certainly be circumstances under which normative information plays a more critical role in efficacy appraisal, such as when a task is novel or ambiguous (France-Kaatrude & Smith, 1985; Marsh et al., 1991). Still, the comparative items are not recommended because they appear to emphasize social comparison more heavily than is theoretically justified. Another MSLQ item, "My study skills are excellent in this class," is also not recommended because it asks about respondents' evaluation of their current skill levels rather than whether they believe they can successfully employ these study skills to realize satisfactory achievement in the given domain.

In many achievement settings, students can predict the form in which the outcome of their new learning will materialize before they are introduced to all relevant skills and tasks. Academic grades are one such outcome. When researchers aim to predict students' grades, they can ask students to rate their confidence in their ability to obtain each of the letter grades in the given subject domain at the end of the course. These self-efficacy questions present the varying levels of performance qualities in the prediction target and, at the same time, provide respondents with concrete anchors against which to estimate their competence (Bong & Skaalvik, 2003).

Judgment Intervals in Self-Efficacy Rating Scales

The most typical self-efficacy response format is the one proposed by Bandura (see the Guide, this volume). Respondents are provided with a 100-point rating scale ranging from either 0 or 10 to 100, divided in 10-unit intervals. To help students understand more clearly what each number represents, the following verbal descriptors typically accompany this type of scale: 0 (not sure), 40 (maybe), 70 (pretty sure), and 100 (real sure).

Whereas the original 100-point response scale was widely used in early academic self-efficacy research, Likert-type scales with slightly different ranges tend to appear more frequently in contemporary academic self-efficacy research. For example, Likert scales of 1 to 5 (Bong & Hocevar, 2002), 1 to 6 (Pajares, 1996), 1 to 7 (Chemers, Hu, & Garcia, 2001), and 1 to 8 (Pajares & Graham, 1999) have been successfully applied to the study of adolescents' self-efficacy. However, when Pajares, Hartley, and Valiante (2001) assessed students' writing self-efficacy using both the traditional 0-100 and the Likert-type 1-6 response scales, the 0-100 scale demonstrated better predictive utility for students' writing GPA, especially in the presence of other motivational variables such as self-concept, apprehension, and task value in writing. Their results are consistent with Bandura's (1997) warning that self-efficacy response scales with too few steps should be avoided because they cannot capture fine distinctions among individuals' efficacy beliefs. Therefore, providing students with a broad enough range of potential responses such as those offered in the original 100-point response scale appears most defensible. When Likert-type scales are used, investigators must ensure that the scale contains a sufficient number of points so as not to miss subtle variations in students' judgments.

Temporal Proximity Between Self-Efficacy and Performance Assessments

According to Bandura (1997), it is important to assess self-efficacy in close temporal proximity to the prediction target. This guideline is reasonable, given that individuals' self-efficacy, situational demands, or both could change during the assessment interval. But such practice sometimes poses a problem, especially when the goal is to predict longer-term outcomes. Educational researchers are often interested in foretelling students' motivation and performance at the end of the semester or school year on the basis of efficacy beliefs assessed at the beginning of the school year. In addition, though self-efficacy is relatively more malleable than are other trait-like self-perceptions, individuals can and do develop a resilient sense of efficacy toward a particular task or domain as a result of their repeated success or failure experiences (Bandura, 1997). This is particularly true among adolescents, who have been dealing with a more or less similar academic subject matter for several years.

Empirical evidence suggests that the issue of temporal proximity may be less relevant in the study of adolescents' self-efficacy when the target of prediction is at the academic subject domain level or beyond. Bong (2002) compared the utility of students' self-efficacy for predicting a number of performance outcomes assessed after increasingly longer intervals from the self-efficacy assessment. Efficacy judgments obtained at the beginning of the semester predicted students' end-of-semester exam performance with the same accuracy that they predicted performance on tests that immediately followed the self-efficacy assessment. Nevertheless, it should be noted that performance scores on these exams typically correlate strongly and hence often demonstrate similar relations with other variables. Therefore, investigators are urged to assess adolescents' self-efficacy and performance in reasonable temporal proximity. This is particularly important when the learning and performance conditions are expected to change and students are required to perform progressively more challenging tasks or when there exists an intervening performance or testing event that may alter students' self-efficacy toward the tasks.

SUMMARY AND CONCLUSION

The primary reason why so many educators and researchers are keenly interested in adolescents' self-efficacy is because of its proven effect on diverse spheres of academic functioning. Whereas past research on various self-related perceptions tried to uncover "what is," research on self-efficacy has instead been emphasizing "what works." Numerous experiments with academically challenged students have demonstrated clearly the modifiable nature of self-efficacy as a consequence of successful instructional interventions. Relatively simple teaching procedures such as modeling, goal setting, and attributional feedback are able to enhance students' success expectations in a fairly short period of time. This improved sense of self-efficacy invariably leads adolescents to function more effectively in taxing academic situations. This modifiability of judgments vividly contrasts with the frustration educators often experience when they strive to augment students' generalized self-perceptions.

It is critical, therefore, to accurately document the malleability as well as the predictive power of efficacy beliefs on important student outcomes. This information aids researchers and practitioners in their efforts to help adolescents become more resilient learners by strengthening their self-efficacy. One major impediment to this is the confusion among investigators as to how best to assess self-efficacy toward the numerous skills, tasks, and domains that adolescents need to master in school. Some researchers hold a misguided assumption that one must always resort to established items and scales, as that has often been the standard procedure with other decontextualized constructs. But published scales are not of much help when they do not match the tasks or domains of interest. To exacerbate the situation, many variations of self-efficacy assessment exist in the study of adolescents, some of which deviate considerably from Bandura's theoretical prescriptions.

As I have explained, the most fundamental difference between self-efficacy and other self-referent beliefs is that self-efficacy beliefs represent context-specific judgments of competence. It is less important what capabilities adolescents believe that they posses than whether they believe that, at the end of their endeavor, they can enjoy success on the given tasks under the given circumstances by successfully applying those capabilities. Research on adolescents' self-efficacy, therefore, must start by asking the right question—"How confident are you that you can successfully perform these tasks?"

REFERENCES

Bandura, A. (1977). *Social learning theory.* Englewood Cliffs, NJ: Prentice-Hall.
Bandura, A. (1986). *Social foundations of thought and action: A social cognitive theory.* Englewood Cliffs, NJ: Prentice-Hall.
Bandura, A. (1997). *Self-efficacy: The exercise of control.* New York: Freeman.
Bandura, A., Pastorelli, C., Barbaranelli. C., & Caprara, G. V. (1999). Self-efficacy pathways to childhood depression. *Journal of Personality and Social Psychology, 76,* 258-269.

Bandura, A., & Schunk, D. H. (1981). Cultivating competence, self-efficacy, and intrinsic interest through proximal self-motivation. *Journal of Personality and Social Psychology, 41*, 586-598.

Bong, M. (2002). Predictive utility of subject-, task-, and problem-specific self-efficacy judgments for immediate and delayed academic performances. *Journal of Experimental Education, 70*, 133-162.

Bong, M., & Clark, R. E. (1999). Comparison between self-concept and self-efficacy in academic motivation research. *Educational Psychologist, 34*, 139-154.

Bong, M., & Hocevar, D. (2002). Measuring self-efficacy: Multi-trait multi-method comparison of scaling procedures. *Applied Measurement in Education, 15*, 143-171.

Bong, M., & Skaalvik, E. M. (2003). Academic self-concept and self-efficacy: How different are they really? *Educational Psychology Review, 15*, 1-40.

Byrne, B. M. (1984). The general/academic self-concept nomological network: A review of construct validation research. *Review of Educational Research, 54*, 427-456.

Byrne, B. M. (1996). *Measuring self-concept across the life span: Issues and instrumentation.* Washington, DC: American Psychological Association.

Byrne, B. M., & Shavelson, R. J. (1986). On the structure of adolescent self-concept. *Journal of Educational Psychology, 78*, 474-481.

Chemers, M. M., Hu, L. T., & Garcia, B. F. (2001). Academic self-efficacy and first-year college student performance and adjustment. *Journal of Educational Psychology, 93*, 55-64.

Damon, W., & Hart, D. (1982). The development of self-understanding from infancy through adolescence. *Child Development, 53*, 841-864.

Díaz, R. J., Glass, C. R., Arnkoff, D. B., & Tanofsky-Kraff, M. (2001). Cognition, anxiety, and prediction of performance in 1st-year law students. *Journal of Educational Psychology, 93*, 420-429.

Dweck, (1999). Caution—Praise can be dangerous. *American Educator, 56*, 4-9.

France-Kaatrude, A. C., Smith, W. P. (1985). Social comparison, task motivation, and the development of self-evaluative standards in children. *Developmental Psychology, 21*, 1080-1089.

Hansford, B. C., & Hattie, J. A. (1982). The relationship between self and achievement/performance measures. *Review of Educational Research, 52*, 123-142.

Harter, S. (1982). The perceived competence scale for children. *Child Development, 53*, 87-97.

Harter, S. (1990). Causes, correlates, and the functional role of global self-worth: A life-span perspective. In R. J. Sternberg & J. Kolligian (Eds.), *Competence considered* (pp. 67-97). New Haven, CT: Yale University Press.

Harter, S. (1998). The development of self-representations. In W. Damon (Series Ed.) & N. Eisenberg (Vol. Ed.), *Handbook of child psychology: Vol. 3. Social, emotional, and personality development* (5th ed., pp. 553-617). New York: Wiley.

Lau, I. C., Yeung, A. S., Jin, P., & Low, R. (1999). Toward a hierarchical, multidimensional English self-concept. *Journal of Educational Psychology, 91*, 747-755.

Lent, R. W., Brown, S. D., & Larkin, K. C. (1984). Relation of self-efficacy expectations to academic achievement and persistence. *Journal of Counseling Psychology, 31*, 356-362.

Marsh, H. W. (1990). The structure of academic self-concept: The Marsh/Shavelson model. *Journal of Educational Psychology, 82,* 623-636.

Marsh, H. W. (1992). Content specificity of relations between academic achievement and academic self-concept. *Journal of Educational Psychology, 84,* 35-42.

Marsh, H. W. (1995). A Jamesian model of self-investment and self-esteem: Comment on Pelham. *Journal of Personality and Social Psychology, 69,* 1151-1160.

Marsh, H. W., Byrne, B. M., & Shavelson, R. J. (1988). A multifaceted academic self-concept: Its hierarchical structure and its relation to academic achievement. *Journal of Educational Psychology, 80,* 366-380.

Mischel, W. (1977). On the future of personality measurement. *American Psychologist, 32,* 246-254.

Multon, K. D., Brown, S. D., & Lent, R. W. (1991). Relation of self-efficacy beliefs to academic outcomes: A meta-analytic investigation. *Journal of Counseling Psychology, 38,* 30-38.

Pajares, F. (1996). Self-efficacy beliefs in academic settings. *Review of Educational Research, 66,* 543-578.

Pajares, F., & Graham, L. (1999). Self-efficacy, motivation constructs, and mathematics performance of entering middle school students. *Contemporary Educational Psychology, 24,* 124-139.

Pajares, F., Hartley, J., & Valiante, G. (2002). Response format in writing self-efficacy assessment: Greater discrimination increases prediction. *Measurement and Evaluation in Counseling and Development, 33,* 214-221.

Pajares, F., & Miller, M. D. (1994). Role of self-efficacy and self-concept beliefs in mathematical problem solving: A path analysis. *Journal of Educational Psychology, 86,* 193-203.

Pajares, F., & Miller, M. D. (1995). Mathematics self-efficacy and mathematics performances: The need for specificity of assessment. *Journal of Counseling Psychology, 42,* 190-198.

Pajares, F., Miller, M. D., & Johnson, M. J. (1999). Gender differences in writing self-beliefs of elementary school students. *Journal of Educational Psychology, 91,* 50-61.

Pelham, B. W. (1995). Self-investment and self-esteem: Evidence for a Jamesian model of self-worth. *Journal of Personality and Social Psychology, 69,* 1141-1150.

Piers, E. V., & Harris, D. B. (1964). Age and other correlates of self-concept in children. *Journal of Educational Psychology, 55,* 91-95.

Pietsch, J., Walker, R., & Chapman, E. (2003). The relationship among self-concept, self-efficacy, and performance in mathematics during secondary school. *Journal of Educational Psychology, 95,* 589-603.

Pintrich, P. R., & De Groot, E. V. (1990). Motivational and self-regulated learning components of classroom academic performance. *Journal of Educational Psychology, 82,* 33-40.

Salomon, G. (1984). Television is "easy" and print is "tough": The differential investment of mental effort in learning as a function of preconceptions and attitudes. *Journal of Educational Psychology, 76,* 647-658.

Schunk, D. H. (1982). Effects of effort attributional feedback on children's perceived self-efficacy and achievement. *Journal of Educational Psychology, 74,* 548-556.

Schunk, D. H. (1983). Ability versus effort attributional feedback: Differential effects on self-efficacy and achievement. *Journal of Educational Psychology, 75,* 848-856.

Schunk, D. H. (1991). **Self-efficacy and academic motivation.** *Educational Psychologist, 26,* 207-231.

Schunk, D. H. (1996). Goal and self-evaluative influences during children's cognitive skill learning. *American Educational Research Journal, 33,* 359-382.

Schunk, D. H., & Hanson, A. R. (1985). Peer models: Influence on children's self-efficacy and achievement. *Journal of Educational Psychology, 77,* 313-322.

Schunk, D. H., Hanson, A. R., & Cox, P. (1987). Peer-model attributes and children's achievement behaviors. *Journal of Educational Psychology, 79,* 54-61.

Schunk, D. H., & Swartz, C. W. (1993). Goals and progress feedback: Effects on self-efficacy and writing achievement. *Contemporary Educational Psychology, 18,* 337-354.

Shavelson, R. J., & Bolus, R. (1982). Self-concept: The interplay of theory and methods. *Journal of Educational Psychology, 74,* 3-17.

Shavelson, R. J., Hubner, J. J., & Stanton, G. C. (1976). Self-concept: Validation of construct interpretations. *Review of Educational Research, 46,* 407-441.

Shell, D. F., Colvin, C., & Bruning, R. H. (1995). Self-efficacy, attribution, and outcome expectancy mechanisms in reading and writing achievement: Grade-level and achievement-level differences. *Journal of Educational Psychology, 87,* 386-398.

Shell, D. F., Murphy, C. C., & Bruning, R. H. (1989). Self-efficacy and outcome expectancy mechanisms in reading and writing achievement. *Journal of Educational Psychology, 81,* 91-100.

Shih, S. S., & Alexander, J. M. (2000). Interacting effects of goal setting and self-or other-referenced feedback on children's development of self-efficacy and cognitive skill within the Taiwanese classroom. *Journal of Educational Psychology, 92,* 526-543.

Skaalvik, E. M., & Bong, M. (2003). Self-concept and self-efficacy revisited: A few notable differences and important similarities. In H. W. Marsh, R. G. Craven, & D. McInerney (Eds.), *International advances in self research* (pp. 67-89). Greenwich, CT: Information Age.

Thomas, J. W., Iventosch, L., & Rohwer, W. D., Jr. (1987). Relationships among student characteristics, study activities, and achievement as a function of course characteristics. *Contemporary Educational Psychology, 12,* 344-364.

Wigfield, A., & Karpathian, M. (1991). Who am I and what can I do? Children's self-concepts and motivation in achievement situations. *Educational Psychologist, 26,* 233-261.

Wilhite, S. C. (1990). Self-efficacy, locus of control, self-assessment of memory ability, and study activities as predictors of college course achievement. *Journal of Educational Psychology, 82,* 696-700.

Yeung, A. S., Chui, H. S., Lau, I. C., McInerney, D. M., Russell-Bowie, D., & Suliman, R. (2000). Where is the hierarchy of academic self-concept? *Journal of Educational Psychology, 92,* 556-567.

Zimmerman, B. J. (1995). Self-efficacy and educational development. In A. Bandura (Ed.), *Self-efficacy in changing societies* (pp. 202-231). New York: Cambridge University Press.

Zimmerman, B. J., Bandura, A., & Martinez-Pons, M. (1992). Self-motivation for academic attainment: The role of self-efficacy beliefs and personal goal setting. *American Educational Research Journal, 29,* 663-676.

Zimmerman, B. J., & Kitsantas, A. (1999). Acquiring writing revision skill: Shifting from process to outcome self-regulatory goals. *Journal of Educational Psychology, 91,* 241-250.

CHAPTER 14

GUIDE FOR CONSTRUCTING
SELF-EFFICACY SCALES

Albert Bandura

Perceived self-efficacy is concerned with people's beliefs in their capabilities to produce given attainments (Bandura, 1997). One cannot be all things, which would require mastery of every realm of human life. People differ in the areas in which they cultivate their efficacy and in the levels to which they develop it even within their given pursuits. For example, a business executive may have a high sense of organizational efficacy but low parenting efficacy. Thus, the efficacy belief system is not a global trait but a differentiated set of self-beliefs linked to distinct realms of functioning. Multidomain measures reveal the patterning and degree of generality of people's sense of personal efficacy.

There is no all-purpose measure of perceived self-efficacy. The *"one measure fits all"* approach usually has limited explanatory and predictive value because most of the items in an all-purpose test may have little or no relevance to the domain of functioning. Moreover, in an effort to serve all purposes, items in such a measure are usually cast in general terms divorced from the situational demands and circumstances. This leaves much ambiguity about exactly what is being measured or the level of task and situational demands that must be managed. Scales of perceived self-

---

Self-Efficacy Beliefs of Adolescents, 307–337
Copyright © 2006 by Information Age Publishing
All rights of reproduction in any form reserved.

efficacy must be tailored to the particular domain of functioning that is the object of interest.

Although efficacy beliefs are multifaceted, social cognitive theory identifies several conditions under which they may co-vary even across distinct domains of functioning (Bandura, 1997). When different spheres of activity are governed by similar sub-skills there is some inter-domain relation in perceived efficacy. Proficient performance is partly guided by higher-order self-regulatory skills. These include generic skills for diagnosing task demands, constructing and evaluating alternative courses of action, setting proximal goals to guide one's efforts, and creating self-incentives to sustain engagement in taxing activities and to manage stress and debilitating intrusive thoughts. Generic self-management strategies developed in one realm of activity are serviceable in other activity domains with resulting co-variation in perceived efficacy among them.

Co-development is still another correlative process. Even if different activity domains are not sub-served by common sub-skills, the same perceived efficacy can occur if development of competencies is socially structured so that skills in dissimilar domains are developed together. For example, students are likely to develop similarly high perceived self-efficacy in dissimilar academic subjects, such as language and mathematics in superior schools, but similarly low perceived efficacy in ineffective schools, which do not promote much academic learning in any subject matter.

And finally, powerful mastery experiences that provide striking testimony to one's capacity to effect personal changes can produce a transformational restructuring of efficacy beliefs that is manifested across diverse realms of functioning. Extraordinary personal feats serve as transforming experiences.

The conceptual and methodological issues regarding the nature and structure of self-efficacy scales are discussed in detail in Chapter 2 in the book *Self-Efficacy: The Exercise of Control* and will not be reviewed here. The present guide for constructing self-efficacy scales supplements that conceptual and empirical analysis.

Content Validity

Efficacy items should accurately reflect the construct. Self-efficacy is concerned with perceived capability. The items should be phrased in terms of *can do* rather than *will do*. *Can* is a judgment of capability; *will* is a statement of intention. Perceived self-efficacy is a major determinant of intention, but the two constructs are conceptually and empirically separable.

Perceived self-efficacy should also be distinguished from other constructs such as *self-esteem*, *locus of control*, and *outcome expectancies*. Perceived efficacy is a judgment of capability; self-esteem is a judgment of self-worth. They are entirely different phenomena. Locus of control is concerned, not with perceived capability, but with belief about outcome contingencies—whether outcomes are determined by one's actions or by forces outside one's control. High locus of control does not necessarily signify a sense of enablement and well-being. For example, students may believe that high academic grades are entirely dependent on their performance (high locus of control) but feel despondent because they believe they lack the efficacy to produce those superior academic performances.

Another important distinction concerns performance outcome expectations. Perceived self-efficacy is a judgment of capability to execute given types of performances; outcome expectations are judgments about the outcomes that are likely to flow from such performances. Outcome expectations take three different forms (Bandura, 1986). They include the positive and negative physical, social, and self-evaluative outcomes. Within each form, the positive expectations serve as incentives, the negative ones as disincentives. The outcomes people anticipate depend largely on their judgments of how well they will be able to perform in given situations.

Perceived efficacy plays a key role in human functioning because it affects behavior not only directly, but by its impact on other determinants such as goals and aspirations, outcome expectations, affective proclivities, and perception of impediments and opportunities in the social environment (Bandura, 1995, 1997). Efficacy beliefs influence whether people think erratically or strategically, optimistically or pessimistically. They also influence the courses of action people choose to pursue, the challenges and goals they set for themselves and their commitment to them, how much effort they put forth in given endeavors, the outcomes they expect their efforts to produce, how long they persevere in the face of obstacles, their resilience to adversity, the quality of their emotional life and how much stress and depression they experience in coping with taxing environmental demands, and the life choices they make and the accomplishments they realize. Meta-analyses across different spheres of functioning confirm the influential role of perceived self-efficacy in human self-development, adaptation, and change (Boyer et al., 2000; Holden, 1991; Holden, Moncher, Schinke, & Barker, 1990; Moritz, Feltz, Fahrbach, & Mack, 2000; Multon, Brown, & Lent, 1991; Sadri & Robertson, 1993; Stajkovic & Luthans, 1998).

Domain Specification and Conceptual Analysis of Self-Efficacy Multicausality

The construction of sound efficacy scales relies on a good conceptual analysis of the relevant domain of functioning. Knowledge of the activity domain specifies which aspects of personal efficacy should be measured. Consider the self-management of weight as an example. Weight is determined by what people eat, by their level of exercise, which burns calories and can raise the body's metabolism, and by genetic factors that regulate metabolic processes. A comprehensive self-efficacy assessment would be linked to the behavioral factors over which people can exercise some control. This would include perceived capability to regulate the foods that are purchased, to exercise control over eating habits, and to adopt and stick to an increased level of physical activity. Behavior is better predicted by people's beliefs in their capabilities to do whatever is needed to succeed than by their beliefs in only one aspect of self-efficacy relevant to the domain. In the present example, perceived self-efficacy will account for more of the variation in weight if the assessment includes perceived capability to regulate food purchases, eating habits, and physical exercise than if it is confined solely to eating habits.

The preceding example further illustrates how different facets of perceived efficacy operating within a domain may weigh in more heavily in different phases of a given pursuit. Perceived efficacy to purchase healthful foods that make it easier to manage one's weight accounts for daily caloric and fat intake prior to treatment when self-regulatory skills are infirm. After self-regulatory skills are developed, however, perceived efficacy to curb overeating maintains reduced caloric and fat intake, and perceived efficacy to manage what one brings home fades in importance. Apparently, savory foods are not a problem as long as one can eat them in moderation. If negative affect triggers overeating, assessment of perceived efficacy for affect regulation will explain additional variance in self-management of weight. Thus, multifaceted efficacy scales not only have predictive utility but provide insights into the dynamics of self-management of behavior.

If self-efficacy scales are targeted to factors that, in fact, have little or no impact on the domain of functioning, such research cannot yield a predictive relation. If, for example, relaxation does not affect drug use, then perceived self-efficacy to relax will be unrelated to consumption of drugs because the causal theory is faulty. Under these circumstances, negative findings will reflect faulty theory rather than limitations of self-efficacy beliefs. In short, self-efficacy scales must be tailored to activity domains and assess the multifaceted ways in which efficacy beliefs operate within the selected activity domain. The efficacy scales must be linked to factors that, in fact, determine quality of functioning in the domain of interest.

Gradations of Challenge

Perceived efficacy should be measured against levels of task demands that represent gradations of challenges or impediments to successful performance. Self-efficacy appraisals reflect the level of difficulty individuals believe they can surmount. If there are no obstacles to overcome, the activity is easily performable and everyone is highly efficacious.

The events over which personal influence is exercised can vary widely. It may entail regulating one's own motivation, thought processes, performance level, emotional states, or altering environmental conditions. The content domain should correspond to the area of functioning one seeks to manage. The nature of the challenges against which personal efficacy is judged will vary depending on the sphere of activity. Challenges may be graded in terms of level of ingenuity, exertion, accuracy, productivity, threat, or self-regulation required, just to mention a few dimensions of performance demands.

Many areas of functioning are primarily concerned with self-regulatory efficacy to guide and motivate oneself to get things done that one knows how to do. In such instances, self-regulation is the capability of interest. The issue is not whether one can do the activities occasionally, but whether one has the efficacy to get oneself to do them regularly in the face of different types of dissuading conditions. For example, in the measurement of perceived self-efficacy to stick to a health-promoting exercise routine, individuals judge how well they can get themselves to exercise *regularly* under various impediments, such as when they are under pressure from work, are tired or depressed, are in foul weather, or when they have other commitments or more interesting things to do (see Appendix).

Constructing scales to assess self-regulatory efficacy requires preliminary work to identify the forms the challenges and impediments take. People are asked in open-ended interviews and pilot questionnaires to describe the things that make it hard for them to perform the required activities regularly. The identified challenges or impediments are built into the efficacy items. In the formal scale, participants judge their ability to meet the challenges or to surmount the various impediments. Sufficient gradations of difficulties should be built into the efficacy items to avoid ceiling effects.

Response Scale

In the standard methodology for measuring self-efficacy beliefs, individuals are presented with items portraying different levels of task demands, and they rate the strength of their belief in their ability to execute the requisite activities. They record the strength of their efficacy beliefs on a 100-point scale, ranging in 10-unit intervals from 0 ("Cannot do"); through intermediate degrees of assurance, 50 ("Moderately certain can do"); to complete assurance, 100 ("Highly certain can do"). A simpler response format retains the same scale structure and descriptors but uses single unit intervals ranging from 0 to 10. The instructions and standard response format are given below.

The attached form lists different activities. In the column **Confidence**, rate how confident you are that you can do them **as of now**. Rate your degree of confidence by recording a number from 0 to 100 using the scale given below:

0	10	20	30	40	50	60	70	80	90	100
Cannot do at all				Moderately certain can do				Highly certain can do		

The sample efficacy scales in the Appendix illustrate some variations in format depending on the age of the respondents and the sphere of efficacy being assessed.

Scales that use only a few steps should be avoided because they are less sensitive and less reliable. People usually avoid the extreme positions so a scale with only a few steps may, in actual use, shrink to one or two points. Including too few steps loses differentiating information because people who use the same response category may differ if intermediate steps were included. Thus an efficacy scale with the 0-100 response format is a stronger predictor of performance than one with a 5-interval scale (Pajares, Hartley, & Valiante, 2001). In sensitive measures, the responses are distributed over a good part of the range of alternatives.

Efficacy scales are unipolar, ranging from 0 to a maximum strength. They do not include negative numbers because a judgment of complete incapability (0) has no lower gradations. Bipolar scales with negative gradations below the zero point that one cannot perform a given level of activity do not make sense.

Preliminary instructions should establish the appropriate mindset that participants should have when rating the strength of belief in their personal capability. People are asked to judge their operative capabilities as of now, not their potential capabilities or their expected future capabilities. It is easy for people to imagine themselves to be fully efficacious in some hypothetical future. However, in the case of perceived self-regulatory efficacy to maintain a given level of functioning over time, people judge their efficacy that they can perform the activity regularly over designated periods of time. For example, recovered alcoholics would judge their perceived capability to refrain from drinking over specified time intervals.

A practice item, such as the capability to lift objects of increasing weight, helps to familiarize respondents with the scale gauging strength of efficacy belief and reveals any misunderstanding about how to use it. With young children, one can use a physical performance task to familiarize them with the scale for rating the strength of their perceived efficacy. For example, one can place markers on the floor at progressively farther distances. Children are asked to rate their degree of confidence that they can jump to each of the distances. They do so by selecting a number from the scale with the following descriptors (e.g., cannot do it, not too sure, pretty sure, certain I can do it). They perform the task after each rating. In this concrete way, children learn how to use numerical scale values to convey the strength of their perceived self-efficacy.

With very young children one may have to use pictorial rather than verbal descriptors of strength of self-efficacy belief. For example, circles with progressively larger size could be used with explanation that the size gradations represent increasing confidence that they can perform the tasks. Happy or sad faces are to be avoided. Children may misread such a scale as measuring their happiness or sadness rather than how confident they are that they can perform given tasks.

Efficacy beliefs differ in generality, strength, and level. People may judge themselves efficacious across a wide range of activity domains or only in certain domains of functioning. Generality can vary across types of activities, the modalities in which capabilities are expressed (e.g., behavioral, cognitive, affective), situational variations, and the types of individuals toward whom the behavior is directed. Assessments linked to activity domains, situational contexts, and social aspects reveal the patterning and degree of generality of people's beliefs in their efficacy. Within the network of efficacy beliefs, some are of greater import than others. The most fundamental self-beliefs are those around which people structure their lives.

In addition, efficacy beliefs vary in strength. Weak efficacy beliefs are easily negated by disconfirming experiences, whereas people who have a tenacious belief in their capabilities will persevere in their efforts despite innumerable difficulties and obstacles. They are not easily dissuaded by adversity. Strength of perceived self-efficacy is not necessarily linearly related to choice behavior (Bandura, 1977). A certain threshold of self-assurance is needed to attempt a course of action, but higher strengths of self-efficacy will result in the same attempt. The stronger the sense of personal efficacy, however, the greater the perseverance and the higher the likelihood that the chosen activity will be performed successfully.

One could also designate self-efficacy beliefs in terms of level, that is, the number of activities individuals judge themselves capable of performing above a selected cutoff value of efficacy strength. However, converting a continuous measure of efficacy strength into a dichotomous measure on the basis of a minimal cutoff strength value loses predictive information. If a low cutoff value is selected, a relatively low sense of efficacy is treated the same as complete self-assurance. Conversely, if the cutoff criterion is set at a high level, a moderately strong sense of capability gets defined as a lack of efficacy. Either too low or too high cutoffs can produce artifactual discrepancies between perceived self-efficacy and performance.

A more refined microanalysis of congruence is provided by computing the probability of successful performance as a function of the strength of perceived self-efficacy (Bandura, 1977). This microlevel analysis retains the predictive value of variations in strength of efficacy beliefs. Because efficacy strength incorporates efficacy level as well as gradations of certainty above any threshold value, efficacy strength is generally a more sensitive and informative measure than efficacy level.

Minimizing Response Biases

The standard procedure for measuring beliefs of personal efficacy includes a number of safeguards to minimize any potential motivational effects of self-assessment. These safeguards are built into the instructions and the mode of administration. Self-efficacy judgments are recorded privately without personal identification to reduce social evaluative concerns. The self-efficacy scale is identified by code number rather than by name. Respondents are informed that their responses will remain confidential and be used only with number codes by the research staff. If the scale is labeled, use a nondescript title such as *"Appraisal Inventory"* rather than *Self-Efficacy*. To encourage frank answers, explain to the respondents the importance of their contribution to the research. Inform them that the knowledge it provides will increase understanding and guide the development of programs designed to help people to manage the life situations with which they have to cope.

People make multiple judgments of their efficacy across the full range of task demands within the activity domain rather than making each judgment immediately before each performance. The assessments of perceived efficacy and behavior are conducted in different settings and by different assessors to remove any possible carryover of social influence from assessment to the performance setting.

Does rating one's self-efficacy affect one's behavior? If merely recording a level of self-efficacy made it so, personal change would be trivially easy. People would rate themselves into grand accomplishments. Nevertheless, the question arises as to whether making efficacy judgments may contribute some motivational inducement to improve the match between self-judgment and performance. Numerous tests for reactive effects of self-efficacy assessment have been conducted (Bandura, 1997). The findings show that people's level of motivation, affective reactions, and performance attainments are the same regardless of whether they do or do not make prior self-efficacy judgments. The nonreactivity of self-efficacy assessment is corroborated for diverse activities, including coping with threats, self-regulation of motivation, pain tolerance, cognitive attainments, recovery of functioning after coronary surgery, and exercise adherence. Nor are efficacy judgments influenced by a responding bias to appear socially desirable, regardless of whether the domain of activity involves sexual behavior, alcohol consumption, smoking, dietary practices, or self-management of diabetes.

Private recording of efficacy judgments may reduce evaluative concerns and consistency expectations, but it could be argued that it does not eliminate them entirely. To the extent that people assume their private recordings will be evaluated at a later time, they may retain some evaluative concerns. However, evidence shows that making efficacy judgments does not increase congruence between perceived efficacy and behavior under either high or low social demand for consistency (Telch, Bandura, Vinciguerra, Agras, & Stout, 1982).

Item Analysis in Scale Construction

Pretest the items. Discard those that are ambiguous or rewrite them. Eliminate items where most people are checking the same response point. Such items do not differentiate among respondents. Items on which the vast majority of respondents check the maximum efficacy category lack sufficient difficulty, challenge, or impediments to distinguish levels of efficacy among respondents. Increase the difficulty level by raising the level of challenge in the item.

The items tapping the same domain of efficacy should be correlated with each other and with the total score. Factor analyses verify the homogeneity of the items. Different domains of efficacy require different sets of scales with item homogeneity within each of the domain-relevant scales.

Reliability places an upper limit on the maximum possible correlation that can be obtained between variables. Internal consistency reliabilities should be computed using Cronbach's alpha. If the reliability coefficients are low, discard or rewrite the items with low correlates. Including only a few items will limit the alpha level. Increase the number of items.

Assessment of Perceived Collective Efficacy

The theorizing and research on human agency has centered almost exclusively on personal influence exercised individually. People do not live their lives autonomously. Many of the outcomes they seek are achievable only through interdependent efforts. Hence, they have to work together to secure what they cannot accomplish on their own. Social cognitive theory extends the conception of human agency to collective agency. People's shared beliefs in their collective power to produce desired results is a key ingredient of collective agency (Bandura, 2000).

A group's attainments are the product not only of shared knowledge and skills of the different members, but also of the interactive, coordinative, and synergistic dynamics of their transactions. Therefore, perceived collective efficacy is not simply the sum of the efficacy beliefs of individual members. Rather, it is an emergent group-level property. A group operates through the behavior of its members. It is people acting coordinatively on a shared belief, not a disembodied group mind that is doing the cognizing, aspiring, motivating, and regulating. There is no emergent entity that operates independently of the beliefs and actions of the individuals who make up a social system. Although beliefs of collective efficacy include emergent aspects, they serve functions similar to those of personal efficacy beliefs and operate through similar processes (Bandura, 1997).

There are two main approaches to the measurement of a group's perceived efficacy. The first method aggregates the individual members' appraisals of their personal capabilities to execute the particular functions they perform in the group. The second method aggregates members' appraisals of their group's capability operating as a whole. The latter holistic appraisal encompasses the coordinative and interactive aspects operating within groups.

Some researchers advocate that perceived collective efficacy be measured by having a group arrive at a single judgment of the group's capability (Guzzo, Yost, Campbell, & Shea, 1993). The discussion approach is methodologically problematic, however. Constructing unanimity about a group's efficacy via group discussion is subject to the distorting vagaries of social persuasion by members who command power and other types of pressures for social conformity. Indeed, a group's collective judgment of its efficacy reflects mainly the personal judgments of higher status members rather than those of subordinate members (Earley, 1999). The discussion approach is likely to produce reactive effects in that persuasory efforts to reach consensus will alter members' views. Assessments that operate through social influence should be avoided. A method of measurement should not change what it is measuring. Moreover, no social system is a monolith with a unitary sense of efficacy (Bandura, 1997). A forced consensus to a single judgment masks the variability in efficacy beliefs among the various factions within a social system and misrepresents their beliefs.

The two informative indices of perceived collective efficacy differ in the relative weight given to individual factors and social interactive ones, but they are not as distinct as they might appear. Being socially situated, and often interdependently so, individuals' judgments of their personal efficacy are not detached from the other members' enabling or impeding activities. Rather, a judgment of individual efficacy inevitably embodies the coordinative and interactive group dynamics. Judgment of efficacy in a group endeavor is very much a socially embedded one, not an individualistic, socially disembodied one. To take an athletic example, in judging the collective efficacy of their football team, the quarterback obviously considers the quality of his offensive line, the fleetness and blocking capabilities of his running backs, the adeptness of his receivers, and how well they work together as an offensive unit. Conversely, in judging the efficacy of their team, members certainly consider how well key teammates can execute their roles. Players on a basketball team would judge their team efficacy quite differently depending on whether or not a key superstar was in the lineup.

Self-efficacy theory distinguishes between the *source* of the data (i.e., individual) and the *level* of the phenomenon being measured (i.e., personal efficacy or group efficacy). As noted earlier, there is no group mind that believes. Perceived collective efficacy resides in the minds of members as beliefs in their group's capability. All too often the source of the judgment is misconstrued as the level of the measured phenomenon. The level is concerned with whether the efficacy of an individual or the group is being judged.

Given the interdependent nature of the appraisal process, linking efficacy measured at the individual level to performance at the group level does not necessarily represent a cross-level relation. The two indexes of collective efficacy are at least moderately correlated and predictive of group performance. The fact that appraisals of group efficacy embody members' dependence on one another has important bearing on gauging emergent properties. It is commonly assumed that an emergent property is operative if differences between groups remain after statistical methods are used to control variation in characteristics of individuals within the groups. The analytic logic is fine, but the results of such statistical controls can be quite misleading. Because judgments of personal efficacy take into consideration the unique dynamics of a group, individual-level controls can inadvertently remove most of the emergent group properties.

The relative predictiveness of the two indexes of collective efficacy will depend largely on the degree of interdependent effort needed to achieve desired results. For example, the accomplishments of a gymnastics team are the sum of successes achieved independently by the gymnasts, whereas the accomplishments of a soccer team are the product of players working intricately together. Any weak link, or a breakdown in a sub-system, can have ruinous effects on a soccer team despite an otherwise high level of talent. The aggregated holistic index is most suitable for per-formance outcomes achievable only by adept teamwork. Under low sys-tem interdependence, members may inspire, motivate, and support each other, but the group outcome is the sum of the attainments produced individually rather than by the members working together. Aggregated personal efficacies are well suited to measure perceived efficacy for the latter types of endeavors.

A growing body of research attests to the impact of perceived collective efficacy on group functioning (Gully, Incalcaterra, Joshi, & Beaubien, 2002; Stajkovic & Lee, 2001). Some of these studies have assessed the motivational and behavioral effects of perceived collective efficacy using experimental manipulations to instill differential levels of perceived col-lective efficacy. Other investigations have examined the effects of natu-rally developed beliefs of collective efficacy. The latter studies have analyzed diverse social systems, including educational systems, business organizations, athletic teams, combat units, urban neighborhoods, and political systems.

The findings taken as a whole show that the higher the perceived col-lective efficacy, the higher the groups' motivational investment in their undertakings, the stronger their staying power in the face of impediments and setbacks, and the greater their performance accomplishments.

Predictive and Construct Validation

As noted earlier, self-efficacy scales should have face validity. They should measure what they purport to measure, that is, perceived capabil-ity to produce given attainments. But they should also have discriminative and predictive validity. The construct of self-efficacy is embedded in a theory that explains a network of relationships among various factors. Construct validation is a process of hypothesis testing. People who score high on perceived self-efficacy should differ in distinct ways from those who score low in ways specified by the theory. Verifications of predicted effects provide support for the construct's validity.

Perceived self-efficacy can have diverse effects on motivation, thought, affect, and action, so there are many verifiable consequences that can be tested. There is no single validity coefficient. Construct validation is an ongoing process in which both the validity of the postulated causal structure in the conceptual scheme and the self-efficacy measures are being assessed.

Conclusion

Scientific advances are greatly accelerated by methodological development of assessment tools for key determinants of human functioning. Quality of assessment provides the basis for stringent empirical tests of theory. Given the centrality of efficacy beliefs in people's lives, sound assessment of this factor is crucial to understanding and predicting human behavior. Human behavior is richly contextualized and conditionally manifested. Self-efficacy assessment tailored to domains of functioning and task demands identify patterns of strengths and limitations in perceived capability. This type of refined assessment not only increases predictiveness, but provides guidelines for tailoring programs to individual needs.

The value of a psychological theory is judged not only by its explanatory and predictive power, but by its operational power to effect change. Perceived self-efficacy is embedded in a broader theory of human agency that specifies the sources of self-efficacy beliefs and identifies the processes through which they produce their diverse effects (Bandura, 1997, 2001). Knowing how to build a sense of efficacy and how it works provides further guidelines for structuring experiences that enable people to realize desired personal and social changes.

APPENDIX

Practice Rating

To familiarize yourself with the rating form, please complete this practice item first.

If you were asked to lift objects of different weights **right now**, how certain are you that you can lift each of the weights described below?

Rate your degree of confidence by recording a number from 0 to 100 using the scale given below:

0	10	20	30	40	50	60	70	80	90	100
Cannot do at all					Moderately can do				Highly certain can do	

	Confidence (0-100)
Physical Strength	
Lift a **10** pound object	_____
" **20** " "	_____
" **50** " "	_____
" **80** " "	_____
" **100** " "	_____
" **150** " "	_____
" **200** " "	_____
" **300** " "	_____

Self-Efficacy to Regulate Exercise

A number of situations are described below that can make it hard to stick to an exercise routine. Please rate in each of the blanks in the column how certain you are that you can get yourself to perform your exercise routine regularly (three or more times a week).

Rate your degree of confidence by recording a number from 0 to 100 using the scale given below:

0	10	20	30	40	50	60	70	80	90	100
Cannot do at all					Moderately can do				Highly certain can do	

	Confidence (0-100)
When I am feeling tired	_____
When I am feeling under pressure from work	_____
During bad weather	_____
After recovering from an injury that caused me to stop exercising	_____
During or after experiencing personal problems	_____
When I am feeling depressed	_____
When I am feeling anxious	_____
After recovering from an illness that caused me to stop exercising	_____
When I feel physical discomfort when I exercise	_____
After a vacation	_____
When I have too much work to do at home	_____
When visitors are present	_____
When there are other interesting things to do	_____
If I don't reach my exercise goals	_____
Without support from my family or friends	_____
During a vacation	_____
When I have other time commitments	_____
After experiencing family problems	_____

Self-Efficacy to Regulate Eating Habits

A number of situations are described below that can make it hard to stick to a diet that is low in fat. Please rate in each of the blanks on the column how certain you are that you can stick to a healthy diet on **a regular basis**.

Rate your degree of confidence by recording a number from 0 to 100 using the scale given below:

0	10	20	30	40	50	60	70	80	90	100

Cannot do at all	Moderately can do	Highly certain can do

	Confidence (0-100)
While watching television	_____
Feeling restless or bored	_____
During holiday times	_____
Feeling upset or tense over job-related matters	_____
Eating at a friend's house for dinner	_____
Preparing meals for others	_____
Eating at a restaurant alone	_____
When angry or annoyed	_____
When very hungry	_____
When depressed	_____
When you want to sit back and enjoy food	_____
When lots of high fat food is available in the house	_____
Feel like celebrating with others	_____
Someone offers you high fat foods	_____
Feel a strong urge to eat foods high in fat that you like	_____
When you are entertaining visitors	_____
During vacations	_____
Eating out with others when they are ordering high fat meals	_____
Parties where a lot of appetizing high fat food is served	_____
At recreational and sport events where high fat fast foods are served	_____
When visiting a city and needing a quick meal	_____
Airplane meals with high fat items	_____
When visiting a city and wanting to experience the local food and restaurants	_____
Holidays and celebrations where high fat foods are served	_____
When upset over family matters	_____
When you want some variety in your diet	_____
When eating breakfast in a restaurant	_____
Others bring or serve high fat foods	_____
When you have to prepare your own meals	_____
When faced with appealing high fat foods in the supermarket	_____

Driving Self-Efficacy

Please rate how certain you are that you can drive in the situations described below.

Rate your degree of confidence by recording a number from 0 to 100 using the scale given below:

0	10	20	30	40	50	60	70	80	90	100

Cannot					Moderately				Highly certain
do at all					can do				can do

	Confidence (0-100)
Drive a few blocks in the neighborhood	_____
Drive around in residential areas	_____
Drive on a downtown suburban business street	_____
Drive on a main arterial road	_____
Drive on a freeway	_____
Drive into the city	_____
Drive on narrow mountain roads	_____

Problem-Solving Self-Efficacy

Please rate how certain you are that you can solve the academic problems at each of the levels described below.

Rate your degree of confidence by recording a number from 0 to 100 using the scale given below:

0	10	20	30	40	50	60	70	80	90	100

Cannot   Moderately   Highly certain
do at all   can do   can do

**Confidence
(0-100)**

Can solve 10% of the problems	_____
" 20% " " "	_____
" 30% " " "	_____
" 40% " " "	_____
" 50% " " "	_____
" 60% " " "	_____
" 70% " " "	_____
" 80% " " "	_____
" 90% " " "	_____
" 100% " " "	_____

Pain Management Self-Efficacy

People sometimes do things to reduce their pain without taking medication. Please rate how certain you are that you can **reduce** the different levels of pain described below?

Rate your degree of confidence by recording a number from 0 to 100 using the scale given below:

0	10	20	30	40	50	60	70	80	90	100
Cannot do at all					Moderately can do					Highly certain can do

	Confidence (0-100)
Reduce a **DULL PAIN**	
A small reduction	_____
A moderate reduction	_____
A large reduction	_____
Reduce an **ACHING PAIN**	
A small reduction	_____
A moderate reduction	_____
A large reduction	_____
Reduce a **PENETRATING PAIN**	
A small reduction	_____
A moderate reduction	_____
A large reduction	_____
Reduce an **EXCRUCIATING PAIN**	
A small reduction	_____
A moderate reduction	_____
A large reduction	_____

Children's Self-Efficacy Scale

This questionnaire is designed to help us get a better understanding of the kinds of things that are difficult for students. Please rate how certain you are that you can do each of the things described below by writing the appropriate number. Your answers will be kept strictly confidential and will not be identified by name.

Rate your degree of confidence by recording a number from 0 to 100 using the scale given below:

0	10	20	30	40	50	60	70	80	90	100
Cannot do at all					Moderately can do				Highly certain can do	

Confidence (0-100)

Self-Efficacy in Enlisting Social Resources
Get teachers to help me when I get stuck on schoolwork _____
Get another student to help me when I get stuck on schoolwork _____
Get adults to help me when I have social problems _____
Get a friend to help me when I have social problems _____

Self-Efficacy for Academic Achievement
Learn general mathematics _____
Learn algebra _____
Learn science _____
Learn biology _____
Learn reading, writing, and language skills _____
Learn to use computers _____
Learn a foreign language _____
Learn social studies _____
Learn English grammar _____

Self-Efficacy for Self-Regulated Learning
Finish my homework assignments by deadlines _____
Get myself to study when there are other interesting things to do _____
Always concentrate on school subjects during class _____
Take good notes during class instruction _____
Use the library to get information for class assignments _____
Plan my schoolwork for the day _____
Organize my schoolwork _____
Remember well information presented in class and textbooks _____
Arrange a place to study without distractions _____
Get myself to do school work _____

Self-Efficacy for Leisure Time Skills and Extracurricular Activities

Learn sports skills well _____

Learn dance skills well _____

Learn music skills well _____

Do the kinds of things needed to work on the school newspaper _____

Do the things needed to serve in school government _____

Do the kinds of things needed to take part in school plays _____

Do regular physical education activities _____

Learn the skills needed for team sports (for example, basketball, volleyball, swimming, football, soccer) _____

Self-Regulatory Efficacy

Resist peer pressure to do things in school that can get me into trouble _____

Stop myself from skipping school when I feel bored or upset _____

Resist peer pressure to smoke cigarettes _____

Resist peer pressure to drink beer, wine, or liquor _____

Resist peer pressure to smoke marijuana _____

Resist peer pressure to use pills (uppers, downers) _____

Resist peer pressure to have sexual intercourse _____

Control my temper _____

Self-Efficacy to Meet Others' Expectations

Live up to what my parents expect of me _____

Live up to what my teachers expect of me _____

Live up to what my peers expect of me _____

Live up to what I expect of myself _____

Social Self-Efficacy

Make and keep friends of the opposite sex _____

Make and keep friends of the same sex _____

Carry on conversations with others _____

Work well in a group _____

Self-Assertive Efficacy

Express my opinions when other classmates disagree with me _____

Stand up for myself when I feel I am being treated unfairly _____

Get others to stop annoying me or hurting my feelings _____

Stand firm to someone who is asking me to do something unreasonable or inconvenient _____

Self-Efficacy for Enlisting Parental and Community Support

Get my parents to help me with a problem _____

Get my brother(s) and sister(s) to help me with a problem _____

Get my parents to take part in school activities _____

Get people outside the school to take an interest in my school (for example, community groups, churches) _____

Teacher Self-Efficacy Scale

This questionnaire is designed to help us gain a better understanding of the kinds of things that create difficulties for teachers in their school activities. Please rate how certain you are that you can do the things discussed below by writing the appropriate number. Your answers will be kept strictly confidential and will not be identified by name.

Rate your degree of confidence by recording a number from 0 to 100 using the scale given below:

0	10	20	30	40	50	60	70	80	90	100

Cannot   Moderately   Highly certain
do at all   can do   can do

                                                         **Confidence
(0-100)**

Efficacy to Influence Decision Making
Influence the decisions that are made in the school   _____
Express my views freely on important school matters   _____
Get the instructional materials and equipment I need   _____

Instructional Self-Efficacy
Get through to the most difficult students   _____
Get students to learn when there is a lack of support from the home   _____
Keep students on task on difficult assignments   _____
Increase students' memory of what they have been taught in previous
    lessons   _____
Motivate students who show low interest in schoolwork   _____
Get students to work well together   _____
Overcome the influence of adverse community conditions on
    students' learning   _____
Get children to do their homework   _____

Disciplinary Self-Efficacy
Get children to follow classroom rules   _____
Control disruptive behavior in the classroom   _____
Prevent problem behavior on the school grounds   _____

Efficacy to Enlist Parental Involvement
Get parents to become involved in school activities   _____
Assist parents in helping their children do well in school   _____
Make parents feel comfortable coming to school   _____

Efficacy to Enlist Community Involvement
Get community groups involved in working with the school   _____
Get businesses involved in working with the school   _____
Get local colleges and universities involved in working with the school   _____

Efficacy to Create a Positive School Climate
Make the school a safe place   _____
Make students enjoy coming to school   _____
Get students to trust teachers   _____
Help other teachers with their teaching skills   _____
Increase collaboration between teachers and the administration
    to make the school run effectively   _____
Reduce school dropout   _____
Reduce school absenteeism   _____
Get students to believe they can do well in school work   _____

Parental Self-Efficacy

This questionnaire is designed to help us gain better understanding of the kinds of things that create difficulties for parents to affect their children's academic development. Please rate how certain you are that you can do the things discussed below by writing the appropriate number. Your answers will be kept strictly confidential and will not be identified by name.

Rate your degree of confidence by recording a number from 0 to 100 using the scale given below:

0	10	20	30	40	50	60	70	80	90	100
Cannot do at all					Moderately can do				Highly certain can do	

	Confidence (0-100)
Efficacy to Influence School-Related Performance	
Get your children to see school as valuable	_____
Get your children to work hard at their schoolwork	_____
Get your children to stay out of trouble at school	_____
Help your children get good grades at school	_____
Get your children to enjoy school	_____
Show your children that working hard at school influences later success	_____
Efficacy to Influence Leisure-Time Activities	
Get your children into activities outside of school (e.g., music, art, dance lessons, sports)	_____
Get your children to keep physically fit	_____
Find time for leisure activities with your children	_____
Efficacy in Setting Limits, Monitoring Activities, and Influencing Peer Affiliations	
Keep track of what your children are doing when they are outside the home	_____
Prevent your children from getting in with the wrong crowd of friends	_____
Get your children to associate with friends who are good for them	_____
Get your children to do things you want at home	_____
Manage when your children go out and when they have to be in	_____
Instill your values in your children	_____
Spend time with your children and their friends	_____
Work with other parents to keep the neighborhood safe for your children	_____
Keep your children from going to dangerous areas, corners, or playgrounds	_____

Efficacy to Exercise Control over High-Risk Behavior

Prevent your children from doing things you do not want them to do outside the home

Prevent your children from becoming involved in drugs or alcohol _____

Prevent your children from becoming involved in premature sexual activity _____

Get your children to quit drugs or alcohol if you found them using it _____

Manage the situation if you found that your children were sexually active _____

Efficacy to Influence the School System

Affect what teachers expect your children to be able to do in school _____

Have a say in what is taught in your children's school _____

Make your children's school a better place for them to learn _____

Influence the social activities in your children's school _____

Get parents involved in the activities of your children's school _____

Make your children's school a friendly and caring place _____

Make parents feel welcome in your children's school _____

Have a say in what is taught in your children's school _____

Affect what your children do after school _____

Efficacy to Enlist Community Resources for School Development

Get neighborhood groups involved in working with schools _____

Get businesses involved in working with schools _____

Get local colleges and universities involved in working with schools _____

Get public funds for specific programs in the school _____

Efficacy to Influence School Resources

Help your children's school get the educational materials and equipment they need _____

Self-Efficacy to Control Distressing Rumination

Stop yourself from worrying about things _____

Take your mind off upsetting experiences _____

Stop yourself from being upset by everyday problems _____

Keep your mind on the things you are doing after you have had an upsetting experience _____

Resiliency of Self-Efficacy

Keep tough problems from getting you down _____

Bounce back after you tried your best and failed _____

Get yourself to keep trying when things are going really badly _____

Keep up your spirits when you suffer hardships _____

Get rid of self-doubts after you have had tough setbacks _____

Keep from being easily rattled _____

Overcome discouragement when nothing you try seems to work _____

Teacher Self-Efficacy to Promote Reading

Ratings for Your Class Only

Listed below are eight different levels of achievement scores on the criterion referenced test (CRT). Please rate how certain you are that **your class** can attain the different average levels of CRT scores by the end of the school year. Record the appropriate number to the right of **each** of the eight levels of school average levels of CRT scores.

Rate your degree of confidence by recording a number from 0 to 100 using the scale given below:

0	10	20	30	40	50	60	70	80	90	100

| Cannot | | | | Moderately | | | | Highly certain |
| do at all | | | | can do | | | | can do |

CRT class average by end of school year:	**Confidence (0-100)**
30% correct	_____
40% correct	_____
50% correct	_____
60% correct	_____
70% correct	_____
80% correct	_____
90% correct	_____
100% correct	_____

Teacher Self-Efficacy to Promote Mathematics

Listed below are eight different levels of achievement scores on the criterion referenced test (CRT). Please rate how certain you are that **your class** can attain the different average levels of CRT scores by the end of the school year. Record the appropriate number to the right of **each** of the eight levels of school average levels of CRT scores.

Rate your degree of confidence by recording a number from 0 to 100 using the scale given below:

0	10	20	30	40	50	60	70	80	90	100

Cannot   Moderately   Highly certain

do at all   can do   can do

CRT class average by end of school year:	Confidence (0-100)
30% correct	_____
40% correct	_____
50% correct	_____
60% correct	_____
70% correct	_____
80% correct	_____
90% correct	_____
100% correct	_____

Collective Efficacy to Promote Reading

Rating for Your School as a Whole

Listed below are eight different levels of achievement scores on the criterion referenced test (CRT). Please rate how certain you are that **your school as a whole** can attain the different average levels of CRT scores by the end of the school year. Record the appropriate number to the right of **each** of the eight levels of school average levels of CRT scores.

Rate your degree of confidence by recording a number from 0 to 100 using the scale given below:

0	10	20	30	40	50	60	70	80	90	100
Cannot do at all					Moderately can do					Highly certain can do

CRT school average by end of school year:	Confidence (0-100)
30% correct	_____
40% correct	_____
50% correct	_____
60% correct	_____
70% correct	_____
80% correct	_____
90% correct	_____
100% correct	_____

Collective Efficacy to Promote Mathematics

Rating for Your School as a Whole

Listed below are eight different levels of achievement scores on the criterion referenced test (CRT). Please rate how certain you are that **your school as a whole** can attain the different average levels of CRT scores by the end of the school year. Record the appropriate number to the right of **each** of the eight levels of school average levels of CRT scores.

Rate your degree of confidence by recording a number from 0 to 100 using the scale given below:

0	10	20	30	40	50	60	70	80	90	100

Cannot   Moderately   Highly certain
do at all   can do   can do

CRT school average by end of school year:	**Confidence (0-100)**
30% correct	_____
40% correct	_____
50% correct	_____
60% correct	_____
70% correct	_____
80% correct	_____
90% correct	_____
100% correct	_____

Perceived Collective Family Efficacy

The statements below describe situations that commonly arise in families. For each situation please rate how certain you are that your family, working together as a whole, can manage them effectively. Your answers will be kept strictly confidential and will not be identified by name.

Rate your degree of confidence by recording a number from 0 to 100 using the scale given below:

0	10	20	30	40	50	60	70	80	90	100
Cannot do at all					Moderately can do					Highly certain can do

Confidence (0-100)

How well, working together as a whole, can your family:

Set aside leisure time with each other when other things press for attention _____

Agree to decisions that require giving up personal interests _____

Resolve conflicts when family members feel they are not being treated fairly _____

Prevent family disagreements from turning into heated arguments _____

Get family members to share household responsibilities _____

Support each other in times of stress _____

Bounce back quickly from adverse experiences _____

Help each other to achieve their personal goals _____

Build respect for each other's particular interests _____

Help each other with work demands _____

Get family members to carry out their responsibilities when they neglect them _____

Build trust in each other _____

Figure out what choices to make when the family faces important decisions _____

Find community resources and make good use of them for the family _____

Get the family to keep close ties to their larger family _____

Celebrate family traditions even in difficult times _____

Serve as a good example for the community _____

Remain confident during difficult times _____

Accept each member's need for independence _____

Cooperate with schools to improve their educational practices _____

REFERENCES

Bandura, A. (1977). Self-efficacy: Toward a unifying theory of behavioral change. *Psychological Review, 84,* 191-215.

Bandura, A. (1986). *Social foundations of thought and action: A social cognitive theory.* Englewood Cliffs, NJ: Prentice-Hall.

Bandura, A. (Ed.). (1995). *Self-efficacy in changing societies.* New York: Cambridge University Press.

Bandura, A. (1997). *Self-efficacy: The exercise of control.* New York: Freeman.

Bandura, A. (2000). Exercise of human agency through collective efficacy. *Current Directions in Psychological Science, 9,* 75-78

Bandura, A. (2001). Social cognitive theory: An agentic perspective. *Annual review of psychology* (Vol. 52, pp. 1-26). Palo Alto, CA: Annual Reviews.

Boyer, D. A., Zollo, J. S., Thompson, C. M., Vancouver, J. B., Shewring, K., & Sims, E. (2000, June). *A quantitative review of the effects of manipulated self-efficacy on performance.* Poster session presented at the annual meeting of the American Psychological Society, Miami, FL.

Earley, P. C. (1999). Playing follow the leader: Status-determining traits in relation to collective efficacy across cultures. *Organizational Behavior and Human Decision Processes, 80,* 192-212.

Gully, S. M., Incalcaterra, K. A., Joshi, A., & Beaubien, J. M. (2002). A meta-analysis of team-efficacy, potency, and performance: Interdependence and level of analysis as moderators of observed relationships. *Journal of Applied Psychology, 87,* 819-832.

Guzzo, R. A., Yost, P. R., Campbell, R. J., & Shea, G. P. (1993). Potency in groups: Articulating an construct. *British Journal of Social Psychology, 32,* 87-106.

Holden, G. (1991). The relationship of self-efficacy appraisals to subsequent health related outcomes: A meta-analysis. *Social Work in Health Care, 16,* 53-93.

Holden, G., Moncher, M. S., Schinke, S. P., & Barker, K. M. (1990). Self-efficacy of children and adolescents: A meta-analysis. *Psychological Reports, 66,* 1044-1046.

Moritz, S. E., Feltz, D. L., Fahrbach, K. R., & Mack, D. E. (2000). The relation of self-efficacy measures to sport performance: A meta-analytic review. *Research Quarterly for Exercise and Sport, 71,* 280-294.

Multon, K. D., Brown, S. D., & Lent, R. W. (1991). Relation of self-efficacy beliefs to academic outcomes: A meta-analytic investigation. *Journal of Counseling Psychology, 38,* 30-38.

Pajares, F., Hartley, J., & Valiante, G. (2001). Response format in writing self-efficacy assessment: Greater discrimination increases prediction. *Measurement and Evaluation in Counseling and Development, 33,* 214-221.

Sadri, G., & Robertson, I. T. (1993). Self-efficacy and work-related behavior: A review and meta-analysis. *Applied Psychology: An International Review, 42,* 139-152..

Stajkovik, A. D., & Lee, D. S. (2001, August). *A meta-analysis of the relationship between collective efficacy and group performance.* Paper presented at meeting of the National Academy of Management, Washington, DC.

Stajkovic, A. D., & Luthans, F. (1998). Self-efficacy and work-related performance: A meta-analysis. *Psychological Bulletin, 124,* 240-261.

Telch, M. J., Bandura, A., Vinciguerra, P., Agras, A., & Stout, A. L. (1982). Social demand for consistency and congruence between self-efficacy and performance. *Behavior Therapy, 13,* 694-701.

CHAPTER 15

SELF-EFFICACY DURING CHILDHOOD AND ADOLESCENCE

Implications for Teachers and Parents

Frank Pajares

I begin this chapter with an assumption I hope readers will find reasonable. The assumption is that the beliefs that young people hold about their capability to succeed in their endeavors are vital forces in the subsequent successes or failures they attain in these endeavors. These *self-efficacy beliefs* provide the foundation for motivation, well-being, and personal accomplishment in all areas of life. This is because unless young people believe that their actions can produce the results they desire, they have little incentive to act or to persevere in the face of the difficulties that inevitably ensue. They can, of course, be cajoled or coerced to complete tasks or participate in activities not of their choosing, but, as soon as they are provided with the option to select their own life paths, they will surely select tasks and activities they believe are within their capabilities and avoid those that they believe are beyond their perceived competence.

Self-Efficacy Beliefs of Adolescents, 339–367
Copyright © 2006 by Information Age Publishing
All rights of reproduction in any form reserved.

Researchers have made noteworthy contributions to the understanding of self-efficacy and its relation to motivation and achievement. But, although parents and teachers may well be impressed by the force of research findings regarding the self-efficacy beliefs of children and adolescents, they are apt to be more interested in useful implications, sensible strategies to help maintain their youngsters' adaptive self-efficacy, and insights on ways to best alter these beliefs when they are inaccurate and debilitating to the young people in their care. In this chapter, my aim is to identify some of the implications that emanate from the findings on self-efficacy obtained by researchers (and presented in this volume). First, however, let me clarify the defining characteristics of this important self-belief and briefly synthesize the major findings on the relation between the self-efficacy, motivation, and achievement of children and adolescents.

SELF-EFFICACY AND SOCIAL COGNITIVE THEORY

With the publication of *Social Foundations of Thought and Action: A Social Cognitive Theory* in 1986, Albert Bandura proposed a theory of human functioning that emphasizes the role of self-beliefs. In this social cognitive perspective, individuals are viewed as self-organizing, proactive, self-reflecting, and self-regulating rather than as reactive organisms shaped by environmental forces or driven by concealed inner impulses. Human thought and human action are viewed as the product of a dynamic interplay of personal, behavioral, and environmental influences. How people interpret the results of their own actions informs and alters their environments and the personal factors they possess, which, in turn, inform and alter future actions. This is the foundation of Bandura's conception of *reciprocal determinism*, the view that (a) personal factors in the form of cognition, affect, and biological events, (b) behavior, and (c) environmental influences create interactions that result in a triadic reciprocality.

The reciprocal nature of the causes of human functioning in social cognitive theory makes it possible to direct attention at personal, environmental, or behavioral factors. For example, well-being can be fostered by improving the emotional, cognitive, or motivational processes of young people that are keystones of their personal factors. Well-being can also be fostered by improving young people's skills or altering the social conditions under which they live. In school, teachers work to improve the competence and confidence of the students in their charge. They can accomplish this by working to improve their students' emotional states and to correct their faulty self-beliefs and habits of thinking (personal factors), improve students' academic skills and self-regulatory practices

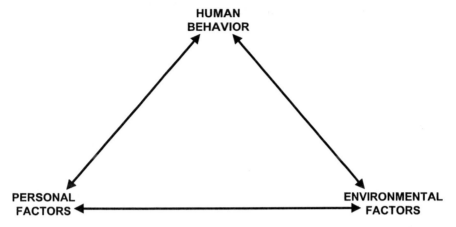

Figure 15.1.   Model illustrating relations between determinants in triadic reciprocal causation.

(behavior), and alter the school and classroom structures that may work to undermine student success (environmental factors).

SELF-EFFICACY AND ACADEMIC ACHIEVEMENT

Empirical evidence supports Bandura's contention that self-efficacy beliefs touch virtually every aspect of people's lives—whether they think productively, self-debilitatingly, pessimistically or optimistically; how much effort they expend on an activity; how well they motivate themselves and persevere in the face of adversities; how they regulate their thinking and behavior; and their vulnerability to stress and depression. As a consequence, these beliefs can powerfully influence the level of accomplishment that people ultimately realize. Self-efficacy is also a critical determinant of the life choices people make and of the courses of action they pursue. Typically, they engage in activities in which they feel competent and avoid those in which they do not. This is particularly critical at the high school and college levels, where young people progressively have more academic choices available to them.

The knowledge and skills that individuals possess will certainly play critical roles in what they choose to do and not do. But it is important to emphasize that people must invariably *interpret* the results of their attainments just as they must make judgments about the quality of the knowledge and skills they possess. Imagine, for example, two students who receive a B on an important exam. In and of itself, a B has no inherent meaning, and certainly no causal properties. How will receiving such a grade affect a particular youngster? A student accustomed to receiving As on exams in this particular class and subject and who worked hard throughout the term and studied for the exam will view the B in ways quite dissimilar from that of a student accustomed to receiving Cs and who worked equally hard. For the former, the B will be received with distress; for the latter, the B is likely to be received with elation. The student accustomed to receiving As is likely to have her academic confidence bruised; the C-acquainted student is sure to have her confidence boosted. Context is not always everything, but it colors everything.

Because people inherently interpret the results of their actions, their choices, behaviors, and competencies can typically be better predicted by the beliefs they hold about their accomplishments than by what they are actually capable of accomplishing. Of course, this does not mean that they can accomplish tasks beyond their capabilities simply by believing that they can. Competent functioning requires harmony between self-beliefs on the one hand and possessed skills and knowledge on the other. Rather, it means that self-efficacy beliefs help determine what people will do with the knowledge and skills they possess. This idea is consistent with the basic assumption with which I began this chapter, that young people's self-beliefs are critical forces in their motivation and achievement in all areas of life. Self-efficacy beliefs are also critical determinants of how well knowledge and skill are acquired in the first place.

Self-efficacy beliefs should not be confused with people's judgments of the consequences that their behavior will produce. Typically, self-efficacy beliefs help foster precisely the outcome one expects, which is the very heart of the *self-fulfilling prophecy*. Confident students anticipate successful outcomes. Students confident in their social skills anticipate successful social encounters. Those confident in their academic skills expect high marks on exams and expect the quality of their work to reap academic benefits. The opposite is true of those who lack confidence. Young people who doubt their social skills often envision rejection or ridicule even before they establish social contact. Those who lack confidence in their academic skills envision a low grade before they even begin an exam or enroll in a course.

When self-efficacy belief and perceived outcome differ, the belief can easily determine the behavior. A student may well realize that strong academic skills are essential for obtaining a good SAT score and being admitted to the college of her choice, and this, in turn, may ensure a comfortable future lifestyle. But if she lacks confidence in her academic capabilities, she may well shy away from challenging courses, will approach the SAT with apprehension and self-doubt, and may not even consider college attendance. In the social arena, a young man may realize that pleasing social graces and physical attractiveness will be essential for wooing the young lass who has caught his eye, which, in turn, may lead to a romantic interlude and even a lasting relationship. If, however, he has low confidence in his social capabilities and doubts his physical appearance, he will likely shy away from making contact and hence miss a potentially promising opportunity. In each of these cases, it bears remembering that, as Henry Ford once observed, "Whether you think that you can or that you can't, you are usually right."

By the year 2005, more than 3,000 articles included the concept of self-efficacy. In a typical Internet search, the term generated over half a million Web pages. Self-efficacy has been the focus of research in areas as diverse as business, athletics, medicine and health, media studies, social and political change, moral development, psychology, psychiatry, psychopathology, and international affairs. It has been especially prominent in educational research, where scholars have reported that, regardless of previous achievement or ability, self-efficacious students work harder, persist longer, persevere in the face of adversity, have greater optimism and lower anxiety, and achieve more. Students who believe they are capable of performing academic tasks also use more cognitive and metacognitive strategies than those who do not. Academic self-efficacy influences cognitive strategy use and self-regulation through the use of metacognitive strategies, and self-efficacy is associated with in-class seatwork and homework, exams and quizzes, and essays and reports. In psychology, "intelligence" (in the form of IQ) has typically been acknowledged the most powerful cognitive predictor of achievement. But when researchers tested the joint contribution of self-efficacy and intelligence to the prediction of achievement, they found that students' self-efficacy beliefs made a powerful and independent contribution to the prediction of their academic performance. Clearly, it is not simply a matter of how capable you are; it is also a matter of how capable you believe you are.

Self-efficacy explains approximately a quarter of the variance in the prediction of academic performances. Lest you think that a modest contribution, consider the many and varied factors that impinge on a student's experience. Any psychological factor capable of explaining 25% of the variance in most academic outcomes merits attention and even a bit of awe. In this next section, I offer some implications that emanate from research findings on self-efficacy.

IMPLICATIONS FOR TEACHERS AND PARENTS

The first few implications emanate from theory and research regarding the genesis, or sources, of self-efficacy beliefs, that is, how they are created and how they can be nurtured. Individuals form their self-efficacy perceptions by interpreting information from four sources: mastery experience, vicarious experience, social persuasions, and physiological reactions. For most people, the most influential source is the interpreted result of one's own performance, or *mastery experience*. Simply put, individuals gauge the effects of their actions, and their interpretations of these effects help create their efficacy beliefs. Success raises self-efficacy; failure lowers it. What could be simpler or more sensible? Students who perform well on mathematics tests and earn high grades in mathematics classes develop a strong sense of confidence in their mathematics capabilities. This strong sense of efficacy helps ensure that they will enroll in subsequent mathematics-related classes, approach mathematics tasks with serenity, and increase their efforts when a difficulty arises.

- **Emphasize Skill Development Rather Than Self-Enhancement**

  The contention that one's mastery experiences are the most influential source of self-efficacy information speaks directly to the self-enhancement model of academic achievement that contends that, to increase student achievement in school, educational efforts should focus on enhancing students' self-conceptions. Traditional efforts to accomplish this have included programs that emphasize building self-esteem through praise or self-persuasion methods. Self-efficacy theorists shift the emphasis from self-enhancement to skill development—to raising competence through genuine success experiences with the performance at hand, through *authentic* mastery experiences. Educational interventions should be designed with this critical point in mind.

  Students' self-efficacy beliefs develop primarily through actual success on challenging academic tasks. As Bandura has written, "let us not confuse ourselves by failing to recognize that there are two kinds of self-confidence, one a trait of personality and another that comes from knowledge of a subject. It is no particular credit to the educator to help build the first without building the second. The objective of education is not the production of self-confident fools." Decades earlier, Erik Erikson argued that "ego identity gains real strength only from wholehearted and consistent recognition of real accomplishment, that is, achievement that has meaning in their culture." It is always important to keep in mind Shel Silverstein's caution that "if the track is tough and the hill is rough, thinking you can just ain't enough."

  Academic work should be hard enough that it energizes, not so hard that it paralyzes. Effective teachers know that tasks and assignments must always be at an accomplishable level of difficulty. Young people themselves well know that successful completion of challenging tasks is self-rewarding and energizing, whereas completion of simple tasks brings little satisfaction. As Thomas Paine said, "What we obtain too cheap, we esteem too lightly."

- **Ensure That Students' Interpretations Are Adaptive**

Sociologist Alfred Schutz observed that, "It is the *meaning* of our experiences which constitutes reality." Recall the brief vignette a few pages back about our A and C students. We saw with some clarity that young people invariably *interpret* their mastery experiences. This can lead to situations in which inappropriate interpretations can diminish the very self-efficacy beliefs required to push on in the face of adversity. In no situation is this more evident than in the manner in which individuals perceive "failure."

Famed psychologist Robert Sternberg received a C in his first college introductory psychology class. His teacher commented that "there was a famous Sternberg in psychology and it was obvious there would not be another." Three years later, Sternberg graduated with honors from Stanford University with exceptional distinction in psychology. In 2002, he became President of the American Psychological Association. Michael Jordan was cut from his high school basketball team. He once observed, "I've failed over and over again in my life. That is why I succeed." Van Gogh sold only one painting during his life. Louisa May Alcott, author of *Little Women*, was encouraged to find work as a servant by her family. Emily Dickinson had only seven poems published in her lifetime. And 27 publishers rejected Dr. Seuss's first book, *To Think That I Saw It on Mulberry Street*, Jack London received six hundred rejection slips before he sold his first story, William Saroyan accumulated more than a thousand rejections before he had his first literary piece published, and Gertrude Stein submitted poems to editors for nearly 20 years before one was finally accepted.

The Roman poet Virgil wrote that "they are able who think they are able." One of the important characteristics of successful individuals is that failure and adversity do not undermine their self-efficacy beliefs. This is because self-efficacy is not so much about learning how to succeed as it is about learning *how to persevere when one does not succeed*. Self-efficacy cannot provide the skills required to succeed, but it can provide the effort and persistence required to obtain those skills and use them effectively.

When failure is normative, resilience is second nature. Adults make a great mistake when they endeavor to prevent young people from failing. Failure, after all, is the price that must be paid for success. Efforts are better aimed at helping young people learn how to fail at those times when failure is unavoidable. To this end, effective teachers and parents treat student errors, missteps, and incorrect answers as positive contributions that lead to subsequent achievement. Often, all that is needed is an adaptive perspective on failure. After Thomas Edison had made 1,000 unsuccessful attempts at inventing the light bulb, a reporter asked, "How did it feel to fail 1,000 times?" Edison replied, "I didn't fail 1,000 times. The light bulb was an invention with 1,000 steps." Author Samuel Beckett put it well: "Ever tried. Ever failed. No matter. Try Again. Fail again. Fail better."

In addition to interpreting the results of their mastery experiences, young people form their efficacy beliefs through the *vicarious experience* of observing others perform tasks. Observing the successes and failures of peers perceived as similar in capability contributes to beliefs in one's own capabilities ("*If he can do it, so can I!*"). Although this source of information is usually weaker than is mastery experience, when young people are uncertain about their own abilities or have limited previous experience, they become especially sensitive to it. If there is one finding that is incontrovertible in education and psychology it is that people learn from the actions of models, and so this is a prominent area of research in the study of self-efficacy. Vicarious experience also involves the *social comparisons* that students make with each other. These comparisons, along with peer modeling, can be powerful influences on self-efficacy beliefs. In situations in which young people have little experience with which to form a judgment of their competence in a particular area, peer models are especially useful.

- **Engage in Effective Modeling Practices**

  Different modeling practices can differently affect young people's self-beliefs. For example, adults who are *coping* models, that is, who good-naturedly admit their errors when they are pointed out ("Oops, I was a little careless. Thanks for pointing that out."), help youngsters understand that missteps are inevitable, that they can be overcome, and that even authority figures can make them. Conversely, adults who are strictly *mastery models*, that is, those who have their authority and ego tied up into their infallibility, respond to errors in a manner that shows they are incapable of making them

("I was just checking to see if you were paying attention."). Mastery models imbue in young people the idea that making errors is unacceptable and just plain dumb.

- **Select Appropriate Peer Models**

A student's peers are also a student's models. Hence, it is important to select peers as classroom models judiciously so as to ensure that students view themselves as comparable in learning ability to the models. There are cautions that should be observed. A model's failure has a more negative effect on the observers' self-efficacy when the observers judge themselves as having comparable ability to the model. Clearly, when someone whom we perceive as similar to us in ability fails, we are likely to believe that we, too, might fail (*"If she can't do it, neither can I."*). If, on the other hand, observers judge their own capability as superior to the model's capability, failure of the model has a minimal effect ("She can't do it, but I can."). When peer models make errors, engage in coping behaviors in front of students, and verbalize emotive statements reflecting low confidence and achievement, low-achieving students perceive the models as more similar to themselves and experience greater achievement and self-efficacy. As is the case with teachers as models, students who model excellence can imbue other students with the belief that they too can achieve that excellence.

- **Minimize the Relative Ability Information Publicly Available**

There are many ways in which young people are not helped by comparing their efforts and accomplishments with those of their peers. Of course, most children and adolescents will inevitably compare their skills and abilities with those of their friends and peers regardless of what well-meaning adults try to do to minimize or counter these comparisons. Nonetheless, young people should be helped to develop their own internal standards for evaluating their own outcomes. The challenge is to ensure that these internal standards are rigorous without being debilitating, realistic without being self-limiting, fluid without being wishy-washy, consistent without being static.

- **Tailor Instruction to the Student's Capabilities**

Educators have long known that when they create classroom structures that are individualized and they tailor instruction to students' academic capabilities, social comparisons are minimized and students are more likely to gauge their academic progress according to their own standards rather than compare it to the progress of their classmates. In cooperative and individualized learning settings, students can more easily select the peers with whom to compare themselves. Individualized structures that lower the competitive orientation of a classroom and school are more likely than are traditional, competitive structures to increase academic self-efficacy.

Self-concept researchers have illustrated the *Big-Fish-Little-Pond-Effect*, which describes how students form their self-beliefs by comparing their academic ability with the perceived abilities of other students in their reference group. Academic self-beliefs are increased when one views oneself as more capable than one's peers but, conversely, lowered when others are viewed as more capable. Social-comparative school practices that emphasize standardized assessments, involve ability grouping and lockstep instruction, use competitive grading practices, and encourage students to compare their achievement with that of their peers work to destroy the fragile self-beliefs of those who are less academically talented or prepared. These are instructional practices that can transform self-efficacy into self-doubt.

- **Exercise Care in Grouping Practices**

  Group dynamics are powerful. If a teacher is not careful, it is easy to create groups in which one or two students monopolize the activities or in which some students feel at a social or academic disadvantage. Effective teachers manage groups with care, and they work hard to provide all students with opportunities for success in group activities. Similarly, wise parents ensure that all siblings experience success within the family. It's difficult to develop confidence or competence when one is not engaged or when others are doing most of the work.

Stephen Sondheim cautioned adults to be "Careful the things you say. Children will listen." Self-efficacy beliefs are influenced by the words (and the actions) of others, whether these be intentional or accidental. Consequently, the third source of self-efficacy information comes from the *verbal messages and social persuasions* that people receive. These messages can help one to exert the extra effort and persistence required to succeed, resulting in the continued development of skills and of personal efficacy. Or they can be powerfully disheartening.

• **Careful the Things You Say, Children Will Listen**

Famed educator Maria Montessori wisely counseled that, "Since children are so eager to learn and so burning with love, an adult should carefully weigh all the words he speaks before them." Young people do listen, often when we least expect them to. The verbal and nonverbal judgments of others can play a critical role in the development of a young person's self-confidence, and these judgments often become the self-talk that youngsters repeat in their own heads further down the road.

Successful persuaders cultivate young people's beliefs in their capabilities while ensuring that the envisioned success is attainable. Positive persuasions encourage and empower; negative persuasions defeat and weaken self-beliefs. When girls receive social messages that they can achieve and succeed in male-dominated fields such as mathematics, science, and technology, these messages are instrumental in their future success in these areas. Ironically, it is the young person who has the greatest self-doubt to begin with who is more affected by negative comments and discouragements. Being counseled at an early age that one is not "college material" can have destructive effects if one is not endowed with a resilience to withstand and counteract such judgments.

• **Praise What Is Praiseworthy**

Effective persuasions should not be confused with knee-jerk praise or empty inspirational homilies. Praise and encouragement should be delivered honestly and in their proper measure when they are deserved. It is of course important that young people feel positively about themselves and about their capabilities, and teachers and parents play a critical role in nurturing the positive self-beliefs of children and adolescents. But heed carefully Erik Erikson's caution that young people "cannot be fooled by empty praise and condescending encouragement. Their identity gains real strength only from wholehearted and consistent recognition of *real* accomplishment ... a strong ego does not need, and in fact is immune to, any attempt at artificial inflation."

Praising a young person for a job well done is an important way of showing encouragement and support. Providing praise when it is undeserved, however, is dishonest, manipulative, and potentially dangerous. When capable people accomplish competent work with minimal effort, knee-jerk praise sends the quite peculiar message that putting forth minimal effort is praiseworthy. Self-efficacy is unaffected when praise is perceived as undeserved, and adults who provide such praise soon lose credibility. Moreover, in such situations the youngster is clearly under-challenged, and teachers and parents are better served by raising standards and expectations and challenging the young person to meet these expectations.

- **Praise Effort and Persistence, Not Ability**

Foster the belief that competence or *ability* is a changeable, controllable aspect of development, and encourage effort, perseverance, and persistence as ways to overcome obstacles. Praising with statements such as "You are so smart!" or "How bright you are!" can often have the opposite effect intended. Praising for "smarts" tells young people that success is a matter of intellectual ability (which one either has or doesn't have). How can young people develop confidence in an ability they believe is beyond their control? Praising for effort tells people that the harder you work the more you accomplish and the smarter you get. Whether at home or at school, rather than praising for ability, make it a habit to praise the *genuine* effort and persistence the young person puts forth.

- **Make a Moment Memorable**

Providing private feedback in a personal encounter can be a powerful way of engendering attention and making a moment memorable. Most of us recall an adult's words provided during a private moment that left a lasting and powerful impression. Positive public feedback aimed at an individual too often will please that individual but displease others who do not receive it. With students, public praise often has the opposite effect that the teacher intends—the student receiving the praise is likely to be teased or ridiculed when the teacher is not present. Private moments take more time, but they pack a stronger punch. Parents, too, can provide these private moments in the home or during an outing. Teachers and parents who proactively make time for such private encounters foster communication and help build memories that are not easily forgotten.

- **Be Alert to the Unintended Messages You Send**

The philosopher Michel Foucault once observed that, "People know what they do; they frequently know why they do what they do; but what they don't know is what they do does." Well-intended messages can have unintended consequences. When a young person encounters difficulty in an academic area or task in which a parent also encountered difficulty as a student, a loving parent will often attempt to soothe the child's frustration with well-meaning statements such as, "Don't feel bad. This runs in the family. I couldn't spell to save my life." Keep in mind that the message the youngster hears is that it is perfectly fine, even admirable, to be incompetent in spelling because the parent was. Too often, they may come to take pride in that incompetence and cease their efforts to improve. Parents must understand that if they were terrible spellers and their child is having difficulty with spelling, they must not commiserate. Instead, parents should challenge their child to improve her own spelling so that she can teach them a thing or two about spelling.

Physiological and emotional states such as anxiety and stress, along with one's mood, provide information about efficacy beliefs. Typically, optimism and a positive mood enhance self-efficacy, whereas depression, despair, or a sense of despondency diminishes it. As with the other sources, it is not the intensity of the physical indicator or mood state itself that is important, but the individual's interpretation of it. People with strong self-efficacy will view the emotional state as energizing, whereas those beset by self-doubt may regard it as debilitating.

- **Help Young People Learn to "Read" Their Feelings**

  We can all get a fairly good sense of our own confidence by the emotional feelings we experience as we contemplate an action. Negative feelings provide cues that something is amiss, even when we are unaware that such is the case. People who approach an activity with dread and apprehension likely lack confidence in their skills in that activity. Moreover, those negative feelings can themselves trigger additional stress and agitation that help ensure the inadequate performance feared. Worse yet, anxiety and dread can be paralyzing. Help young people read their own emotional feelings. Teach them that, if they find themselves experiencing undue anxiety when faced with a task, this is an appropriate time to discuss their feelings with a teacher, parent, or counselor. Help them understand that these feelings should not be ignored. It goes without saying that one should not confuse the typical butterflies that may accompany specific performances and activities with the anxiety that has its roots in more complex causes.

- **Identify Self-Handicapping Strategies**

  When young people fear failure, they can engage in all sorts of self-handicapping strategies to avoid feeling the anxiety that accompanies this fear. One of the most common self-handicapping strategies is to put forth little or no effort on the task in which the young person has little confidence of success. It is less anxiety-producing to fail believing you didn't try than to fail knowing you tried your best. When one puts forth little or no effort and fails, it hurts less when one explains the failure by claiming that "I didn't do well because I didn't try. I could do well if I wanted to. I just don't want to." That sort of self-deception inevitably leads to lower and lower competence, missed opportunities, and a vicious cycle of continued failure. Other self-handicapping strategies include self-deprecating talk, deliberate procrastination, setting goals so high and unattainable that failure can be self-viewed as "failing with honor," and setting goals so easy that one cannot fail.

- **Foster Optimism and a Positive Outlook on Life**

  Winston Churchill once said that "a pessimist sees the difficulty in every opportunity, but an optimist sees the opportunity in every difficulty." Energizing as that is, optimism has even greater powers. Researchers have found that optimism is related to adaptive academic benefits, including academic achievement, positive goal orientation, and use of learning strategies, whereas pessimism is associated with negative outcomes and with learned helplessness. Moreover, optimism is correlated with self-efficacy, self-esteem, and even with using self-regulatory strategies. Optimism is also associated with tranquility, lower stress, and numerous health indexes. As Bandura once observed, people live in psychological environments that are primarily of their own making. Not only should parents and teachers foster optimism in their children and students, they should faithfully model it themselves.

The implications above emanate from findings regarding the sources of self-efficacy beliefs. The following result from findings on the relationship between self-efficacy, motivation, and achievement.

- **Foster Competence *and* Confidence**

  Albert Bandura has cautioned that "educational practices should be gauged not only by the skills and knowledge they impart for present use *but also by what they do to children's beliefs about their capabilities*, which affects how they approach the future. Students who develop a strong sense of self-efficacy are well equipped to educate themselves when they have to rely on their own initiative." Competence *and confidence* should be fostered in tandem as students progress through school, or indeed through life. Recall that the results of our previous actions are always filtered by the beliefs that those actions create. For this reason, nurturing adaptive and beneficial self-beliefs is a clear imperative of psychological and educational practice.

Some self-efficacy researchers have suggested that teachers and parents should pay as much attention to young people's self-efficacy beliefs as to actual competence, for research findings have demonstrated that the beliefs are better predictors of motivation and future academic choices and career decisions than are factors such as preparation, knowledge, competence, or interest. College undergraduates select majors and careers in areas in which they feel most confident and avoid those in which they lack confidence to compete. And it is unrealistically low self-efficacy, not lack of knowledge or skill, that can be responsible for maladaptive academic behaviors, disciplinary problems, and diminishing school interest and achievement. Given the generally lower confidence of girls related to boys in some areas of mathematics, science, and technology (despite possessing equal capability as boys), the beliefs of adolescent girls may be especially vulnerable in these areas.

- **Challenge Underconfidence**

Many talented individuals suffer frequent (and sometimes debilitating) bouts of self-doubt about capabilities they clearly possess. There are few things sadder to a teacher or parent than being faced with capable young people who, as a result of previous demoralizing experiences or self-imposed mind-sets, have come to believe that they cannot succeed at a task or activity when all objective indicators show that they can. Often, much time and patience are required to break the mental habits of perceived incompetence that have come to imprison young minds.

In school, many students have difficulty not because they are incapable of performing successfully but because they are incapable of believing that they can perform successfully—they have learned to see themselves as incapable of handling academic work or to see the work as irrelevant to their world. As a consequence, students' difficulties in basic academic skills are often directly related to their beliefs that they cannot read, write, handle numbers, or think well—that they cannot learn—even when such things are not objectively true. In addition to continued skill improvement, adults must work to identify the inaccurate judgments of youngsters and implement strategies to challenge these judgments. Alexandre Dumas made the wise observation that when people doubt themselves, they make their own failure certain by themselves being the first to be convinced of it.

By adolescence, many self-beliefs have taken hold in powerful ways, for good or for ill. Like bad habits of action, inaccurate self-beliefs become bad habits of mind that can be frustratingly difficult to break. With time and use, self-beliefs become robust, and people hold on to beliefs based on incorrect or incomplete knowledge even after correct explanations are presented to them. Closely-held beliefs can persevere against reason, experience, time, and learning. John Dewey observed that "it is not uncommon to see persons continue to accept beliefs whose logical consequences they refuse to acknowledge." Young people who consider themselves failures at a particular thing will reject or distort evidence that contradicts their belief. As educator William Stafford commented, "If I know I am stupid, ugly, awkward, and I receive a grade of A, win a beauty contest, or perform an acrobatic feat, I will chalk it off as a fluke, error, or dumb luck." Psychologist Arthur Jersild suggested that young people are active "in the maintenance of the self picture, even if by misfortune the picture is a false and unhealthy one." Because bad habits of mind can resist change, adults must work to prevent them from forming in the first place and to challenge them when they do.

- **Ask Young People About Their Self-Efficacy**

Self-efficacy beliefs are not always self-evident. Capable individuals often hold deep insecurities that they will not readily admit. In school, assessing students' self-beliefs can provide teachers, counselors, and administrators with important insights about their pupils' academic motivation, behavior, and future choices. As I have pointed out, in many cases, young people avoid particular academic routes, career opportunities, and life paths because they lack confidence in their capability rather than because they lack competence or capability. Inaccurate self-beliefs, rather than poor knowledge or inadequate skills, are often responsible for people shortchanging themselves personally, socially, and academically. When low self-efficacy is identified early, youngsters can be helped to develop a better understanding of their potential to succeed in a desired path. Often, under-confidence is due to an inaccurate understanding of what skills a task or activity demands. In such cases, young people can be helped to better understand what abilities and skills a course of action will actually require. Identifying, challenging, and altering low self-efficacy is essential to success and adaptive functioning.

- ## Help Young People Maintain Adaptive Self-Efficacy

Philosopher and theologian Teilhard de Chardin wrote that "it is our duty as human beings to proceed as though the limits of our capabilities do not exist." de Chardin's exhortation notwithstanding, adults often work to lower the self-efficacy of young people in the well-meaning hope of making them more "realistic" about what they can and cannot do. These adults fear that it is not wise for a young person to hold "unrealistic" and lofty aspirations that are unlikely to be met. Reality and potential, the caring adult argues, should be well matched. But who can ever assess a person's *full* potential with complete accuracy? People surprise us all the time, just as we surprise ourselves. And who has the key to understanding the precise nature of reality?

Bandura emphasized that successful functioning is best served by reasonable efficacy appraisals, but the most functional self-efficacy judgments are those that slightly exceed what an individual can actually accomplish, for this overestimation serves to increase effort and persistence. Manipulating the "accuracy" of self-efficacy beliefs so that they are better matched with some perceived potential is an enterprise fraught with danger. American students are often viewed as too academically overconfident for their own good. Perhaps. But remember that the stronger the self-efficacy, the more likely are persons to select challenging tasks, persist at them, and perform them successfully. Efforts to lower young people's efficacy beliefs should generally be discouraged. Strategies to improve the match between belief and reality should emphasize helping children and adolescents to better understand what they know and do not know so that they may more effectively deploy appropriate cognitive strategies as they perform a task and engage in activities. Keep carefully in mind that the issue of "accuracy" cannot easily be divorced from issues of well-being, optimism, resilience, and optimal functioning.

Research supports the notion that, as people evaluate their lives, they are more likely to regret the challenge not confronted, the contest not entered, the risk un-risked, and the road not taken as a result of under-confidence and self-doubt rather than the action taken as a result of overconfidence and optimism (and, yes, even the occasional foolhardiness). The challenge to parents and educators on this account is to make young people more familiar with their own internal mental structures without lowering confidence, optimism, drive, and passion. The shakers and movers of this world believed they could shake and move the world even when those around them ridiculed their beliefs. If our reach cannot exceed our grasp, what is a heaven for?

- **Foster Authenticity**

  Help young people avoid the *illusion of incompetence* and the *illusion of artificial limits*. The *impostor syndrome*, as it is often called, is the belief that one is not truly competent to perform the tasks that others erroneously believe he can perform. This phenomenon has been found to be associated with stress, anxiety, and depression. It also fosters a sense of learned helplessness and helps debilitate students. This is hardly a surprise. After all, hiding your perceived incompetence is a heavy burden. The fear of discovery and ridicule is ever present. There is some evidence to suggest that high-achieving girls can be especially prone to these illusions in certain situations.

- **Make Self-Regulatory Practices Automatic and Habitual**

  Home and school are the primary settings in which self-regulatory practices are developed and maintained, and the use of these strategies is intimately connected both with social and academic success and with the positive self-beliefs that accompany success. The importance of self-regulatory practices is that they can be used *across* tasks, activities, and situations. This means that effective self-regulatory practices can result in stronger self-efficacy and achievement in various areas. Consequently, they are at the very heart of improving self-efficacy beliefs and achievement. Barry Zimmerman and his colleagues have outlined a number of these practices in school. They include

  - Finishing homework assignments by deadlines.
  - Studying when there are other interesting things to do.
  - Being able to concentrate on school subjects.
  - Taking useful class notes of class instruction.
  - Being able to use the library for information for class assignments.

- Effectively planning schoolwork.
- Effectively organizing schoolwork.
- Being able to remember information presented in class and in textbooks.
- Arranging a place to study at home without distractions.
- Being able to motivate oneself to do schoolwork.
- Participating in class discussions.

For William James, the critical challenge that parents and educators face is making children's self-regulatory practices automatic and habitual as early as possible. There is evidence to support James's contention that the self-regulatory processes that individuals use to make most of their decisions soon become automatic and are exercised primarily unconsciously. Many psychologists contend that individuals perform the bulk of their actions on autopilot, as it were. What this means is that people are, in later life, slaves to the self-regulatory practices and inclinations that they mastered during their youth. These habitual ways of behaving exert a powerful influence on the choices that people make and on the success or failure they experience. As a consequence, *habitual* self-regulatory behaviors are the very stuff of which the Self is made. According to James, when sound self-regulatory practices are handed over to "the effortless custody of automatism," higher powers of mind can be freed to engage other tasks.

- **Set Proximal Rather Than Distal Goals**

Working toward long-term goals is a necessary ingredient of life, but it can be tough on a young person's motivation. Proximal (short-term) goals are more easily digestible than are distal (long-term) goals. Proximal goals have the added benefit of raising self-efficacy. Not only do they make a task appear more manageable, but the more frequent feedback can convey a sense of mastery. Dale Schunk and his colleagues have demonstrated that self-efficacy and skill development are stronger in students who set proximal goals than in students who set distal goals, in part because proximal attainments provide students with evidence of growing expertise. In addition, students who are verbally encouraged to set their own goals experience increases in confidence, competence, and commitment to attain those goals. Self-efficacy is also increased when students are provided with frequent and immediate feedback while working on academic tasks, and, when students are taught to attribute this feedback to their own effort, they work harder, experience stronger motivation, and report greater self-efficacy for further learning.

- ## Provide Instrumental Rather Than Executive Help

When young people require help, adults should of course endeavor to provide it. But there are powerful differences between *instrumental help* and *executive help*. Instrumental help consists of providing just enough information to enable young people to succeed on their own. Executive help consists of providing the solution to a problem. It goes without saying that executive help is not particularly helpful if the aim is to foster problem-solving, authentic mastery, and self-reliance. Clearly, executive help is "over-help," and over-help diminishes motivation. Moreover, self-efficacy is unlikely to be affected by success brought about by having had the solution provided. Sometimes, well-meaning parents and teachers will offer excessive help to youngsters they perceive to be academically weak or learning disabled. Two consequences inevitably ensue from this intrusive practice: The young person will read the adult's intention, and whatever success is obtained will undermine intrinsic motivation. To paraphrase the wonderful Chinese proverb, give young people executive help and you feed them today; give them instrumental help and you feed them for a lifetime.

In school, teachers must also teach students how to provide help to their classmates. Students often seek help from each other to a greater degree than they seek help from the teacher. Like many of us, students often interpret a plea for help as a request for a solution to the problem in question. Part of creating an effective classroom climate involves teaching students how to provide instrumental rather than executive help. Teach students that executive help breeds dependence. A teacher can teach students to provide instrumental help in large part by modeling such help-giving, but explicit explanations, instructions, and monitoring help ensure that bad habits don't resurface.

- ## Create Opportunities for Self-Efficacy Beliefs to Generalize

Self-efficacy beliefs can generalize across activities or situations. That is, beliefs acquired as a result of one set of experiences can influence new experiences. When people are confronted with a novel task that requires performing skills similar to those that were required to accomplish a familiar task, the beliefs about the familiar task will generalize to the novel task. In sports, a young athlete who believes herself competent at basketball will receive her introduction to volleyball with the attitude that this is a game she can master. In school, a student who has grown confident in his capability to write stories will welcome his introduction to poetry with the attitude that this, too, is something he can do. In these cases, strong self-efficacy maximizes the chances of success in related activities.

As success beliefs generalize, so can failure beliefs. Young people who have developed self-defeating beliefs in their capability to accomplish tasks will approach similar tasks with apprehension and pessimism ("*If I'm no good at basketball, I'll surely suck at volleyball.*"). When one ability is valued and highly rated, a failure of that ability can lower one's self-efficacy in other abilities. Repeated failure in a valued skill may have profound effects in seemingly unrelated skills. This *spread-of-effect phenomenon* has been well documented. The dangers of the self-fulfilling prophecy are evident.

Beliefs can also generalize when skills required to accomplish dissimilar activities are acquired together under the supervision of a competent instructor. Great coaches can create all-around athletes whose beliefs about their capabilities cut across various sports. The skills required to organize any course of action are governed by broader self-regulatory skills such as knowing how to diagnose task demands or constructing and evaluating alternative strategies. When young people possess these self-regulatory skills, they can improve their performances across a range of activities, in part because they believe in their ability to solve the problems required to succeed.

Self-efficacy beliefs also generalize when the effects of these beliefs are cognitively structured across activities. For instance, if a young person can be helped to realize that increased effort and perseverance will result in academic progress and greater understanding in mathematics, connections will be made to achieving success in other academic areas. Generalizable coping skills work in similar fashion by reducing stress and promoting effective functioning across a range of activities.

There are also "transforming experiences" that come about as the result of powerful performance attainments and can serve to strengthen beliefs in diverse areas of one's life, areas often greatly unrelated. Wandering into a school's theater club, trying out for a play, and finding that she loves and excels at acting can alter a young person's life in profound ways. The confidence of youngsters so transformed often reaches into many and diverse areas of their lives. When opportunities are created for them to generalize their self-efficacy beliefs, the net these self-beliefs cast can be both wide and strong.

- **Emphasize a Mastery Goal Orientation**

Young people engage tasks and activities for a variety of reasons. Goal theorists have identified three such reasons, which they call *achievement goal orientations*. Researchers describe these goal orientations in terms of either *mastery* or *ego*. Mastery goals (sometimes called task or learning goals) represent a person's concern with mastering material and concepts, challenge-seeking, and viewing learning as an end in itself. Ego goals (also called performance goals) represent a concern with doing better than others, appearing smart, or avoiding appearing incompetent.

Research findings show that holding a mastery goal orientation has motivational and learning benefits whereas having an ego goal orientation can be detrimental and maladaptive. In school, students who engage their academic work with a mastery goal orientation tend to exhibit greater self-efficacy, use deeper processing strategies, show increased task engagement, attribute their success to effort rather than to ability or external causes such as luck, and persist longer in the face of difficulty. Ego goals are related to maladaptive behaviors such as lack of persistence, use of shallow cognitive strategies, avoiding help seeking, and attributions of failure to lack of ability.

It is not surprising that holding an ego orientation is also associated with pessimism and with the impostor syndrome. People whose achievement efforts are grounded on the fear of appearing incompetent, being embarrassed, or looking stupid are prone to view the fruits of their labors through the lens which that fear provides. There can be little psychological distance between the fear that others will think us incompetent and the suspicion that we may indeed be so, the suspicion that our accomplishments are illdeserved. And how could fear and suspicion not be chaperoned by pessimism?

When teachers create a classroom climate in which mastery goal orientations are encouraged and ego orientations are discouraged, students approach their academic work with greater enjoyment and serenity. Of great importance, when encountering failure (and who doesn't encounter failure?), mastery oriented students prove resilient and resourceful, whereas ego oriented students experience greater stress, anxiety, depression, and shame. When parents foster a mastery goal orientation in their children's activities, children engage in those activities with joy and enthusiasm and without fear of the missteps and errors that inevitably arise.

- **Encourage a Proactive Sense of Personal Agency**

No one should ever feel like a pawn on a chess board. Personal agency is the ability to act intentionally and exercise a measure of control over one's environment and social structures. Personal agency is about will, drive, and self-determination. Bandura rightfully contended that self-efficacy beliefs constitute the key factor of human agency. A century earlier, William James had observed that "our self-feeling is in our power." A great many of the things in our life happen to us because of the choices that we make. Young people must be helped to understand earlier than later that they are the engine that drives the train of their life.

- **Self-Efficacy Is Contagious—Nurture and Model Your Own Self-Efficacy**

The philosopher Joseph Joubert once observed that young people have more need of models than of critics. Children and adolescents look to adults for guidance on what to believe. Researchers have reported that the confidence that teachers have in their capability to affect their students' learning affects their instructional activities and their orientation toward the educational process. Teachers with a low sense of efficacy tend to hold a custodial orientation that takes a pessimistic view of students' motivation, emphasizes rigid control of classroom behavior, and relies on extrinsic inducements and negative sanctions to get students to study. Teachers with strong self-efficacy create mastery experiences for their students, whereas teachers with low instructional self-efficacy undermine students' cognitive development as well as students' judgments of their own capabilities. Teacher self-efficacy also fosters student achievement and students' achievement beliefs across various areas and levels. Self-efficacy is contagious, which is to say that students can easily "catch" a teacher's own sense of confidence. Self-confident teachers help create self-confident students and, regretfully, unconfident teachers help create unconfident students.

Similarly, parents' self-efficacy in their own parenting capabilities influences the development of their children. Gian Vittorio Caprara and his associates have studied the influence of parental self-efficacy beliefs on the well-being and adjustment of their children. Parents with strong parental self-efficacy monitor, support, protect, guide, encourage, and make time for their children, dispense needed discipline with emotional closeness, and maintain open communication with them so that disagreements do not escalate into open conflict. Parents confident in their parenting skills contribute to the development of young people by cultivating their potential. They foster the aspirations and capabilities of their children, thereby improving their social relations, emotional well-being, academic development, and career choices.

- **Maximize the Collective Efficacy of the Classroom or Home**

Self-efficacy is both a personal and a collective belief. Collective systems such as homes, neighborhoods, communities, classrooms, teams of teachers, schools, and school districts develop a sense of collective efficacy—a group's shared belief in its capability to attain its goals and accomplish desired tasks. Children, parents, teachers, and school administrators operate collectively as well as individually. Schools develop collective beliefs about the capability of their students to learn, of their teachers to teach and otherwise enhance the lives of their students, and of their administrators and policymakers to create environments conducive to those tasks. Schools with a strong sense of collective efficacy exercise empowering and vitalizing influences on their constituents, and these effects are palpable and in evidence—visitors speak of the schools' "atmosphere" or "climate" and describe them as "can-do" or effective schools.

Families too have a climate and "feel" generated from the collective action of their individual members. As is the case with schools, fostering the collective efficacy of a family pays dividends both for parents and for children. Beyond the sense of togetherness that binds the individual members, the collective beliefs can foster all the qualities essential to adjustment and well-being.

Bandura found that collective efficacy mediated the influence of socioeconomic status, prior academic achievement, and teachers' longevity on the academic achievement of students in various middle schools. The collective efficacy of a school is also related to the personal teaching efficacy of its teachers, as well as to their satisfaction with the school administration. The classroom's and school's sense of collective efficacy can undermine or enhance students' and teachers' own sense of efficacy. Caprara and his associates discovered parallel benefits of collective family efficacy.

- **Foster and Model Self-Reflection**

Socrates was wise to observe that the unexamined life is not worth living. Noted educator John Dewey expounded on the human capability, and need, for self-reflection. Bandura similarly noted that, "if there is any characteristic that is distinctively human, it is the capability for reflective self-consciousness." Playwright, poet, and moral leader Václav Havel once wrote that the salvation of the world itself lies in the human power to reflect. Even little Calvin, of *Calvin and Hobbes* fame, took some time from mischief making to reflect that "sometimes one should just look at things and think about things without doing things."

Without the capability to self-reflect, human beings would be reactive souls without the capacity for self-improvement. Purposeful and proactive self-reflection has powerful adaptive qualities. Naturally, it is the key to self-regulation. How can young people self-correct if they do not reflect on the corrections required? Such reflection should be proactive rather than reactive, and it should also be shared, which is to say that it should take the form not only of purposive and reflective self-thought but also self-reflective dialogue between the child, parents, and teachers.

- **Confidence is a Habit of Mind—Cultivate it Early**

William James wrote that "education is for behavior, and habits are the stuff of which behavior consists." Self-efficacy beliefs ultimately become habits of thinking that are developed like any habit of conduct, and teachers and parents are influential in helping young people to develop the self-belief habits that will serve them throughout their lives.

There is a proverb to the effect that "instruction in youth is like engraving in stone." Researchers know that the earlier a belief is incorporated into our belief system, the more difficult it is to alter it. Newly acquired beliefs are the most vulnerable to change. Once solidly established, our beliefs tend to self-perpetuate, persevering even against contradictions caused by reason, schooling, or experience. People tend to hold on to beliefs based on incorrect or incomplete knowledge even after correct explanations are presented to them. For these reasons, adults face the critical challenge of making the positive self-beliefs of youngsters automatic and habitual as early as possible. After all, good habits are as hard to break as are bad habits.

- **View Young People as Capable and Let Them Know It**

As young people strive to exercise control over their surroundings, their transactions are mediated by adults who can empower them with self-assurance or diminish their self-beliefs. As do we all, children and adolescents rely on the judgments of others to create their own self-efficacy beliefs. In 1902, Charles Horton Cooley introduced the metaphor of the *looking-glass self* to illustrate the idea that our sense of Self is primarily formed as a result of our perceptions of how others perceive us. That is, the appraisals of *others act as mirror reflections* that provide the information we use to define our own Self.

The mirrored appraisals of others can be so powerful that it is not at all unusual for children to become the very sort of people they believe others believe them to be. I recall one discussion with a doctoral student who was struggling with a portion of her dissertation that was giving her no end of trouble and undermining her confidence. At a particularly difficult juncture she said to me, "You know, Professor, I've come to the realization that, although it is important for me to believe that I can do this, it seems equally important for me to believe that you believe I can do this."

Over a century ago, William James ended his lectures to the nation's teachers with the gentle admonition that if they could but see their pupils as individuals composed of good intentions, and love them as well, they would be "in the best possible position for becoming perfect teachers." As this is our aim, we do well to take heed.

CONCLUSION

To many readers, and certainly to all effective teachers and parents, many of the implications I have offered will sound like little more than educational principles grounded in simple common sense. Indeed. But two observations merit making. First, good psychology should always be allied to common sense. Second, as Voltaire wrote, common sense is not so common. Regrettably, it is too seldom common practice. There is often a fine line between what individuals perceive as common sense and what they have been doing for years, taking for granted that their actions are grounded in their own sense of common sense. Often, these actions reflect the simple repetition of habitual behaviors long established, seldom evaluated, and long unquestioned. Bertrand Russell once observed that in all affairs, "it's a healthy idea, now and then, to hang a question mark on things you have long taken for granted." The implications I have offered emanate from research findings in which question marks have been hung on critical educational assumptions long taken for granted. As such, they represent the best answers that researchers have obtained when these assumptions have been subjected to scholarly scrutiny.

But let me add a word about the danger of *formalizing* generalizations. Lee Cronbach cautioned that "when we give proper weight to local conditions, any generalization is a working hypothesis, not a conclusion." All implications should be viewed through that cautionary lens. None should be taken as a formal principle that becomes a rule or precept to be followed independent of context. When implications are disjoined from their contextual safeguards, the danger is that they can become one-size-fits-all recipes for instruction. John Dewey worried that the use of these recipes is antagonistic to education, for when research findings are reduced "to a rule which is to be uniformly adopted, then, only, is there a result which is objectionable and destructive of the free play of education as an art." In offering implications that emanate from research findings, I seek only to provide a "starting point" from which teachers and parents may begin to seek the solutions to the challenges they face. All generalizations, however, must be tested against the reality of a particular setting and the particular individuals within that setting.

A third caution is warranted. Many critics have quite rightly railed against the tyranny that can result from an unbridled self-oriented emphasis in psychology and in education. It can be a short voyage from self-reflection to self-obsession, self-absorption, self-centeredness, self-importance, and selfishness. Young people who believe that the nurturance, maintenance, and gratification of their sense of Self is the prime directive of their own personal and social development do not easily learn to nurture others, to maintain lasting and mutually satisfying relationships, or to defer or postpone their own perceived needs. Artificial self-esteem is naked against adversity; unwarranted confidence is cocky conceit. When what is communicated to young people from an early age is that nothing matters quite as much as how they feel or how confident they should be, one can rest assured that the world will sooner or later teach them a lesson in humility that may not be easily learned. An obsession with one's sense of self is responsible for an alarming increase in depression and other mental difficulties.

As is evident from the proliferation of self-esteem kits, programs, and gimmicks, complex issues related to the Self are often oversimplified and caricatured. In most cases, efforts are better aimed at transforming schools, classrooms, families, and teaching and parenting practices than at altering young people's psyches. But institutional, curricular, familial, and pedagogical transformation and a focus on the self-beliefs of young people need not be incompatible with concern for their personal, social, and psychological well-being. Warranted self-confidence need not result in arrogant self-satisfaction. Personal, social, emotional, and academic difficulties, as well as the misdirected motivation and lack of commitment often characteristic of the underachiever, the dropout, the student labeled "at risk," the troublemaker, the delinquent, and the socially disabled, are in good measure the consequence of, or certainly exacerbated by, the beliefs that young people develop about their capabilities and about their ability to exercise a measure of control over their environments.

All parents and teachers have the responsibility of preparing self-assured and fully-functioning individuals capable of pursuing their hopes and their ambitions. Philosopher Nel Noddings observed that their ultimate aim should be "to produce competent, caring, loving, and lovable people." Parents and teachers can aid their children and students in these pursuits by helping them to develop the habit of excellence in scholarship and in action while at the same time nurturing the self-beliefs necessary to maintain that excellence throughout their adult lives. One need only cast a casual glance at the world's landscape to see that attending to the self-beliefs of young people is both a noble and necessary enterprise.

SUGGESTED READING

Bandura. A. (1982). Self-efficacy mechanism in human agency. *American Psychologist, 37*, 122-147.

Bandura, A. (1986). *Social foundations of thought and action: A social cognitive theory.* Englewood Cliffs, NJ: Prentice Hall.

Bandura, A. (1993). Perceived self-efficacy in cognitive development and functioning. *Educational Psychologist, 28*, 117-148.

Bandura, A. (Ed.) (1995). *Self-efficacy in changing societies.* New York: Cambridge University Press.

Bandura, A. (1997). *Self-efficacy: The exercise of control.* New York: Freeman.

Caprara, G. V., Scabini, E., & Sgritta, G. B. (2003). The long transition to adulthood: An Italian view. In F. Pajares & T. Urdan (Eds.), *International perspectives on adolescence* (pp. 71-99). Greenwich, CT: Information Age.

Hackett, G. (1995). Self-efficacy in career choice and development. In A. Bandura (Ed.), *Self-efficacy in changing societies* (pp. 232-258). New York: Cambridge University Press.

Multon, K. D., Brown, S. D., & Lent, R. W. (1991). Relation of self-efficacy beliefs to academic outcomes: A meta-analytic investigation. *Journal of Counseling Psychology, 38*, 30-38.

Pajares, F. (1996). Self-efficacy beliefs in academic settings. *Review of Educational Research, 66*, 543-578.

Pajares, F. (1997). Current directions in self-efficacy research. In M. Maehr & P. R. Pintrich (Eds.). *Advances in motivation and achievement* (Vol. 10, pp. 1-49). Greenwich, CT: JAI Press.

Pajares, F., & Schunk, D. H. (2001). Self-beliefs and school success: Self-efficacy, self-concept, and school achievement. In R. Riding & S. Rayner (Eds.), *Self-perception* (pp. 239-266). London: Ablex.

Pajares, F., & Schunk, D. H. (2005). The self and academic motivation: Theory and research after the cognitive revolution. In J. M. Royer (Ed.), *The impact of the cognitive revolution on educational psychology* (pp. 165-198) Greenwich, CT: Information Age.

Pajares, F., & Urdan, T. (Eds.). (2005). *Self-efficacy and adolescence*. Greenwich, CT: Information Age.

Schunk, D. H. (1995). Self-efficacy and education and instruction. In J. E. Maddux (Ed.), *Self-efficacy, adaptation, and adjustment: Theory, research, and applications* (pp. 281-303). New York: Plenum.

Schunk, D. H., & Pajares, F. (2002). The development of academic self-efficacy. In A. Wigfield & J. Eccles (Eds.), *Development of achievement motivation* (pp. 16-31). San Diego: Academic Press.

Schunk, D. H., & Pajares, F. (2004). Self-Efficacy in education revisited: Empirical and applied evidence. In D. McInerney & S. Van Etten (Eds.), *Research on sociocultural influences on motivation and learning. Vol. 4: Big theories revisited* (pp. 115-138). Greenwich, CT: Information Age.

Zimmerman, B. J. (1999). Self-efficacy: An essential motive to learn. *Contemporary Educational Psychology, 25*, 82-91.

Zimmerman, B. J., & Schunk, D. H. (2003). Albert Bandura: The scholar and his contributions to educational psychology. In B. J. Zimmerman & D. H. Schunk (Eds.). *Educational psychology: A century of contributions* (pp. 431-458). Mahwah, NJ: Erlbaum.

Printed in the United Kingdom
by Lightning Source UK Ltd.
108346UKS00001B/5